Intranets

What's the B

WITHDRAWN

Randy J. Hinrichs

Sun Microsystems Press
A Prentice Hall Title

The publisher offers discounts on this book when ordered in bulk quantities. For more information,
contact Corporate Sales Department, Prentice Hall PTR, One Lake Street, Upper Saddle River, NJ 07458.
Phone: 800-382-3419; FAX: 201-236-7141.
E-mail: corpsales@prenhall.com.

Editorial/production supervision: *Nicholas Radhuber*
Cover designer: *M&K Design, Palo Alto, California*
Cover design director: *Jerry Votta*
Manufacturing manager: *Alexis R. Heydt*
Marketing manager: *Stephen Solomon*
Acquisitions editor: *Gregory G. Doench*
Sun Microsystems Press publisher: *Rachel Borden*

10 9 8 7 6 5 4 3 2 1

ISBN 0-13-841198-0

Sun Microsystems Press
A Prentice Hall Title

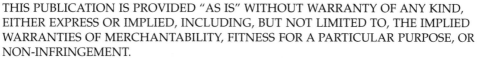

THIS PUBLICATION IS PROVIDED "AS IS" WITHOUT WARRANTY OF ANY KIND, EITHER EXPRESS OR IMPLIED, INCLUDING, BUT NOT LIMITED TO, THE IMPLIED WARRANTIES OF MERCHANTABILITY, FITNESS FOR A PARTICULAR PURPOSE, OR NON-INFRINGEMENT.
THIS PUBLICATION COULD INCLUDE TECHNICAL INACCURACIES OR TYPOGRAPHICAL ERRORS. CHANGES ARE PERIODICALLY ADDED TO THE INFORMATION HEREIN, THESE CHANGES WILL BE INCORPORATED IN NEW EDITIONS OF THE PUBLICATION. SUN MICROSYSTEMS, INC. MAY MAKE IMPROVEMENTS AND/OR CHANGES IN THE PRODUCT(S) AND/OR THE PROGRAMS(S) DESCRIBED IN THIS PUBLICATION AT ANY TIME.

Sun Microsystems Press
A Prentice Hall Title

This book, like all my accomplishments, is a family effort.
Janice, my wife, my soulmate, was there without exception. Je t'aime.
My three older children, Colin, Anna, and Claire, brilliantly
managed the house and took care of each other with selfless consistency.
And to Evan, who entered our world at a late stage of our life,
to move us into a new direction.
I dedicate this book to my family for whom I've only got
two words — let's party!

Contents

Chapter Three   What's It Made of? **50**

Chapter Nine   Interviews with CIOs, Webmasters, and Other Visionaries **332**

Chapter Ten   Top Ten Lists **396**

List of Figures

List of Tables

Acknowledgments

This book is the effort of many individuals. It demonstrates the work of dozens more. All of them deserve a very warm and grateful thank you.

Sun Microsystems played a significant role in providing key information for the development of this book. Many people were helpful in providing insight, methods, screen shots, internal processes, and support. Key among them are Judy Lindberg, Internet Program Manager; Debra Winters, Intranet Webmaster; Karin Ellison, SunSoft Internet Manager/Web Architect; Pat Baldwin, Director of Business Simplification; David W. Thompson, Manager of Communications Technology, SMI Employee Communications; Carl Middlehurst, Sun Legal; Gary Adams, Senior Staff Engineer; Rick Levine at Java Soft; Alan Nichols, Video Expert; Robert Cruz, Sun Professional Services; Rand Lindsley, Senior Staff Engineer; Jakob Nielsen, Sun's Internet Designer, Senior Staff Engineer; and Wayne Gramlich from SunLabs. My special thanks to Jerry Neece, Internet Marketing Manager, for providing significant cost data.

I'd especially like to thank the interviewees who agreed to take time off from their busy schedules and spend over an hour on the phone, then another couple of hours editing their interviews. Thank you very much for your insights and leadership. These memorable interviews came from Bill Raduchel, CIO Sun Microsystems; Larry Geisel, CIO Netscape Communications; John Connors, CIO Microsoft; Bill Prouty, Chief Webmaster Sun Microsystems; Ken Trant, Webmaster SGI; Tim Horgan, Webmaster CIO Communications; and the visionaries Patricia Seybold,

Patricia Seybold Consulting; Chris Locke, VP Business Strategy DisplayTech; and Dr. Steve Telleen, Director of Business Strategy and Development, Intranet Partners.

Many people contributed conversations, white papers, web sites, screen shots, international perspectives, advice, and plain old friendly support. Thank you for your contributions. They provided the support structure for the book. George Gilder, Gilder Technology; Tim-Berners Lee at the World Wide Web Consortium; Lou Tice at the Pacific Institute; Peter Senge at MIT; Lew McCreary CIO Communications Publisher; Charles Brownstein, Corporation for National Research Initiatives; Don Tapscott, author of The Digital Economy; Dave Weiden, Kurt Wedel, and Lee Baldwin at Netscape; Wayne Erickson at Patricia Seybold Group; Matthew Cutler of The Webmaster's Guild; Dave Trowbridge at Hummingbird Communications; Frank Brunotts and Jay Whittle of the Internet Society; Fred Courtot at Verity, Inc. Thanks to Jim Newton and the entire staff at Laurel Systems (http://www.laurel.com) for designing and producing the new look of Sun Microsystem's SunWeb intranet. Special thanks to Kaoru Yoshino for the Japanese translation.

I'd like to extend my thanks to Doug Rutherford and Lee Kurnoff from Zona Research; Sarah Norton from Business Research Group; Joe Clema from Neurosystems; Steve Finegan, President of The Huntington Group; Barbara Lang at Abitec; Tristan Louis at iWorld; David Strom of David Strom, Inc.; Linda Barlow at Monash Information Services; Malcolm Humes of Total Entertainment Network; Jean Macdonald at MIT; Jean Clegg at Microsoft; Mike Pettejohn at Netcraft; Murray Smith of Internet Media; Richard Karash, Host for Learning-Organization Mailing List; Rob Barrow, CEO of JSB Corporation; and Steve Whan, Corporate Webmaster at BC Hydro.

A special, warm thanks to Greg Donech, Lisa Iarkowski, and Nick Radhuber, an incredible editor, at Prentice Hall. Thanks also to my friends Rachel Borden and John Bortner at Sun Microsystems Press.

This book was reviewed in whole or in part by many people from many disciplines. Their wide-ranging perspectives kept me on track. The review staff includes Dave Walden from the Center for Quality of Management; Tim Horgan from CIO Communications; Brian Duelm from Compaq Computers; Mary E. S. Morris, co-author with me on Web Page Design: A Different Multimedia; Norman Gary from Sun Microsystems; Jason Couchman from Internet Developers Association; Janice Cowsert from Air Liquide; and Malcolm Humes, Total Entertainment Network.

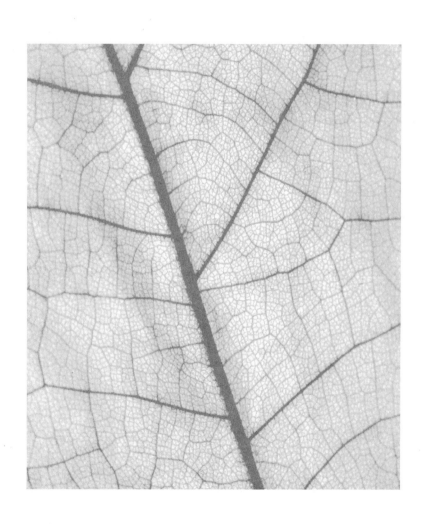

CHAPTER

1

Introduction

Overview

The Intranet

Picture this. You're at the client's headquarters. You're on a break. You've got some additional items to look up. The client has asked some questions that you know are going to close their buying decision. You securely log on to your intranet from your laptop from one of the offices they've loaned you. The main intranet web page comes up. You double-click on the Sales and Marketing web page, click on the search box, and type in your question. Within seconds, you've got an answer.

Then, you click on an interactive Sales Expert web page and answer some questions regarding the client. You identify the key selling points, the person you're talking to, and what questions they've been asking. You click on Enter, and within seconds, the latest breaking information about the customer is sent to your laptop (press releases, announcements, analyst information, stock quotes), even information about which of your competitors has already seen this client. You click on a chat room to see if anyone else has sold to this client recently and begin open discussions with co-workers, one who knows the MIS Director and lets you know his preferences for certain products.

Your e-mail flashes, suddenly, and a product update announcement about your product appears on the screen. The price has dropped. You've got what you need. You close your laptop after the 20-minute break, and you're back in the conference room, answering questions and signing contracts.

How did you adjust to change so fast? It's easy when the intranet generates intelligent information when you need it, right on the points you want, and right when you want it. In a generation when you're asked to work smarter, work faster, work with less, you finally have a tool that focuses the entire company's resources behind you like a single laser beam.

Whenever you need to make a decision about something crucial or risky, you can enter the intranet and line yourself up with the experts. Instead of one systems engineer, or one sales representative, you now have the entire knowledge base of systems engineers or the entire sales force to work with you. Instead of files, reports, and books, you have complete corporate libraries on-line. Best of all, you have an environment where every department in the organization can develop their best applications for enterprisewide access and you can get to them.

The Bottom Line

This book is about using an intranet to align the workplace, improve workflow, create learning organizations, leverage corporate intelligence, and develop a corporate culture that is ready for the 21st century. This book will make you proactive, providing you with the forward thinking and management techniques that need to be put in place, with a manager's perspective on technical issues and insider information on how to evolve your intranet.

Intranet technology is altering the culture of international corporations, qualifying employees worldwide to understand key issues facing their business, to exchange ideas in real time, and to collaborate on solutions—regardless of geographic location or time zone. If you're doing business over a network, this book is for you.

This book will explain what an intranet is and how to use it within your organization. At the core are improved communication, enhanced creativity, and the development or emergence of critical thinking knowledge workers. This is a book to stimulate thinking about how to use an evolutionary networking concept, the intranet, to transform your organization into an integrated, global, human intelligent network.

An important caveat: You cannot implement the technology for the sake of technology. You must align the visions, the mission, and the goals of your organization to identify the best way for your organization to evolve and mature into a 21st century organization. Then apply the technology to realize your plan for the future.

There is no need for reengineering the organization or reskilling large workforces. The focus is to move the decision making, the actions, the problem solving, and the responsibilities closer to the people who understand the opportunities and possess the skills to react quickly and efficiently. When a problem needs an organizational solution, users can then reach out to the expertise, power, and wealth of the intranet and focus the total resources on the problem.

The intranet is about being linked together like some great collective consciousness, where people can cultivate their intelligence or call on networked intelligence as a powerful resource. The intranet deals with the issue of how to make your organization smarter, where the combined intelligence is greater than the individual intelligence in the group. It's up to you to leverage this combined intelligence into a smarter, faster, and friendlier organization.

Audience

This book is designed for decision makers who want bottom-line intranet information. *Intranets: What's the Bottom Line?* is a strategic book. It is a manager's intranet handbook. It focuses on how you'll use an intranet once it is installed. It answers the basic business questions on building an infostructure that meets employees' 21st century information needs. The road you take to the 21st century is up to you.

What's in This Book?

In this book, we'll answer some very basic questions for you on how and why intranets are going to cut costs, increase productivity, streamline business processes, improve quality, and rightsize your organization, plus get you ISO 9000+ compliance, improve human resources, strategically align your organizational infrastructure, and help you emerge as a learning organization involved in principle-centered self-improvement.

We'll provide ample executive overviews, tables, figures, interviews with key players in the field, anecdotes, and analogies that are easy to understand, plus statistics and business computing models. This book is meant to take the jargon out and teach you some new concepts and stimulate your existing ideas into an action plan. Every effort has been made to make the readability international, so everyone in the company's global infrastructure can start thinking about how to evolve their organizations into powerful, global intranets.

What's an Intranet?   Using simple language and easy to follow analogies, this chapter explains to you that an intranet is more than the wires and servers. Internet technology has provided us with an organizational tool for the 21st century, the intranet. It's a tool that sharpens our minds, prepares us for rapid change, enables our creativity, and provides us an opportunity to create an intellectually creative society within the walls of our enterprises.

What's It Made of?   This chapter identifies key components for building various generations of intranets: Internet standards, web servers, web browsers, database programs, legacy system integration, security, new web competencies and skills, seamless integration between you and your partners. It gives you a feel for the whole system.

What's It Buy Me?   This chapter discusses leveraged intelligence, single-point contact, workflow improvement, collaboration for project development, reduced product life cyles, strategic alignment of departments and projects, ISO 9000+ compliance, empowered workforce, quality, and continuous process improvement.

What's It Going to Cost Me?   This chapter examines direct costs and identifies four different tiers of intranet development to evaluate these costs. It discusses cost drivers and how they influence buying decisions. It provides some cost tips for saving money. Cost savings is the premier cost topic, and ROI (Return on Investment) is tied to productivity gains.

How Do I Make It Work?   This chapter introduces tools, processes, templates, procedures, and action plans to set up your intranet. It provides a road map to make it work for you and it looks at what you need to do to set the stage, architect a plan, develop the intranet, and manage your intranet site.

How Do I Know It's Working?   If you can measure it, you can improve it. This chapter provides you with a discussion on web measurement systems for both technical performance and human performance and examines web metrics, access control logs, improved productivity, internal client satisfaction, accelerated development cycles, external client satisfaction, using cookies to profile internal users and feedback mechanisms to improve communication.

What Do Other People Say about Intranets?   What are leading analysts' viewpoints on the industry. This chapter is a snapshot of some key analysts' thoughts and predictions. It also looks at the key players' strategies and product lines (to provide a baseline). Resources for more information follow.

Interviews with the Key Players. This chapter features interviews with CIOs of Netscape, Microsoft, and Sun Microsystems, with Webmasters from Sun, SGI, and CIO Communications, and other intranet visionaries.

Intellectually Creative Society of the 21st Century

At the core of this book converge many of the leading business strategies and methodologies that have influenced business in the last couple of decades—ideas like rightsizing and client/server strategies, reengineering and empowerment, principle-centered leadership, *kaizen*, learning organizations, networked enterprises, quality, and ISO 9000+. These timeless business philosophies find their powerful truths being realized through the organizational tool that connect people's knowledge and performance from around the globe—the intranet.

In a networked age, where being on-line is everything to business success, the opportunity for creating intelligent companies with smart workers is at hand. The move away from an industrial society to an intellectually creative society seems inevitable. Already, the World Wide Web has empassioned the creative entrepreneur and has affected every organization: education, the stock market, the economy, the government, international business, worldwide entertainment and broadcasting, plus nearly every society across the globe.

Something bigger is happening though. It is the union of digital companies, organizations, and enterprises. It is the internetworking of individual and cultural identities, wrapped in the web of global knowledge that harnesses the potential of improving universal knowledge. It is the effects of universal knowledge on society as a whole that are evolving us into an intellectually creative society, populated with knowledge workers, knowledge creation tools, and knowledge management expertise. In such a society, based on high-performance infostructures, the most important and social economic resources and assets are the free creation, distribution, and sharing of these resources.

Organizations need to create a social environment that can fully capitalize on information and knowledge in order to resolve the increasingly more complex problems facing the world and to build a society that emphasizes intellectually creative activities.

Why I Wrote This Book

My bottom line is that intranets are about people empowerment, not technology. Almost all the intranet resources I reviewed were concerned with technical discussions. The core issues of knowledge creation, collaboration, communication, and information sharing are hardly ever mentioned. I've visited companies with all the technology in the world but no corporate culture to do anything with their resources, while other companies were creating magic with e-mail.

I wanted to write a book that explored the inner workings of an organization as a learning organization, one that values its culture, views the processes for design and development as treasures, and understands the potential of web technology to enhance intellectual potential for self-improvement and increased creativity IQs.

This lifelong study of computer-based expert systems, language simulators, computer-based training, multimedia development, and interactivity design has led me to write a book about a dream of interconnected, distributed communication tools that would affect the way we are doing business, the way we're performing our jobs, the way we're learning, and the way we're entertaining ourselves in the discovery and use of knowledge and intelligence.

With the generous help of so many individuals within the industry, I have built a body of information here that will focus on what to do with an intranet. I'm focused on developing on answer for how to use an intranet to prepare for highly competitive on-line 21st century electronic commerce. There are principles that underlie the magnitude of sharing organizational memory across all employees. The goal is to work smarter, not harder, to collaborate, not store and hoarde information, and to steel yourself for the future paradigm shifts that are going to rock the foundations of our industrial society.

CHAPTER 2

What's an Intranet?

Evolution of the Internet

Technical Definition   An intranet is a heterogeneous computing environment connecting different hardware platforms, operating system environments, and user interfaces in order to seamlessly communicate, collaborate, transact, and innovate.

Organizational Definition   An intranet is a learning organization, capable of integrating people, processes, procedures, and principles to form an intellectually creative culture dedicated to implementing total organizational effectiveness.

Where Are We Today with Intranets?

History   Intranets have actually been around for quite some time. Several people claim to have originated the term that describes the development of an internal client/server solution based on web technology. Dr. Steve Telleen at Amdahl was using the term IntraNet as early as 1994 in a paper he wrote on IntraNet methodology which resided on Amdahl's internal intranet and then was placed on Amdahl's external internet site.

The first commercially printed appearance of the term is found in Stephen Lawton's article on intranets in *Digital News & Review* in April 1995. In it he discusses Fortune 1000 companies posting web pages and installing telnet and ftp servers. The pioneers were Boeing, Schlumberger Ltd., Weyerhaeuser Corp., Sun Microsystems, and Digital Equipment Corp. The advantages were listed as low cost of setup, ease of writing HTML, and access to various kinds of documents on-line such as employee manuals, research material, and individual home pages.

Popularization   The popularization of the term is due in large part to Netscape™. When Netscape began to develop their business strategy around the full-service intranet, it put the term in our everyday vocabulary. None of us, however, can claim to be the first to build intranets. The use of the web technology in ways that today we would call intranets was happening not only at Amdahl in 1993, but also at Schlumberger, Lockheed, and NASA AMES. The phenomenon was happening before the term was around to describe it.

Bottom Line: The most impressive contribution an intranet will make to your organization is its communication and collaboration benefits.

Use It, Use It, Use It   Much like learning new information, it is not so much a matter of accessing information as it is using that information effectively and in a timely manner. The key is how are you going to use intranet technology. What is it ultimately going to do for you? The payback is going to be much more than you imagined if you know what you're going to do with it, rather than waiting for it to magically have an effect. If deployed properly, the fundamental organizational benefit will be a place in the 21st century digital economy.

Intranet Evolution

Intranets evolve. They start as basic web pages shared among a few technical people. These people educate a few others, and horizons are soon perceived. Cross-functional teams spring up, and suddenly a general awareness regarding paradigm shifts and 21st century business replaces industrial attitudes. With each level of evolution, you discover new capabilities. Some capabilities open new ideas for innovation, and then on to the next evolution.

In Table 2–1, we've listed five levels of intranet evolution. Many corporations, organizations, and universities have passed through only the first three levels. It is few that are seen in the fourth and fifth. The levels are Basics Intranets, Publishing Library Intranets, Collaboration Intranets, Transaction Intranets, and Extranets. The differences can be summarized by the level of integration into your organization. We list the characteristics of each intranet level by description, architecture, people and processes, value added, major cost features, and key limitations. You can examine the cost features in Chapter 5.

Table 2-1 Intranet Evolution

	Basic Intranet	Publishing Library	Collaboration Intranet	Transactions Intranet	Extranets
Description	Small web site. +50 pages. Text, links, graphics.	Production and access to company documents and on-line resources. Fairly large (static).	Interdependent group sites. Department pages. Centralized intranet home page. Advanced toolset.	Integrated with legacy systems and network applications. Uses Java and ActiveX and other APIs.	Full-service intranet, capable of interenterprise networking outside the firewall.
Architecture	TCP/IP. Central web server & browser. Server software. Editing tools.	Basics plus, publishing software, document management, search engine, database integration.	Full-service intranet with directory, file, print, mail capability. Integrate with groupware, project management software, and e-mail systems.	Full-service intranet server. Secure integration with corporate legacy databases and all applications.	Full-service intranet with encrypted escort software, that communicates with external partners.
People and Processes	A single individual, or small group, doing all design and development. Educating others is key responsibility.	Requires publishers, editors, and writers. Needs processes for submitting work, and a centralized web site to act as a single point of contact.	Requires sophisticated infrastructure. A cross-functional web council, webmaster, gatekeeper, application programmers and content provider. Needs templates, guidelines, and principles for doing business.	Reskilling of most labor processes at all levels. Requires integration of processes with network tools, databases, and metrics. Training required to orient work force.	Defined processes for doing business. Strong metric system to determine effectiveness. Integrators and augmented partnering.

Table 2-1 Intranet Evolution *(Continued)*

	Basic Intranet	Publishing Library	Collaboration Intranet	Transactions Intranet	Extranets
Value Added	Presence on-line.	Access to org. information.	Reduced development cycles.	Organizational effectiveness.	Wealth creation.
Cost Drivers	Minimal outlay of hardware/software.	Employee costs and tools. Increase in equipment and process	Exponential increase in overall operating costs. Development costs are pivotal.	Complete integration of all MIS costs.	Bandwidth. Partnering. Security.
Limitations	Capability.	Accuracy.	Maintenance.	Security.	Competition.

An Intranet Does What?

It *unifies the people,* the business processes, the corporate knowledge, the suppliers, the partners, and the customers through the technology of the Internet. Your business information, business processes, and corporate strategies are protected from outsiders behind a firewall (software and hardware that prevent electronic access from outside the organization).

It *provides a collaborative technology and a communication infrastructure* (people, processes, procedures) that permits your organization to behave as a whole entity, a group, a family, where everyone knows their roles, shares a common knowledge base, is strategically aligned to the organization's mission, goals, and objectives, and produces intellectual artifacts in the form of web pages for shared use throughout the organization.

It *uses a "single, universal" interface.* By identifying and communicating missions, goals, processes, relationships, interactions, standards, projects, schedules, budgets, and culture on-line in a "single, universal" interface. An intranet becomes the voice and the combined intelligence of the organization.

It *builds* **a learning organization**. In a word, an intranet represents your organization's "intelligence." The purpose of this intelligence is to organize each individual's Desktop with minimal cost, time, and effort to be more productive, most cost-efficient, more timely, and more competitive. Everyone uses and adds value back to the intranet, creating a dynamic learning organization, capable of creating a participative and rapid response workforce.

It **focuses us** *on co-existence, co-location, co-creation.* "Intranets make it possible for people to fulfill their own information needs and to easily locate people with similar interests or skills they need to get their jobs done. In some cases the intranet enables people to explore new ways to do their job or new business opportunities" (Gary Adams, Internet Pioneer, Sun Microsystems, Inc.).

What Value Do Intranets Add?

Apart from adding value such as presence on-line, access to organizational information at your fingertips, and reduced development cycles, the intranet adds value in powerful transformational ways to your organization. These may come because you planned them and then deployed an intranet to create the transformation. Or they may occur because of the organic and systemic nature of the intranet. Either way, I've observed the following:

- leveraging intelligence

- creating a single point of contact

- optimizing organizational focus

- securing a communication and transaction environment

Leveraging Intelligence   Effectively building an intranet is similar to building individual intelligence. Naturally, core basic skills are required for employees to be able to learn from an intranet and to derive complete, complex, and interesting solutions to current business problems. Self-paced learning and critical thinking skills are prerequisites to leveraging intelligence. It requires learning, applying the learning to practical decision making, and acting on the intelligence with solid, clear tasks and responsibilities. It requires modifying the learning for improved performance in the future and making sure all of this is communicated all of the time to everyone. It requires feedback and challenge from your organization's employees. This book is about using the intranet to leverage your organization's intelligence.

Creating a Single Point of Contact   The intranet probably already exists in your organization, or at least the components do. You need a Local Area Network (LAN) if your organization is regional, or a Wide Area Network (WAN) if your organization is international. You need servers (workstations, powerful PCs), you need clients (PCs, UNIX workstations, Apples, etc.), and you need software (server software, browser software, software tools for creation, maintenance, and analysis, and database connectivity software).

An intranet connects people together no matter what their hardware or software. Projects are linked together. Processes are linked together. Expert information is updated instantly for everyone to see at the same time. This is done with web servers (you've already got the technology), web browsers (download one), and data warehouses (you've already got information in your company, somewhere).

You've been using these components all along in your organization to do your work, improve efficiency, and communicate with others. The problem, of course, is that the machines, software, and communication systems don't necessarily talk to each other. You couldn't have internal communication of all data and information without a team of programmers and new software for every new cut on the information.

With an intranet, you have access to all the information, applications, data, knowledge, processes, and so forth, available in the same window, or the same browser. The key advantage is really what people want to know. And, you give it to them in an easy to use, easy to access, easy to produce environment. For Netscape Communications it was just a matter of fitting all the puzzle pieces into one screen.

In Figure 2–1, Netscape uses a logo name W3 as a brand recognition item for a company culture. It divides the company up into areas of functional or information access. Legal, Website Team, Engineering, Human Resources, Marketing, Finance, and OEM Marketing are a few of the functional pieces of the intranet puzzle. Test!, JAVA! Bugs, External Server, and Data Warehouses are the informational pieces. And, an empty puzzle piece remains for future planning. Any Netscape member could be the innovator of that piece. It identifies the culture as a participative, intellectually creative organization, comprised of individual units that collectively make up the whole. It is a single point of contact for Netscape.

Netsite: http://w3/

Welcome to w3.netscape.com

This is the launch point for Netscape's internal web. Use these links to view the company's development and business websites.

If you would like to add or update your group's information, send an email to manual3@netscape.com.

Here are some useful suggestions on setting up your group's website.

Figure 2–1 Netscape's Single Point of Contact

Netscape does not worry about conversions to different formats, accessing incompatible legacy systems, tying to the data warehouse, or accessing human resource information. They have created a single point of contact where the entire corporate information knowledge base is accessible.

No more missed opportunities because the technology is not compatible. No more trying to figure out where you stored certain information. Instead, the intranet connects people together with Internet technology, using web servers, web browsers, and a data warehouse in a single view that everyone can easily learn while still using their old software.

Bottom Line: An intranet is a single point of contact for leveraging your organization's knowledge.

Optimizing an Organizational Focus   The intranet is your opportunity to define your organization's culture and to display it for everyone to see in a graphical international format. If the major groups inside the corporation know what the company stands for, what the company's strategic vision is, what the guiding company principles are, and who the clients and partners are, they can then focus more clearly on what their own contributions are to the organization.

A clear, single web site (or home page) representing the values of the company is tantamount to success. Figure 2–2 shows Sun Microsystem's newly redesigned intranet web site. Clearly, Sun communicates an optimized organizational focus.

Securing a Communication and Transaction Environment   The intranet is the evolution of e-mail and network technology. Secured behind something called "firewalls," hardware, and software that screen, secure, and encrypt data passing through your network, the intranet allows communication between internal employees that cannot be perceived outside the company.

Transactions occur on the inside without any external peeking or poking into the intranet. Likewise, internal intranet users can communicate, collaborate, and even establish secure transactions outside of the intranet. Some companies restrict external access, although that is changing rather quickly. For example, reseller webs with passwords allow passing of internal information out to qualified, secured reseller web sites. These work over the Internet, the outside worldwide network that links all companies.

The level of encryption and security protection is unparalleled in electronic history. Secured intranet servers are very sophisticated, perhaps offering security that is unprecedented even by American Intelligence standards. A concern for many users is the ability for hackers to penetrate your intranet with the slightest connection to the outside world. The secured systems used in enterprise servers is highly sophisticated, using complex mathematical solutions. Nevertheless, many people are still unconvinced. Consequently, there is an issue with paranoia of risk

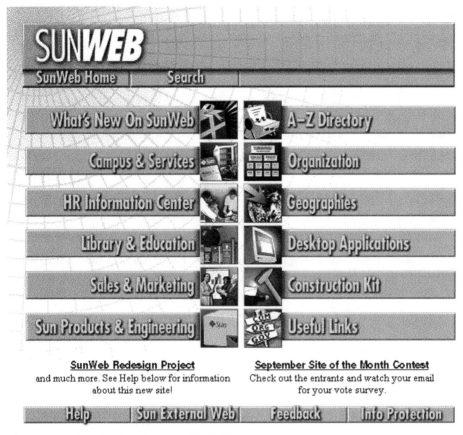

Figure 2–2 Sun's New Intranet Web Site.

and exposure in the hearts and minds of many who don't fully understand the technology. Only education and experience will help provide the understanding needed to ensure that intranets are secure.

Extranets

One of the anticipated value addeds is the extranet. Extranets will allow you to do direct on-line business with other companies' intranets directly over the Internet. Extranets are full-service intranets that combine all network services with all web technology services, including the Internet and the World Wide Web. This means e-mail, directory maintenance, log-in access control, and print services are united with open systems access, standardized data formats, legacy integration, and interactive web site development that is network-centric and provides communication and global collaboration. Security is achieved internally with encrypted intranets and externally with firewalls.

Most companies do not have full-service intranets yet and are not ready for this kind of deployment. Some companies are starting slowly, putting in a web server and having a smaller group within the organization develop web pages to examine the capabilities of the technology. Some organizations have moved a significant portion of their documentation on-line for easy access but are still designing and developing their overall strategies, watching, waiting. Other companies possess fully integrated intranets with legacy systems and advanced, interactive web-centric applications that focus on business simplification. The move to an extranet is reserved for those organizations that have developed a robust, cohesive intranet managed securely behind the firewall.

Enterprises need to allow customers access to their internal information for various reasons. Many processes in an organization begin outside the organization. In order to integrate the process, it may be necessary to extend out of the intranet through the secured firewall to interact with customers. This is one of the reasons that security is a significant issue with intranets.

Zona Research brilliantly captured their separate environments: the intranet (inside), the Internet (outside), and the extended intranet (inside, reaching outside), also called the extranet. In Table 2–2, as you can see, business productivity, processes, and company communications are the focus of the intranet. Developing marketing presence, placing orders, and providing decision-making information are the strengths of the external internet site. And the extended intranet (extranet) provides transaction processes for customers outside the intranet where internal databases are being updated.

Table 2-2 Internet, Intranet, Extended Intranet

Intranet Productivity Enhancement	Internet Productivity Enhancement
Internal E-mail	Product/Company Information
Collaborative Processing	External E-mail
Access Enterprise Memory	Place Orders
Order Processing	Order Tracking / Order Fulfillment / Customer Support / Transactions / Product Development — **Extended Intranet or Extranet**
Personal Pages	
Dept. Pages	
Group Communications	
Enterprise Communications	Business Enhancement
Product and Company Information	External Presence / Outbound Marketing / Catalogs, Product Information / Order Placement
Courtesy of Zona Research Inc.	

FedEx in Figure 2–3 is a good example of the extranet (extended intranet). You can track your packages directly by looking into their internal tracking systems. You have a limited access to a functional part of FedEx's intranet. Such a service creates a more supportive, more competitive service organization.

No matter what stage of development an intranet is in, the good news is that all the work is modular in nature. This means that if you're working on a small project or a large complex intranet project, the ability to cojoin any part of a smaller intranet project with a large-scale intranet is seamless when standardizing on TCP/IP and common international publishing standards. Just this alone makes this technology very palatable.

Countrywide Home Loans, the nation's largest independent mortgage lender, has developed a powerful extranet accessible only to Countrywide's lending partners and brokers today and to real estate agents in the near future. These parties require secure access to valuable information such as account and transaction status, loan status or "pipeline queries," company contacts, and company announcements. Called Platinum Lender Access, the service operates from a single Sun system running Netscape Server software. A total of 500 Countrywide lenders use

Netscape Navigator client software to access Platinum, with 300 regularly logging on to receive multiple-account updates each day. The Platinum system uses a sophisticated, Netscape-enabled routing system that automatically identifies each lender and provides them with their own customized information on premium rates, discounts, and special arrangements.[1]

Bottom Line: The extranet integrated with interenterprise intranets is the wave of the future.

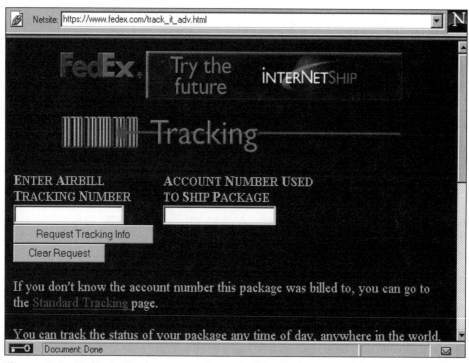

Figure 2–3   FedEx's Consummate Extended Intranet Example

---

1.   Copyright 1996 Netscape Communications Corp. All Rights Reserved. This page may not be reprinted or copied without the express written permission of Netscape.

Intranet as a Critical Thinking Tool

The intranet is not the perfect tool, but it is certainly being honed as a tool that will enable critical thinking. Most organizations rely on data, information, and knowledge to create products, services, education, and entertainment. Industrial development promoted *information is power.* In the past, it was always difficult to get hold of enough information, or reliable information, or information quickly enough, so those who could, seized the opportunities to use the information. They were reluctant to share and were dominated by the fear of losing power.

No matter what the user's information needs, the MIS department was more concerned with processing information, rather than allowing users to access information. For MIS, processing information is a repeatable filtration process, turning MIS into a filtration factory. Someone gets the information, reformats it for the audience, and redistributes it to the next person in the info-line.

With intranets, we not only enable access to information for all users, but we also empower the user to create knowledge products, innovate processes, improve workflow, and accelerate product development. Rather than processing information and moving it down the line, intranets create the ability to analyze interrelated events and to critically integrate these events into the work process. Intermediation between knowledge users and knowledge factories is eliminated.

Models of Information Flow

The flow of information has changed in business. In older models of information flow, information flowed through a series of information processing managers, who aligned work products with strategic goals. Managers acted as approving filtering bodies, delegating action plans to technical specialists who partnered with the workforce to produce goal oriented products. See Figure 2–4.

Managers acted as unwilling bottlenecks in a way because they needed the time to analyze information, filter it, and prepare it for well-planned information streams that helped improve the manufacturing and industrial processes. This method worked fine as long as most employees were focused on the repeatable processes of an industrial organization. The minute workers began creating knowledge products and reengineering business processes, the need for an information manager between the client and the worker changed radically.

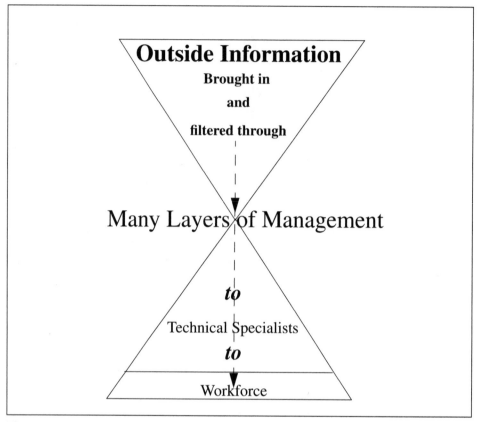

Figure 2–4 Management Model of Information Flow in an Organization

The Paradigm Shift

The quality movement, competition, and an expanding market into the development of knowledge products or knowledge processing forced organizations to change the way they were working. No longer was it sufficient to repeat processes and manufacture goods. Instead, people were required to innovate, to streamline processes, to improve workflow, to focus on the business of doing business, and communicate directly with the customer during the entire product development cycle.

The manager became a negotiator, bringing the right people together to solve problems. They helped identify root causes, perform process analysis, and act as consultants between departments. Managers started to focus on eliminated obstacles and to shop for opportunities. They moved away from information processing to knowledge management.

The intranet changes the model of filtered information flow. Managers are no longer the filtration system for all information. Instead, the focus on aligning information with business goals. Information access is replaced by information alignment. Information is localized and distributed out onto the intranet, like a magazine subscription, and at the same time can be internationalized to fit the needs of the enterprise.

In Figure 2–5, the intranet connects groups of people inside the organization differently. Each group has their own web site. Anyone on the intranet backbone can access information or knowledge easily. Corporate goals and strategic alignment can be viewed at the executive level. Managers have their own web sites to manage. The individual user accesses information from across the intranet. The customer has a single point of contact into the intranet, when authorized. Firewalls separate the outside from the inside. Electronic escorts allow outside movement to come inside with limited access. The model is elegant, it's simple, it's secure.

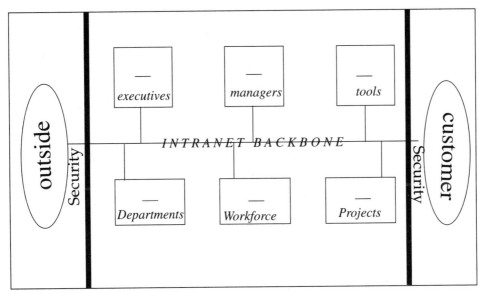

Figure 2–5 Information Flow with an Intranet

The Intranet as a Business Tool

A Collaboration Tool

Think about what happens when an easy-to-use, easy-to-learn, powerful tool for collaborating, project managing, data collecting, managing knowledge and information is handed to everyone in your networked organization. Imagine a tool that empowers people to put their best foot forward, proudly displaying their quality products, sales tips, marketing messages, internal customer services, technical procedures, processes, departmental goals, frequently asked questions, shortcuts, tips, tricks, and self-images in a place where anyone who subscribes can access them.

Imagine collaborating with each other without wading through e-mail, or playing telephone tag sessions, or missing your chance to input at a meeting. And, think of forums where people with common interests meet and hash out issues until the best possible solution is achieved. Then, add video-conferencing, electronic white- boards, single document sharing, and you've got a collaborative tool—the intranet.

An Expert's Tool

Who knows their job the best in any organization? The individual or group(s) performing the jobs. Experts are responsible for sharing their expertise and are responsible for communicating it to others so it can be understood. Being linked to real-time expert support by experts who add depth and breadth to their site while you incorporate their levels of expertise into your workflow is tantalizing.

It is equally possible to chat directly with the top, essential consultants and knowledge czars within your organization. On an intranet, capturing all that information in threaded databases so anyone can look at it, at any time is the stuff this new technology is all about. Sharing tips, tricks, pitfalls, analysis, and bottom line information about any topic allows you to minimize the innumerable hours researching, thinking, and putting ideas into action. Instead, you're performing and moving ahead faster than ever. In Figure 2–6, you can see how Amdahl uses its intranet as an expert tool. They use a combination of a well- designed page with commentary on key expert information in the company.

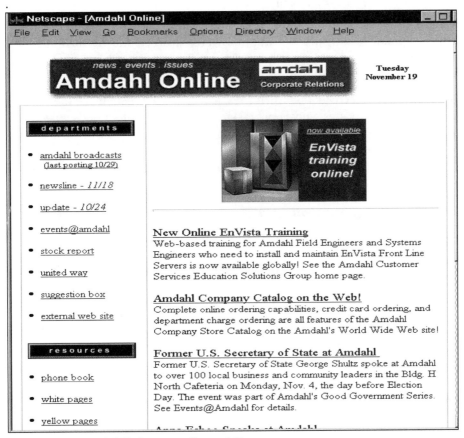

Figure 2–6 Amdahl's Intranet Central Site.

A Single Invention Tool

An intranet enables employees to find information when they need it and to cut and paste it into their presentations, sales pitches, marketing messages, or training modules. People save time not reinventing the wheel. Duplication of effort is eliminated. Instead of company information stored in filing cabinets, desks, garbage cans, huge piles on desks, hard drives, or floppies, information is on-line in your intranet, available for use by anyone working on similar topics.

An intranet provides one view into the organization. Through a common look and feel and through common goals and messages repeating across the organization, everyone in the organization tells the customer the same story! Once again— a single point of contact, a single source.

A 21st Century Telephone

The intranet is a tool that has already become a utility in many companies, much like the telephone. Use it, and you are empowered to accelerate production cycles, to focus on expert information, to customize products and services for customers, to educate yourself immediately, and get hold of anyone in the organization.

Allow individuals to create their own sites, just as you let them make their own calls. Creating group sites, departmental sites, and project sites builds an empire of knowledge in which the organization knows what they represent, how they fit into the organization, and how to speak and listen to the customer with this focus in mind. The level of interaction becomes more intelligent and more streamlined to business goals and corporate missions.

A Process Identification and Process Improvement Tool

Ever wondered how your sales cycle really worked? Or have you ever dreamed of a system that would show you where any transaction was within an accounting cycle, so you could apply the most appropriate resources? Because an intranet produces a visual representation of the processes within the organization, everyone in the organization can examine the elements of the process that it is representing.

With an intranet, you observe the way cross-functional teams integrate their needs, products, and services. You develop awareness of how your way of doing business makes your internal client's job easier. Does it include the necessary pieces of your overall organization, department, or group? Is your group giving others what they need? Is the workflow timely and effective?

Where are they getting their information? Do *you* have anything to make their job easier? Or vice versa. Can you clearly see your own inputs, what process activities you're responsible for, and what your outputs are? Can you observe the workflow among your team members, identify the process, and provide ways to improve it continuously? Companies with established, integrated intranets have only one word: "Yes."

A Competitor's Tool

It seems almost every company in the world has created at least one page on the Internet. If you want a real taste of what millions of people are doing on the outside Internet, you'll find Internet statistics at

- IDC [http://www.idcresearch.com/git96.htm]

- Dataquest, a Gartner Group company [http://www.gartner.com/] and [http://www.dataquest.com]

- The Burton Group [http://www.tbg.com]

- Zona Research [http://www.xbg.com/Pubs/inet.html]

- Forrester Research Group [http://www.forrester.com/]

If this much activity is occurring on the outside Internet, just imagine what's going on behind the firewalls: something akin to a competitive assault. We've summarized some of the facts for you in the chapter called"What Do Other People Say About Intranets?"

A Partnering Tool

With this information explosion, the idea is obviously to hook up with your partners as well if they're going on-line. Doing so provides accurate, precise, up-to-date information on products and services, competitive advantages, current trends, late breaking news, technologies, and on and on. What a wealth of information you can feed your intranet.

Also, with an intranet, you can integrate internal processes with partners and streamline the way you do business. You can incorporate their sites into your web site for a more robust internal intranet, track projects, manage vendors, channel partners, manage requirements, and link to one another's excellence and processes.

A Customer Tool

Your customers have gone on-line as well, describing their processes, their services, their products, and often their competition. Linking into these sites provides you a much quicker reference point for getting to know what your customer is thinking. *You can connect to your customer's clients and analyze solutions or opportunities from a different vantage point.* This connection is an internet tool, meaning it is outside your company's security firewalls. But, having the information about your customer at your fingertips can decidedly impact how you deliver to them, so keeping that intranet/internet awareness is very important.

An ISO Tool

The intranet can satisfy a lot of your ISO 9000+ requirements. First of all, you can provide all information on-line in a single location. Secondly, you can identify processes, metrics, and project contacts on-line. Since everyone can access the intranet, it becomes a solid singular source or repository which stores data satisfying many of the ISO requirements for accessing information. Similarly, intranets help with the following tasks:

- Management responsibility

- Quality system

- Contract review
- Design control
- Document and data control
- Purchasing
- Control of customer-supplied products
- Product identification and traceability
- Process control
- Inspection and testing
- Control of inspection, measuring, and test equipment
- Inspection and test status
- Control of nonconforming products
- Corrective and preventive actions
- Handling, storage, packaging, preservation, and delivery
- Control of quality records
- Internal quality audits
- Training
- Servicing
- Statistical techniques

As mentioned before, it is up to you to use the intranet to make your work easier. The intranet is the undisputed tool for working on hefty requirements like those of the ISO 9000 Certification group. See http://www.iso.ch/welcome.html for more information on ISO.

A Target Marketing Tool

Steve Finnegan, president of the Huntington Group, Inc., says:

> The elements of a traditional business-to-business marketing and sales program can be integrated within the web environment in order to create target marketing, which attracts highly qualified customer/client prospects and engages them in an ongoing product/service sales dialogue, a definitive competitive advantage realized through an intranet.

> The end result can be more profitable, long-term customer/client relationships. These issues include a shift in emphasis from sales transactions to the lifetime value of business relationships, from one-way information flow to two-way

dialogue and collaboration, and from mass markets to market segments, each demanding more customization and faster response times.

The intranet permits you to build on external profiling. Your outside Internet collects row data about its visitors. The data can be used to prequalify users on intranet tools. You can then leverage off of internal resources to identify customer requirements more accurately. The customer will be delighted to see how well prepared you are.

A Human Resource Tool

It takes systematic rethinking about the nature of employee-to-enterprise and employee-to-employee relationships now that every employee has the ability to instantly communicate work, thoughts, gripes, experiences, and solutions to every other employee. The power of the employee also creates a set of value-added responsibilities for all members of the organizational community.

You're going to have to start thinking about infrastructure, policies, procedures, roles and responsibilities, templates, and legal issues. The intranet may cause your company to reevaluate itself entirely. But haven't we been told that for the past five years— Reengineer your corporation, rightsize it, turn it into a learning organization, focus on principle centered leadership so your employees can build quality products, services, education, and entertainment? Yes, we have. The difference is that we've finally got the tool to do it with. Chapter 6 will explain how to use the tool, so you can get back to the business of making your products and services work right the first time, every time.

Bottom Line: Intranets are merely the tool for shaping your organization into a 21st century powerhouse.

Differences Between Intranets and the Internet

Basically, these two technologies are the same. Both are based on Internet technology. In Chapter 2, we'll discuss Internet technology more thoroughly. The bottom line is that the technology is based on standardized TCP/IP communication protocols, HTTP protocols, web servers and browsers, HTML publishing, and web application programming. These technologies enable the rapid, graceful development of internetworked web sites that communicate across all platforms and across most international networks.

Bottom Line: What separates the Internet and intranets is their use, not their technology.

The Internet Comparison

The Internet is designed for public consumption. The Internet so far only focuses on marketing and advertising environments. It focuses on product orientation and company profiles. Its audience is primarily the consumer, the customer, and the student. The Internet is also an excellent source of educational research, where you can access vast databases around the world, from the Library of Congress to Yahoo's varied multiple topical sites.

The Internet is a vast clearinghouse for individuals who present their ideas, products, wares, and families in an act of community sharing. Users are on their own, deciphering the quality of the information they experience and trusting in the reliability of company names, or reputations. The search tools are abundant and the quality of information is extraordinary. However it is not driven by a single purpose or raison d'être. It simply provides information that an individual or a company thinks should be freely distributed.

Many users are familiar with the Internet, either for shopping for products or just looking for "cool sites" that deal with topics of interest. One of the key features of the Internet is its global searching capability. A simple example is at http://home.netscape.com/home/internet-search.html, which hosts at least 20 different search tools for you to find everything you want on the Internet.

Currently with the advent of secured on-line transmissions, the Internet is evolving into an environment of financial transactions, where electronic commerce is starting to take place. The Internet has become an integral part of the sales cycle. This means that an Internet site is meant to prequalify the customer by identifying needs and expectations and educating on features, benefits, and competitive reasons to select their products or services.

Bottom Line: The Internet focuses people on how to make money and how to get smarter.

The Intranet Comparison

Intranets, on the other hand, are meant to strengthen the intelligence and capability of a workforce developing, disseminating, and supporting products and services. An intranet is designed to focus on employees, on improving workflow. It is process oriented, providing an environment for employees to streamline how work is done and how to expedite the creative and developmental processes.

Intranets should be used for collaborative processing. This means that the minute a project is identified at a company, a web site can establish project management. Contacts, schedules, timetables, resources, interdependencies, and competitive information can be posted to the web site to allow the quick retrieval of relevant information. See Microsoft's Outlook product that accompanies Office 97.

Problems, questions and answers, and software bugs can all be maintained at the site to provide a collaborative environment for individuals participating in a group. Threaded conversations, which are ongoing e-mail with subject headings, can also be maintained on the site, so the history of the project can be used in the future. Additionally, any group that wants to link to the project site can do so to assist in their projects as well. This is corporate intelligence leveraged to optimize the organization's effectiveness.

Intranets rely on the company's internal information and intelligence. It is only as good, though, as the tools used to display the information. This is where the real payoff is— in *leveraging the company's intelligence.* Your inside knowledge is the greatest competitive advantage that you have. No one has the repository of information that you do about your company. Plus, you've got the people and the expert resources to interact with the information and to draw on when there is a need to expedite a response.

Bottom Line: Intranets focus on improving business processes and reducing development life cycles.

In Table 2–3 below, you can find a summary of the differences.

Table 2-3 Differences between an Intranet and the Internet

An Intranet	The Internet
Proprietary information	Public information
Security is mission critical	Security is mission critical and competitive
Focused on employee communication	Focused on customer communication
Collaboration transactions	Financial transactions
Designed for workflow	Designed for customer interaction flow
Process oriented	Sales and marketing oriented
Optional connection to the Internet	Mandatory connection to the Internet
Transforms organizations	Transforms the customer/sales cycle
Emphasis on work groups, teams, and intradepartment flow	Emphasis on single point of contact with the organization and user profiling
Used for development	Used for implementation
Creates a learning organization	Creates brand awareness and Net-citizen status
Needs to be highly decentralized	Needs to be highly centralized

Users are less familiar with the inner workings of an internal intranet. Some companies, Amdahl, SGI, Sun Microsystems, Inc., Schlumberger, and Eli Lilly, have been using the intranet for a very long time. They use it successfully to promote company innovation, company collaboration, and company process improvement.

The On-line Services Comparison

On-line services, such as Prodigy, AOL, CompuServe, and Microsoft Network, are designed to provide "on-line communities" for the general public. On-line services provide a single source of information and transaction capability for their subscribers. The source is proprietary in nature, meaning that the service provider decides what services and products will be put under their domain. They also provide on-line business environments for small companies to go on-line and provide an electronic community for individuals to set up their individual web pages, for whatever purpose they see fit.

On-line services are designed for a large amorphous customer. They have the same daunting task as the Internet. However, on-line services are comprised of a single company, which collects, compiles, filters, and designs information for its huge, undefined audience. They make critical decisions, they buy and manage content and databases, and provide whatever appropriate tools they believe their audience needs. One of their most popular features is their chatting rooms where individuals can speak freely about any number of topics.

Are they robust financed environments for creating vast wealth? No. They are too focused on pushing content to the customer. They are too expensive to subscrive to. They do not add enough value; nor do they position you for being in control of your business evolution.

They cannot focus the piercing light of intelligence as an intranet can. They are disparate and trying to be all to everyone. What they do well is to pull people together in an electronic community in chat rooms, creating the metaphor of the cafe or bar where people come to talk to each other about their problems, hobbies, or business needs. Some of the on-line tools are splendid, and intranet technology could benefit from paying attention to their success and best practices.

Table 2–4 below summarizes the differences between these three services—the internet, intranets, and on-line services. Each has their own strengths and weaknesses. For you, for internal communications that provide the most value to your organization, the intranet is the best show in town.

Table 2-4 Internet, Intranet, On-line Service Comparisons

The Internet	An intranet	On-line Services
Key strategies: Branding, partnering, and electronic commerce	*Key strategies:* Collaboration, improved workflow, global communication, and rapid development prototyping.	*Key strategies:* Advertising, ease of use. Access to stylized sites, so look and feel are consistent.
Access and speed are based on 14.4 and 28.8 modems most often. Browsers are usually memory efficient.	*Access and speed* are based on internal lines, T1, T3, ISDN, and ATM.	*Access and speed* are based on 14.4 and 28.8 modems, and interfaces are graphic intensive.

Table 2-4 Internet, Intranet, On-line Service Comparisons *(Continued)*

The Internet	An intranet	On-line Services
Interaction is transactional. Most interaction occurs in written form, with check boxes, radio buttons, and pull- down menus. Other interaction is threaded e-mail.	*Interaction is collaborative.* It occurs in the corporate meeting room with intranet access from computerized overheads. Also, people work together on-line, over the phone in real time for development purposes.	*Interaction is social.* It happens in chat rooms where social conversation occurs in electronic forums.
Cost is dependent on internet service provider.	*Cost* to the user is not apparent, but cross-charging is popular.	*High cost* of subscription and additional connect times. Uses native browser for Internet access.
Communication is not done well. The customer communicates through feedback forms. Rarely do you see contacts to web ownership.	*Communication* is the major benefit. Projects, schedules, e-mail, repositories, and links are managed well to stimulate communication and team work.	*Communication* occurs in chat rooms. The environment is one of a community of individuals with the same interests. Strongly socialized.
Content is filtered by public law, corporate policy, and individual expression.	*Content* filtered by individual organization publishing the web site, the gatekeeper role.	*Content* is filtered by public law and strictly at the on-line service's discretion.
Content providers can be independent of any corporation. Or they can be selected by marketing communications to represent the corporate site.	*Content providers* interact without going through gatekeepers for official approval. But, when web sites are pushed up for position on the intranet, gatekeepers approve content.	*Content is purchased* and distributed en masse to the public.
Future. Telecommunications companies will bundle Internet access or an Internet-based on-line service with long distance, paging, cellular, and satellite-delivered video.	*Future.* Will see enhanced use of video, training, and very capable data warehouse querying for decision support. Capability is based on the original architecture of the intranet. Plan well.	*Future.* Will change its proprietary nature and prohibitive costs. May emerge as unique broadcasting channels to enable one-stop shopping.

Pros and Cons of an Intranet

Benefits of an Intranet

The key benefits include lowered network costs, ease of learning, goal-oriented self-development, and open standards that allow software to run without relying on an operating system. Communicating company focus and tracking to the mission statement or individual department goals make an intranet a winner.

Access to data warehouses makes the intranet worth its weight in gold. Other key benefits are improved business models, enhanced communication, collaborative work group environment, with continuous process improvement principles underlying the intranet infrastructure.

Limitations of an Intranet

The limitations are important in developing an intranet strategy. These limitations may or may not have immediate solutions in your organization; however, identifying them up front can save you lots of development time. So in planning, you must weigh them carefully.

Rand Lindsley, Senior Engineer at Sun Microsystems, says:

> Before you can start addressing the issues of improved business processes, you have to look at the bigger problems first. Most importantly, look at architecture and infrastructure. How are you going to configure everyone's systems (so they have TCP/IP capability and a client browser)? What kind of search engine are you going to incorporate? And what are the processes and policies for getting your messages on the intranet site.

These are not daunting. Instead, they are plans for action.

Another limitation is determining the reliability and currency of the content. It's difficult to say who the experts are in this area, unless they are well recognized. Corporations push what an expert is on the Internet, but on an intranet, the technical people tend to be experts. But, are they expert at delivering their expertise on the intranet?

Controversies of an Intranet

The most salient controversy is security. Security is an issue for the intranet and the Internet. Security issues have to be addressed fully. Not all information can be put on-line: payroll, personal employee information, engineering prototypes, company secrets, and so forth. However, in order for the intranet to be fully functional, this information needs to be available on-line. Information like this needs to be secured behind fire ridges (security that allows access only by authorized members). The Web does not handle login, security, access control, authorization, or replication very well yet. So, setting up fire ridges like this is challenging.

Issues of directory and security interoperability are significant hurdles as well. With the introduction of directory servers and new Internet protocols for dealing with directories and operating system differences, these issues will be resolved. However, the maturation of the technology must take place to handle these hurdles. We're not as open as we want.

Should You Be Centralized or Decentralized?

A centralized model as in Figure 2–7 focuses all the attention, approval, decision-making and policy decisions in the center of the technology. An MIS or IT department is usually responsible for all information needs within an organization. This is a pre-intranet model, and it used to work well when organizations were industrial manufacturing houses where process was the key focus. There was only one way to manufacture something.

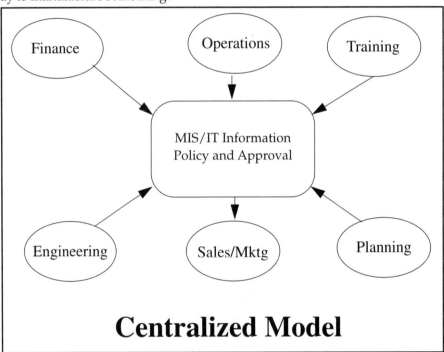

Figure 2–7 Centralized Model of Information Technology

In a decentralized model as in Figure 2–7, each individual organization has their own intranet, and subscribes to the main intranet page where common information and tools are provided from a central group (service providers). The decentralized groups focus on how the intranet can help users. They also add the specific information and tools that content providers need to be successful. This way users can manage their own information, hide proprietary information for unauthorized access, and innovate and develop according to the principles of their discipline.

The decentralized model provides more flexibility and access to information expertise from the source. Separate intranets can operate managing their workflow and business processes best at their own level. When integrating with other web sites, standards, mutual practices, and policies must be available for coordination, if necessary. These standards and policies can be centralized at the top level for easy compliance. The idea of decentralization is independence and robustness. Each group deals with its own customers and interdependencies. No reliance is placed on a centralized information group.

However, the architecture should be centralized by the IT group. Management, support, capacity planning, load balancing, and rightsizing are handled more elegantly. Centralized architecture is the true distributed model that creates reliable, available, and serviceable intranet systems.

Bottom Line: Centralize your architecture, decentralize your content.

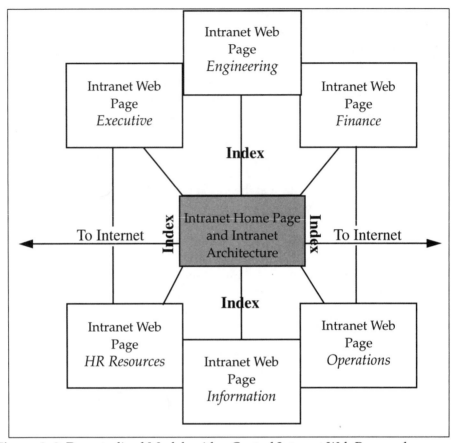

Figure 2–8 Decentralized Model, with a Central Intranet Web Page and Architecture

Summary of Issues

In Table 2–5 below, we've summarized some of the benefits, limitations, and controversies. We look at organizational focus, company goals, ownership, metrics, workflow, usage, validity, communication, collaboration, and development. How will these affect your business? How will you plan accordingly?

Table 2-5 Pros and Cons of an Intranet

	Benefits	Limitations	Controversies
Organizational Focus	Focuses the organization with a centralized web page, centralized tools, and processes.	Requires content management and access control to organizational areas requiring security.	Security, HTML standards, conflicts with organization versus individual needs.
Company Goals	Coordinates interdepartmental goals and strategies.	Needs to centralize at a high level, and streamline departmental visions.	Highlights incongruities and inconsistencies in company.
Ownership	Builds company values.	Requires conversion of old systems and disperses accountability.	Creates turf wars. Builds information silos.
Workflow	Enhances group communication to improve workflow.	Can create pockets or islands of excellence.	Groups guard or hide information.
Usage	Stimulates critical thinking processes.	Have to use it to be good at it.	Employees will play on it.
Validity	Focuses on expert content.	Can experts design good sites?	Is information valid and authentic?
Communication	Universal communication.	English is the predominant language.	Translating sites is hard, plus is it worth it?
Collaboration	Collaborative environments easily developed and customized.	Intranets do not provide replication, where the most current version is updated, providing version control.	Many of the maintenance features of collaborative applications have to be built in.

Table 2-5 Pros and Cons of an Intranet *(Continued)*

	Benefits	Limitations	Controversies
Development	HTML easy to learn and program.	HTML not powerful enough to develop web applications.	Java and ActiveX™, web application development tools, are programming intensive, increasing development time.
Metrics	Observes company behavior, focuses on positive and minimizes the negative.	Usage statistics are not robust.	ROI is difficult to evaluate. Can human performance be measured?

An Intranational Explosion

The United States has certainly gotten a running start on intranet development. Many of the technologies were born here, and much of the research was done in the labs in the Silicon Valley, the Silicon Forest, and the Silicon Desert. However, this is a global environment. Corporations are global, doing business in the 90s is global. The intranet must become intranational in order for it to work right.

Various demographic surveys regarding Internet usage declare that a considerable amount of commercial traffic is coming out of the United Kingdom, Germany, Japan, and, of course, the United States. These statistics reveal a notable rise in European and Japanese presence on the Internet, suggesting that international electronic commerce is on the rise worldwide. Many enterprises are international, and intranets are developing internationally as well.

There are many international corporations that can get along without Microsofts, Netscapes, and Sun Microsystems Inc. and develop sophisticated intranets based on internetworking technology their own way. They, in fact, can start to set world standards and develop their own electronic environment for commerce, education, and entertainment. They, can, in fact, develop their own encryption technology and distribute it throughout the world over the Internet. But, if the 21st century is going to become the Global Digital Economy Century, the need to communicate international standards, open architecture, and repeatable processes is imperative.

Your organization has to internationalize. You have to begin trade agreements, learn about information exchange, understand the differences in culture, integrate cultural icons into your web environment, and develop sophisticated security mechanisms. The point here is to leverage corporate intelligence (national or international). It opens up the international market and lets companies globalize.

Your customers, and equally important your employees, come from everywhere around the world. Doing business with each other internationally impacts the effectiveness of your global presence. How is your organization's intranet transforming your company into an international competitor? Planning an answer is crucial.

Common Global Link

While each international issue requires multifaceted strategies depending upon the politics and relationship between countries, the common link is the *need to enable and expand global communications within the organization*. Once intranets are clearly established, an integration with international partners and the global marketplace can be established. The internal adoption of intranet technology to leverage organizational international intelligence can make significant contributions to the global economy.

In "The Intranet: A Corporate Revolution"— from UK-based JSB Computer Systems—Rob Barrow, chief executive officer, identifies "the impact of the intranet on a corporation's operation, efficiency, development and even its culture." The cultural effect is what is revolutionizing the enterprise. Organizations are becoming smarter, more critical in their thinking, and more connected to the organization. The culture is evolving.

Identifying cost, quality, changing markets, and business models as critical success factors for international success, JSB believes that global collaboration, internationalization, and simulated environments will be the call of the day. These solutions will require an in-depth knowledge of intracultural needs and expectations.

Understanding and integrating with other cultures are imperative to a global digital economy. However, remember a new culture is being forged as well, a cyberculture, where new ways of communicating (video, icons, audio, simulated 3D environments, colors, branding, headlines, mindmaps) define the evolving language of the intranet. English, by far, dominates as the key language. But, leveraging off an intranet in Japan, France, or Singapore will require some knowledge of moving around communication structures of other cultures. Get used to it.

Internationalization

If your company already works in the international sector, localization and internationalization are important factors to consider. If you're a global company, no matter what you do on your intranet site, recognition of various languages and cultures is imperative. Opening up the borders within an intranet will bring your international organization full circle. If you're not in the international arena, these words provide guidance when you take on international partners, customers, and locations. Simply put, internationalize.

What Is the Intranet? Cos'e l'Intranet? Was is das Intranet? Wat is Intranet?[2]

English   In simple terms, the intranet is the descriptive term being used for the implementation of Internet technologies within a corporate organization, rather than for external connection to the global Internet. This implementation is performed in such a way as to transparently deliver the immense informational resources of an organization to each individual's desktop with minimal cost, time, and effort.

Italian   Detto semplicemente, intranet è un termine che descrive l'implementazione di tecnologie Internet all'interno di un'impresa invece che per collegamenti all'Internet globale esterno. Questa implementazione viene attuata per far sì che le immense risorse informative di un'organizzazione vengano rese disponibili, in modo del tutto trasparente, al desktop di ciascun individuo, col minimo di costi, tempo ed energie.

German   Einfach ausgedrückt könnte man sagen, daß das intranet die Einführung der Internet Technologie innerhalb eines Unternehmens beschreibt, im Gegensatz zu einem externen Anschluß an das globale Internet. Durch diese Einführung läßt sich eine transparente Weiterleitung des umfangreichen Informationsmaterials innerhalb eines Unternehmens an den Desktop eines jeden einzelnen Mitarbeiters mit einem geringen Kosten-, Zeit- und Arbeitsaufwand verwirklichen.

---

2.   Courtesy of JSB Corporation.

Japanese

日本語：簡単に言えばイントラネットとは、
グローバルインターネットという外界への
接続に対して、組織集団内でインターネット
テクノロジーを用いることである。これは、
最低限のコストと時間と努力で、組織の
莫大な情報源を個人個人にそのまま伝える
方法である。

Let the translating begin. Or visit http://www.aleph.com. This is a site that helps you translate from almost any spoken language. They use the best translators in the world and can help profile you and your translator to make the experience as seamless as possible.

The Intranet Computing Model

The intranet computing model is based on the network services model, which suggests that a full set of interoperable network services be available for an organization's infostructure. These services include: file, print, directory, security, messaging, Web, and management.

The Network Is the Computer

Sun Microsystems coined the phrase "The Network is the Computer." By this they mean that every computer, desktop, or workstation is connected to the Network and can share files, directories, and software in a common environment, or graphical user interface. The intranet computing model extends that definition. The network is the computer—the web is the network—therefore the web is the computer. Another way to say this is network-centric computing is replacing desktop-centric computing. This is why companies like Microsoft are embracing Internet standards and technologies.

Sun's model for computing is at the very foundation of its own success as an organization. Using Internet technology, TCP/IP protocols, Sun built itself into an organization that was seamless, open, and integrated. In effect, Sun has been working on an intranet model during its entire life span. Sun has a computer, or a workstation, on every desk. Each one of those units is TCP/IP friendly, connected to the network, and uses standard Internet protocols. Someone saw the vision a while back. Now the vision is clear to the critical mass.

As the World Wide Web technologies emerged, Sun used the opportunity to align more closely with its partners, clients, and investors. The Internet served as a direct line of communication between Sun and the outside world. Sun began to demonstrate to their clients how their internal intranet worked, and an intranet computing model was born.

The Network Is the Web

Evolution dictates that we expand beyond our concept of reality, examine the new features of our ecosystem, and adjust both physically and psychologically. Intranets will change the way business is done. Business will not look the same in the 21st century.

Each web site is independent, designed, maintained, and administered by the owner. It contains intelligence the way the independent originator knows how to display it best. At any point, another site can link to the expertise of the web site. At any point, another site can go to the outside through a firewall to retrieve, explore, or research other web sites. There are no central content developers. Everyone is a webmaster.

Each node on the Web constitutes a higher state of intelligence for the enterprise. As everyone uses their intelligence, and equally contributes to the Web, the intranet becomes a gigantic neural network. Focused on the right spot, at the right time, an organization can develop anything better (in shorter time, for less cost, with better quality—a new paradigm emerges).

What Are the Key Features of an Intranet Computing Model?

Certainly, it is true that we must figure out the value the intranet has for the organization in some measurable way so that appropriate resources can be directed toward developing it. We need to answer simple questions, such as, Do we need web experts in each department or for each project? Does everybody need to be able to write HTML? What is the payback for this effort? Should the effort be centralized? Which functions should be centralized and which should be distributed to the work groups? While all of these questions need to be answered individually by each company, we need to define an intranet computing model, or at least identify aspects of the model that we can start to put into place, since intranets are developing in organizations without official planning.

Co-Evolution and Co-Location

The intranet must be designed to evolve at the granular level of the individual, reflecting contributions and intellectual artifacts from all the various contributors around the organization. Also, it must evolve at the systemic level, where all contributions from all departments evolve interdependently. What affects one, affects all. With this design, you can accommodate for the distribution of workers across multiple locations, localizing some information while internationalizing other intranet information simultaneously.

Individual Organization and Access

An intranet must be designed to allow individuals to organize, publish, create, and develop their own infostructures as they see fit. This means individual, group, project, and departmental freedom of expression. Also, this means that the individual is responsible for access to information. This competency needs to be a part of the individual's base for success. In other words, workers who know how to research information are your greatest assets.

Centralized Communication and Coordination

An intranet needs to have a centralized location, a single point of contact. At any level, this is the home page. It is a web page designed to communicate collective, shared information, including tools and organizational focus. Centralized coordination means access control and security enforcement.

Rapid Response to Change

Rapid response to change must be a part of the intranet model's requirements. People leave, processes change, customers alter their thinking, and market trends affect decision making. A broadcast model must be established to inform users of rapid change. When needed, the entire organization must be behind the individual during transitions.

Management Becomes a Negotiator

Management as discussed previously becomes a negotiator between content providers. This model is important, as it reflects the general trend in business today. Someone in the organization still needs to architect information models, workflow, and system views of organization.

Bottom Line: There is no revolution going on here. There is only evolution.

Summary of Key Points

• WHAT'S AN INTRANET?

An intranet is a client/server technology based specifically on Internet standards, especially TCP/IP. It is used specifically within your organization to leverage company intelligence to improve business processes, improve workflow, empower with collaboration, and articulate vision and strategy in a secure communication and transaction environment. Also, the extranet or extended intranet is defined as the external transactions between intranets over the Internet or World Wide Web.

- INTRANET AS A TOOL

  The intranet is a tool for collaboration, workflow, process improvement, process identification, decision support, ISO compliance, communication, and customer partnering and interaction.

- KEY FEATURES, KEY COMPARISONS

  When you indentify how you're going to use your intranet, start first by understanding the differences between an intranet and the Internet. Also, make sure you understand the difference between on-line services, client–server, and the Intranet. The principle benefit is decreased cost and increased productivity. The greatest limitation is having to build Web-friendly applications. And, the biggest controversy is security.

- INTRANET COMPUTING MODEL—*"The Web is the Network"*

  Everything moves to the intranet. Servers are multifunctional, and clients are thin (storing little data). The model is based on TCP/IP, where co-evolution and co-location must occur, with centralized communication and coordination and distributed content development.

- AN INTRANATIONAL EXPLOSION

  Simply put, you've got to prepare for an intranational audience. The global economy requires your intranet to reach out across the world for electronic partnerships. Globalization of companies is requiring international appeal and cultural sensitivity.

Bottom Line: Now you know what to plan for.

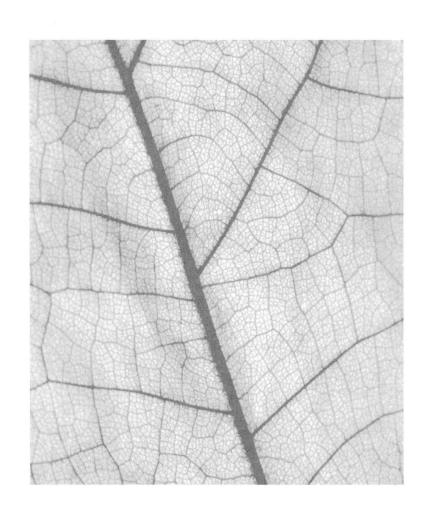

CHAPTER 3

What's
It Made of?

In order for you to make good decisions about introducing, analyzing, budgeting, staffing, administering, maintaining, or using a corporate intranet, you need to know what they are made of. This chapter provides you with an overview of the key issues regarding the makeup of an intranet. It will help you perform an intranet feasibility analysis and determine your intranet strategy development. We've chosen simple terms and colorful analogies to help you understand these terms, rather than use "tech talk."

- Intranet Architecture (hardware, software components, and standards)

- Intranet Infrastructure (tools, people, and processes)

- Intranet Interactivity (talking to legacy systems, databases, and customers)

- Intranet Security (firewalls, policies, risk)

- Intranet Design (four tiers: site creation, content creation, site maintenance, site analysis)

Intranet Architecture

This section will describe some of the architecture issues relating to intranet sites as they relate to making business decisions. This section is meant to be a decision-making session. It provides a working knowledge of architecture terms to assist in making strategic intranet decisions. It covers issues regarding internet standards, networks, servers, clients, and browsers. It also includes internet connectivity and Independent Service Providers (ISPs).

Open Standards

Talking about intranet architecture means talking about open standards. Open standards means that the software you use to transform your data into company intelligence can run on any hardware, over any network. It also means that anyone can quickly develop software without having to make sure it is compatible with every network operating system. The days of proprietary software and hardware, of divergent operating systems, have ended with intranet architecture. Or are they? Interoperability still depends on disclosure of extensions to standards and existing proprietary protocols. This means such openness as Windows, Novell, Java, and any HTML extensions being incorporated. This is the reason for standards bodies. We are close to complete open systems. Close enough to create intranets today.

Figure 3–1 paints a clear picture of open standards. Any client (PC or workstation) uses TCP/IP (Internet standards) to communicate with any server. It just doesn't get simpler than that.

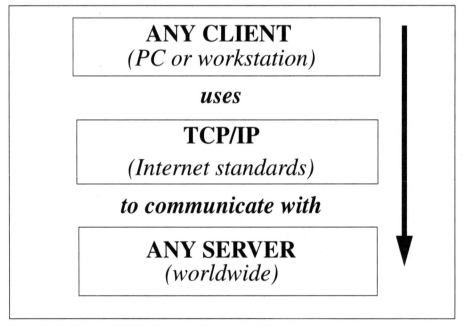

Figure 3–1 Classical Web Browser-Server Architecture

Business Implication—Right Tool for the Right Job   Nobody owns the internet standards on which intranets are developed. This means that anyone using internet standards can develop an application and make it available on the intranet. This frees up software development enormously, helping to bring to market the right tool for the right job, on time, under budget, and with excellent quality. Making applications available over the intranet reduces the cost of distribution and improves the licensing and upgrading process.

Intranet Standards

You really needn't spend much time thinking about intranet standards as they are based on established internet protocols. You need to understand them to build your intranet framework. Intranet standards are made up of internet protocols, programming languages, and Application Programming Interfaces (APIs).

Table 3–1 below summarizes the key internet standards that facilitate the flow of information. We include them here because you will need to have a working recognition of the terms. Because this industry is technical, you'll need to have a bit of information about internet standards to help position your intranet solutions appropriately. I've deviated a bit from traditional definitions, only to make them readable.

Table 3-1 Internet Standards

Internet Standard	What's it do?	How's it do it?
TCP/IP	Acts as a post office between global networks.	Gives each PC or workstation its own address, so packages can be sent to the right place.
HTTP	Enables browsing across global networks.	Delivers and tracks information packages between clients and servers. It's like Fed Ex.
HTML (for text); CSS and DSSL (for stylesheets)	Publishing system for documents, graphics, videos, audio, etc.	Makes files have the same codes behind the scenes, so any platform with a browser can view the web page.
FTP, WebNFS	Moves anything digital (files, audio, software) across the network.	Converts all imaginable data into 1s and 0s and ensures the integrity of moving across telephone lines.
SMTP/IMAP4/ POP	International e-mail.	Transports e-mail across all networks.
IP address	Provides you a unique number on the Internet.	Creates a number like 205.124.234.1 that only represents you.

Table 3-1 Internet Standards *(Continued)*

Internet Standard	What's it do?	How's it do it?
SNMP	Supermanagement.	SNMP takes on numerous jobs specific to devices such as printers, routers, and bridges, thereby providing a standard mechanism of network control and monitoring.
NNTP	Provides on-demand news to the desktop.	Streamlines news data so you can follow others' views on news.
DNS/NIS+	Provides names for your website. Like yahoo.com.	Assigns a name like www.hot-company.com to an IP address like 205.124.234.1.
LDAP (Light Directory Access Protocol)	LDAP provides a standard way for internet clients, applications, and servers to access directory services.	LDAP bases its directory model on entries. Entries are common across all directories, so it's easier to refer to an entry without ambiguity.
MIME	Provides multimedia to be delivered over e-mail.	Uses a translation schema when the file is transferred or launches an external application for viewing.

These are the key internet standards that essentially make intranets work. Other standards exist but are not discussed here. The bottom line is that intranet technology has standardized on internet standards to communicate across networks worldwide. This is what makes your intranet compete in a global environment.

TCP/IP—the Post Office Between Networks   It doesn't matter so much that TCP/IP stands for Transport Control Protocol/Internetworking Protocol. Most desktop operating systems today include TCP/IP because it allows each computer to have its own, unique address. TCP/IP is an addressing and delivery system designed for allowing information to travel between clients.

A good analogy is the post office. You package information in an envelope, put an address on it, and send it out. It goes to a unique address and zip code. This is why you have universal communication. Each computer can reach any other computer, no matter what kind of computer it is, as long as it has an intranet address or an IP address and runs over TCP lines. It is the browser, like Netscape Navigator or Microsoft's Internet Explorer, that makes it possible to look at data on other computers. The TCP/IP simply gets you to that computer.

IP addresses are únique for each computer. They look like this: 130.148.177.31. They are represented by a decimal number between 0 and 255, separated by periods. They can be permanent for each computer, or they can be dynamically assigned every time the computer boots up. This is in wide use in larger companies. A single IP address can represent an entire organization. Then, a series of subnets, IP addresses under the roof of a single IP address, can be utilized for simplicity and security.

Business Advantage. You can share information globally.

Business Risk. Your IP address is trackable as you move around the intranet. No anonymity, or casual looking around. Hackers can enter your intranet looking like someone else. Use security software to disguise IP address.

HTTP—An Internal Web FedEx   Again, it doesn't matter that HTTP means HyperText Transfer Protocol, anymore than it matters that DOS means Disk Operating System. What is important is that HTTP moves information around the intranet. It moves information packages back and forth between computers over TCP using IP addresses to get from here to there. With HTTP you can hyperlink all your electronic files, media, packages, software, graphics, and photos together and make them available for anyone around the company to look at. Think of HTTP as a FedEx-like carrier who moves packages around your organization. Because of HTTP, you can click anywhere on a page, and your package is right there. An overview of HTTP's functionality can be found in Figure 3–2.

Business Advantage. You can request information globally.

Business Risk. HTTP is an evolving standard. Future changes will occur. Hopefully, there will be backward compatibility. but the push to broadcasting and multimedia intensive design may cause some problems.

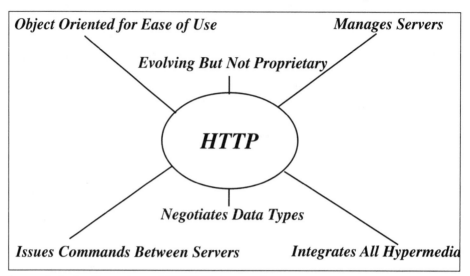

Figure 3–2 An Overview of HTTP Functionality

HTML—Publishing Language Supreme   HTML is simply a way of designing web pages in order to put them on the intranet. HTML is the reason everyone who can get on the intranet is already on the intranet. HTML is easy to learn and easy to use. WYSIWIG programs like Netscape's Navigator Gold, Microsoft's FrontPage for Windows, and Adobe's PageMill are available to make webtop publishing as easy as desktop publishing or word processing.

In just a few lines of text, you can have your web pages up on the intranet within a couple of hours, complete with graphics, links, audio, clickable maps, frames, tables, color, backgrounds, and e-mail addresses embedded in your pages. Also with HTML you can integrate video, software, business applications, and multi-media presentations into your intranet. Figure 3–3 identifies the key components of HTML: access to documentation, menus, e-mail, hypermedia, database forms and results, graphics, hypertext, and spreadsheets.

Business Advantage. Huge amounts of data can be made available with a few clicks of the mouse.

Business Risk. Lack of bandwidth will limit movement, causing added expenditures. No solution. You're going to have to pay for increased bandwidth and for reliability of delivery.

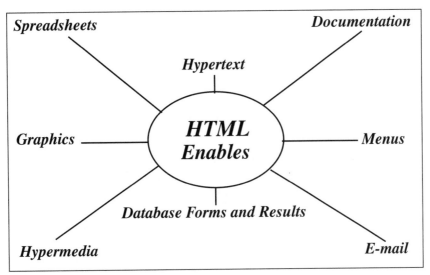

Figure 3–3 HTML Enables Multimedia Integration

FTP (the Old) and WebNFS (the New)—Moving Files across the World
Because Internet standards have been chosen to navigate your data around the intranet, you need a standard way of moving files so they can be viewed on any hardware platform. You rely on File Transfer Protocol (FTP) or the newer Web-NFS, which allows you to share files with other people. You can send any kind of file you want: text, graphics, audio, software applications, and video using the FTP or WebNFS service.

Business Advantage. The capability allows you to share work with others and leverage off expert sites that provide value to your business methods.

Business Risk. Viruses can be easily transferred into your system when you downloading software executables. Educate users and set up an automated warning when downloading to prevent such a disaster.

SMTP, POP & IMAP—International E-Mail   Also, with the internet standards, you get an international e-mail protocol called Simple Mail Transport Protocol (SMTP) for internet mail (POP3 and IMAP are the PC mail protocols). Of course, you want internet mail so you can e-mail to anyone with an IP address. This includes anyone inside the company as well as anyone outside the company. You just need to know their e-mail name. For example, John.Doe@anycompany.com, or John.Doe@aol.com, or John.Doe@internic.org.

Business Advantage. Information dissemination is global, intercompany, intercontinental. You can e-mail any individual or group in the world. this promotes rapid, collaborative decision making.

Business Risk. Company secrets can be moved easily outside the company. Determine a security plan for tracking e-mail movement, and educate the employees about the risk of leaking proprietary information.

SNMP Management Is Network Management   Simple Network Management-Protocol (SNMP) is a network management system protocol. Another way to look at is as a network Mom. It watches over every aspect of your network life. The SNMP manager continuously polls network devices, collects network statistics, and stores them in a database for cross-tabulation and correlation. SNMP provides the capability to manage networks incorporating components that come from a variety of manufacturers with a single application. SNMP allows management remotely, as well. Single-console control for worldwide operations is a powerful idea—the ultimate in centralized support.

Business Advantage.   The capability to have a device from one vendor managed by a device from another vendor is the key advantage. No longer do you need software administration tools for every additional software that you incorporate.

Business Risk. SNMP is a highly complicated protocol to implement. Many SNMP vendors seem to see network management activities in terms of Graphical User Interfaces (GUIs) with point-and-click controls instead of automated systems for configuring devices, gathering data, and conduct corrective procedures on large networks

NNTP—Network News   Network News Transfer Protocol (NNTP) allows news to be delivered on-demand on a real-time basis (much like Reuters ticker tape services of the past). This includes daily news, competitive news, press releases, product announcements, and so forth. It includes special interest USENET newsgroups to keep you informed all the time.

News is extremely helpful when you're researching an innovation or the competition. Addressing newsgroups and using news contribute to the cutting edge of your employees' readiness to perform. Examine your competition's marketing behavior, partner with others who are actually doing e-commerce, learn more about intranet design; it's all there for the taking. Usually your intranet will have a newsgroup tool so you can browse through the news as though you were standing in front of a kiosk.

Business Advantage. Being on top of the daily news and finding timely expert information are competitive advantages.

Business Risk. Employees could fritter away their time following personal news events. So, create a usage policy and educate. But, allowing for discovery, encouraging reading, and following newsgroups you never know exactly where you will get a good idea.

LDAP—Talking with Directories Lightweight Directory Access Protocol (LDAP) is an open standard protocol for directory services on the Internet. It is important because it provides a standard way for internet clients, applications, and servers to access directory services across platforms. It's network glue.

Business Advantage. As LDAP becomes more widely used, it will provide customers with a standard way to access directory services in different environments, making it easier for organizations to communicate with each other.

Business Risk. LDAP doesn't support generalized browsing, directory administration, schema management, full authentication, and the infrastructure for internationalization.

MIME—Multimedia e-mail MIME, the Multipurpose Internet Mail Extensions, is a specification that offers a way to interchange text in languages with different character sets. It also allows for multimedia e-mail. It's the network translator.

MIME allows mail messages to contain:

- Multiple objects in a single message.
- Text having unlimited line length or overall length.
- Character sets other than ASCII, allowing non-English language messages.
- Multifont messages.
- Binary or application specific files.
- Images, audio, video, and multimedia messages.

Business Advantage. MIME allows the transfer of files with different extensions through e-mail, including graphics, audio files, and executables. It can also launch native applications once the character set is recognized.

Business Risk. No authentication, confidentiality, or data integrity properties are provided for security when transferring files across e-mail. Also, certain viewers must be available to view some kinds of data, most notably Microsoft products. For now at least.

Intranet Application Development Environment

Many attempts have been made to standardize applications so various clients on a network can use the same information. The need to scale from the PC to the LAN to the intranet saw the appearance of network and application standards like TCP/IP and simple mail transport protocol. These protocols unified the organization's internal infrastructure. These are the same protocols upon which you are building your intranet.

As the intranet transports your applications to web technology, and ultimately to the Internet and World Wide Web, we see a surge in application development for the Web. Application programming interfaces will enable workers to collaborate with their colleagues, partners, and customers in rich new ways, incorporating databases, spreadsheets, and interactive multimedia and broadcasting capability. The potential of business events being captured into objects on the screen is tantalizing. If you want to look at Payroll, you click on the payroll icon, and the web application opens up and you securely log in. If you want to transfer information from one application to the next, you simply drop and drag, and all databases are updated because of the power of the application programming interfaces.

An extranet will unify computing infrastructures across organizations, and you'll want to use an application standard that will assist you in integrating with these e-commerce services. Additionally, the interfaces will become more sophisticated, integrating the visual features of multimedia to transact business processes.

CGI—Creating On-line Forms, Talking to Databases   The basic development environment beyond HTML is called Common Gateway Interface (CGI). HTML offers you text, hypermedia links, graphics, audio, and video. However, for more interactivity, including forms, and database access, the CGI is required. This entails programming. Most of it is very simple and straightforward for average programmers, but it is not as easy to program CGI scripts as it is to produce HTML. These skills usually need to be subcontracted out.

The CGI is a standard for interfacing external applications with information servers, such as HTTP or web servers. A plain HTML document that the Web retrieves is *static*, which means it exists in a constant state: a text file that doesn't change. A CGI program, on the other hand, is executed in real time, so it can output dynamic information that changes at each request.

CGI is widely used for interactive forms development in early intranets. CGI is not as robust as its descendants, Java and JavaScript. CGI scripts can be written in almost any scripting language—Perl, C, C++, FORTRAN, or TCL. CGI scrips must be kept on the server in their own subdirectory for security purposes.

The more you envision building full-scale applications on your intranets, you'll need to consider using some of the application programming interfaces developed for a more robust software solution, rather than rely on CGI.

Business Advantage. CGI programs allow you to interact with users, gathering information in forms and integrating it with your database. Users can perform queries on your databases.

Business Risk. Since a CGI script is an executable program, it exposes your server to security risks and viruses. Security precautions are required. CGI programs need to reside in a special directory, so that the web server knows to execute the program rather than just display it to the browser. This directory is usually under direct control of the webmaster.

Java   Java is a complete programming language that allows true network-centric application development. It was developed by Sun Microsystems. Java creates "applets" which are securely downloaded from any node in a network to any other node. The application is dynamically loaded and executed immediately. This frees up the need to have software residing on your client in order to process applications. Java integrates directly into HTML and VRML (Virtual Reality Markup Language) documents so with the click of a button, you get virtually unlimited dynamic content that may have originated anywhere in the network.

Business Advantage. Java was designed with network applications in mind. It provides solutions to a number of issues— platform independence, location independence, versioning, security, and multithreading.

Business Risk: Java requires learning and programming specialty. It can slow down development of applications on-line, when you could easily launch the application directly from your web browser.

Javascript   JavaScript is a scripting language for the creation of applications that may be embedded entirely within HTML documents, rather than calling up "applets" as Java does, or programming CGI scripts. JavaScript works with an event model, providing immediate feedback to the user when a transaction event takes place. Processing is performed on the client, so the speed of interaction is accelerated. JavaScript will provide powerful interaction between web pages and relational databases.

Business Advantage. JavaScript is easier to program for HTML authors who are not object-oriented programmers.

Business Risk. JavaScript is not good at screen I/O (Input/Output) or memory-intensive text or number manipulation, like spreadsheets.

VRML   VRML, the Virtual Reality Modeling Language, is a standard scripting language for creating applications that enable users to navigate through three-dimensional information. VRML is 3D and manipulates data in a different environment than traditional application software offers.

Business Advantage. VRML is not a language for only developing games and web curiosity. With its compatibility with JavaScript it is also able to analyze complex business problems, such as stock market results, company performance statistics, and sophisticated scientific data.

Business Risk. VRML is a new environment for users to move in. A strong learning curve is expected both in writing VRML and in learning to manipulate the environment.

NSAPI and ISAPI   These two application programming interfaces, one from Netscape (NSAPI [Netscape Application Programming Interface]) and one from Microsoft (ISAPI [Internet Server Application Programming Interface]) are designed to provide developers with the ability to extend the native capabilities of their servers and integrate with databases like Oracle, Sybase, and Informix. They allow developers to exert a great deal of control over the server's behavior by creating high-performance applications.

Bottom Line: Until easy application programming evolves on the Web, network-centric applications will be slow in coming.

Emerging Standards

There are standards being crafted daily to make the deployment of intranets much easier across the network. WebNFS is by far a more transparent file-sharing mechanism than FTP and will probably be quickly integrated as soon as the standard is formalized. I don't think Netscape is waiting that long. If a standard is superior to an existing one and is at the same time a superset, then by all means ratify the standard and let's get on with development.

Also, X.400 e-mail is another emerging standard to dress up SMTP. X.x00 has been around for a long time, but was usually too cumbersome to use. Nonetheless, it is growing in use and usability, so you can prepare to see some assimilation there as well.

Standards will continue to emerge. Keep aware of them by visiting Netscape's web site and the standards organizations listed below.

Standards Organizations   To learn more about standards and protocols go to the sources. *The Internet Society* has a great paragraph that sums up the standards hierarchy:

> At the technical and developmental level, the Internet (the Intranet, as well) is made possible through creation, testing and implementation of Internet Standards. These standards are developed by the Internet Engineering Task Force. The standards are then considered by the Internet Engineering Steering Group, with appeal to the Internet Architecture Board, and promulgated by the Internet Society as international standards.

These are the internet standards committees that are undoubtedly responsible for many of the emerging standards and for formalizing the standards proposed by governing bodies. The World Wide Web Consortium is the main point of contact for the World Wide Web and the standards required for integration into the web.

See Table 3–2 below for the URLs for these groups.

Table 3-2 Intranet Standards Organizations

URL	Organization	Main Focus
http://www.ietf.cnri.reston.va.us	Internet Engineering Task Force (IETF).	Develops standards.
http://www.ietf.cnri.reston.va.us/iesg.html	Internet Engineering Steering Group.	Considers standards.
http://www.iab.org/iab/	Internet Architecture Board.	Appeals standards.
http://info.isoc.org:80/standards/index.html	The Internet Society.	Promulgates standards.
http://www.association.org	The Association of Web Developers.	Develops standards.
http://www.w3.org/pub/WWW/Consortium/	The World Wide Web Consortium.	Web Standards.

Networks Evolve to the Intranet

From Proprietary to Open   In the last decade, firms have invested enormous time and money in hooking up personal computers and workstations to networks. They were fraught with significant hurdles, among them linking cross-platform applications, proprietary-specific solutions, sharing files and e-mail systems, and securing access to sensitive information. The choices were daunting, the investment risky. Many network attempts were successful; others failed miserably. Getting people, processes, and projects to work together was a challenge.

Novell brought the Network Operating System (NOS) to sort out the problems of collaborative computing. NOS was not based on internet standards. Other NOSs competing with Novell widened the gap even more on interoperability. When internet standards are integrated with Novell's NetWare 4 in the form of IntranetWare™, the bridge to intranets is strengthened. Many NOS are upgrading their systems for intranet compatibility. This means integrating internet protocols with their NOS.

Let's look at Table 3–3 for additional guidelines on how to evolve your network to an intranet.

Table 3-3 The Network Evolution: Intranet Components

Component	Hardware or Software	What do I need?
Intranet Client Is a user environment, made up of hardware components and software components	Hardware	Can be a PC* or workstation, running any operating system with TCP/IP. Needs to be connected to the LAN/WAN. Needs client browser software.
Intranet Client The software components are made up of the OS, the GUI, plus some service software	Software	Mainly an operating system that is TCP/IP favorable (UNIX, NT, or Windows 95), a browser, e-mail, FTP, or WebNFS software on each client. Need HTML software for publishing.
Intranet Server	Hardware	Can be a PC or workstation running server software. Servers have various distinct functions. Some perform all the business processing, some software and file distribution, and some maintenance.

Table 3-3 The Network Evolution: Intranet Components *(Continued)*

Component	Hardware or Software	What do I need?
Intranet Server	Software	HTML interface to install, administer, and maintain intranet and network
TCP/IP Connection, LAN and WAN	Hardware and software	Requires Ethernet cards, cabling, hubs, and routers. Provides international, internet-related communication.
Bandwidth (the measure of TCP/IP pipe size)	Hardware	Use at least 28.8 modem, cable modem, T1–T3 lease lines, ISDN or ADSL. Video servers for increased multimedia, video, and graphics use are gained.
Optional Cache Server	Hardware	Same requirements as the server. Use this for performance. It stores most frequently accessed pages for quicker retrieval.
Security firewall or Proxy Server	Hardware	Requires a PC or a workstation. Prevents unauthorized traffic and protects from worms which are unauthorized entry.
Proxy server	Software	Block URLs. Proxy servers also hide the identities of internal users by acting in their place.
Navigation and Access Tools	Software	Search engines and indexing software are required for easy access and navigation to information.
Robots, Spiders, and Web Crawlers, Agents	Software	Robots, spiders, and web crawlers are the collector arms of the search services. Intelligent agents proactively search and deliver information to users based on their personal profiles.

*The minimum PC configuration should be at least one 486 with 16 megs of RAM and 1 gigabyte hard drive, with a 28.8 modem. You can use any platform that conforms to these standards.

Guidelines for Minimum Intranet Requirements

First Generation (Basic Intranets, Publishing/Library Intranets)   For first-generation intranets, publishing on the intranet is all that is necessary at first. You must get your feet wet working with browsers, integrated hyperlinks, and graphics, working both layout and content design issues. Most importantly, you need to figure out how to publish on the Web. So, these are your bare minimum requirements:

- TCP/IP-based network with LAN (10-Base-T minimum speed)

- Web server software

- Client browser software

- Client e-mail software and FTP (File Transfer Protocol) software—e-mail and FTP are often included in the browser and with the advent of Microsoft and Netscape's going head-to-head on the desktop solutions, FTP will be passe. However, integrated e-mail solutions aren't always optimal.

- Log maintenance

Second Generation (collaborative, interactive, and transactional intranets)

Second-generation solutions tend to start putting a premium on security and developing workflow/interactive solutions. This means they need user authentication and a common user database (name service) as well as access control for security implementations. Digital certificates are optional but highly recommended.

For interactive/workflow intranets, back-end programs (either CGI or proprietary, that is, NSAPI, Oracle specific, Java, JavaScript or whatever) are needed. Server-side includes aren't mandatory and are often better implemented through a back-end program such as HTMLscript.

IBM, Sun, Oracle, and Netscape jointly announced a set of guidelines for developing intranet-centric network computing devices. These are their bottom-line requirements for an intranet configuration on the network.

Hardware Equipment

- Minimum screen resolution of 640x480

- Pointing device—like a mouse

- Text input capabilities—keyboard, text editor

- Audio output—speakers

- Distributed application servers (with business applications)

Network Standards Stuff

- TCP/IP-based network with LAN (10-Base-T minimum) with multiple sub-nets and a high-speed WAN backbone

- UDP—wireless, connectionless transport service for information

- IP—individual number for every computer client on the intranet

- Bootp—starting program

Internet Services and Standards

- FTP—moves files around globally or WebNFS—file structure for directories, files, and so forth (when it is formalized as a standard)

- Telnet—for logging into off-site computers

- HTML—for writing and publishing intranet documents

- HTTP—for making documents, graphics clickable

- Java Application Environment—for adding interactivity

- SMTP—for international e-mail

- IMAP4 —IMAP4 includes operations for creating, deleting, and renaming mailboxes; checking for new messages; permanently removing messages set-ting, and clearing flags

- POP3—for PC mail to the Internet

- Firewall software for secure access to the Internet

Format Standards for Graphics, Audio

- JPEG—graphic format for photolike quality

- GIF—graphic format widely used on the intranet

- WAV—audio file type

- AU—audio file type

For Performing Transactions on the Extended Intranet

- Optional ISO 7816 (SmartCards) security standard

- Optional European MasterCard/Visa security standard

Third Generation (Extranets)   Extranets have not arrived yet, as they require full-service secured transactional intranets to be installed in each company that is conducting e-business. The emphasis will be on security and authentication of data. Authorization software requiring digital certificates and sophisticated access control and accompanying logic must be in place.

Network/Intranet Bottom Line

Intranet technology enhances your network technology by standardizing internet standards. Using your existing networks, network hardware, software, and business applications, you can use intranet technology to link people, processes, and projects together. You do this using web browsers and servers to enable a focused view into the network with a common global interface.

Each department builds their own web site with most of the network administration, directory and file maintenance, network access, and security managed by your network. The intranet configuration enables all your users to publish using HTML and HTTP—two universal communicators that make intranets, the evolution of the network.

All this occurs behind the scenes, unless you're one of the technical managers. What you'll need to do is figure out how to improve performance using intranets. You'll need to determine what new capabilities you have over the network. Intranets extend your network capabilities.

Intranets Improve Network Functionality   With intranet technology, employees overcome the obstacles and limitations of networks. They maintain their own home pages or group pages on web servers that can be accessed easily across the network, using a simple browser. Instead of working through the network administrator for development and maintenance, home pages and group pages supplant the central administration of information. This greatly enhances communication.

Home pages empower employees to focus on creating knowledge repositories of their progress, programs, contacts, methods, discoveries, and linkable expertise. Anyone in the organization can potentially link into any part of that knowledge repository. Intranets offer this networked view of individual functionality, where anyone can examine the work in progress of any and all interdependent departments with the organization.

In Figure 3–4, you can see that networks haven't gone much beyond the filing cabinet. Your data are still stored in network archives, accessible only by reporting software, and programmers who can process data warehouses and pull out information as you require it. Information access is blocked, slowing down the development process to almost a crawling pace. Because every node, or organization, or group, or individual can create their own home page, web site, and attached it to the intranet web server, a major evolution in individual expertise is about to be launched.

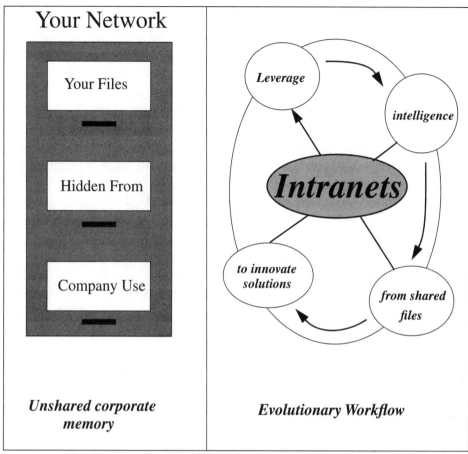

Figure 3–4 Networks Evolve into Workflow Intranets

Users Give Back to the Intranet   Networks have made several attempts to make workflow easy. They strive to enhance internal communications, improve collaboration across the organization, share files, streamline work processes, and provide software for everyone in a consistent system. With your network, you share tools. You share applications. With intranets, the users give back to the network, by establishing, publishing, or operating part of the business on-line. They share their information and develop knowledge products to do so.

The intranet will not work unless this openness of data and giving back to the intranet are part of the culture. A paradigm shift in trust and honesty is upon us. We must prepare for a biological or organic growing pattern. As long as the individual parts of the intranet are contributing to its growth, its maintenance, and its security, then the intranet will thrive. If individual parts only take resources, hide them behind fire ridges, never revealing participative processes, then the intranet body will soon degrade. The only way for an intranet to work is much like the way a human body works—all systems must be designed to feed back information to the brain center in order to preserve the species.

Network Risk and Considerations

Take a second look and reflect on some of the negative arguments. This is the tool of compare and contrast. Why would it be better not to go to intranets?

Web Anarchy. Is Web anarchy taking place in every organization? It seems that it's very easy to set up a server using Netscape Suite Spot, Microsoft Back Office, or Apache servers without telling anyone. Even smaller PC servers are set up everywhere and serve pages to small groups. Do you network administrators know this is occurring? Probably not.

 Intranet web sites are appearing everywhere. Content and ownership issues bubble up. Suddenly, a pull on network traffic causes attention to be drawn. Suddenly, there is a flurry of Net activity that is not being managed by centralized data groups. No serious planning is going on. Is this anarchy, or is it an organic evolution of human communication? Developing in chaos is a good thing as out-of-the-box thinking for data moguls. They need to know how to control the network without squashing effort and innovation, especially when it is accelerating beyond control. You cannot stop an organic process—you have to assimilate. But assimilation can be planned and implemented to preserve the integrity of the network and promote individual intranet growth.

Support Problems   Evolution has happened to the network, and most of the network administrators haven't been paying attention. Even worse, employees are finding uses for intranet technology that MIS cannot support. Individual groups are setting up servers, and serving information, databases, multimedia presentations, company resources all over the organization. Will the network scream to a halt? And, who is going to support and pay for all of this?

You've got to get your arms around the idea of centralized intranet administration with decentralized, distributed content development. This allows for integrity of the network and freedom of the individual departments.

Playing or Discovering? There is a fine line between discovery on the intranet/Internet and playing or surfing. Some companies initiate policies on use, while others allow free, self-controlling reign. Activity on-line can be tracked, so either you use that information to control the access rights of your knowledge to workers, or you use it to profile your users in order to provide more quality information. As with any other communication evolution, the good use will rise to the top.

There is a honeymoon period when the users simply play and try to get to know the intricacies and strengths of the intranet. Then, the user evolves to leveraging the tools and knowledge gathered from the play stage. Then, the user focuses on getting information, creating solutions, and expediting transactions. When the rest of the company can see what you've harvested and how you put your harvest to use, you tend to perform at optimal efficiency.

Productivity Loss   A psychological warning. Using information all day on-line can cause people to lose concentration. Short-term memory can handle only between five to seven concepts at a time. If users aren't skilled at navigating or analyzing logical points of information, their analytical capabilities can be severely impaired. Good design eliminates this problem. But, too much exposure to badly laid out web sites can impact your company's information processing capabilities.

Browser Jihad   Will the competitive development of browsers bury us in a proprietary jihad? This is intolerable in a world where customers are demanding open standards and dismantling proprietary systems. As developers of intranet architecture and intranet infrastructure, we need to rely solely on the bottom line—open standards and independent platforms. The client, I mean the user and customer, needs to be kept right in the center of these providers' eyesight, in order to help the flow of information across Internets, intranets, and eventually extranets.

Visionary Solutions   In the laboratories of Netscape, Sun Microsystems, Oracle, Microsoft, IBM, Lotus, Apple, and others solutions are being crafted to help move people away from web anarchy. Across the network, an intranet model of computing is unfolding. It is evolving into a full-service environment taking care of directories, files, e-mail, administration, configuration, performance and tuning, publishing, information serving, and fully integrated, customizable business applications that improve business processes, delight customers more readily, and provides collaborative partnerships for future accelerated development. These visionary companies are defining the solutions every day. We are in a unique period, where we are pioneering many of the technological solutions of tomorrow.

Servers

Intranets are made of servers.

- Hardware servers (PCs and workstations, Sun's Netra™ intranet server; BSDI and Hewlett-Packard also have exceptional servers).

- Software servers (Netscape's Suite Spot, Microsoft's Internet Information Server (IIS); see http://www.netcraft.co.uk/Survey/Reports/) for more.

Hardware Servers   Hardware servers are computers, workstations, and sometimes mainframes that are operating using Internet standards. This is why you probably have some intranet architecture already in your organization. You can purchase intranet servers that are more finely tuned for rolling out your intranet from the start (like Sun Microsystem's Netra line), but any computer can be configured as a server, using any operating system. It is recommended that you start with at least a 486, 66-megahertz machine, with at least 16 megs of RAM, and a 28.8Kpbs data modem (for going out to the Internet, which we call the extranet). Anything less would be too slow. Then, the sky's the limit.

Features to look for in investing in hardware servers:

- A company mission statement and action plan for deploying and supporting an intranet server solution

- Access to corporate hardware already in place

- Scalability

- Security features

- Competitively low prices. Some companies are giving away software

- Maintenance optimization. Someone has to keep things updated, and that takes time. Make realistic estimates of how many resources you can dedicate to your intranet

- Ease of installation

- Ease of use

Netcraft provides a comparative view of various web servers on the market. This site provides ample statistics and evaluations of the servers. It's a good place to start. See Figure 3–5 below.

.

Server Hardware and Operating System. When building and designing a Web site, the hardware and Operating System (OS) decision is crucial. Your choices include UNIX for scalability and robustness of high transaction environments, and NT or Microsoft solutions, which leverage off application software for desktop-centric computing. Common trade-offs include performance versus ease of use, and maturity versus cost of ownership. Performance, price, and cost of ownership will dictate which hardware and OS option is the correct one for any Web site.

Figure 3–5 Netcraft's Directory of Web Server Home Sites

Hardware Server Issues to Consider:

• Can you run the web server on multiple hardware and OS environments?

• Is there a migration path to scale your web site as traffic grows?

• Can you easily tune the hardware and OS for enhanced performance?

These are technical issues for you to hand over to your technical group. Beware, however, that decisions of this nature must be made before moving ahead with the intranet. The eternal question is: Am I building for the present, or am I scaling up and preparing for my future needs? You will be running video servers, and high-end transaction secured servers soon too. Your needs will grow as this technology becomes facile.

Software servers The key component of any intranet is the web-server software. This software runs on a central computer and acts as the clearinghouse for all available data regardless of its source. Document requests, e-mail, database queries, news feeds, home pages, transactions—everything must go through the Web server before it is sent to a user.

Make sure your server provides adequate access to corporate data. Consider Apache Servers, UNIX Servers, NT Servers, or the low-end Windows 95 as a software server solution. Build according to your needs. Careful study will reveal which software will be best for you.

Key features to look for in a good server administration interface include:

- Single interface which can manage multiple servers

- Ability to manage servers from any client, anywhere on the Web

- Intuitive interface with good navigation

- Complete map of server management

- On-line performance monitoring and tuning

- On-line security management

- Secure management via user authentication

- Ability to undo changes

- SNMP support

- Built-in reports for one-step log file analysis

The *Gilder Technology Report* identified which servers were most popular. Apache Servers came out as the number one server in use around the country, with NCSA servers running close behind.

Apache Servers (Best of Breed). Apache is now the most popular web server in the world. The August World Wide Web server site survey by Netcraft [http://www.netcraft.co.uk/Survey/Reports/] found that more web servers were using Apache than any other software. Apache is run on 36 percent of all web servers in the world. The Apache httpd server is a plug-in replacement for NCSA 1.3. It fixes numerous bugs and security holes seen in NCSA 1.3 and 1.4 and it is free. Refer to http://www.apache.org/info.html. Their high-end secured server, Stronghold, costs $495, commercial free for noncommercial users.

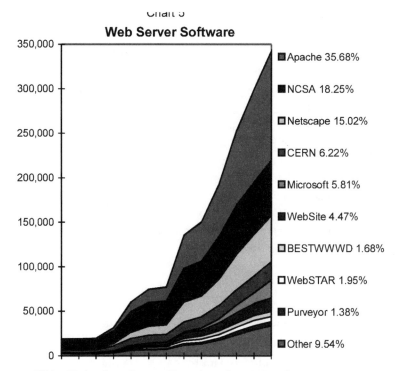

Chart 3

Web Server Software

Apache 35.68%

NCSA 18.25%

Netscape 15.02%

CERN 6.22%

Microsoft 5.81%

WebSite 4.47%

BESTWWWD 1.68%

WebSTAR 1.95%

Purveyor 1.38%

Other 9.54%

Figure 3–6 *Gilder Technology Report* Tags Apache as Top Server

UNIX Servers (Work Horses That Scale Up). UNIX supports the widest range of servers. Netscape is the most widely known server software. Sun Netras, UNIX servers, are capable intranet machines. They are configured for Internet standards and can scale up very well to handle larger and larger customer needs. If you want to deploy a well-integrated server that handles on-line transaction process-ing, back-office applications, high-volume transactions, extensive news and mail-ing lists, moderated chat rooms, and supports dial-up terminal users, then UNIX is a good solution.

The cost is not as prohibitive as you might think. The low end of the Ultra line of Sun computers costs less per operation than an NT counterpart. It is also in line with the cost of a high-end Pentium Pro box. After adding the cost of the NT Server OS software and enough seat licenses, the cost is often very close. Add to that the ability to build from the bottom up, and you have some compelling argu-ments to rethink your OS strategy.

NT Servers (Popular Enterprise Solution). Windows NT Server comes with a free web server. Windows NT Servers are quickly becoming popular due mostly to the pervasive mind-share Microsoft holds over the desktop application environment. Microsoft is ready to move into the enterprise market with their Back Office solutions, robust web server, and network-ready office applications.

Zona Research predicts that 68 percent of the market will be dedicated to NT by the end of 1997. Microsoft promotes NT Server by giving away its powerful Internet Information Server to licensed NT Server users. Windows NT Server offers system-level security and the ability to scale up to more powerful hardware as your needs grow. Whether the NT Server can provide for the needs of the next century will be seen. It is based on an operating system that will ultimately get in the way of the network. If you intend to connect out to the Internet and start interenterprise networking, you might want to take a harder look at UNIX. However, never underestimate Microsoft.

Again, the point is that the server you use, be it NT, Apple, or UNIX simply needs to satisfy your performance requirements. You will decide based on the open standards of the Internet, and whatever your installed base is. The budget for upgrading to higher-end technology is reserved for your planning meetings.

Windows 95. Windows 95 is inexpensive. You can use Windows 95 as a low-end intranet server. Don't expect to have more than 10 people working on the server at the same time though and don't expect to be able to scale up later, when you discover you need a more robust system. If you need robustness, go for NT. If you need mission-critical on-line transaction processing, go with the UNIX servers, until NT has more proven experience in the enterprise.

Server Types   By now you've heard there are different types of servers. Server software comes in the form of proxy servers, caching servers, administrative servers, and the list goes on. What you have is the server performing different functions. Distributing functionality across various servers is what intranets are all about.

Distribution accelerates performance and simplifies maintenance and support. For complex intranets, serving thousands of internal users, you'll want to consider these options carefully. We've compiled a list in Table 3–4 to help you sort them out.

Enterprisewide Server. The enterprise server is a basic web server used as the core of your intranet architecture. It is the server that is used to administer the centralized design of your intranet. If you are a high-traffic site and you need your intranet to work like a work horse, you'll need a robust enterprisewide server.

Administrative Server. Once you install server software, you administer and manage it using a forms-capable network navigator. It is the server software that allows you to control who has authorization and who doesn't to access the server. Having a single administrative server improves maintenance, support, and administration of your intranet. More importantly, it provides the best security, as access control can be managed centrally.

Table 3-4 Server Types

Server Type	Functionality	Architecture Issues	Examples
Administrative Server	Puts administration in one central location. Improves security. Manages user authentication.	Is a standard part server, not a specific product of its own. Bundled as part of the enterprisewide server.	Sun Netra Internet Server BSDI Server. Microsoft Exchange Server.
Enterprisewide Server—High-End Server	Task master server, handles web pages, connections to databases, administration, and application software.	Manages multiple servers from one interface. Manages servers from any client, anywhere on the Web. On-line performance monitoring and tuning.	Apache Server. Netscape Enterprise Server. NCSA HTTPd CERN Server. Microsoft IIS.
Proxy Server	Increases performance and security.	Manages secured IP addresses for increased security. Acts as a go-between for security as well.	Netscape's Proxy Server. Microsoft's Catapult Server Software.
Caching Server	Stores frequently accessed web sites for quick retrieval.	Performance improvement.	Netscape's Caching Server.
Staging Server	Testing ground for your official web site.	Does not have to be on a separate server.	Any hardware server.
News Server	Provides incoming news.	A news server serves Usenet. Manages the peculiar nuances of news services.	Any hardware server will do.

Table 3-4 Server Types *(Continued)*

Server Type	Functionality	Architecture Issues	Examples
Database Server	Accesses databases at your site.	Improves performance. Provides access to heterogeneous databases.	Netscape's Database Server. Microsoft SQL Server.™ Oracle, Sybase, and LiveWire Pro.
Mail Server	Distributes e-mail information over the network.	Simple SMTP, POP, or IMAP protocol integrates heterogeneous e-mail systems.	Netscape's Mail Server Metainfo Microsoft's Exchange Server.
Catalog/Index Server	Dedicated to searching capabilities.	Frees up the network for long searches.	Netscape's Catalog Server Verity's Information Server.
Mainframe Connection Server	Connects directly to mainframe.	Improves workflow to mainframe.	Attachmate Microsoft's SNA Server.
Name Server or the Directory Server	Stores directory information.	Breaks down the proprietary walls between directories.	Netscape's Directory Server Standard X.400 Microsoft's Cairo Directory Server.
Certificate Server	Allows you to manage your own certificate infrastructure.	Vital for security with on-line transactions.	Netscape RSA.
Mirrored Server	Backs up your entire web site at a remote site.	Improves network traffic provides backup for emergency recovery.	Configure with the same set up you have for the original server.

Proxy Servers. A proxy server acts as a gateway between an HTTP client and a server which may be HTTP-based. Document caching is performed at the gateway to speed retrieval time and mitigate network bandwidth. With a proxy server you can restrict the movement of data types to avoid security leaks. FTP (transferring files and software) is one of those services that might be restricted as complete autonomy in moving files from network-to-network can open some considerable holes for prying eyes. A proxy server is good to use on a firewall to hide the users behind it and manage proprietary information.

We advocate internal use of proxy servers to protect proprietary information within your intranet. Eighty percent of the information leakage is done internally. If you want to move information back and forth between the Internet and the intranet, you can block certain data types or IP addresses through a proxy server. In order to block all FTP traffic, you must use a firewall. You can also use the firewall to make sure that FTP only passes through the proxy server as well. This is also true of e-mail, Netnews, and other services.

A firewall is designed to examine each and every packet of data that passes through it. The packet of data will only be passed if the firewall is configured to pass it. The general areas that can be used in screening are

- Source location—restrict access to certain geographies (for example, no access to China, or http://www.playboy.com).

- Destination location—restrict access to only certain employees or force traffic to only go through specific systems such as secondary firewalls or designated servers.

- Service type—this is actually service numbers not service names, thus web servers placed on nonstandard service ports can be and often are hidden. Each service—ftp, http, e-mail, netnews—uses a specific service port by default.

Caching Server. A caching server is a proxy server that writes to the disk to accelerate access to frequently used web pages. Caching servers retain local copies of pages so that the small pipes aren't repeatedly taxed. For example, a cache is usually placed on the company's side of the Internet connection to save on repeated traffic on the T-1, T-3, or ISDN.

At Sun or most other distributed companies, caching servers are also placed at the local end of small pipes. For example there are a few caching servers in the main European hub cities that cache for European sites instead of having repeated traffic return to the United States.

Verity's Information Server manages "corporate memory." Through the Information Server, users can access and mine this catalog of information using their SEARCH'97 interface or any standard Web browser. Information Server provides the key integration point for additional search components such as the Agent Server and Information Gateways. See Figure 3–7.

Staging Servers. Ideally, it is good to have a staging server (it doesn't have to be a different system—you can put two web server software packages on the same piece of hardware). However, it is very important to keep the staging and produc

Figure 3–7   Verity's Information Server to Manage Corporate Memory

tion areas distinct to keep problems from being seen by the masses. All Quality Assurance (QA) should be done on the staging server and only approved material passed on to the production server.

Mirror Server. A mirrored server creates a "mirror" or "replica" by replicating the data from one server to another off-site, for backup and ease of downloading from distant sites. Software for mirroring is available.

Directory Server. This is an attempt by Netscape, IBM, Novell, Inc., Microsoft, Banyan Systems, Inc., and AT&T Corp. to close the gap on universal directory systems. With the directory server, corporate users can quickly and easily query directories of people and information stored on both corporate intranets and the Internet. Information such as user names, e-mail addresses, security keys, and contact information can all be organized and published in searchable, structured, scalable directories.

An excellent directory server lets businesses freely choose operating systems, directory, and client components, eliminating the time and exorbitant costs of reconciling incompatible, proprietary directory systems.

Certificate Server. This is a new class of software that is based on open industry standards. It enables organizations to issue, sign, and manage public-key certificates using a Secure Sockets Layer (SSL) for secure, private communication over the Internet or a corporate intranet.

Catalog Servers. Netscape Catalog Servers allow you to set up and automatically maintain Yahoo-style services for your intranets. This server manages your company's knowledge base and makes it easy for employees to navigate. Create a multimedia catalog service and ease the burden of long, arduous searching and navigating a large web site.

Server Management Issues   Your server demands will grow. Keeping things transparently scalable is very intelligent. In general, you can put a wide range of server products on the same box if you want to maximize your resources. It is important to refer to all servers via aliases to make expansion transparent to the user. All names can be aliased to servername.company.com and then as your resource needs grow, you can create another server and move some resources over to it.

Web Site Performance Issues and Criteria   As the Web evolves, performance rises as one of the top management issues. There are four major areas to look at when optimizing the performance of a web site:

- Web server content (file size, dynamic vs. static: reduce file size; create web pages on the fly; avoid useless multimedia presentations; use metatags for quick searching).

- Web server software (use robust software that scales; UNIX choices are superior for scalability at this time, but if you're willing to wait, NT solutions will make your choices wider).

- Server hardware and OS (distribute the functions across hardware pieces; use robust operating systems that are network-centric).

- Network bandwidth (consider ISDN, T-1, or T-3 leased lines, or HDSL [High-speed Digital Subscribe Lines], or consider PairGain's IDSL [Internet Digital Subscribe Lines] to bypass the telcos and absurd T-1 tariffs).

Tuning a web site for high performance involves optimizing each of these components. Failure to optimize any of these areas can result in poor performance and an unreliable site.

Clients

Once a web server is in place, setting up the client is simple. A client is nothing more than a PC or a workstation with browser software, TCP/IP connection, and additional intranet software for extending functionality. You need web browsers compatible with your users' systems. Macs, SPARCStations, x86, and Pentium Pros all have supporting browsers.

Use Your Old Machines as Clients   Clients drive the industry. Clients represent the reason why open standards and independent platforms are hard requirements for the intranet. People have many years of learning invested in their tools. In order to remain at the peak of their performance, using these tools is critical. Stick with your client's machines, with their current configurations, and current software tools. The client browser on top will be capable of reading any file you have created on your client.

Webtops   Many progressive intranet players envision Internet access devices that will be able to easily take advantage of accessing large worldwide databases, other intranets and the Internet. Webtops, or thin clients, represent the concept of a web-ready terminal that requires no hard drive or operating system. Webtops have appeared at Sun Microsystems, Oracle, and Microsoft. The idea is somewhat reminiscent of dumb terminals, except webtops are graphic intensive, prescribe to Internet standards, and are quite economical.

Webtops are inexpensive, intranet/Java friendly, user-friendly, low-maintenance, high-speed, and high-capacity machines that will proliferate making intranet access a priority. Over time, if clients are not able to be made intranet ready, they will most likely be obsolete by the end of the century.

Browsers

- Browsers for navigation
- Niche browsers
- Database browsers
- Browsers on the horizon

Browsers are software. They enable your PC, workstation (client) to communicate with any data type, any other client on the network with an IP address, and any server on the network with an http address. You have seen http://www.whatever.com all over the place.

Browsers for Navigation   Netscape Navigator, NCSA's Mosaic, and Microsoft Internet Explorer have done well as browsers for navigation. They allow users their first glimpses into an intranet and into the Internet, as well. They provide features that allow the pleasure of learning, reading, listening, filling out forms, and navigating through invisible database repositories. They provide a means of getting to information through navigation browsers. They allow entry into the HTML worlds of their creators. Each browser navigates people right into enterprise's inner world of development, marketing strategy, rapid development, user input, and wide area feedback mechanisms.

Commercial browsers typically are minimal in cost, and, some can be downloaded and used for free. The indisputable king of browsers is Netscape's Navigator 3.0. See the graph on browser from the August issue of *Gilder's Technology Report* in Figure 3–8. But expect Microsoft's Internet Explorer to give Netscape a serious competition. The focus, however, *must be* on the customer, not on the browser.

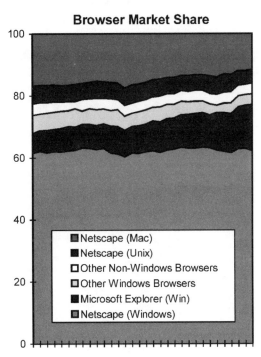

Browser Market Share

Figure 3–8 *Gilder Technology Report* on Browser Use

Niche Browsers   Although it seems that the ultimate browsers for viewing data on your intranet already exist, other companies are creating browsers for easy access for novice users and specific populations of niche browsers. These browsers reside mostly within commercial packages, such as AOL, Prodigy, Compuserv,

PointCast, and Microsoft Network. They are designed for specialized audiences. They claim that the "Internet is intimidating," and that their specialized browser makes surfing on the Internet easier. They have little to do with intranets.

As many people know, the PointCast Network™ is designed to provide the latest news and information to viewers via the Internet. The free service can be personalized by viewers to suit their own interests.

PointCast I-Server extends the capabilities of the PointCast Network by allowing corporations to post a "private" company channel alongside the public PointCast channels. Companies can use PointCast I-Server to broadcast 401K updates, training schedules, sales successes, and press releases. You can stop filling your bookmark coffers with URLs that map your needs and use PointCast I-Server to customize the kind of news you need to read about the company.

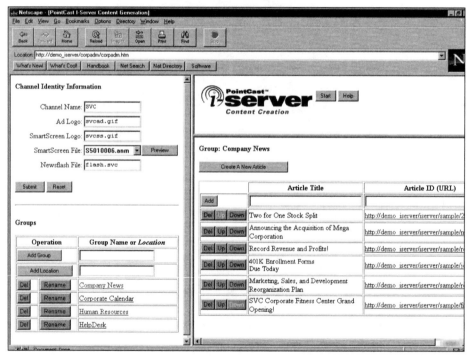

Figure 3–9 PointCast News, Corporate News Broadcasting

The Browser Site   For the consummate site on browsers, see
Figure 3–10 for http://www.browserwatch.com[1]

Figure 3–10 Browser Watch.

Database Browsers a.k.a. Database Servers   Some large database companies offer a web solution to communicate directly with their giant repositories of data. The companies feature their web savvy application software as database servers. Oracle, for example, offers the WebServer and Designer/2000, Sybase uses web.sql, and Informix uses Webkits.

Oracle.   Oracle WebServer 2.0 is the first web server to support next-generation intranet applications. At the core of Oracle WebServer 2.0 is the Web Request Broker which provides a scalable application platform that uses a cartridge architecture for building applications. Designer/2000 enables developers to create visual representations of their applications to communicate with the intranet. Designer/2000 makes use of the Oracle WebServer, an HTTP server tightly integrated with Oracle7, to create web applications. The Oracle WebServer retrieves data from the database and formats it into HTML pages using the PL/SQL language, Oracle's standard extension to SQL.

---

1. Browser Watch appears courtesy of iWORLD (http://www.iworld.com).

Sybase. Sybase offers web.sql which provides easy access to relational databases from the World Wide Web and allows you to dynamically generate customized Hypertext Markup Language (HTML) documents. With web.sql, you can insert SQL statements and Perl scripts into the text of HTML pages. When a client browser requests these pages, web.sql runs the scripts and the resulting output is interpolated into the file. web.sql requires HTML 2.0 at a minimum, but HTML 3.0 is recommended since it supports tables. Sybase web.sql does not preclude using any Web browser.

Informix. Informix offers webkits to assist developers in connecting Informix databases to the World Wide Web. Each webkit contains a library of functions or classes to help you write CGI programs that can interface with Informix databases. A CGI program is executed in real time by the Web daemon and transmits the information to the database engine. The goal of the Informix Webkits is to simplify the programs you write to achieve web connectivity with, and still conform to, Informix standards.

Using a database web solution like this avoids the time delay for creating an application plug-in to customize your database information for the intranet. The drawback to these solutions are that they require you to have a homogeneous database environment, in other words, Oracle is Oracle, Informix is Informix, Sybase is Sybase, and so forth.

Browsers on the Horizon   Is the browser market closed? There are features not available in Netscape's Navigator or Microsoft's Internet Explorer. Netscape's strategy extends the Navigator functionality considerably with plug-ins. Plug-ins are software solutions created by independent partners. Microsoft, on the other hand, manages the software development within the various releases of their browser. There may easily be others, but not with the great head start these two browsers have. Look at the niche browsers for competition.

Browsers limit functionality. They are read oriented, not write oriented. That means you must accept the functionality you get, because you cannot alter the software code to customize the browser. You can, of course, download helper software, or plug-ins. How that will be handled on webtops is a good question. All the applications that need to run as tools can be launched from a single view on the intranet. But, to really get a good customizable "Desktop" with rich functionality, you need an object-oriented drop-and-drag software builder. It must integrate with any operating system, your intranet, and all your database partnerships. To create the niche worlds that are required for unlimited functionality, the operating system and the browser must become one.

Look for applications that look like browsers but are designed specifically with a niche market in mind. Financial browsers, stockbroker browsers, educational browsers, with tools wrapped around the browsers for developing or capturing input from the web experience will be appearing on the scene soon.

Internet Connectivity

Bandwidth Needs to Be Bigger   As mentioned before, you do not have to hook up to the Internet to have an intranet run effectively in your organization. However, many companies hook up in order to have access to universal e-mail and to scope out the competitor. *Zona Research Reports*, 1996, reports that "the commercial on-line service providers and major bandwidth providers will usurp much of the individual business which is being serviced by Internet Service Providers." Whether AT&T can provide adequate connectivity is to be seen. The smaller ISPs are just as capable of innovating bandwidth solutions.

In order to connect to the Internet, which most intranet users want, you'll need to hook up with companies like AT&T, BBN, UUNET, PSINET, or MCI.

George Gilder dedicated the August 1996 issue of his prestigious *Gilder Technology Report* to bandwidth. In it, he clearly positions ISDN as a technology not on the rise for bandwidth expansion. He chides the telcos for creating "parasite farms," where ISDN is the cash cow. He suggests bandwidth organizations that use the telephone companies' 65 million tons of copper to their economic advantage are going to be fulfilling the bandwidth needs of the future.

> ISDN has enough momentum to carry it for another year or so, but it will then hit a wall. What is needed today is not more fat and happy vendors of gear fitting into the present pricing structures and telco architectures, but more aggressive entrepreneurs such as Tut and AIR, Echostar and @Home, Teledesic and Globalstar, Winstar and Associated Communications that can up end this government guarded parasite farm. (courtesy of George Gilder)

What is Bandwidth?   "Bandwidth" is a measure of the amount of data that can flow through a channel in a given amout of time. In general, bandwidth is measured in bits (b) per second or bytes (B) per second. Expect anything that sends information serially (modem, ISDN, networks) to be measured in bits per second, and anything that sends information in parallel (SCSI [Small Computer System Interface], parallel port) to be measured in bytes per second.

In general, bandwidth can be measured across any two computer components that store or manipulate data. Bandwidth is comprised of CPU (Central Processing Unit) memory, disk memory, network throughput, and operating system efficiency.

- CPU—Memory bandwith is generally good and keeps getting better.

- Memory—Disk bandwidth is often one of the biggest bottlenecks in a system, and the one that is not getting faster by leaps and bounds. Webtops, thin clients, or web-ready computers with no hard drives may be the solution.

- Networks—The Internet and the proliferation of networks in general have brought network bandwidth into focus. This is one of the areas that has the most variation in options, and variations in costs as well, in part because you tend to pay ongoing costs for network bandwidth.

- The operating system needs to be built in a way so no barriers are put in the way of data flowing through the system, and to always be prepared to do something useful. This is where concepts such as multiprocessing and multithreading are useful, because they allow the system to have multiple processes or threads running at the same time.

Intranet-Oriented Suites   Look to see more intranet-oriented suites. Suites will provide enterprisewide software solutions within the browser. These packages are designed for all environments. Some are large providers of services, clients, servers, authoring tools, and management software for the enterprise intranet. Others are providers of PC X server and NFS technology. These are great solutions for companies that don't want to piece every part of their intranet together.

Instead of collecting all the components of an intranet, you can rely on products designed for use within the enterprise which incorporate enabling connectivity and management software within the browser. Look for good management features, and good end-user and connectivity features.

Pay attention to companies like Attachmate, FTP, Hummingbird (see Figure 3-11), NetManage, Microsoft, Hewlett-Packard, and Netscape who will be the significant players.

Figure 3–11 Hummingbird's Intranet-Oriented Products

The Internet Service Provider's List (ISPs)   ISPs also provide a service for smaller end intranet sites. Many of these larger organizations can provide storefronts for you and manage all of your intranet requirements in their offices. You can shop for these at The List[2] (see Figure 3-12).

2.   The List appears courtesy of iWORLD (http://www.iworld.com).

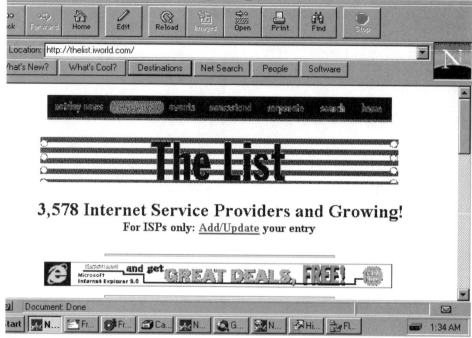

Figure 3–12 The Place to Find ISPs on the Net

Intranet Infrastructure

This section encourages you to investigate possible intranet infrastructure scenarios. It includes vision, mission statements, policies, job competencies and skills, processes, procedures, libraries, and design issues.

The intranet is made up of an elaborate, yet commonsense infrastructure. By infrastructure, we are referring to processes, people, and policies. In order to completely understand the intranet, you must understand its processes. In doing so, you understand the skills and people required to do the job. Once you have processes and people in place, you must set policies defining official, legal positions on intranet use.

Common Infrastructure Characteristics

The National Information Infrastructure is attempting to define common infrastructure characteristics. They are extending the work of the intranet leaders into society and the information superhighway. The objective is to stimulate, educate, and motivate users into action.

In the "National Information Infrastructure: Agenda for Action," President Clinton presented a vision of a National Information Infrastructure (NII) for the 21st century and articulated the benefits it will provide to our society. In the document, infrastructure characteristics are identified. They are worth repeating here as they describe intranets well.

Useful, well-planned infrastructure generally has in varying degrees the following characteristics:

- *Shareability.* Common resources offer economies of scale, minimize duplicative efforts, and if appropriately organized encourage the introduction of competing innovative solutions.

- *Ubiquity.* All potential users can readily take advantage of the infrastructure and what it provides.

- *Integrity.* The infrastructure operates at such a high level of manageability and reliability that it is often noticeable only when it ceases to function effectively.

- *Ease of use.* There are logical and consistent (preferably intuitive) rules and procedures for the infrastructure's use.

- *Cost-Effectiveness.* The value provided must be consistent with cost or the infrastructure simply will not be built or sustained.

- *Standards.* The basic elements of the infrastructure and the ways in which they interrelate are clearly defined and stable over time.

- *Openness.* The public infrastructure is available to all people on a nondiscriminatory basis.

Processes

Understanding the processes you have to go through to build such an intranet will benefit you greatly in setting up the rest of the infrastructure. In this work, the infrastructure consists of process, people, and procedures. Here we'll discuss the following:

- Executive buy-in process—suppliers of shareable resources
- Design process—vision behind ease of use and cost effectiveness
- Legal process—action that drives integrity
- Library process—repository for standards
- Development process—manages openness
- Maintenance process—ensures 7x24 customers' expectations

- Site Analysis Process—identification of ubiquity

Executive Buy-In Process   Getting your upper management committed to adopting intranet/web technology is a primary step. You must get a vision statement or a mission statement articulating exactly what the purpose of the intranet is at your company. You must show how this technology works and how the mission will be carried by the intranet. Clearly identify your action plan for achieving results. Identify how long the migration will take place and exactly what resources are required to make it happen. Get a budget approved by the executive sponsor.

Create an intranet prototype that features a mission-critical function for the executive team. Include two-way communication, master scheduling, and live stock quotes from the intranet. Use interactive e-mail and a map that identifies key processes within the executive management function. Then clearly explain what intranets are, what they're made of, what they buy the executive and the rest of the organization, what the costs are, including cost savings and productivity improvements, identify workflow improvement, and show off the library and publishing aspects of the intranet for access to key documents.

Explain ROI in terms of revenue, cost savings, and reduced cycles. Caution against high expectations on revenue and emphasize an incremental return based on reduced production cycles over time and reduced time to market.

Thoroughly explain the required resources, emphasizing the gradual reskilling of the internal staff by level of intranet maturity. Show how intranets directly streamline processes that have an effect on the customer, satisfying customers and enabling vendor and reseller partnerships to emerge.

Bottom Line: Once executives see how to use the technology for their own improvement, understand a clear cost benefit analysis, and see a direct impact on customer perception and loyalty, then your intranet is on the way to the planning stage.

Planning Process   Planning for intranet deployment starts with reviewing the organizational mission statement and aligning the intranet goals with it. Focus on what is required for successful intranet deployment. During planning, clearly identify what the intranet will do and how the company will do it. The purpose of the plan is to provide a framework or a guideline for evaluating the intranet's accomplishments. Internal uses focus on guiding and improving performance of the organization, and external uses focus on relations with outside partners, especially investors.

Internally, you must plan how you're going to communicate the intranet expecta-tions to the staff. Plan for coordinating activities across functions and depart-ments. In grass-roots (or bottom-up) intranets, these planning activities are too restrictive, disallowing the natural development of the free-flowing intranet. But once your intranet moves from a publishing/library intranet, then you'll require more vigorous planning. It is never too late to start, and starting early will get you to your goals faster.

Your plan must include a marketing and revenue-generating strategy. It may be difficult to think of intranet marketing strategies among internal customers, but you must find out what information can be brokered in an organization, to whom, in what quantities, and at what price. What are your strategies for promoting intranet information availability? What is the payoff for providing information to others? And, what is the best intranet design for distribution of effective content?

At some point in time, the intranet must justify itself and produce revenue. Plan what that revenue stream will look like. Sure, at first information is quite free and available to everyone. But as all organic markets grow, the same issues of supply and demand take effect, and the customer (although internal) will somehow have to identify the financial viability of maintaining the intranet. The primary sources of uses of funds must be identified.

Bottom Line: Information at your fingertips is powerful. Knowing how to get it is career enhancing.

Because many industries and organizations today find themselves in an environ-ment which can be characterized by rapid, frequent technological advances, they need to prepare a research and development strategy for ensuring the intranet is part of a highly competitive strategy in which new refined products are intro-duced frequently. This means keeping up with intranet and Internet technology to enhance the interactive, two-way customer-to-customer contact essential to intra-net success, and preparing for critical thinking knowledge workers whose demands for intelligent interactions are demanding.

Make sure all the appropriate staff is involved in planning for intranet deploy-ment and use. When you have involved the right staff, it is easier to ensure that appropriate assignment of responsibilities will speed the development of the intranet, with fewer interdepartmental conflicts or unnecessary omissions.

Create a formal business plan and distribute it on-line on the intranet, so the entire staff can understand how to relate directly to the plan. Perhaps there are participants within the group who could enhance the planning process. A formal plan brings planning to a closure, but closure doesn't happen unless everyone has responded. Above that, it confirms to the organization that the intranet is a serious plan for the improvement of communications and whatever other outcomes you've decided are important. With such a framework, moving into the development stage of an intranet is much simpler.

The production strategy for the intranet must be planned. Usually this falls into the same hands as the builders of networks and technology centers. Nonetheless, the process and technology that will be used to deploy an intranet must be clearly planned. As always, you need to account for materials, equipment, facilities, and staff. Where will the facilities be located? What are the costs associated with intranet deployment? Communicate the budget, resource allocations, and variances publicly. Use discretion within group definitions. But anyone within a project must see the financial detail.

Planning resource and staff strategies focuses on identifying responsibilities of the intranet staff and how they will be assigned. Identify the overall staffing requirements for the level of intranet you're building. You'll also need to plan what management controls you'll have to have in place. The more intranets I have reviewed, the more I have seen the intranet reporting into the top executive level, especially the CIO (Chief Information Officer). Some organizations have developed a position called the CKO (Chief Knowledge Officer).

You need to understand what role the various groups in your organization will have on the intranet. You need to include legal, and IS (Information Systems), sales and marketing, and Human Resources. You need to anticipate a training program. Planning is fundamental to success. Anticipate the unknown.

Design Process   If you care enough to create an intranet site for the organization, you must remember that the main purpose of an intranet site is communication and information sharing among internal divisions and departments. The key to your site is how well you all are informed and how you manage openness of information with each other. Communicating values is imperative.

Design Corporate Standards. Standards or even the need for standards vary across organizations. However, before you go much further, develop a statement regarding proprietary information. This is an organizational standard that cannot be overlooked. Certain levels of information simply cannot be cut and pasted and sent outside the intranet through e-mail. This standard or policy must be made clear to all the employees creating and using content. If you do not have these definitions well articulated and communicated throughout the company, you could be headed for trouble. To clarify, consider identifying all departmental documents as *"For internal use only."*

Initiate Corporate Guidelines. To avoid everyone going crazy, organize a committee to determine what the least common elements of each page should be. Make sure you get equal representation from the various departments or divisions. Buy-in is paramount to successful acceptance. Common elements include headers, footers, e-mail address (i.e., the Webmaster should receive all known bugs or broken links, or the owner of each page should design in their e-mail address). Do you need dates on each page? What is the common look and feel of the intranet site? Concentrate on navigation and graphic elements—how easily can people find information. Make sure you provide a site map, where any user can glance at a single page and overview the site. Remain flexible, but consider the entire population needs as a whole.

Document Ownership. A key factor in maintaining a streamlined, well-oiled intranet is to identify who owns what documents. A key method for doing so is to provide a contact alias at the bottom of each page. When someone leaves the company, make sure these pages are turned over to a working manager, so they can be updated regularly and so somebody can be responsible for the validity of the content. Or provide feedback forms, or any mechanism of interaction.

Enhance Your Corporate Culture. When creating a corporate information server, don't limit yourself to just product information and human resources manuals. The intranet is a perfect place to create or enhance your corporate culture.

Personnel On-Line. In addition, intelligent use of the security features of current commerce servers can allow management to share private information and employees to use on-line registration and changes of personnel information. Design some way of getting hold of anyone in the organization. Create a database that identifies each employee's function, location, special capabilities, or whatever other necessary information the entire company can benefit from by using an intranet personnel searching page.

Connections. Remember the design of an intranet is about connections among people, processes, procedures, information, and so forth. The primary purpose of an intranet is to provide an organization with a sense of "interconnectedness" (awareness of how things relate to one another in the organization) and "connectedness" (how the individual relates to these connections). This means, make it clear in your design, or the offerings on your key menus, the ways employees can contribute, and the ways they can learn.

Technical Design. The technical aspects of design must be considered as well. All the architecture issues discussed in the beginning of this chapter also must be designed into the intranet. Also, decide what effects the graphics, video, and audio will have on your site. What does the top page look like? What kind of search capability will you design into the site? What is the format—a magazine cover, a menu driven page? What common information will be on all pages? You'll need to account for issues like content overload, navigation, and human factors design as well. Either that, or you can roll up your sleeves, pump some HTML pages out there, announce the URLs, and watch what happens.

For a more detailed explanation of intranet design, see Chapter 4 where you'll explore the details of intranet design. This section was intended to introduce the process.

Legal Process. What is the process for labeling content for security access? Leveling should be made available, such as Need to Know, Company Confidential, Proprietary, and so forth. What does the official logo of the company officially look like? Who is legally liable for content? How does an employee know which data can be made publicly available in the company? The legal part of the organization need to get involved from the very beginning of the intranet design process. Laws vary state to state, country to country. For example, in many places human resource information legally must be available on a 24-hour basis. Get legal involved and find out what is permissible, and what methods are available for getting permission.

Library Process. Indexes and catalogs have to be established on-line for rapid development. Libraries of common elements, graphics, fonts, audio, video, logos, and so forth. need to be set up and maintained. Any reusable scripts, or templates for designing web sites must be made available and customizable. This is a common process for the library services in most organizations. Intranets provide some of the first library-like functions within an organization, making the intranet extremely valuable just for the availability of expert information. Library science is a recommended competency in intranet design.

Development Process. Once you've gotten executive buy-in, designed an elegant intranet plan, passed through the design, legal and library processes, you're ready for rapid development. If you cleverly managed these processes by using the intranet as a management, tracking and oversight environment, you've got a lot of information already on-line. If you used a centralized web site to communicate the processes to all the participating members of the intranet, you've got a head-start in the development process. If you have the internal skills, start developing now. Remember, you'll need to install and configure all the technical pieces, and the various servers. You'll need to configure all the clients, or at least automate the client configurations.

You'll need to start writing web pages, working on the overall site map, scripting in CGI, Java, ActiveX, designing memory-friendly graphics and clickable image maps, videos, and sound clips, and so forth. If you've got the talent fine, if not outsource. Get the outsource developers to produce quick results. Find out what tools are required and make them available on-line as soon as possible. Focus content at the employee level and develop a site that enables/empowers users to produce content in your designed intranet framework.

From here on, you can rapidly develop over the intranet by putting your site up and inviting interactive feedback from interested parties, reviewers, and testers. You can make incremental changes, constantly improving the quality of the site, yet making as much information available as possible. This is not ad hoc development. It is instead a process called rapid collaborative development.

Maintenance Process. Web servers have to be maintained. As problems occur or bugs appear in the software, someone has to respond as quickly as possible. Johnson and Harris in their book *Managing the New Enterprise*, a Sun Microsystems Press book, discuss the maintenance process for client/server very well. They discuss help desks as a premier interactive maintenance process.

Site Analysis Process. Process statistics can be maintained very easily in this environment. Statistics provide site activity analysis. Strategies can be developed to influence site behavior. Statistics are used to manage processes more effectively with on-going site analysis so a potential for observing human performance may be possible. If it is, intranet use may be a significant factor in continuous improvement which affects an organization's bottom line positively.

Most organizations have avoided statistics to describe organizational behavior because they've never had the ability to review as much spontaneous, random, interactive behavior among employees in the process of doing their work. The individual worker enjoys a lot of freedom and anonymity, while at the same time providing IP trails[3] that indicate exactly where they've been, how long they spent there, where they went next, and other information that contributes to a profile of the individual's work behavior.

---

3.   An IP trail is your unique intranet number that leaves its number at every site you visit. Behavior can be observed as a result.

When more organizations feel confident about moving to a statistical model of observing and measuring human performance on an intranet, the procedures and processes for doing so will grow in demand. Deming's work with internal performance statistics attests to the positive power of observing human variability and altering processes to accommodate for accelerated growth.

People

Job competencies and skills   Once certain tasks or processes have been clearly defined, you can begin to see what job competencies and skills are required to create an intranet. You do not necessarily need to look for new skills and competencies, at the beginning. It is best to leverage existing employees' knowledge and provide the intranet tools required to permit users to publish and link on-line.

Employees need to use intranets to perform existing tasks, concentrating first on accessing and using available data. Next, they'll need to be able to easily update them, then publish on them. Learning to convert existing documents and publishing robust intranet web pages will become increasingly important. Either they can learn how to perform some of the more complex development tasks, or they can manage vendors performing the technical pieces.

Management competencies dominate intranet deployment. Publishing and document creation are skills learned fairly quickly. It is difficult to move away from the model of managers' controlling the information flow through an organization, to managing information flowing freely among the appropriate decision makers and the individuals carrying out their respective tasks. Management must develop and maintain an infrastructure upon which independent decision makers can use the intranet to speed up decision making and get more core people involved at the right time.

One principle task of the management group is to ensure that certain management controls are integrated into the intranet in order to manage the ebb and flow of information. Information must be consistent, reliable, accurate, current, and resolved of conflict within the organization. Management must prepare for the rapid growth the intranet will experience and manage the acquisition of required skills and competencies of the intranet staff and the internal users.

Later when the intranet develops into a high-transaction environment, you'll need to look for competencies and skills in knowledge management, information architecture, cognitive resonance, human factors and ergonomics, knowledge representation, and very high information security.

Intranet technology and administration will most likely be handled by the current technology groups within your organization. Since the network must integrate with the intranet, the information technology group is the appropriate developer and caretaker. The content will not be placed in this group's hands. They will not develop content, and they will not manage content. Content development and content management will happen at the level of its creation, and managed at the level of its most powerful users.

People are required to run the intranet. Their skills and competencies grow with the power of the technology, but at the same time, they must have additional skills to fall back on when they hit up against the limitations of the technology. We'll discuss the individual roles and responsibilities later in this chapter.

Policies

You must also set up some policies. These are tried and true lessons of business that protect your organization legally and securely. These issues have been hashed out by many corporations. The distinction lies within how much employers are willing to trust their employees with information flow. Does information flow entirely freely, or are there restraints? Information movement and the freedom of speech are not necessarily common practice, among most cultures of the world. You must adhere to culture and political differences as well. What are the international constraints on information proliferation? Find out. That is the stuff of policies.

Six Types of Policies   Let's look at six policy types to help you prepare some team meeting agendas. The types are content, design, administrative, security, legal, and usage.

Content Policies. Until you have problems putting content on the intranet, you won't understand how important these policies are. You need to clearly identify what can and cannot go onto the intranet. You need to identify ownership and accountability of information and communicate these policies beyond a shadow of a doubt. Information experts who own the information must be held accountable, too. You need a buffer zone, or a staging area, where content can flow freely and actually be accessible by others. The content approval and review process pushes this information up to the "organizational tiers" of the intranet, and gets pushed to the customer when it clearly represents the voice of all and resonates with truth.

You must have a process for getting something pushed out onto the intranet site. This means you need some guidelines for submitting and an approval process for letting something go on-line. Be protective of your intellectual capital. At the same time, allow the freedom of speech.

Table 3-5 Policy Types: Content, Administrative, Legal, and Security

Policy	Purpose	Contents
Content Policies	Determine ownership and accountability. Define content creation, review, approval, and maintenance standards. Provide a flexibility clause—a creative foundation for freedom of speech.	Policies that tie corporate goals to information ownership. Procedures for submitting content to the intranet. Approval process for publishing content. Revision control procedures.
Design Policies	Develop a common look and feel, with appropriate tools, and available procedures.	Templates. Common look and feel. Authoring standards. Maintenance policy.
Administrative Policies	Provide overall design of infrastructure to ensure a smooth running intranet. Align your architecture with your IP client server distributed model.	Mission statement. Executive ownership statement. Funding. Roles and responsibilities. Usage policy.
Legal Policies	Ensure that proper legal procedure is being followed regarding information access and dissemination.	Logos. Proprietary information. Trademark. Copyright. Permissions.
Security Policies	Protect your network from viruses and loss of intellectual capital.	Download software Information protection.
Usage Policies	Identify what your thinking is on internet usage and the funding for usage.	Policy for internet usage. Funding model for who's paying for internet access.

Design Policies. You need a common look and feel to facilitate access to information and to group like ideas or concepts together. Common look and feel reside on the home page and are reflected on group and department pages for consistency and ease of navigation. You need to determine which repeating navigational devices you'll use. Decide what minimal information you need on each page. Things like date, e-mail address of author, and link to a home page are key. See Sun Microsystems Press and Prentice Hall's *Web Page Design: A Different Multime-*

dia by Morris and Hinrichs, 1996, for more information. This chapter also has some great recommendations on how to design your intranet site. In summary, know how to

- design content for your unique data

- design navigational devices

- design cognitive friendly sites

- lay out hypermedia economically

- incorporate interactivity

- plan for experiential content

Administrative Policies. It is important to let the entire organization know what their common goal is. Create it and post it. Also, you need to identify how the infrastructure of your intranet works. Get job responsibilities on-line. You need to explain to people how to get support and how to maintain their sites. You must have a policy on usage. How much usage is allowed on the intranet? Will you allow unlimited use? Tools are available for monitoring usage, so you have an automatic way of enforcing such a policy if you desire. You must have policies on the following:

- Version control

- Link integrity checking

- Graphical site management

- Image and document conversion support

- Support for search engines

Legal Policies. Get your legal department involved up-front. There are many issues to consider, such as copyright protection for using links and cutting and pasting text and graphics from other pages, authentication and authorization, proper use of logo on web pages, trademark status of any products you mention. These issues may be critical in your organization, or there may be others that your legal department needs to convey about information dissemination, for example, what is confidential and proprietary.

Legal processes can be put on your intranet as well. Sun Microsystems, for example, created an interactive screen so you could speak directly to the lawyers in the company. See Figure 3–13. Also, confidentiality agreements were placed on-line to speed up the process of approval and getting subcontractors working more quickly

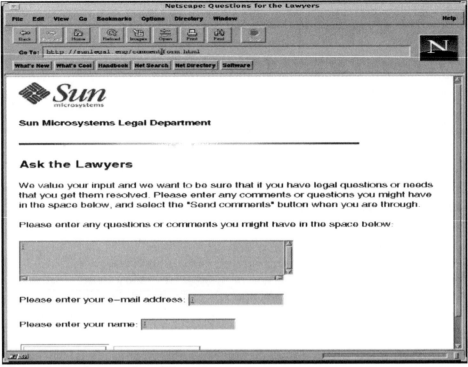

Figure 3–13   Intranet Legal Processes

Security Policies. Viruses over the net! No way. Yes, way. Provide a policy for downloading software, especially executables. Either provide a standardized virus checker, or simply forbid the downloading of these potentially infected files. Also, protect the kind of information your employees may inadvertently throw out. How do you protect confidential information? Do you prevent ftp capability outside of the firewall? You must decide. Track downloads.

Usage Policies. Currently, many corporations are feeling the pains of intranet growth. Naturally, they are hooked up to the Internet for outside commerce and research. But, are employees using the Internet side strictly to analyze the competition or purchase corporate required products? Or are they spending time on their own? Research indicates that user surfing dissipates after the glow wears off. You need a policy to indicate complete freedom, no tell policy, or usage restrictions. A funding policy must support the usage policy.

Intranet Interactivity

This section describes what interactivity pieces intranets are made up of. Interactivity helps communicate and collaborate within the organization. Requirements of users are identified, and responses to feedback can be captured and reintegrated back into the web site. This includes using e-mail, searching mechanisms, interaction with databases and legacy systems, connection with newsgroups, interfacing with experts, video-conferencing, electronic whiteboarding, and creating both human and automatic feedback mechanisms for site improvement and evolution.

Forms

One of the fundamental interactions with the client is through the use of forms. Forms can be used to collect information. However, users are reluctant to give out information freely unless they have a need. This has less to do with privacy than it does with taking the time to fill out a form. If you want to collect information, make sure the form has relevance to the user.

Other forms are useful for acquiring information so action can be taken. Help desks are a typical example. There is something wrong with your workstation, or your office furniture, or the temperature of your room. You want to develop an on-line assistance, or a help desk, to take the person's call, put their request into a queue, and develop an interactive e-mail autoresponder (automated e-mail responses) that provides the user with updates on the status of the help. In Figure 3–14, Netscape uses a simple screen form to assist users with installing and setting up software. The user fills out the form, submits it, and waits as it queues up for 24-hour turnaround .

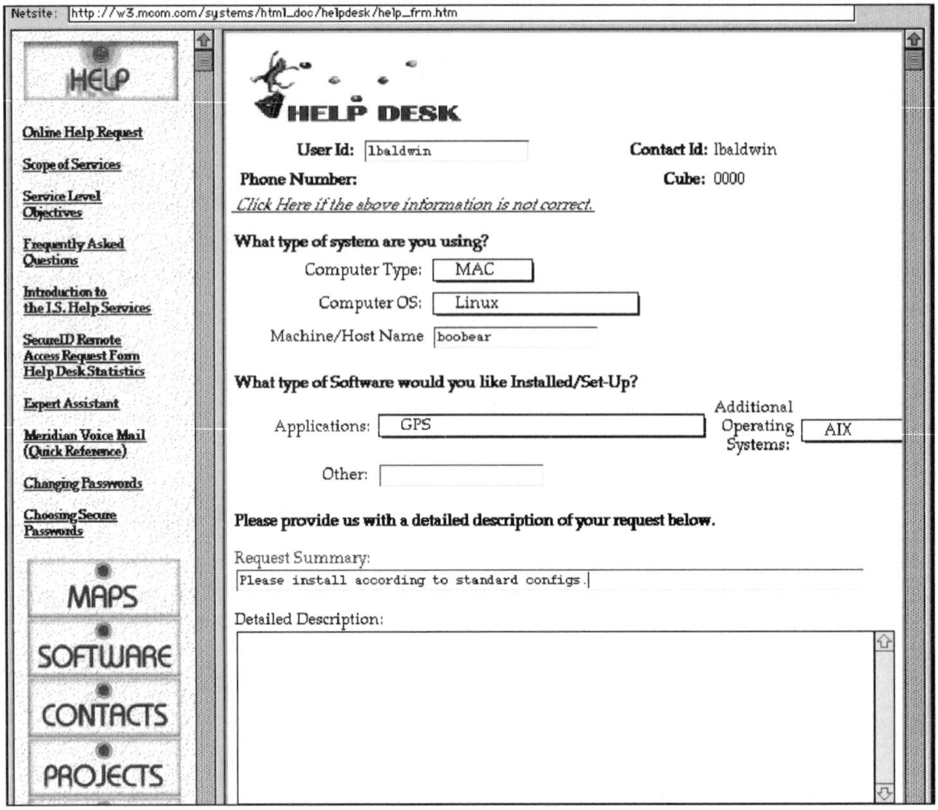

Figure 3–14 Netscape Uses Forms to Provide On-line Help

E-mail

Don't start an intranet without an excellent e-mailing system. Use SMTP, POP, or IMAP protocols as discussed earlier in this chapter. Make sure everyone in the organization has an e-mail address and that you maintain a robust e-mail support system. Include e-mail contacts on all web pages. Each author should be held responsible for the integrity and validity of published intranet web pages. Whenever possible, add the contacts or interdependent e-mail address of anyone associated with the intranet site. Encourage your staff to save their e-mail in e-mail folders and verify that they know that all e-mail is proprietary. Define education or policies for using personal e-mail and for sending attachments.

Search or Find Tools

Don't even think about an intranet without creating a publishing system that includes a search tool. Intranets are made up of search and find tools. So far, tools search two ways—text-based searching and concept-based searching. A form based on case-based reasoning is appearing.

Text-Based Searching   You have a variety of search engines to use—text-based search tools crawl all over your intranet site and find matching text. If you're looking for "How to request travel authorization," somewhere on your intranet, someone must use the term "How to request travel authorization" to provide an exact match, thereby accelerating your navigation to the information you need.

Text-based searches have problems concerning relevancy. You may pull up several hundred documents with the keyword that was an exact match, but the documents are not relevant, because you cannot drill down much deeper. You're stuck reading hundreds of documents. Text-based searching alone will not endure much longer, it will evolve to incorporate conceptual-based searching, metainformation, and case-based reasoning.

Concept-Based Searching   Unlike keyword indexed-based systems, concept-based searching uses concepts or ideas and searches your intranet site more intelligently. Essentially, concept-based search engines explore your entire intranet for dominant themes. It indexes the themes in a database and checks them for frequency of use against the concept you are searching for. You may look for "Intranet publishing, policies, in the United States," and the concept builder will look for the documents with the highest frequency of these words. The more frequently a word appears in a document, the higher its percentage of relevance.

Conceptual search tools may even provide you with documents that do not have the exact keywords of your search, but are linguistically, or conceptually related. See http://www.excite.com for an example.

Visit the Search Information site in Figure 3–15 for greater detail (http://www.monash.com/spidap.html). Whichever web search technology you use, make sure it performs both textual and concept-based searching.

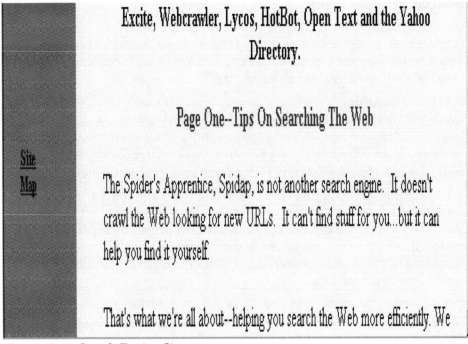

Figure 3–15 Search Engine Site

MetaInformation and Case-Based Reasoning (CBR)   Metainformation is information *about* a document. This information is used to index the site more efficiently, keeping documents timely and providing filtering where content may be inappropriate for some audiences and providing appropriate bibliographic information about each document for distributed reference.

Visit http://www.scit.wlv.ac.uk/wwlib/position.html for more discussion on this topic.

Case-based reasoning (CBR) solves new problems by adapting solutions that were used to solve old problems. CBR analyzes historical information against the search words you use to seek a solution to an existing problem. A new problem is matched against cases in the case base and one or more similar cases are retrieved. A solution suggested by the matching cases is then reused and tested for success. Unless the retrieved case is a close match, the solution will probably have to be revised, producing a new case that can be retained. As you can see, you have a system capable of learning with you about a specific problem. Tools based on CBR will provide increased relevancy to the information you seek. Visit the *CBR Virtual Library* for more at http://146.87.176.38/ai-cbr/SERV06.HTM.

Video-Conferencing and Whiteboarding

Meeting on-line around the globe is a part of advanced intranetting. You might not be ready for it, but you need little to get going. You'll need to configure video cameras on each client and add video-conferencing software to your workstation or PC. Much more information can be transferred when people see each other over the intranet and react face to face. Individuals, leaders and experts bring more spontaneity and openness to meetings when conducted together in a Net meeting.

To accompany the video-conferencing experience, electronic whiteboards are available. Like whiteboards or chalkboards, electronic whiteboard software allows multiple users to draw or create on screen and share the results simultaneously. The ability to go to the whiteboard and show a concept by example is interactivity worth having. More than a trend, videoconferencing and whiteboarding enhance on-line collaboration. The ability to meet together in intact shared work groups adds value to the workflow and improved productivity cycles of an organization.

Interaction with Databases and Legacy Systems

No doubt you'll want to be interactive with your databases and legacy systems. If you want to move your company beyond mere web page publishing and into interactivity applications, you'll need to access and update corporate databases from the web browser. What components of the intranet work with databases and legacy systems?

Web Browser as an Application Launcher Only   There are many kinds of database applications you have set up already on your internal network. You probably have Human Resource databases which certain application programs access each time an on-line employee transaction takes place. This is to assume that you've automated your processes and are using database technology to accommodate the automation.

At Sun Microsystems, Inc., for example, Pat Baldwin, director of business simplification, designed and implemented internal network applications to automate HR processes relative to Sun's "human assets" applications. She invested smartly in internal net products. So, when the World Wide Web touched Sun headquarters, Baldwin opted to maintain her popular applications and wrap a web interface around her entire product suite. Accessing existing databases without missing a day was a key objective. Her solution allowed Sun's 14,000 employees to access HR tools through Sun's intranet SunWeb site. The internal employees were delighted because there is now one common access point to all HR tools.

Data are being managed by the original database application, not by the web site (see Figure 3–16). Notice in this example how the internal interface has taken over. The web browser has subordinated the HR application. You leave the web browser, run the application, all data are updated at the application level, then you return to the web browser.

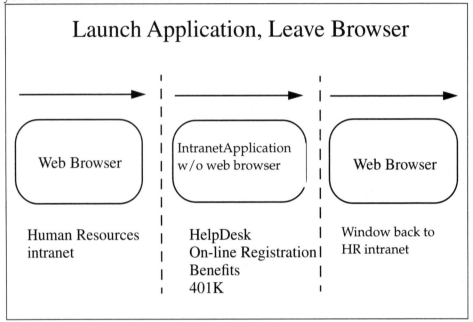

Figure 3–16 Launch Intranet Applications from Browser

Web Browser Form Is the Database

CGI (Common Gateway Interface) and SQL. A common form of intranet interactivity is the web form. Forms technology is becoming very popular on the Web. You can create any kind of form in any browser. You access simple databases using CGI scripts to make SQL queries to the database. The databases update automatically. See Figure 3–17. This may be an intermediary methodology for the present, but the consistency of the forms and the ease of use of the forms provide the same power as desktop publishing database software. They link graphical interfaces directly with databases.

The web browser is always visible but is working extra in the background to update existing relational databases. With web browser forms you can attain common look and feel and easy change management.

Bottom Line: You cannot create web forms that perform heavy on-line transaction processing with CGI scripts.

With CGI interactive forms, you lack security and performance suffers. CGI scripts are good for simple databases. For more heavy-duty ones, you need to consider either launching a proprietary database program, or evolve to Java, ISAPI (Microsoft), or NSAPI (Netscape).

Web Browsers Use OBDC and JDBC for Multiple Databases   The Internet's World Wide Web provides businesses and consumers access to millions of web pages. But it requires more interaction to enable access to the trillions of bytes of data stored in conventional databases (Oracle, Informix, Sybase). ODBC (Open Database Connectivity) standards (Microsoft) and JDBC (Java Database Connectivity) standards (Sun Microsystems, Inc.) are two important application programming interfaces for databases that move you beyond CGI scripts.

Both of these protocols allow embedded Java applications to access conventional databases, providing security and boosted performance. ODBC is Microsoft's WINTEL (Windows/Intel) desktop database access solution. JDBC protocol provides SQL-oriented connectivity to databases, and is considered an all inclusive network-centric database connectivity solution. Bridges between the two now exist.

Bottom Line: There is a dichotomy between the ODBC and JDBC, threatening open standards and database integration.

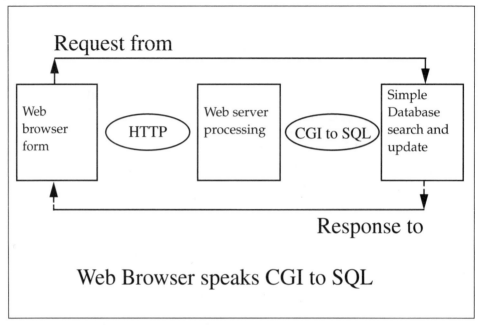

Figure 3–17 Web Browser to Database Process

The divergence of database protocols fragments the open philosophy of the intranet. The user is not the focus. It seems there is only a desire to dominate the standards whether the customer has to take the pain or not. This idea of customer pain rather than customer delight or customer loyalty is frightening. Convergence of technology and true open standards is what drives customers, not proprietary jihads. Look for JDBC becoming the superset standard for network-centric applications that emerge to make the intranet dynamic and database friendly. Or look for an integration of ODBC and JDBC tolead the way in true customer delight. See Figure 3–18 to see the possible streamlined integration.

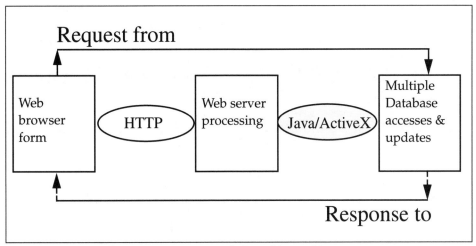

Figure 3–18 Database Interactivity with Java/ActiveX

Connecting to Legacy Systems

In order to create a complete intranet solution, intranets must connect to a data warehouse, a structure which stores enormous amounts of historical data. The data are extracted from large legacy systems and placed into a relational data model for use in a data warehouse. Once these data are placed into a data warehouse, a decision support system can allow users to drill down into company data to predict future corporate and market trends. Drill-down functionality allows end users to determine the root of a problem by providing direct access to specific levels of data.

Various software solutions exist for connecting the intranet to your legacy systems. Some of the software comes directly from your database vendor.

Other software solutions exist that help to create effective web end solutions. DSS Web[4] is an example of such a software solution. Their software illustrates the ease of drilling down into corporate data stored in a data warehouse.

In Figure 3–19 is an example of how the intranet site looks using DSS's solution. This example looks at a clothing data warehouse. The user wants to look at profit margins from four different regions and three different classes of clothing. The tabular format is useful for easy analysis of the figures. But, with the additional value of being connected to the intranet, the checkboxes can be used to drill down into the data warehouse for additional analysis.

4.   http://dssweb.strategy.com/projects/feature/dd1.html-ssi.

The user wishes to examine profit margins in the Mid-Atlantic region for just women's clothing. Without programmers and without structured query reports, two checkboxes are marked. You click on Drill-Down and the intranet accesses the legacy database and responds immediately as in Figure 3–19.

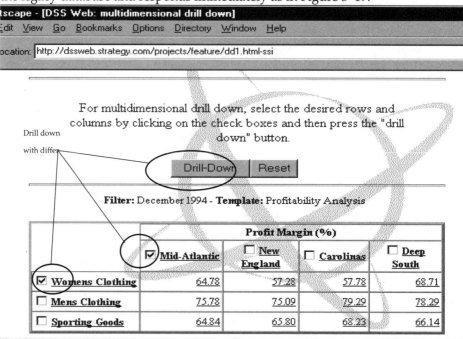

Figure 3–19 Drill-Down in a Data Warehouse on the Web

This is only a small example of integrating your legacy data in a data warehouse and using a third-party solution as a front-end to your data over an intranet. Many other solution providers exist that have created similar functionality. You, in fact, can design and program them using your internet suite of office products.

Again, the main point of intranet interactivity resides in making it all work together—old software, new software, stored data, databases, web technology, andmost important your need to see it all integrated together. The intranet is that integrator.

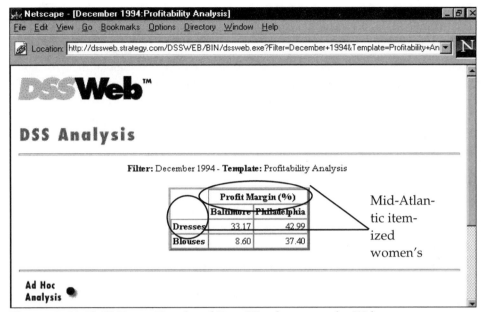

Figure 3–20 Drill-Down Results of Data Warehouse on the Web

Each data warehouse requires a software interface, like DSS Web, to analyze their data. You will need to research various decision support vendors to determine which system works best with your database and to discuss the best methodologies for analyzing data via the intranet. You will want to operate from a standard web browser, creating forms that query directly into the data warehouse. Look for the decision support system that provides "complete" solutions and offers clear results.

Connection with Newsgroups, Threads, and Chatting

In order to keep your site as interactive and real as possible, it is an excellent idea to incorporate newsgroup interactions. Newsgroups allow you to peek inside ongoing discussions. You remain anonymous if you want, or you can become an active participant. The goal is to share resources and seek answers. There are some informal rules. Always be polite. Support your opinions with facts. Stick to the subject. Contribute back.

The software is exemplary of human interaction in a forum. You begin a thread of a conversation about a topic of interest simply by posting a question, or a comment. Everyone interested views the threads of conversation and can comment on any one. This is public information you're using to share common solutions. It can be stimulating and rewarding. For example, networking with people, the old-fashioned way, happens very actively in newsgroup discussions. This is where chance meetings take place and the passing of important spontaneous information takes place.

Someone asks a question, and several people respond, leaving calling cards, e-mail addresses, telephone numbers, URL sites, and appointments. It is a community clearinghouse. In Figure 3–21 below, you see an example of a threaded conversation. The *Intranet Journal* and *CIO Communications* provide on-going discussions in this area. You can use these areas as though you were speaking directly to web consultants. Be careful to verify information as always.

Intranets: Networking with Peers

Welcome to the moderated message exchange dedicated to Intranets. Express yourself freely. This is an open forum, and will only be moderated to remove foul language, and offensive behavior. Click on *policies* for more detail.

Post a Message	*FAQ*	*Post a Follow-up*

1. What is a Webmaster? Randy Hinrichs, 10/1/96. 35 Responses
    Re: What is a Webmaster? Colin Louis, 10/2/96. 11 Responses
    Re: What is a Webmaster? Anna Barry, 10/3/96. 9 Responses
    ...

2. Intranets and Novell Netware. How do you upgrade?
    Re: Intranets and Novell. Tyler James. 10/15/96. 6 Responses
    Re: Intranets and Novell. Evan Jay, 08/10/96. 1 Response

3. Hare Virus. What is it? Claire Soleil, 12/8/96. 8 Responses

---

Figure 3–21 Example of a Threaded Newsgroup

You can set up chat rooms to discuss issues. Chat rooms are web sites that promote on-going discussions among special interest groups. The various participants log on to the web site. Once inside the chat room, you can see whom the other participants are and address them directly. Or you can observe by reading the general discussion that is taking place. At any point, you can either speak directly to a participant, or speak to the entire group. Discussing issues in this way considerably helps users streamline their processes for looking for information.

Feedback Interactions for Site Improvement and Evolution   Feedback is essential to improving your site's architecture and infrastructure. Users are engaged with your information and become voices of customers. Pay attention, and you will increase your value seriously. Feedback comes in many forms:

- e-mail address to the content owner of the page

- web form to become acquainted with user

- pages of contacts within the organization

- open-nded discussions in a chatting session

- survey forms

- call support or help desks

- white boarding

- Net meetings

Intranet Security

This section[5] will explain to you the components of intranet security. It will introduce you to the concept of firewalls, fire ridges, and secure electronic transactions. It will also advocate changing your security paradigm in order to achieve higher learning among your employees.

Although security degrades performance, your intranet with enterprise connections is subject to attack. Eighty percent of the break-ins within an organization originate from the inside. Local employees can hack into the system files, or alter or remove important documents. An Internet connection compounds the problem a hundred times unless security precautions are taken and followed rigorously. The benefits of the intranet and internet connections are too compelling to ignore. In order for you to protect your data, databases, and system configuration files, you must set up security on your intranet.

The moment you install a web server on a network, you've opened a window into your local network. The entire intranet can peer in and break in if you do not take precautions, see Table 3–6. Security issues can be complex. A basic understanding of the issues and policies is essential.

---

5.   Material in this section has been adapted from "How to Develop a Network Security Policy: An Overview of Internetworking Site Security." Copyright 1996, Sun Microsystems. Inc. All rights reserved.

Bottom Line: Any system can be broken into if the break-in artist is determined.

One consolation is the complexity of secure encrypted firewalls. Hackers usually do not have the computing power and the volume of time to breach through mathematically complex encryption. If they do try, they are detected fairly soon, as the activity is viewed as an anomaly bombarding the site.

Remember though, that's why hackers are criminals. They know how to get around security and break in. They know how to take what they need and get out equally as well. Security is a key issue on the intranet.

Security Policies Are Subjective.   No single site security policy is best for any two businesses. And, just as your business evolves to adapt to changing market conditions, your site security policy must evolve to meet changing technology conditions. Security is subjective. Degrees of freedom exist. It is up to you to establish what the security policies are. Below are some recommendations.

Table 3-6 Potential Security Problems and Their Resolutions

Culprit	Problem	Resolution
CGI Scripts	Plant bugs between systems	Restrict scripts to the cgi-bin directory. Set up limited permissions so that only the web administrator can install quality scripts. Use ODBC or JDBC. Use Java.
Confidential Documents	Unauthorized on-line access.	Keep off the Net, or Encrypt.
Dial-in Users	Dial in behind firewall and move data in and out through e-mail.	Limit the number of login accounts available on the machine. Delete inactive users. Implement strong authentication measures. Consider point-to-point tunnelling
Credit Cards	Numbers being intercepted.	Encrypt using certificate keys.

Table 3-6 Potential Security Problems and Their Resolutions *(Continued)*

Culprit	Problem	Resolution
WWW Server or FTP Server	Leaks out information about itself.	Turn off unused services, especially the finger daemon. Set file permissions in the document and server root directories so that only trusted local users can make changes.
Bugs	Allow outsiders to execute commands on host machine.	Don't allow unknown executables to be downloaded.
Operating Systems	UNIX is complex with many portals of entry. Powerful NT secured systems can be set up wrong.	Use Java. Automate NT security setup.
Experience of Operator	Novice security managers can create havoc.	Rigorous hiring policy and supplemental training policy.

Official Policy   The Internet Standards group has issued a document regarding security policies. RFC 1244 can be found at ftp://archie.au/rfc/rfc1244.au.gz or at http://ds.internic.net/ds/dspg2intdoc.html.

Developing a Site Security Policy   The first rule of network site security is easily stated: That which is not expressly permitted is prohibited. Simply, a security policy should start by denying all access to all network resources, and then expressly add back access on a specific basis. Implemented in this way, your site security policy will not allow any inadvertent actions or procedures.

Internet vs. Intranet   Naturally, you do not need the full level of security services required by your internet connection. However, if you are planning on having an active internet connection as a major feature of your intranet, you need to take every precaution to set up security. Many companies unknowingly increase the vulnerability to their computer network, all in the name of improving productivity.

DoD Security Levels—a Guideline   The United States Department of Defense has defined seven levels of computer OS security in a document known as the Trusted Computer Standards Evaluation Criteria, otherwise known as the Orange Book. The different levels are used to define different levels of protection for hardware, software, and stored information. The system is additive—higher ratings include the functionality of the levels below. The definition centers around access control, authentication, auditing, and levels of trust.

Table 3-7 Guideline: DoD Security Policies from the Orange Book

Name	Policy	Comments
D1	System is untrusted.	No security at all. Rarely used.
C1	File and Directory read and write controls. User login authentication.	Root directory is unsecure and auditing is not available.
C2	Same as C1, with auditing function records all security-related events.	Stronger protection of password file.
B1	Same as C1–C2. Users cannot change permissions on files or directories.	Secret and top secret security.
B2	Every object and file labeled according to its security level.	Labels change dynamically depending on what is being used.
B3	Terminals can only be connected through trusted cable paths. Specialized system hardware employed.	System hardware is secured to ensure there is no unauthorized access.
A1	Mathematically verified user authentication and movement of files.	Highest level of security. All hardware and software protected during shipment to prevent tampering.

Most OSs and Network Security software falls here

Physical Security

If you don't want people to see it, or get to it, simply lock it up away from your physical site. Don't allow physical access to your secured servers. And if something is extremely sensitive, don't put it on your intranet.

Operating System Security

UNIX and Microsoft Windows NT have C2 level security imbedded. C2 provides access control—file and directory read and write permissions—and auditing and authentication controls.

Firewalls

Firewalls are either hardware devices or software that reside in a router, a common hardware device. The firewall restricts the types of traffic that it allows into the intranet. It determines which type of access (e-mail, telnet, ftp, etc.) is allowable to a user. It manages the source or destination of data, and always records the time of day.

Firewall systems protect and facilitate your network at a number of levels:

- They set up a security wall between the outside and the services you use to go outside, that is, e-mail, ftp, and remote login.

- They authorize access to only specific users or applications through the firewall.

- They track usage and signal warnings at specified events.

- They hide user's real names, for example webmaster@anycompany.com, instead of janice.queenofwebs@anycompany.com.

- They provide encryption and virtual private network capabilities.

- Encryption scrambles data. It requires code keys to decrypt data.

- Virtual Private Networks employ encryption to provide secure transmissions over public networks such as the Internet. Firewall systems can also be deployed within an enterprise network to protect classified areas within the intranet.

- Compartmentalizes different servers and networks. For example, Accounting and Payroll servers.

Firewalls are required for any kind of transaction outof your intranet and onto the Internet. You may consider a firewall around an area within your intranet as well. Confidential and even top secret information resides on your intranet. You may consider C1 level security around that data.

Security Techniques

Besides firewalls there are many different security techniques. See Table 3–8.

Table 3-8 Security Techniques, Risks, and Solutions.

Security Techniques	Risk	Solution
Passwords for access	Flood access gateways with dictionaries. Users loan out passwords to others.	One-time password use. Password aging (change after a certain amount of time). Minimum and maximum combinations of alpha and numeric. SmartCards, challenge-response schemes. Different passwords for different parts of the intranet.
Encryption	Supercomputer decryption attacks. DES Encryption is not available for export from the U. S. E-mail messages not secure	56-bit key length passwords. Private key and public keys RSA encryption (public key) (can be used in Europe/Asia). Uses PGP encryption for e-mail encryption.
Authentication	Users are not who they say they are.	Different passwords for different parts of the intranet.
Integrity	Message has been altered.	Digital Signature (RSA and PGP [Pretty Good Privacy] only).
Physical Privacy	Minimal risk	Ensure secrecy of location.
Authorization	Impostors can break in and authorize illegally.	Use digital signatures internally.

An Example   Kerberos is an add-on system that can be used with any existing network. Kerberos validates a user through its authentication system and uses DES (Data Encryption Standard) when communicating sensitive information—such as passwords—on an open network. In addition, Kerberos sessions have a limited life span, requiring people to log in after a predetermined length of time and disallowing would-be intruders to replay a captured session and thus gain unauthorized entry.

Good Password Procedures

- Do use a password with mixed case.

- Do use a password with nonalphabetic characters (digits or punctuation).

- Do use a password that is easy to remember, so you don't have to write it down.

- Do use any password except your first, middle, or last name or the names of your spouse or children

- Do use passwords that are nonsense words with a digit or punctuation mark somewhere in the password

- Don't use your login name in any form (as is, reversed, capitalized, doubled, and so forth).

- Don't use other information easily obtained about you. This includes license plate numbers, telephone numbers, social security numbers, the make of your automobile, the name of the street you live on, and so forth.

- Don't use a password of all digits, or all the same letter.

- Don't use a word contained in English or foreign language dictionaries, spelling lists, or other lists of words.

- Don't use a password shorter than eight characters.

Assessing the Risk

There has been lot of publicity about break-ins on computer networks. The actual loss of security in fact comes from people within the organization. Risk analysis is important in securing on-line intelligence. You must determine what needs to be protected, whom you need to protect it from, and how to protect it. It is the process of examining all your risks, and ranking those risks by level of severity that provides you with your security insights. This process involves making cost-effective decisions on what you want to protect.

Defining a Policy for Acceptable Use

The tools and applications discussed in the previous section will form the technical foundation of your site security policy. But this is only part of the solution. How users interact with the network is just as important as the tools that serve them. The creation of a policy for acceptable use should consider the following:

People

- Who is allowed to use the intranet resources?
- Who is authorized to grant access and approve usage?
- Who may have system administration privileges?
- Who will interpret the policy on electronic communications (mail forging, etc.)?
- What do you do to those who violate their rights?

Rights and Responsibilities

- What are the users' rights and responsibilities?
- What are the rights and responsibilities of the system administrator versus those of the user?
- Are users permitted to share accounts or let others use their accounts?

Procedures

- What is the proper use of the resources?
- What do you do with sensitive information?
- How do you handle the disclosure of information that may be proprietary?
- What guidelines do you have regarding resource consumption (whether users are restricted, and if so, what the restrictions are)?
- How "secret" should users keep their passwords
- How often should users change their passwords (and any other password restrictions or requirements)?
- How often do you provide backups or expect the users to create their own.

Definitions

- Define what might constitute abuse in terms of system performance.
- Provide a statement on electronic mail privacy (Electronic Communications Privacy Act). Specifically, does the company consider electronic mail private to each employee, or do they consider it the property of the organization?
- Define your policy concerning mail or postings to mailing lists or discussion groups (obscenity, harassment, etc.), and on representing the organization to these areas.

<u>*Auditing Log Files.*</u>

- How will you track and maintain login procedures? Most users have patterns, so to avoid security leaks, it is sometimes necessary to monitor them.

- Will you examine failed, repeated login attempts?

- Who will check authorized user's application program usage?

- Will you run various monitoring commands at different times throughout the day?

Last Word   Reviews are imperative due to today's changing computing environments. It is getting astoundingly easy to break into intranet sites through available user-friendly point-and-click packages. Security is a dynamic process. Only by assembling the core team or a representative subset and reviewing how well things are working, what the latest threats and security tools are, and assessing the risk against new assets and business practices, can an organization stay secure and productive.

Communicating Security to Users

The site security policy should include a formalized process which communicates the site security policy to all users. In addition, an educational campaign should make users aware of how computer and network systems are expected to be used and how to protect themselves from unauthorized users.

All users need to be informed about what is considered the "proper" use of their account or workstation. This can most easily be done at the time a user receives their account by giving them a policy statement. Proper usage policies typically dictate things such as whether or not the account or workstation may be used for personal activities (such as checkbook balancing or letter writing), whether profit-making activities are allowed, whether game playing is permitted, and so forth.

Users should be told how to detect unauthorized access to their account. If the system prints the last login time when a user logs in, he or she should be told to check that time and note whether or not it agrees with the last time he or she actually logged in.

Bottom Line: Ideally, the security policy should strike a balance between protection and productivity.

Security Hacker Tools

Some security experts advocate the proactive use of the very tools which hackers use in order to discover system weaknesses before those with less than honorable intent do. By discovering weaknesses before the fact, protective action can be implemented to fend off certain attacks. Perhaps the most famous of these tools is called the Security Analysis Tool for Auditing Networks, which is publicly available on many WWW sites. According to the National Computer Security Institute, many companies are using this tool on their own network to uncover vulnerabilities. Look into such self-protective tolls and use them in your site!

The Security Paradox

We have a paradox. We need security for some information, but need most information to flow freely. Content is an asset. Access to all content is a privilege. Your methods of doing business, your performance results, and other inside information are intellectual capital. It needs to be secured to ensure validity. Most computer organizations are rushing to either join the Internet, or directly interface with partnering groups. How they manage the flow and security of information is tantamount to their success. While "bulletproof" security is a red herring, reasonable security levels can be attained cost-effectively with today's technologies *by explicitly managing risk.* The paradox: provide all information, but not some.

Intranet Design

This section explains how an intranet is made up of certain design elements. We'll discuss audience considerations, tying intranet design to goals, content design, and cognitive design. We'll also explain a bit about preparing your site for search design. Also, we'll cover layout, navigational design, and graphics design. We'll explain what to consider for time, interactivity, and experiential design.

This discussion on intranet design is by no means an extensive discussion. More detail is provided elsewhere in this chapter. The idea here is to make you aware of intranet design components.

Design for the 21st Century

Intranets have quickly become highly interactive, collaborative, process streaming communication tools. The intranet is more important than the telephone. With the telephone you make a point-to-point connection either directly with the person you're calling or with their voice mail. Intranets open communication in providing the receiver with as much information and transaction as desired before initiating verbal contact. The user comes to the conversation prepared. The communication experience is enhanced enormously.

Bottom Line: Remember two things about designing for the 21st century: Intranets are organic and intranets integrate the enterprise with the public.

Intranets Are Organic   The intranet develops as a whole. This means that as intranet technology evolves, so does the use of the technology. As the use improves, so does human performance. All the components of information exchange and human participation in an electronic environment engage the user in a struggle for information survival. The intranet becomes the environment; the user becomes the living form adapting to that environment. As the users' abilities to utilize information improve, so do the skills for manipulating the environment. Expertise and intelligence improve and so does the quality of the experience. We enter the psychozoic era—where mind and body join together for co-evolution.

Think of an intranet as a live system, ever changing, ever evolving, with new faces and new opportunities, and with dead things breaking off naturally. This means the intranet develops simultaneously with the organization's growth and with the employee's growth as well. The infrastructure grows, the individual adapts and finds a niche within the intranet. The organic message resides in the interdependencies of the information system. The parts must stay healthy to feed and nurture each other. Intranet web sites must work together to provide the best infrastructure, the story, the best tools, and the best solutions for users.

Intranets are the Public   Remember first that you are developing your intranet for your organization. This means that the intranets must be designed for ease of use, for efficiency, for human performance. There is no precedent for the public ownership of such an enormous wealth of information. The intranet belongs to the citizen. It is by far their most prestigious invention.

You need to create an environment that can sustain all of the employees at the individual level, yet at the same time never be dependent on any single one of them. Employees come and go, your intranet stays and adapts to the change naturally. Intranets are bodies of people, tied together, with an incredible palette of tools for creation and innovation.

Four Tiers of an Intranet Design

Your intranet needs to be designed to provide access to your employees, easily and productively. You must design the site as a whole. Create an overall concept and break it into its systemic parts. To make the job easier, design in four separate tiers (see Table 3–9). Remember these tiers can be developed in unison with one another. If you understand, however, that the tasks belong in different tiers, then it makes the job easier to break up and carry through.

- Tier 1—Site Creation

- Tier 2—Content Creation

- Tier 3—Site Management

- Tier 4—Site Analysis

Table 3-9 **Four Tiers of an Intranet Design**

	Tier 1 Site Creation	Tier 2 Content Creation	Tier 3 Site Management	Tier 4 Site Analysis
Audience	Determine information needs and hypermedia literacy.	Create appropriate content, navigation, and cognitive design.	Manage the file and directory structures to match audience expectations.	Maintain feedback mechanisms with the audience for improving the site.
Architecture	Design intranet architecture, servers, browsers.	Develop hypertext, graphic design, and applications, common look and feel, templates, libraries.	Server management (caching, mirror, proxy, administrative), link management.	Usability test for ease of use and navigability and for architecture performance.
Central Control	Tie business goals into the site's design.	Design interactive and experiential sites between departments (i.e., web home pages).	Maintain template, library, style sheets, legal, security, and administrative policies sites.	Create focus groups to discuss efficiency of the site.
Services	Determine network services and applications that must be accessed.	Design database connectivity, create customized collaborative applications.	Manage services from the server side as much as possible; push content.	Analyze server logs for improving cycle time.

Table 3-9 Four Tiers of an Intranet Design *(Continued)*

	Tier 1 Site Creation	Tier 2 Content Creation	Tier 3 Site Management	Tier 4 Site Analysis
Security	Install and configure web server security software.	Develop applications using secured processes.	Use security hacking tools; keep a human eye on transactions.	Analyze for security and policy compliance.
Support	Select and standardize on browser, helper applications (if possible).	Create a support environment, a Help Desk. Publish procedures. Provide a good security system.	Provide database support, and push database processes to the web application.	Analyze and advise on plug-ins, help applications, development tools. Develop competency tracking.
Tools	Choose publishing tools, maintenance tools, data conversion tools, and make available to all.	Use search design for access to all information, tools, etc.	Update tools on server side, so everyone has latest tool; maintain search database.	Search term analysis and click stream analysis to determine usefulness of provisions.

Tier 1—Site Creation

Consider the Audience. Intranets are designed as communication and transaction devices. Define and categorize your audience well. Understand their expectations, needs, and known desires. Here are some guidelines to follow.

- Design for the reading and cognitive skill level of the user
- Consider the technological expertise of the user
- Factor in web skills: surfing, searching, navigating
- Study the international audience's needs well
- Anticipate age differences, job functions, and positions in the organization
- Be tuned to linguistic differences, that is, jargon, respect, humor
- Make feedback a number one feature
- Write to a common reading level
- Remember users only spend between 20–30 seconds on a page

Design Intranet Architecture. We've discussed servers, software, and browsers in the previous section on infrastructure. Make sure you've got the system you need to support your publishing needs. And ensure you've planned for growth. Your intranet will grow rapidly.

You'll add new software titles. Depending on the browser you're using, will you be able to add the software you want? Software is still being sold directly over the Internet. If there isn't a package for you to purchase, can you find the resources to create what you need?

Your same purpose and goals for choosing the servers, software, and browsers apply to the design of your site. Your site serves you, your employees, your customers, and your partners. Are they getting the best deal?

Tie to Organizational Business Goals. Only design when your organizational business goals are truly understood by all the people involved in your site design. Everyone must understand how the intranet will help you to achieve your goals, and exactly what they have to do to achieve them. One of the key goals is to communicate company activity, processes, well-being, and educational opportunities to your employees. Certainly other goals are customer focus and quality. What do these mean to your intranet design? Each organization is different.

Bottom Line: Plan your intranet, execute your plan, review your plan, then revise it. Then, do it all over again.

Network Services. Your network services and applications will affect your design. Windows users will need the same kind of menu-driven look. Lotus Notes users would like to see a collaborative, work group looking environment. Forms-based users would like to see their forms replicated on the intranet. Some people will change, but most prefer their work to be easier, not different. Learners will be less burdened if you do this for them.

Launch applications directly whenever possible. Start designing web sites that resemble your data environment that you're used to. You can't afford to miss a single day of work, so do everything you can to make your intranet leverage the programming expertise in-house. It's amazing what your internal staff already knows. They do know your business processes better than anyone, and they probably know your internal customers well too.

If you're going to use FTP, e-mail, Telnet, newsgroups, and other network services, you'll need to figure out a way to design these features into your intranet site, so your users learn how to use them, and then use them. We're talking adult learners here. Remember the limitations on information processing. For example, users are capable of handling only five to seven different concepts in their short-term memory at one time. Design the simplest, most intuitive intranet you can!

Security Design. You must understand what your security needs are. Start by defining what can go on the intranet and what cannot. You are less likely to damage your corporation if you keep highly confidential information off the intranet. Better yet, design secured sites within your intranet, so secured access to confidential information can be maintained. Install firewalls and configure for the kinds of services you want.

Support Design. You need to standardize as much as you can, so you can support your users. Start designing a help desk and work the issues for support of the intranet user. Create an application that will allow users to log in and identify the kinds of problems they're having. Integrate these forms with the support group to disperse assistance and support out as quickly as possible. Categorize the kinds of problems and support that people need, and include them in your web site.

Tools. You'll want to hear streamed radio. That's what you're used to hearing in your car—continuous radio with multiple channels. This is a helper application and can be tied to your browser. The same holds true for video, Microsoft Word and Excel viewers, compressed graphics, and a host of other multimedia programs you're used to using. If you'll be working with these programs, consider designs that will use less memory, integrate office products, and are easy to use. Examples are http://www.realaudio.com for RealAudio, and http://wwwiterated.com for viewing compressed images.

Data Conversion Tools. So you want to put your data on the intranet? Well, whatever you're going to put on, what does it look like in your browser? Are you going to have to publish it in HTML? Does your current software vendor have document conversion tools? Do you go out and look for them in Yahoo? Be prepared to convert documents or retag documents with HTML codes. You will spend a considerable amount of time in this area.

One of the first questions you must ask yourself is: What format is my data in now, and is it feasible to convert over? As we've discussed above in Helper Applications, many plug-ins can be added to your browsers to convert data. Visit the Netscape plug-ins and App Foundry sites at http://home.netscape.com for more information.

Tier 2 - Content Creation

Audience Literacy. Remember when you create content, forms, and applications make them user-friendly. Knowing what your audience is capable of on the intranet is fundamental to designing content correctly. You must use navigation design principles and cognitive principles.

Navigation Design. The key issue is to determine how to navigate through your sites. The intranet is not linear; it is instead a fourth-dimensional space. There may be a central position called home, but it is possible to live on an intranet without ever going to the home site. So, include search engines and intelligent agents to help users move around the site more quickly. You may choose to wait and do this in the next review and revision of your intranet, especially if you're only in the basic stage.

To facilitate the navigation design, you can group items together in a way to choose quickly which site you want to move to next. Grouping, in fact, assists greatly in navigation. It allows users to view information in "chunks" and leap more quickly between information structures. Navigation leads you closer to improved human performance. You need to get in, get out, and apply the information you sought. Here are some navigation design tips to help speed up information access.

- Navigate with embedded links
- Jump to sections inside a document, rather than to the top
- Use icons in menu bars
- Provide a search mechanism for your site that uses conceptual searching techniques
- Provide TOCs or site map access at the top of the page
- Provide help by providing definitions, glossaries, clickable words, and so forth

Cognitive Design. In order to prevent your employees from becoming overwhelmed by the vast amount of the information on the intranet, you must consider cognitive design elements. In short, cognitive design deals with how you design your intranet to prevent information overload and enhance information processing and information analysis. Use tables, group graphical icons together, use frames. Keep text to a minimum. Provide the lengthy content at a lower level, or a hyperlink level. Keep different kinds of items to five to seven items per page. The bottom line is to design to optimize the user's information processing capability.

Content Design. Content is what you choose to put on a web site. Content is also the amount and the quality of information you put on the intranet. People believe the information they access on the intranet is valid and authentic. In reality, just because a URL exists doesn't mean the content is valid. Therefore, in order to maintain the reputation of being reliable and accessible, you have to make sure the content is valid, up to date, and well researched. The facts must be straight, the spelling must be impeccable. The content has to be relevant to the intended audience, and you want to be able to drill down into more detail on almost any content topic.

Content is the purpose for creating an intranet. Intranets are made up of content, just as the planet is made of soil. Let people know who you are, so they can interact with your contact. Encourage interaction with the content, it can only result in improving, tweaking, and providing the best content available. Tell your readers what to do with the content, and recommend ways to use it. Explain why you are providing the content, and set up the user to start thinking critically about the meaning of the content.

Graphic Design and Animation. Graphics on the intranet take up memory, degrade performance, and grow stale when seen frequently. Design with common sense in mind, rather than working for the pure aesthetic value of the graphic. Graphics need to be designed so as not to slow down your web site. Observe the graphical element size recommendations in Table 3–10 below.

Table 3-10 Graphical Element Size Recommendations

Graphical Element	Maximum Byte Size (for Performance)	Comments
Overall Composition	70K	Chunk text into 5–7 main categories, keep graphical elements down to 3–5.
Photos	30K	Use GIF or JPEG.
Site Logo	12K	Will be cached probably.
Image Maps	30K for image maps with other elements. 60K for image maps as complete pictures.	Limit color blends.
Main Image	30K	Generate on the fly with Java.
Bullets	2K	Make them small.

Table 3-10 Graphical Element Size Recommendations *(Continued)*

Graphical Element	Maximum Byte Size (for Performance)	Comments
Custom Icons	10K/icon	Common menu items.
Custom Horizontal Rules	5–10K	The lower the better.
Background Images	4K	Will be cached probably.

Animation. Animation is an attention getter. Use it sparingly; it also fades after viewed repeatedly. Pause animation for dramatic effect. In doing so, you can get the reader to focus on the exact message that you're trying to convey. Blinking and marquees parading across the screen are a lower form of animation but nonetheless are effective attention grabbers.

Blinking is considered negative by some, yet useful by others. Do realize that any novelty repeated often becomes a cliche and very boring for the user. Again use these features sparingly. The greatest winner of animation is instruction. Many procedures can be demonstrated more effectively with moving, animated arrows, boxes, movements, and so forth. Training and instruction will easily take over as the premier user of animated intranet content.

Layout. Layout enhances the ease of use on a web site for the individual page. Properly designed layout dictates you limit paragraph size, use wide margins, and 30 percent brightness changes or white space. Mix your long and short thoughts to add variety. Create different visual blocks to avoid boredom. Provide common look and feel, and make sure common elements appear as intranet groupings.

These groupings repeat across the intranet as headers, footers, search tool icons, site map access icons, and quick routes home. Dates on and ownership on each page are recommended. Use tables, frames, and style sheets whenever possible; they make reading much easier.

Sun Microsystems, Inc. , Before and After Layout Design. Look at these two graphics of Sun Microsystem's intranet page. The original in Figure 3–22 was built with the creative pioneering efforts of Judy Lindberg, Will Shelton, Daryl Sano, and Carl Meske. It has recently been retired to be modernized with new web tools like Java.

You can observe many well-designed features that were originally robust allowing the page to last until today. It used minimalist graphics to reduce load time. The layout is fairly clear with each icon identifying internal information warehouses. The site was not originally usability-tested until after its appearance. But, when users became familiar with the location of certain data, they could click through the pages and find what they were looking for. The intranet at Sun was indeed quite functional and visionary.

But, behind the design lay chaos. The Web was developing in its organic state, each individual group adding more information, or slapping up more servers to accommodate for various data domains. The maturation of the intranet as a functional, everyday environment was not anticipated at first. The intranet warehouses grew exponentially. The need for a redesign grew. It was borne out of a cultural need to help people solve problems more easily and without any conflict of interests or information.

Sun immediately saw a need to design an infrastructure that would work. Since they used web technology and had been building with open standards in HTML, they were able to realign the information fairly quickly and integrate a web technology and infrastructure onto the vast stores of data that were becoming commonly in use.

In Figure 3–23, you can see the redesign. It still chunks the information units into separate areas. It adds the flavor of another tier of information which is searchable. In the retired intranet web site the concept of tiering was not in place. Searching was available but only used the limited UNIX searching capabilities that searched exact string matches in the directory. According to Debra Winters, Sun's intranet Webmaster, the purpose of redesigning the site can be summarized as follows:

- to give SunWeb a new, updated graphical look
- to overhaul the HTML and come up with standards, metatags, and so forth
- to clean up the directories and files that had collected over time
- to identify and resolve content integrity and ownership issues
- to move to the new Sun web server
- to test better search services

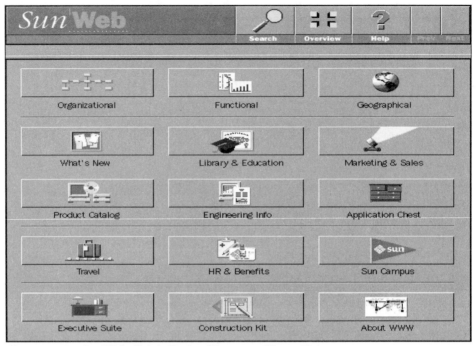

Figure 3–22 SunWeb: Sun's Retired Intranet Home Page

You can see that the content remained fairly stable. Usually functionality changes when intranets grow from basic to publishing, to collaboration, to transactions, and finally to the extranet stage. Chunking your content is imperative, and if done right at first, you'll have very little content redesign. What is underneath the page is better administration, directory maintenance, navigation, server management, and database support

Interactivity Design. The future of your intranet depends on the way you handle e-mail, data collection, forms, feedback, and ways of enhancing the user's experience. Plan and develop a lot of interactivity. Interactivity can be simple links to other sites, or filling out forms and getting feedback. Interactivity can be the creation of custom content for each user. Interactivity can be chatting with experts on specific topics, or multiuser experiences such as video-conferences, live intranet events, whiteboard sharing, and collaborative processing. Interactivity will grow into direct communication with vendors and partners, as well as database integration.

Interactivity will ultimately be a complete immersible experience. The user will confront a game-like environment, where discovery skills are required. Scoping out the terrain in a real-time simulation scenario, the user will take on a business persona and use all available tools for networking, interconnecting, partnering, negotiating, and working directly as a single point of contact for the customer.

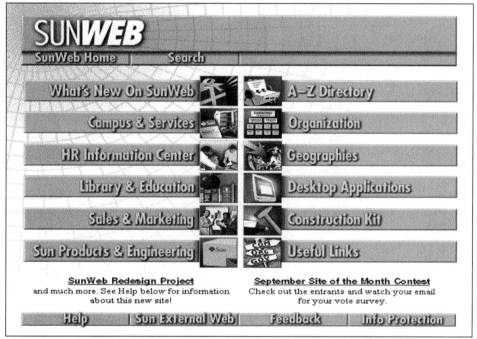

Figure 3–23 un's New Intranet Page—Common Look and Feel

Experiential Design. If users are going to stay on the intranet for long periods of time, create experiences for them. Experiences enhance the discovery process and accelerate data exchanges. Experiences need to be systematic. The sales cycle and where you enter it represents an experience for an employee. Also known as simulations, design an environment that resembles the user's world. Virtual reality is the tool to create simulation.

Motorola, for example, uses virtual reality training models to teach students how to operate manufacturing robots. The simulation is incredibly real. The users can touch any part of the robot, examine its parts, literally tear it apart. This environment creates an almost real experience for the user, enhancing their learning experience as well as their time spent on the intranet using technology to become performance oriented. Users who have gone through the training, show a 95 percent increase in performance ability with working on the robots in the manufacturing labs.

Creating an intranet that enhances and captures experience is perhaps the fundamental building block of tomorrow. In order to effectively capture experience, users will need to participate openly. Programmers are going to be very busy in the next couple of decades. So are intranet users.

Database Connectivity. If you are connecting to databases, then you've got some design choices. Either you design the intranet page to connect directly to the database program interface, or you design a forms-based intranet page to interact with the database. These forms can be customized to fit the user's application, enabling many windows into the database. An additional choice is to utilize the web-based interfaces that the database vendor supplies. These tools are available with Oracle, Sybase, and Informix.

Database integration is at the heart of Java. CGI scripts and links to SQL commands are cumbersome and not network robust, even with CGI scripts. Two key issues with Java are finding programming expertise and selecting a database web solution that meets your database needs.

According to Wayne Eckerson, editor-in-chief and senior consultant of the Patricia Seybold Group in *Open Information Systems*: at Patricia Seybold Consulting.

> In the next two years, one-third to one-half of all queries and analyses will be launched from a Web browser. Why? The Web provides cheap, universal connectivity, allowing companies to instantly deploy new reports to workers in the field or even customers and suppliers. The Web also eliminates the overhead involved in distributing and maintaining client software, including programs, network drivers and middleware. In the future, expect to see companies with large databases, such as Dun & Bradstreet or American Express, allow Web users (either businesses or consumers) to pay a nominal fee to perform wide-ranging, ad hoc analyses of their data.

Collaborative Design. A new body of application for the intranet is collaboration, in which individuals from various parts of the organization communicate, share documents, follow schedules, post discussions, and track e-mail messages, bugs, testing procedures, and so forth. The intranet competes with Lotus Notes in this category only from a naive viewer's perspective. Lotus Notes has a serious leg up on collaborative processing. Its convergence with the intranet is inevitable, though, because work group models must communicate across intranets, the extended intranet, and the World Wide Web. Look at Domino by Lotus.

Nevertheless, collaborative design will be subjective, responding directly to the needs of the participants. This is why the intranet is moving beyond Lotus Notes, because of its ad hoc design capability. Encourage collaborative designs and try to publicize the designs when you can for reuse among your employees.

Help Desks with Case-Based Reasoning. Design your help desks with case-based reasoning. Case-based reasoning is a problem-solving paradigm that solves problems based on the solutions of similar problems stored in a knowledge database. It is based on the concept of using common, intuitive knowledge to adapt old solutions to troubleshoot current problems. When you use old case histories to explain new situations, as doctors do, you have the ability to critique new solutions to problems so you can determine if your immediate answer is correct.

Search Design. When planning your intranet, plan for using search engines. Search design requires the use of Metatags. Metatags, or metainformation, is information about information. Metatags are used to index the site more efficiently. Your search engines will rely on the elasticity of metatags for categorizing and indexing information more quickly, getting your users the right information, at the right time. See "Adding Meta-Information" in *Web Page Design: A Different Multimedia,* by Mary E. S. Morris and Randy J. Hinrichs.

Tier 3—Site Maintenance

File and Directory Structures. Since the intranet works across platforms, file and directory structures are different. Some conventions for file naming must be considered. UNIX is capable of long file names but can get truncated easily when moving to Intel-based systems. Apple has its own file maintenance capability. In order to manage the vast amount of files and directories, consider a directory server and use its capabilities to manage all of the variation in your intranet.

Link Management. In order to maintain your intranet, you have to consider how you will manage the links. Naturally, the best solution is to have ownership of pages and sites, and have those owners manage the links. But employees leave, company reorganizations happen, entire web sites are suddenly retired.

- Are the links broken? Fix them.

- Have they changed and no longer fit in with your site? Get rid of them.

- Do you have authority to link? Get it.

- Is linking appropriate? Tie it to business goals, or the objectives of the web site.

These are some of the questions to grapple with. Some software packages provide some cursory looks at link management. They determine whether links are broken or not. But, someone needs to manage the links as they manage the content.

Server Management (Caching, Mirror, Proxy, Administrative). Someone also has to manage the servers. Usually a central administrator, like IS, manages the servers. It is best to keep management of servers centralized as much as possible.

In the book, *Managing the Enterprise* (Sun Microsystems Press), the authors they describe how to manage the server side of client/server very well. Suffice it to say that with the introduction of directory servers, all servers will be managed centrally. This is akin to a central subway station, running the various subway lines from a single point of contact. Presently, cookies are managing various service activities. See the section on Metrics.

Template, Library, Stylesheet Management. Keep the libraries updated and stocked with fresh templates, standards, and common look and feel objects that can be downloaded. Provide graphics libraries and audio libraries. It is important to realize that all the data on the intranet do not have to be created. It probably already exists. It is important to categorize and catalog as much as you can to enable rapid development within the organization.

It's not enough to have templates, graphic, sound, and video libraries, or even stylesheets, unless you manage them. You need to provide a service to your users to make these available, and then constantly update them for usability.

Database Support. If you are connecting to databases, the intranet pages and programs written behind them must be managed. This is appropriate for the management of the databases in the first place; however, they may not possess the appropriate intranet skills to manage and support the database. So, you'll have to decide how this is going to be properly done.

Bottom Line: Your databases will most likely be more and more integrated into your intranet, perhaps even replacing older, antiquated systems. Plan for this transition.

File and Directory Management. As the intranet is provided with a full-scale information solution to clients, file and directory management needs to be attended to with the same robustness as they are at the operating or system administration level. Currently, network operating systems working with Web-NFS are superior solutions for dealing with file and directory management. Look for web server products with specific attention dedicated to file and directory management. Also look at LDAP (Lightweight Directory Application Protocol) in anything you choose.

Disaster Recovery. Don't even think of not having a disaster recovery plan. Certainly, your central administrator for information services has a disaster recovery program. Make sure! You need mirrored servers that contain all the necessary hardware and network connections needed to run your intranet in the case of a disaster. Good backups can suffice too, if you have a smaller site. Also a small server that keeps an up-to-date record of all the backup tapes and system configurations of all the servers needs to be maintained. Locate your mission-critical servers near you. And make sure that your WAN has sufficient bandwidth to support the burst of network traffic following a disaster.

Security Watchdog. It is imperative in designing an intranet to be able to keep your eye focused on intranet movement all the time. Simply put, the security staff must not only use hacker tools and stage security maneuvers but should also be able to use intuition and "gut feeling" to understand exactly what is moving across the intranet. This means that e-mail, FTP, application use, access logs, unusual repeated movement around the intranet, frequency of use, and so forth, are integral activities to be watched. The purpose of doing this is not to breach privacy, but to be on the lookout for unusual activity that could indicate internal hacking into secured areas. A security watchdog who knows the network intimately is an excellent resource for detecting disaster before it happens.

Tier 4—Site Analysis Analyzing your intranet is important. You need to know about traffic over the network. Who is accessing what sites? Which sites are gaining more attention than others and why? What is your audience like? How are people clicking around the intranet to get to certain spots? Is your top design working? How are you getting feedback? Are you using it properly.

Analyzing this information enables you to create a more responsive intranet. Site analysis tools come with server software. Learning to use them is pretty simple. Interpreting trends is a little more challenging.

Audience Feedback and Contact Mechanisms. It is a confident site that puts feedback and contact information on each page of their web site. Your users are your best testers. Provide ways for them to speak to you, so you can analyze the site and ensure it works as you designed it. Make sure that it is obvious whom to contact. Accountability enforces reliability.

Usability Analysis. Design your usability tests to bring users in off the street and observe them as they are using your web sites. Engage them in conversation, so you can understand how they are developing their strategies for moving around the site. Prepare tasks that are relevant to their jobs and ask them to carry them out, using the web sites you've developed. Use people from all levels to ensure that you've designed for the lowest common denominator. Try to avoid "aesthetics" issues, whether someone likes a graphic or not. Look for functionality, navigability, and ease of use.

Focus Groups. Once usability testing has accommodated for individual differences, bring together focus groups to determine how to measure the effectiveness of the web site. These are like editorial meetings, in which all the key players who either create or use the information are available to discuss cross-functional needs. Be prepared to diagram workflow and ensure you have intranet capability so you can look over the design as a group.

Analyzing Intranet Usage. Most server software lets you generate useful statistics about your web server: Which pages are being accessed the most, how high the load on your web server is, what times of day have the most hits, and so forth. Logging server access helps you understand your employees' behavior. You can measure employee interests, productivity, and network utilization. The reports you get regarding intranet usage help make decisions about site maintenance and growth, network capacity, acceptable use policies, and other management issues.

Search Term and Clickstream Analysis. Search term analysis provides you with the terms people are using to search the intranet. It is an indicator of the kinds of information people are looking for. Clickstream analysis looks at access to web pages and provides a trail of information about the searching strategies for individuals looking for information. If you compare clickstreams, you can analyze information flow more accurately. Best data comes form human interaction, however.

Intranet Future Components

This section discusses the future trends of intranet development. The bottom line is the future of the intranet will be comprised of advanced multimedia experiences which will enhance the intranet experience, increase motivation, productivity, and change the way we're doing internal business forever. They include multimedia components: Shockwave; interactivity components: Java, JavaScript, ActiveX; audio and video components: RealAudio streaming, video streaming; simulation components: VRML; development components: connecting with object-oriented technology.

Beyond TCP/IP

By the year 2000, intranets will utilize technology way beyond the simple movement of data between computers, and the hyperlinking capability that excited us so much in the '90s. Full service networking operating systems will be in full swing. You'll be able to do everything over the intranet—directory, e-mail, file, print, talk, meet in cyberrooms, build, and buy. This is evolution. Linking to the Internet via wireless communication will become the norm, so the intranet will become the singular repository of corporate intelligence, accessible by any employee from any location. Let's examine the different components of what's to come in the future of the intranet.

Multimedia Component

Multimedia and CD-ROM will continue as presentation and learning environments: large multimedia libraries, references to tools needed to improve workflow, or processes to speed up development, or reusable functional object libraries that become indispensable tools.

The most recent advance is the development of interactive multimedia technologies such as Shockwave by Macromedia, Inc. Once these kinds of references are located on your intranet, you become not only a corporate memory library, but also a human knowledge repository for references and job aids that empower your employees. 3D animated virtual multimedia, is next. This is where innovative applications will appear on the intranet.

At Silicon Graphics (SGI) the intranet sites are becoming productions. Ken Trant, Webmaster at SGI, says, "these guys are really becoming competitive in the production of their sites. They try to outdo one another." Multimedia capability in an outfit like SGI can be a powerful weapon. Perhaps weapon is a strong word, but communication in a fast, reliable format can provide intelligence quickly to learners. At SGI, all employees are learners. Multicasting live interactive video will come of age very quickly, as well. Already, MSNBC is cast over internal intranets within Microsoft. Data exchanges are accelerating exponentially.

Interactivity Components

Java applications are changing the face of interactivity on the intranet. Although users are required to rely on programmers again, Java is capable of creating the true learning organization. Java can interact with users and validate their input. Java can prompt users for confirmation, or provide a set of responses that provide more information to the user to help them make their decision. Answers to questions can change depending on the user's input. Isn't this what teachers and marketing folks do? And Java can do it with incredible agility and speed, especially on the technical side. Such an interactive mechanism breeds improved learning on demand.

The ability to easily specify whether code runs on the server or the client simplifies programs, reduces software maintenance cost, and eliminates software distribution. Today, the industry-standard client languages are Java and Javascript, so if you want to write a Web application using one language, Java and Javascript are the best choice.

Audio and Video Components

Radio and television stations are also making their broadcasts available on the Internet. This means that high-value content will be available to use inside your intranet. As it becomes available as a knowledge product, on-demand multimedia technologies will be part of your key services. On-demand audio technologies, such as RealAudio, begin playing a sound file as it is being downloaded. On-demand video technologies such as VDO Live begin playing a video file as it is being downloaded as well. The use of images, audio, and video impacts the impact and perception of your intranet.

Alan Nichols, video engineer at Sun Microsystems, breaks down the video components as follows:

Encoder

This is the piece that will take analog video and create digital video—most likely that digital video will be MPEG. The options and possibilities here range from digital cameras to special purpose encoders, to general-purpose boxes enhanced with video capture hardware and software.

Video Server

This is what will store and play back video. This class of machine will need to know a lot about real-time/continuous media storage and scheduling, as well as some form of admission control (knowledge of what load will cause the machine to start missing deadlines and causing jitter in the outgoing stream, and refusing requests that would put it over that point).

Transport

This is what gets the video from the server to the client. This can be many different things: a cable network, a dedicated ATM video network, or video carried over an existing data network. The direction we're headed is to have all services (including phone and video) carried over data networks (like the Internet). An important technology here will be RSVP (Resource reSerVation Protocol). This allows you to request performance guarantees from the network that are not possible today due to a "best effort" design.

Client

This is what actually does the video playback. Again, this can be any number of things (cable box, dedicated video terminal, smart TV, Java station, general purpose machine), but it will need to have the ability to decode and display video in real-time.

More broadly, it may be necessary to talk about the different models of video usage. Here, we are looking at it in terms of broadcast video, video playback on demand, and videoteleconferencing.

Broadcast video

This is the ability to have one machine send a video stream to multiple receivers. The analogy here is that broadcast video is like your TV: The individual user has no control over what gets broadcast when, but can use their receiver to tune into any available broadcast at any given time.

Video On Demand (VOD)

This is a phrase that gets batted around a lot, so I am not sure that it is well understood or understood the same by everybody. What Nichols defines is the ability for an individual user to request a private viewing of any available video. This best analogy is that VOD is like your VCR—you can, at any time, put a tape in the VCR and control the playback of that tape completely.

Video-Teleconferencing (VTC)

This is the ability to set up a live, real-time point-to-point (or possibly multi-point) communications session. Of course, the analogy here is that VTC is just like your phone.

This covers, in general, any way that you can use video. There are ways to mix the various concepts together: For example, Lyceum,[6] a sample distance learning/distributed video application from Sun Microsystems, uses video broadcast and also has some limited teleconferencing abilities (Figure 3–24).

6.　Courtesy of SunSoft, Sun Microsystems, Inc.

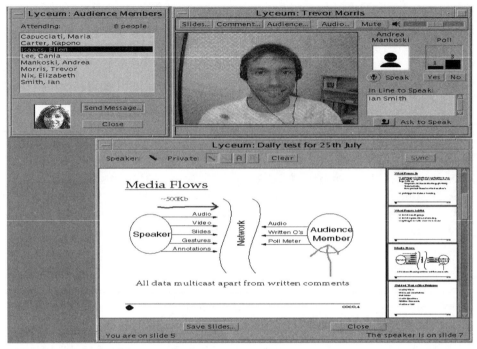

Figure 3–24 Video Uses on the Intranet.

Simulation Components

SimCity™, SimEarth™, SimIsland™, SimAnt™—are virtual worlds where users enter into a world and use all the variables for survival. SimSales, SimMarketing, SimManagement, SimNewEmployee are opportunities waiting that will provide e-worlds on-line for e-commerce, e-education, e-socialization. The applications in business include simulated meetings, simulated engineering design, simulated training, simulated staff meetings where you meet with the entire organization, but what you see is a customized view of your needs reflected against the corporate body's needs. Look at http://www.alphaworld.com. These are all the future of virtual reality.

Development Components

Java Applets and ActiveX development environments provide a wide variety of capabilities. Most important are the reusable objects they'll produce. These applets, or functionality objects, are modular software features to be used in any web site. Huge reuse libraries will exist, where you can reach in, and get a graphic that performs tasks. You can piece these graphics together to create new software with focused functionality. The user will develop in the environment more freely (as in the days, when HTML was the only language you needed to speak). The development environment must move into the hands of the users. The expertise, the quality, and the economic functionality is there. This is a time of empowerment, of liberation.

Summary of Key Points

- INTRANET ARCHITECTURE—*HW and SW Connectivity*

  > This section described some of the architecture issues relating to intranet sites as they relate to making business decisions. It is meant to be a decision-making section. It provides a working knowledge of architecture terms to assist managers in making strategic intranet decisions.

- INTRANET INFRASTRUCTURE—*People, Processes, Policies*

  > This section encouraged you to investigate possible intranet infrastructure scenarios. It includes vision, mission statements, policies, job competencies and skills, processes, procedures, libraries, and design issues. It provides the manager with the breadth of business decisions that need to be made. It is a framework.

- INTRANET INTERACTIVITY—*Database Management Systems*

  > This section described what pieces intranets are made up of to be interactive. Interactivity helps communicate and collaborate within the organization. This includes using e-mail, searching mechanisms, interaction with databases and legacy systems, connection with newsgroups, video-conferencing and electronic whiteboarding, and creating feedback mechanisms for site improvement and evolution.

- INTRANET SECURITY—*Firewalls and Fire Ridges*

  > This section explained why intranet security is important, and points you to some areas for further study. It introduces you to the concept of firewalls, fire ridges, and secure electronic transactions for the extended intranet. It also calls you to change your security paradigm in order to achieve higher learning among your employees. It suggests the quality of knowledge is Truth.

- INTRANET DESIGN—*Site Design*

  > This section explained the Intranet as an organic environment. It discussed audience considerations, tying design to goals, content design and cognitive design. It explained about preparing your

site for search design. Also, it covered layout, navigational design, and graphics design issues, uniquely relevant to intranets, as well as designing for time, interactivity, and experience.

- INTRANET FUTURE COMPONENTS

    This section discussed the future trends of intranet development. Many of these trends are becoming the mainstay of the technology. They include Java, JavaScript, VRML, RealAudio streaming, video streaming, and connecting with object-oriented technology.

CHAPTER

4

What's It Buy Me?

The intranet buys you a tool that will empower the workforce to move the decision making, the actions, the problem solving, and the responsibilities closer to the people who understand the opportunities and possess the skills to react quickly and efficiently. When a problem needs an organizational solution, then users can reach out to the expertise, power, and wealth of the intranet and focus the total resources on the problem.

Intranets pay off in these distinct strategic areas:

- Wealth creation
- Organizational transformation
- Productivity
- Competitive advantage
- Distributed computing or the collective consciousness
- Web space for the future

Wealth Creation

An intranet does not automatically buy you all of these organizational benefits. In fact, the benefits you achieve will occur only if the organization has already determined it wants these benefits. Then, the intranet will help provide them. If the organization, however, doesn't want them, they'll be rejected regardless of intranet availability.

The initial benefits that will cause the wealth creation infrastructure to be put into place are as follows:

- replace existing corporate network infrastructure with the intranet

- use the intranet to publish existing documents currently distributed by other means, using form-based transactions

- create a virtual file system, like WebNFS

- think about how to use for corporate MIS, like SAP (Systems Applications and Products in Data Processing)

- think about how to use the intranet for workflow and EDI (Electronic Data Interchange)

- use the intranet to try to create a learning organization culture

When the intranet is in place, you have an integrated workforce ably using the publishing and library features to store documents, graphics, audio, video, and other intellectual treasures on-line. The more use employees get out of the organizational intellectual property, the more they will learn to create automated processes, like form-based transactions, to speed up their interactions. It will become necessary to have virtual file systems which allow intranet management to successfully administer the enormous files and subdirectory structures within the organization. This is the basis of your organizational wealth.

The natural evolution is to tie your processes together in a fashion as SAP technology does, where all of the back-office and front-office activities are interconnected. A well-structured intranet like this enables the ability to conduct transactions between customers and your purchasing department, or other interactive interdependencies between your intranet and the external Internet. Customers will appreciate having EDI transaction capability.

Getting the organization and the customer aligned is a major win for wealth creation. Your customer is already poised for doing business on-line. Your workforce is integrated organizationally. You've got processes in place, streamlined, and created empowered, focused teams. You communicate rapidly. You solve issues instantly. Consensus is arrived at easily. Now you have workers changing the way products and services within the organization are created, marketed, and distributed. Wealth is created by the knowledge worker.

Rapid, Participative Decision Making

What does the Intranet buy your organization? The answer is a lot. The intranet allows your company to be participative and very quick to act in decision making. The ability to make decisions quickly, get everyone involved without any concern for time or distance, makes the intranet as important as the telephone.

Access to Corporate Powerhouses

Employees with access to an intranet system that allows them top level information about the organization, access to experts about any part of the organization, and high bandwidth development environments are going to become power workers. The new knowledge worker "works smarter," and does so in less time. Those who have access to company intelligence make better business decisions.

Outsourcing: Who Gets the Wealth?

A word of caution though. It is quite possible that outsourcing your intranet to outside vendors will enter the picture. In fact, outsourcing will distribute the wealth created by your company's intelligence even further. They add value to your organization surely. However, maintaining the information and integrating it into your organization and into your customer's extended intranets may prove slow. A middleman not involved in the dynamics of the company may bottleneck the rapid response and participative nature of the intranet. You may be filtering the wealth in the wrong place, unless you integrate your outsourcing vendor with the very principles of your inner organization.

Outsourcing may be good for the initial architecting and building of your intranet. Some of the knowledge moguls of the industry have the ability to identify knowledge structures, review corporate intelligence, map corporate memory to key knowledge domains, and build an architecture to aim that corporate intelligence at the bull's eye of customer loyalty. Look for companies experienced at building a collaborative, high transaction processing, self-teaching, production-oriented on-line environment in half the time.

Bottom Line: Quickly put the control of the content into the hands of your employees.

Depending on the organization's goals, wealth creation will have a symbiotic effect with reduced cycle time, more coordinated work processes, streamlined organizational structure and systems, and more work time spent on customer deliverables rather than internal politics. Soon, you'll be able to integrate the customer as well. The customer is the true source of wealth creation.

Organizational Transformation

Principle-Driven Enterprises

- Current themes in business today discuss the need for developing a principle that drives the organization. This principle defines your organization and enables the organization to move forward as a whole. Individual parts of the organization can define themselves based on this principle.

- Current business literature suggests that principle-driven enterprises rally the organization behind leaders who clearly articulate their organization's driving principles. The principles are then communicated throughout the organization with clear strategies. Such strategies allow organizations to prevent problems before they occur. It allows employees to seize opportunities more quickly because they know what is driving the organization.

- When principles tie a workforce together, building long-term relationships and negotiation strategies, then the character of the workers is rewarded more effectively. The employee understands the level of competence and the required skills to perform a job. Innovation is rewarded especially when it interacts closely with processes that are known to work for the organization. The Intranet provides a physical backdrop for communicating and realizing the central principle of the organization. Some call it the prime directive.

- Within an intranet, an executive section on the web site provides the prime directive, the sets of principles, the mission statement, the goals of the company, the company culture. It provides information and profiles of executive leaders. It provides a place for rewards and recognition of individuals contributing to the principle-centered corporation. Done right, it can be the vision that leads the corporation to unified thinking and organizational transformation.

Mission-Driven Enterprises

The mission statement builds the foundation for a cohesive intranet. In order to develop critical thinking workers who participate in the organization as leaders and quality team members, you must have a credo to live by (no matter how conservative or radical). You must publish that mission statement and make sure all your staff knows what it is and feels that they can provide input directly to you about the mission statement. The statement must permeate your site. You should be able to point to any position in your site and show how it supports the mission statement.

Informed Intelligent Quality Team Members

Once a collective body of individuals agrees on a principle and communicates it in a mission statement, everyone is prepared with a clear-cut picture of how to best accomplish the tasks to meet the mission statement.

Each individual can assume responsibility for growth and competency development. Each individual can concentrate on their propensities and enhance their ability to develop themselves at their own accelerated pace. Suddenly, creative, innovative, effective people at all levels are working together to create quality services and products. The effect on the bottom line is dramatic—increased revenue, lower costs.

Learning Organization

Enterprises, corporations, organizations and companies are living systems. In order for them to evolve into the 21st century, they must increase their ability to learn. Learning rapidly is key to survival. Learning how the enterprise works and how to contribute to the goals of the enterprise are key to individual success within an organization.

Learning means changing. Self-paced learning and continuous adult learning are principles that many organizations want to attain. When adult learners continually examine, explore, and discover the system in which they operate, a foundation for organizational self-knowledge is at hand. Organizations that understand themselves are more effective and more driven to succeed with clearly defined and researched goals.

The enterprise directs their collective knowledge at the customer in order to understand what they think and what they need. They must learn who their customers' customers are and learn what their businesses do. They must share their learned experiences within the organization and focus their intelligence on creating new ways to customize products and services. They must learn how to work together in intelligent teams, focusing on improving their process for learning at all times.

Learning Organization Definition   A good definition of a learning organization is when the organization as a whole and the people who comprise it are continually increasing their capacity to produce the best results they really want to produce.

Team Building and Systems Thinking   On an intranet, learning improves our capacity for effective action and quick response. We are able to act more quickly, decide more confidently, and reinforce our positions more readily when we combine the learned knowledge of a team with the interdependencies within the organization.

The intranet is comprised of hundreds of project web sites, linking to relevant sites that provide critical project information. The knowledge of the corporation fuses together in a coherent, powerful voice where anyone can follow information to the source. Intranets foster team building and systems thinking by providing the organization with a potent tool that provides both a sense of belonging to the intranet, a powerful language to speak in, and a learning environment to excel in.

Knowledge Workers Perform   Employees are knowledge workers in a learning organization. They access information more quickly and analyze it in consensus-driven groups. They know how to learn, how to improve, how to communicate. They are quick to develop and articulate their requirements for information and streamline interdependent processes effectively. They understand their intellectual capital and manage their collaborative partnering. They do this simply by creating a web site that explains what they're doing, how they're doing it, who is helping them, and how can they improve themselves. The intranet is the knowledge worker's toolkit.

Learning Equals Performance   In simple terms, we use learning in an organization more in the sense of learning to do, rather than in the sense of learning just to know things. We do this because it is our performance that counts on the job, not our potential. Our performance directly affects the performance of the organization. The intranet visually reflects our ability to perform, which is one of the major reasons we want more interactive and collaborative environments on-line.

In a Web environment, we demonstrate our competence and our depth of education in the presentation, navigation, content, and cognitive design of a web site. Today's performance requirements make it essential to have some local repository, or local space on the network that we can use to showcase our efforts inside the organization. Then, think of the potential, when that information can be viewed and shared by others.

We find that in industry after industry, the performance challenge comes from stiff competition, highly political globalization, dizzying technology changes, demand for shorter cycle times, high-impact customer delight. The way business is being done today is remarkably intense. Not just in commercial enterprises, either, but also in government, health care, and nonprofit organizations alike. The pressures are just as high. Many leaders assert that business strategies require them to become more of a learning organization to impact performance. Many are turning to intranets to help them do that with the least amount of money, but the highest rate of success.

Peter Senge in his book *The Fifth Discipline* provides us with the tools to create learning organizations. They are personal mastery, shared vision, mental models, team learning, and systems thinking. Intranets build learning organizations, almost as a side effect. If content is highly decentralized, and the infrastructure is highly centralized, your intranet becomes the enabler for a most powerful learning organization. Imagine how you will be able to focus this intelligence on doing what you do best!

Personal Mastery (Senge). This is the phrase Senge uses to describe the discipline of personal growth and learning. People with high levels of personal mastery, he says, are continually expanding their ability to create the results. From the continual learning of the individual comes the spirit of the learning organization and learning to expand personal capacity to create the results we most desire.

Personal Mastery (on the Intranet)—Each individual on an intranet is capable of capturing knowledge and recasting it to complete thoughts and actions that are meaningful both to the individual and to the organization. A user navigates through the universe of organizational knowledge. In jumping between information and application, the user becomes facile at improving their personal mastery. Encourage creating web sites that clarify what is the most important principle to you. Then achieve it and tell us how you did it. We learn from mastery, doing, and reflecting. Create a legacy of your contribution and growth.

Shared Vision (Senge). Shared vision is vital for the learning organization because it provides the focus and energy for learning, where each person's personal vision illuminates different facets of the whole. Only when individuals are striving to accomplish something that matters deeply to them, do they learn how to contribute to the whole. A shared vision is a vision that many people are truly committed to, because it reflects their own personal vision. Develop shared images of the future and show how to get there.

Shared Vision (on the Intranet)—Develop an organizational vision that is shared with all the individuals in the organization. This means that they must have input into the vision so they can truly ensure it satisfies their view of what the vision should be too. The patterns of success are in your shared information. Share them with everyone, and encourage a broadly-held common sense of direction. Create a web site that clarifies what the most important principle is to you. Then achieve it and tell us how you did it. We learn from your mastery.

Mental Model **(Senge).** Mental models are deeply ingrained assumptions, generalizations, or even pictures or images that influence how we understand the world and how we take action. The discipline of working with mental models starts with turning the mirror inward—learning to unearth our internal pictures of the world, to bring them to the surface, and hold them rigorously to scrutiny.

Mental Model (on the Intranet)—The personalized web page is a fundamental mental model of each employee in an organization. In it lie assumptions, generalizations, and pictures about the person's perceptions of their job and of the organization. The links and experience provided by the user leads others into the mental model of the author. Group mental models exist in threaded conversation areas, where individuals reflect on their internal pictures of problem solving, or troubleshooting. This incredible feedback model shapes both individual and group thinking and actions. Project web sites with ongoing discussions are building blocks to your actions and decisions.

Team Learning **(Senge).** Team learning is the process of aligning and developing the capacity of a team to create the results its members truly desire. Team learning builds on personal mastery and shared vision. Team learning requires insightful thinking about complex issues, need for innovative, coordinated action, and the success of working with interdependent teams.

Team Learning (on the Intranet)—Create team intelligence, so the team is smarter than any of the individual team members. Develop multiple web sites, project pages, and so forth, that index and collect project intelligence. Keep a cross-functional bias. Highlight meaningful accomplishments. Post problem areas. Provide a collaborative web site where the team can learn anything about the project, from anyone on the project. Build your library of procedures and processes and convert them into object-oriented links.

Systems Thinking **(Senge).** Systems thinking fuses the other disciplines into a coherent body of theory and practice. System thinking makes the individual components and processes of an organization make sense. The subtlest action of the organization is understandable.

Systems Thinking (on the Intranet)—Develop a site map of the complete organization. This exercise will enable you to see the system as a whole. Provide a view of the whole corporation in a common language or metaphor. Your intranet sets the cultural standard, evolving the symbols of the intranet, creating language, establishing culture. Use the corporate voice, the corporate inner voice, to tell the story of the intranet in a way that each individual will see who they are, how they belong, and what the meaning and consequences of their actions are. Systems captured in a web site perceive long-term patterns, understand interdependencies, and better recognize the consequences of the enterprise's actions.

Learning on Demand

Undoubtedly, one of the key features of an intranet is to expand your ability to train various people, in various places, across various time zones. With full multimedia capability over the strong T1–T3 lines running into most organizations, interactive, feedback-driven training occurs over an intranet, delivering fundamental behavior changes in your workforce. This happens rapidly when training becomes learning on demand.

The ability to impact a market with training over the intranet is a potent concept. Training over the intranet

- *increases the speed, flexibility, and reach of training* and education with an intranet. It is widely distributed, easy to manage content, and reaches throughout the globe for anyone with a TCP/IP connection. Drawback is the need to program in more interactive languages than HTML and ensuring TCP/IP connectivity.

- *reduces costs* associated with traditional classroom training by delivering class on-line, on-demand with collaborative participation. Intranets with Java can create highly interactive, high-touch electronic classrooms at a fraction of the cost of traditional classroom training.

- *leverages instructor's expertise* to a broader population of participants by using the intranet to host live training events. Programs with training functionality, like *Forum* at Sun Microsystems, Inc. provide on-line instructional expertise, and can reach many people at the same time around the world.

On-line training, distance learning, collaborative learning, and leveraged team learning within an organization contribute directly to the performance of the team. Learning on demand transcends time and space. It provides wider and more flexible communication structures, contributing directly to organizational memory.

Recommendations for Learning on Demand   Training on-line is not new. Learning on demand is new. CD-ROM and CBT (Computer Based Training) gave us packages for on-line training. They have two big drawbacks—updating the CBT, or the multimedia CD-ROM training package in real-time doesn't exist. The quality of the information fades quickly. Secondly, getting and receiving valuable feedback in computer-based on-line training environments simply doesn't exist. The feedback you can get from the user is limited to e-mail or to developers guessing what feedback response may occur between the instructor and the learner.

When you have learning on demand, you improve learning substantially. Learning over a distributed system that has direct connections to experts, to live information, to intranet services that enhance feedback, and distribution of vast levels of information accelerates student learning and provides an overview mechanism for ensuring the transfer of knowledge to the workplace.

Learning on demand unites you with the technology of the intranet. With live distributed environments, you can obtain constant learning support, obtain access to expert knowledge and develop intensive feedback mechanisms with development environments like Java and ActiveX. Below in Table 4–1 you'll find some recommendations for using web technology to further your training needs in your corporation. This list is just the beginning of what you can accomplish.

Table 4-1 Recommendations for Learning on Demand

Recommendation	Technology
Orient New Hires	Create a new employee and new manager site that mirrors the orientation package you give each employee. Keep the site fresh with input from recent hires, culture descriptions, easy to access information about the company. Make it self-paced with connections to on-line support.
Align Jobs with Web Sites	Use a web crawler to look at mission statements and key words at each project site (encourage using metatags so this can be done). Map to job descriptions, competencies, and goals of the department. Make available to all users so they can evaluate their own performance. Tie training goals to learning paths to jobs.
Promote Collaboration	Provide threaded conversations on-line and develop a web page on top that manages and monitors the conversation with search tools.
Self-Evaluation	Create web pages that identify key expert competencies and invite the entire organization to publish key knowledge, processes, white papers that expound on expert knowledge. Create on-line testing at the expert sites to provide students with ability to self-test; then use the expert materials for further study. (i.e., Java training, sales training, tuning and performance, managing the new enterprise).
Design for Knowledge Transfer	Encourage individual to develop a web site to chronicle their development. Then, track on-line training goals and objectives to the performance of the individual's web site. Embed in manager sites.

Table 4-1 Recommendations for Learning on Demand *(Continued)*

Recommendation	Technology
Maintain a Training Library	Create an internal university, or an internal education library, where all the training is cataloged and indexed for easy access by search engines. Identify media (text, interactive web site, video, audio program).
Build in HR Training	Turn human resource information into a training event. Train people in how to interpret policies. Create training that demonstrates procedures: that is, how to fill out a travel request form, or make a contribution to a 401K, or look up your health benefits. Integrate with HR applications.
Create a Procedural Library	Put procedures on-line: how to fill out a form, how to track a customer's order, where to go for support, how to change my 401K. Procedures are training in small packages. Use multimedia to make the training tidbits more interesting. Get the owners of the procedures to maintain the pages on-line.

Training may be ending as we know it. Self-paced education will undoubtedly supersede training. We don't need an intermediary between our knowledge needs and our knowledge suppliers. Training implies a single point of interpretation, whereas self-paced education weaves together multiple levels of interpretation and focuses them on you, the knowledge worker. It is now your responsibility to integrate the relevant knowledge into your work processes and measure your knowledge acquisition with experts and a focused peer worldwide audience.

Employee Empowerment

The intranet empowers people with the ability to engineer corporate intellectual property and disseminate it throughout the organization. The content delivery model is decentralized, like the telephone, thus allowing the sharing of corporate intelligence throughout the organization. Sharing information with everyone is the cornerstone for empowerment. Being able to build it yourself and distribute it on-line is efficient empowerment.

Sharing information throughout the company is a risk. Yet without information, people cannot possibly be responsible for streamlining processes, reducing cycle times, improving workflow, collaborating with the right people. The risk revolves around validity of information, or the posting of information that isn't for everyone's consumption. Still, in an empowerment model, the distributor of the information is held fully responsible. Sharing information enhances trust between managers and employees, between internal customers and external customers.

Intranets create empowered employees. They create a break from the hierarchical history of the manager passing information down (filtered information) to the employees. When an intranet publishes its visions, values, procedures, goals, and training on-line, employees have direction. They can interact with the architects of the visions and values and consistently align goals with overarching goals. Two wins for empowerment are performance effectiveness and process effectiveness. In Table 4–2, we've summarized some of these advantages that intranets buy you.

Table 4-2 Intranets Enable Performance and Process Effectiveness

Performance Effectiveness (Products and Services)	Process Effectiveness (Actual Behaviors)
Empowered teams using the intranet communicate requirements and manage change with their clients. Their performance standards are more measurable and can be viewed by the entire team.	An empowered team polishes processes continuously. They put in maximum effort to simplify or automate tasks to speed up delivery of products.
Empowered teams build successful performance methodology for others to take in the future. They also leave a legacy of successful co-development which can benefit them for their next project.	An empowered team applies refinements to their processes with the appropriate level and mix of skill, knowledge, and expertise to the task
Empowered teams enable their members to learn, grow, experience well-being, and develop professionally.	An empowered team identifies appropriate performance strategies to accomplish tasks much faster.

Intranets enable teams to form rapidly, and to centralize information in one location (web site) for easy access. Teams empowered by the intranet make decisions based upon consensus. Intranet teams make decisions faster and with more participation. They are held accountable for their results, so they produce better quality in less time. Isn't it unbelievable that this can happen just because of enterprisewide communications over an intranet?

Sharing information builds trust. When employees share, they begin to feel a renewed sense of trust among each other. They become a well-oiled machine, focusing on continuous process improvement. This break from history exhilarates a team's enthusiasm. Workflow is improved, and teams measure each other's performance against the group. The intranet site reflects their performance and processes and establishes ownership. The team becomes smarter. The partnerships are more long term and rewarding.

Bottom Line: Self-directed teams architect web sites that position them in the big picture, rather than in the little picture.

Business Simplification

Certainly one of the best features an intranet buys you is its ability to simplify the way you're doing business. Instead of filling out various forms for travel expenses, passing the paper through an approval process, collecting reimbursements, and so on, an intranet web site rolls all these processes into one web site. The form is on-line to fill out (Figure 4–1). The information is distributed to everyone in the process, approvals are determined by e-mail, and reimbursements are ordered and sent either through the mail or electronic fund transfer.

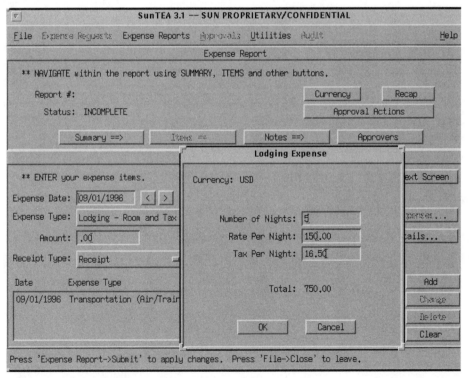

Figure 4–1 SunTea, Sun's Internal Travel Expense Intranet Application

Processes like these can be easily identified in an organization. Simply walk around the office and look for the desk with a lot of paper on it, then ask that person what they do. More than likely all their paper and communication processes can be automated over the intranet.

Using a form-based web site, you can provide an overview of the process to the user. Within a couple of web pages, a click of a few buttons, an entire transaction takes place. This is a vast improvement over the intercompany mail, distributing forms, and processing manager's approvals. To make it even better, users are invited to feed back improvement suggestions right on the same web form. The owner can update the web site instantaneously, when a good suggestion is made.

Netscape is making a business of selling processes that are already automated. They have created the Appfoundry On-line™ (Figure 4–2) to aid in business simplification. They are providing streamlined processes to be added to your intranet. These processes integrate with your web site and help increase the functionality of your web site. Because they are streaming processes from experts through their site to yours, you have more assurance that the application is going to work over the Web, over any platform, for any client.

Figure 4–2 AppFoundry On-Line Provides Business Simplification

Accelerating business simplification within your organization is a win situation. Future revenue potential can be seen in the selling of business process, or the development of business software that operates over the intranet. The business of selling processes is exactly what your intranet developers are capable of doing as well. Only you know which business processes to use with your products and services. You can capture these in web sites, beta test them with your employees, dynamically change the functionality, and automate a process for corporate standard use, or market it and sell it. Business simplification is profitable.

Workflow

Companies using intranets understand the importance of efficiency. They appreciate the significant cost savings they are achieving by streamlining their core business processes. Intranets empower professionals to continually improve their processes. Intranets understand that staying ahead of the competition demands the capability to respond immediately to customers and react quickly to change. Since intranets facilitate automating business processes, the workflow within a corporation can be seriously affected. The dramatic affects of workflow evolution can either propel your organization to the number one position, or mire you in confusion, downsizing, and staff reduction.

In order to improve your workflow over the intranet, you might look at how the intranet improves workflow:

- visualizes business processes (multimedia, browsers)

- automates processes (CGI scripts, Java, ActiveX)

- integrates processes (on-line partnering, collaboration, and mutual product development)

- monitors employee progress (discussion groups, feedback forms, and web profiling)

- modifies processes in real time (administrative control at the server distributed equally to all web top clients)

- responds immediately to changing business (can cut and paste processes into the web site, changing functionality instantaneously)

Workflow Efficiency   The corporation has evolved. Workflow has changed many times within an organization. Personal multimedia and PCs graduated the individual into an effective communicator. Workflow that would go to secretaries, or administrative assistants is rerouted directly to the manager through automated processes. Managers can grab employee profiles, schedules, progress reports, and group commitments on-line by creating a manager's web page and linking it to the other team players. This is known as process efficiency.

Managers redirect their responsibilities into high-performance teams, or work groups. Workflow is automated through software tools and hardware infrastructure, namely e-mail, LANs, and intranets. Sharing decision-making information is encouraged. Information flows more quickly, processes are defined more rapidly, and collaboration among "best resources" is expedited, despite geographical and time differences.

Workflow is captured in project management paradigms. Employees co-locate with team members and share information on a web site. This means that no two people have to be in the same physical location to operate as team members. The web site is maintained by all of the users. Workflow is improved for the project and passed over to the next user, or cooperative team. The following are some suggestions for those team members:

- Build a strong team, include technologists, managers, end users, and other stakeholders.

- Prepare for a thorough analysis of the work processes. You'll need to define the people, the work activities, and interactions along every step of the way.

- Plan for change. Workflow strategy is not a static technology.

In moving workflow to the intranet, company efficiencies are radically altered. The more you create visual objects to represent business events, the more easily you'll be able to manipulate workflow in an intranet environment.

Interenterprise Workflow   At times, expertise will not be available inside the company. In order to improve the workflow in the company, you'll have to look outside. However, because your model for workflow is electronically based, you can easily integrate your external customers and their appropriate internal electronic processes with yours in order to affect the workflow between your organizations. This new area of the extended intranet, or what Don Tapscott calls "Interenterprise computing" (in his book *The Digital Economy, Promise and Peril in the Age of Networked Intelligence)* will dominate workflow thinking between your intranet and other intranets, with whom you'll want to partner.

Secure Workflow—Electronic Escorts   Certainly not all intranet activity can be shared between organizations. Intranets will not be fully interlinked with other intranets. Third parties will be allowed access only in a secured fashion. "Electronic escorts" will greet them and escort them around the appropriate areas of the intranet, for a limited amount of time. In order to complete a project or share resources with an internal project or process, they'll have limited access.

To stay and look around on the intranet when your given electronic access is inappropriate in any organization. The future holds some surprises in this area. Extranets will be necessary for interenterprise commerce. If you're willing to remain competitive, start thinking carefully about how you'll work with other organizations over the Internet. You do not work in a vaccuum. Doing anything on the intranet that touches the customer has a significant impact on your intranet, an even more profound one on your customer. Think about ways you'll be integrating your intranet with other intranets. However, demand robust, impenetrable security and nothing less.

Human Resource Effectiveness

The intranet was designed for Human Resources (HR), if even for access to company information, medical benefits, 401Ks, salary planning, bonus and incentives programs. In fact, so many processes can be automated within HR, that you can almost consider using your intranet in place of your HR software. HR has always been plagued with reams of paper, changes in information, HR directories, cataloges, services, and so forth. They have been plagued with an equal amount of telephone calls to access this information as well.

Standard HR Goes On-Line   Put it all on-line. Create an HR button at the top of your intranet home page and make sure everyone in the company knows it's there. If you have Health Maintenance Organizations (HMOs) and Preferred Provider Organizations (PPOs), put the preferred physicians list on-line, or partner with your provider and get them to put it on-line, and you link to it (extranet). Get all medical and dental benefits on-line and make sure there is an adequate search engine, so employees can drill down quickly to the information they need.

Employee directories with complete and full information on employees (that which is publishable and not private, of course) can go on-line so people know how to get hold of someone in the organization. Make sure this database is comprehensive, so an employee could search for a "SalesPerson, who sells Product X, in the Telco section, living in Atlanta."

The list is not exhaustible. However, one thing to keep in mind; by law, many of the HR documents and services must be available on a 24-hours-a-day, 7 days a week timetable in many different areas. Make sure that your network can sustain this availability over the intranet. There are times when financial operations may require full use of the network for closing books. Make sure that your HR legal information gets on the mission-critical list, so there are no interruptions to service.

HR Intranet Agents   Intranet technology can go even further than accessing documents on-line. You can develop an interactive environment with the user, which places the user in the HR process of their choice. Using the vast resources of human resource databases and automated processes, the interaction occurs in the form of an interview. Once, the needs of the user have been identified, the intranet tools can follow a path that would suggest to the user what HR services would help them the most. In this way, the user is advised by an expert system on how to handle a human resource issue. This is an advance over the user knowing which form to fill out, filling it out, and pushing it through the approval process.

Eventually all the management tools in an intranet are integrated. All interactions are maintained in the database, and the HR Intranet becomes smarter, as it acquires interactive processes in many different forms. The HR intranet system has one level for managers, and another for users. The managers, who are human intelligence agents, base decisions on stronger, more effective data. Users, who are intelligence consumers, perform the transactions that create the data.

Pat Baldwin, director of business simplification at Sun Microsystems, Inc., says that HR systems like these "will deliver back to the bottom line. Surveys and estimates predicated about $325K in management and finance time is being saved by using Sal Tool, Sun's automated HR tools for the annual salary increase process. The savings is in the streamlining and automating of the HR processes, taking time out of the people part of processes. The total savings from all the automation would be hard to estimate. It involves saving not just mananger time, but also line HR, HR specialists (like benefits, administration, and compensation). Additionally, there is a significant savings in non-bay-area (San Francisco) organizations from elimination of Fed Ex costs to route forms for signature and submission." Baldwin estimates that before processes were automated in her HR organization, managers at Sun were spending at least 50 percent of their time processing forms and engaging 18–25 percent of management time building HR processes. Quick access, automated workflow, and automated approval mechanisms have reduced these percentages significantly.

HR Concerns   HR has a traditional cultural bias to sharing information and maintaining high touch with people. This dichotomy makes their service providership difficult to interpret. In fact, HR is usually the most misunderstood organization in a large infostructure enterprise. However, learning how to use information technology and to transfer the right kind of knowledge throughout the organization is their job, no matter how difficult. How does HR keep the human in human resources with high electronic touch?

Many people in many corporations are still afraid of information technology. They simply won't go near it. Information in HR must be kept secure, yet at the same time needs to go on-line for access by those who have authority. Processes are guarded, change is slow, automation is the benevolent enemy. They want to understand how to make information available and secure. They want to reduce the risk factors. Perhaps some reflection on the dichotomy of HR will reveal the answers.

Positives for HR

- shared ownership of the accuracy of information

- speed (access, updating, and distribution) of HR data

- common "source" of answers which is easier to comprehend for the user

- ease of posting to the intranet

- moves groups to document information that they might not otherwise get around to

Negatives for HR

- difficulty in controlling what gets posted on the intranet, specifically where there are legal implications (i.e., HR policies)

- dealing with HR issues that are intranet related, that is, hacking, installing viruses, posting incorrect or illegal information, libel

- need to build intranet operation into more and more position descriptions

- need to familiarize and train staff for optimized efficiency

- identify resources for technological transfer

Effective HR Help and Training Systems   HR can train itself fast enough to maintain status as a viable resource and watch itself take charge of process automation, human resource needs analysis, and a metric system to identify how well they do business.

The call for on-line development has never been stronger. It is the linking of good thoughts, great web events, streamlined processes, proven business models, and closely aligned statistics that improve the growth of a company, exponentially. Netscape's rise to fame in less than two years is a direct result of being an intranet company and having their on-line act together. Everything is on-line. Access to on-line services is always available. Personal mastery is achieved through link partnering. Process improvement is achieved through rapid collaborative prototyping with half the world as beta testers. What an idea.

Once you create procedural web pages that escort users through a form-like adventure, launching policies, linking processes to policies, flying over the entire HR system to position your next move, spinning in a multimedia show that engages the user for interactive input, testing their competencies for survival, then you'll have an integrated intranet HR system that feeds the organization like a farm.

Intranationalize Human Resources (HR) On-line   We are all in a global digital economy, attempting to communicate worldwide to share ideas, conduct business, enhance our knowledge and the quality of our life. Many are sacrificing hours of language learning to contribute, share, and explore on the international Net. Many cultures hold treasures of information that can be unleashed, translated, and synthesized into a format that creates relationship building, and mutual knowledge transfer. We simply blend cultural icons of true meaning.

Incorporate knowledge of international trading law, commerce, legal restrictions, cultural information, and relative analytical information for partnering internationally. Use the technology to communicate HR's global viewpoint and perspective for all organizational employees. The concept to share an enterprisewide culture is a challenge to any HR department. An intranet will facilitate that communication if a common language and international standard for conducting business emerges.

This is a call to help evolve the language of the international intranet. Our spoken language is limited by its borders. The intranet knows no borders, so the language you use to create your intranets must reflect an international awareness, a sensitivity to the creation of new terms that capture ideas and meanings that haven't traditionally been translated.

How to learn this language, or how to help it evolve? Start small. Translate as much as you can if possible. Use international graphics on web sites. Foster localization in a globalized, common culture intranet interface. Provide two-way links to international web sites, international offices, contacts, and organizations that might provide more information to the internal user. Reserve real estate on your intranet for international awareness and business.

Use the Internet for helping you out with translation services. Use Aleph to translate. See Figure 4–3. Aleph is an electronic marketplace for locating and doing business with professional language translators. You can hook up easily with tried translators capable of translating your documents quickly, and getting to you over the Internet. Aleph provides an extensive database of translators and will be involved in profiling customers and matching the right people to the right job. Translation is just one of the ways to improve international relations with other groups within your intranet. Each country has its distinct needs for doing business both in the real world and in the on-line environment. Take the time to perform some audience needs analysis on this group. If you can capture surveys or other marketing time information to understand the international group, then use it. Electronic research turns into web site material.

Figure 4–3 Aleph, the Global Translation Alliance

Productivity

The three pillars of productivity are timeliness, quantity, and rate. Intranets are very capable of improving the timeliness of product development, as employees are united by strategic direction, known corporate values, information about the company's products and services, and project management maintained on web sites. As production accelerates, quantity of output increases, and the production rate is competitive. This provides leverage to the organization when dealing with sales.

Intranets are excellent at providing every employee with knowledge of the strategy of the company and with how each employee's goals contribute to that strategy. Project managers maintain web sites, manage priorities, adjust virtual schedules, and track changes easily. A workforce improves its efficiency when their goals for cooperating and methods for collaborating are linked together through web pages over an intranet.

How does the intranet improve productivity?

- Accelerates communication
- Accesses shared enterprisewide knowledge
- Engenders an innovation/creativity culture
- Enables rapid collaborative prototyping
- Provides a collaborative environment
- Satisfies quality requirements

Accelerated Communication

Ad Hoc Water Cooler Talk   The most valuable information is often transferred over a cup of coffee as service people trade war stories. This often tacit knowledge can't be "rationalized" or automated but can only develop through unstructured, bottom-up, ad hoc conversations. E-mail and newsgroups are great for that, especially if you jettison the old addiction to command and control. With everybody wired, the organization can use these conversations as a vital source of information about real market needs and perceptions, as well as gather process savvy. Unlike the automated information systems designed for mass production, intranets facilitate knowledge exchange.

Take a look at the way Microsoft's ITG uses the intranet to communicate information relevant to the group. The tone is office friendly, while the information mixes leadership goals and missions with tools for on-line production and late breaking information on product announcements. The idea of personalizing a site for a group centralizes key issues and focuses the group's attention.

Multiple Communication   No other technology environment has allowed users to talk to each other as well as e-mail. You can initiate an e-mail in a few seconds, when an idea hits you. You send the e-mail out immediately, and within seconds it arrives in the mailbox(es) of all interested parties. If sitting at their desk, you get a response almost within minutes. If you know someone's e-mail address, you can ask them any question, make any comment. You can write to the President of the company or you can request an extra key be made for your office from facilities.

Now with intranets, users can belong to e-mail groups that specialize in areas of expertise, called aliases. Employees share company e-mails that cross through departments and learn about interdependencies and issues that might not have been covered until much later in the process of development. Instead of losing

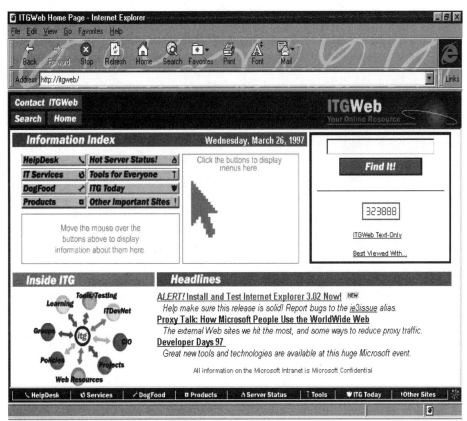

Figure 4–4 Microsoft's ITG Intranet Site

precious one-to-one e-mails between employees, all conversations can be stored in data warehouses and instantly accessed with search tools or agent technologies.

Intranets allow you to study before contacting people personally. You can attend meetings or make more informed conversations over the telephone after you have studied an intranet site of a group, a project, or an individual. You can examine principles, organization structure, the project milestones, the frequently asked questions, the services the group offers *before* you make initial contact, or request assistance. You can get to the right place quickly and base the conversation on your intelligence of the group. This is akin to prequalifying a customer before you decide what to help him buy.

Intranets, web sites, newsgroups, and e-mail accelerate access to information, enable cross departmental communication, and provide casual, spontaneous interactions with other workers.

Communicate Goals and Strategies   Company presidents clearly articulate goals and strategies of a company. Scott McNealy does a radio show for his employees once a month over the company's intranet. In the radio show McNealy motivates, educates, teases, and builds the company culture. With information coming directly from a leader, employees feel connected, in-tune, and know why things are happening in the organization. CEO's and task masters must have a forum on-line to provide information to users.

The CEO at SGI uses the intranet to advertise hands-on meetings, announce company policy changes, praise with rewards and recognition for valued employees, stock quotes, all on a front web page for everyone to share in the common messages and focused thinking of the company leader. How can you not know what you're doing is valuable, when you understand why your company is performing the way it is? Everyone sees the soul of the company when they turn on their intranet. They see the company's symbolic self on-line.

Shared Enterprisewide Knowledge

Today's business climate is characterized by constant and dramatic change. Organizations are struggling with how to sustain their competitive advantage in a climate of globalization, changing customer expectations, explosion of technology, and market unpredictability. The challenge is how to create an environment where all individuals are engaged and contributing value to the organization's success. The only successful way of doing that is through shared knowledge. Shared knowledge improves productivity, especially if designed as a data warehouse.

An intranet assists in facilitating the sharing of knowledge and makes the reuse of knowledge bases and knowledge-based systems more accessible. Web pages or web sites can be created that encompass a project's schedule, time line, key contacts, white papers, leading competitive concerns, design specifications, customer input, and so on. Because this knowledge can be captured and showcased in one single area, many users involved in the project can share an overview of the project. They can contribute to the web site, question the validity or accuracy of information at the web site, and they can cut and paste critical success factors onto other web pages.

Collaborators need the ability to establish and customize knowledge sharing agreements (i.e., mutually agreed-upon terminology and definitions) that are usable by people and their machines. Alphabetized glossaries and search engines can assist in this endeavor. More standards are borne from the publication of standards. Users can share their knowledge of what would be the best way to represent information or knowledge in their key field.

Intranets track the relationships between the elements of a design. So, managing relationships is crucial to the success of intranet activities. By tracking relationships, you can head off conflicts between employees working on the project as those conflicts arise, rather than at the end of a design cycle.

Shared enterprise knowledge works its way up to an intranet web page that encompasses all corporate projects, white papers, threaded discussion groups, and so on. Only with shared knowledge can organizations evolve into communication, high-touch, customer loyalty organizations that build their relationships on trust, and the sharing of information.

Innovation/Creativity Culture

Innovation means that you are using the talents of all the team members against the common purpose or goals to produce an "out-of-the-box" solution. This means finding solutions to problems that have never been thought of before. It means creating products that go beyond satisfying the customer and moving into the realm of delighting the customer. It involves valuing differences and engaging in mutual influence to create innovative, breakthrough solutions that help drive the strategy of the organization. Intranet sites fundamentally help ensure the competitiveness of the organization by promoting an innovative/creative culture.

When you create a shared knowledge environment, in which individuals are contributing their best to their web sites, linking to partners that provide expert content, and providing tools like glossaries, indices, libraries, and search tools, you create an environment in which individuals can focus on their creative and innovative potential.

Creativity comes from critical thinking, questioning the context of a situation, and exploring alternatives. Identifying and challenging assumptions is central to critical thinking. Web pages and web projects focus user's attentions on key pieces of a project as in Figure 4–5 that provides the foundations of creative thinking.

It would be better to include these five elements in your intranet in order to create an environment in which your knowledge workers will be able to focus on creativity solutions. These elements fit nicely on an intranet. They're visible, linkable, and live communication to their creators.

> **Principles.** Service, quality, excellence, integrity, honesty, and trust are principles. Representing these principles at your web site, directly provides your employees with a mature environment in which to create and re-create always developing in the bounds of organizational needs and the creativity of the individual.

Mission. An intranet has to have a mission statement. Mission statements need to reflect the deep shared vision and values of everyone within the organization. The mission statement provides a frame of reference or a set of criteria or guidelines. It must be designed by the core team and endorsed by the entire organization. Create it in an on-line forum, then display it on the intranet.

Problems. An area of the intranet that is key to creativity is the ability to challenge assumptions about the mission, the decisions, the process, the people, and the price. Information made available will certainly uncover key issues regarding accuracy and validity. Problems require immediate action and ownership. An intranet assigns action and owners to show how the corporation is doing. Once a problem has been identified and is posted, it sits out there like a glowing beacon trying to attract the attention of passersby. Present problems to everyone and provide immediate feedback mechanisms, so even casual observers can provide insight on solving problems. Bug Lists are a common example, with forms to describe how to fix the bug.

Discussions. Running an organization requires some serious debate. Procedures or processes that need improvement are discussed here. Threaded discussion groups provide a key question or problem, then indented below you'll find several answers, with names, dates, and e-mail address to continue discussing either in private or publicly. Live chatting events, or radio shows with keynote addresses, are more advanced ways to provide an environment for discussion on your intranet. The purpose is to contribute to the identification and solving of problems. From the interaction, creativity springs out, creating innovative solutions and synchronous partnerships.

Project Management. Scheduling, oversight, tracking projects, tracking costs, resource allocation, lead time, lag time, interdependencies—all are managed in a single web site. As an intranet producer, you can create your own web environment to manage your projects, make the information available to all, and provide the counters of time and money for both customer and supplier. Again, this information is available to all the people working on your Intranet, or on your project. When problems arise, the team is focused with all possible resources at their disposal. An intranet allows the rapid, collaborative decision making companies need in a rapidly changing environment.

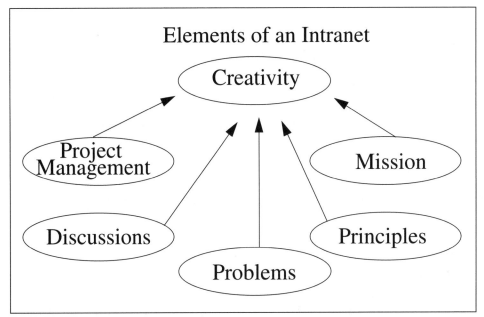

Figure 4–5 Elements of Creativity to Include on a Web Site.

Rapid Collaborative Prototyping

One of the nicest aspects of an intranet is rapid collaborative prototyping. That means that you put something up on the web immediately, once you've decided to take on an intranet project. Start with something very simple: the name of the project, the key players, the purpose of the site telephone numbers, dates, budgets, whatever you have that you think necessary in terms of building the project. This is nothing new, but putting it in HTML, linking anything on the intranet that is relevant, and providing automatic e-mail addresses start the ball rolling fairly quickly.

When you've met with your team and honed a project plan, put it on the intranet site. Make sure to design it so it is easy to read, easy to navigate, and easy to link to. Next determine what the structure of the site will be like—a complete road map. Then make that road map available as something called a "Site Map."

Get the graphics workers designing graphics, or looking through the graphics libraries, and post them as soon as they're complete. If the graphics are going to be clickable maps, add that feature. Everyone on your team can own an area, or a responsibility for developing the web site. Make those responsibilities clear, create a "to do" list, or an action list, and keep it on-line so everyone knows who is supposed to do what. And, create some way of prioritizing the action list, with dates attached, so it is clear where the project is going.

Using telephones and PCs or workstations, you can build sites on-line fairly quickly. You can update simultaneously, work while speaking on the telephone, and watching modifications happen as soon as one of the developers presses the ENTER key. Slowly but surely, add pieces to the site. Add a financial spreadsheet, a clickable map of the regions that you are covering, or whatever you find appropriate to add to this site.

When everyone is contributing their work to one place, one web site on the intranet, you are in the process of rapid collaborative prototyping. The web site is a prototype or a model as long as you have it under construction. There is no reason to publish the site, or even move it onto the central intranet reference pages, until you have promoted the site from collaborative prototype to collaborative product. Stories from interviews reveal that some prototype turn into projects and into products in 75 percent of the time as stand-alone desktop tools.

Netscape Anecdote   Netscape reminisces that when a competitor announced a bundled deal with a major financial newspaper, a senior vice president (VP) at Netscape surprised the competitor with a rapid collaborative response. Within one week, the VP delivered a competitive bundled deal with 20 publishers to deliver personalized content via e-mail. The web site was built while all the developers were on the phone.

Sun-on-the-Net Anecdote Sun Microsystems, Inc. wanted to tell their internet story so everyone in the world could see how Sun has been building intranets for years. So they created a spot on their home page called Sun-on-the-Net. This site was practically built overnight. The designers and the developers never met face to face. They created it over the telephone, writing HTML, importing graphics, partnering with marketing, engineering, sales, human resources, MarCom (Marketing Communications), legal, security, and training and linked content to Sun-on-the-Net within three weeks. The idea was to push out a story as quickly as possible for both the consumer and the salesperson.

Rapid collaborative prototyping on the intranet gives you a cutting edge in developing your web sites very rapidly. You accelerate communications because the team can follow through easily on items that are maintained on the web site. Posting status, links, forms, objectives, and procedures make for strategic alignment. Many divergent departments can contribute simultaneously. In essence, this kind of collaborative workflow is a precursor to rapid, dynamic e-commerce that will affect your products and services dramatically.

Collaboration

The intranet is forcing people to reconcile isolation, ivory tower thinking, noncollaborative environments. We keep hitting against each other's dysfunction each time we try to align marketing requirements with engineering specifications, documentation, testing, and quality. The lack of collaboration is due more to the absence of good tools, than it is on the willingness of individual groups to work together. PCs isolated people from each other, and even worse from each other's rich content. Networks enabled sharing some of the work. But the world was represented as a series of subdirectories and file folders. Who could expect to get anything done working in someone else's mess?

All the different business units ended up re-creating the same customer solutions from different perspectives, and by the time the customer dealt with four or five different departments solving their problem in unique ways, they become discouraged and started looking for other solutions. If the enterprise cannot tell its story of how they collaborate with their own internal customers to plan, design, develop, test, implement and support any product or service, the customer is simply not willing to share in the mayhem.

The intranet provides a collaborative environment. Users are able to share documents, graphics, designs, history, corporate information, and all other relevant media in a single location. They can build project management environments with or without helper applications. They focus attention on the customer and customer requirements by studying the customer on the outside Internet and by linking to partner sites in group web pages. They allow partnering, sharing, and negotiating between functional groups to bring together the right people.

Collaboration means working together as a common body. Lotus Notes provides such an environment. In fact many organizations have already begun some intensive projects with Lotus Notes. Lotus has created a simple solution for organizations to leverage this original infrastructure. With Domino, the Lotus intranet product for collaboration, intranets can align with the Lotus Notes structures that have already been created. With continued integration like this, collaboration will become a core competency within the organization.

You may not need to go to the level of sophistication that these programs offer. An intranet is already collaborative because of its e-mail and hypermedia linking capabilities. You can still get away with creating a collaborative environment simply by linking home pages together. As long as someone has the role of project manager, or gatekeeper for the collaborative home pages, you have the flexibility of building customizable collaboration.

Bottom Line: Collaboration, either in large packages or small intranet packages, buys you rapid development and quality products.

What does collaboration buy you?

- Local and global sharing of product, project, manufacturing, and marketing plans and information

- On-line documentation of policies, processes, and procedures so everyone is on the same page

- Salesforce automation, especially any repeatable process

- Training on-demand, because training requires collaboration between subject matter experts, instructional designers, and development groups

- Document management and cataloging

- Data warehousing

- New Graphical User Interface (GUI) front end for existing applications

- Software management and distribution

The advent of the computer with e-mail allowed project members to be better informed. A few software programs like Microsoft's Project Management software allowed a more structured view into a project. The intranet takes us beyond. It takes us to the land of cross-functional teams who create common web page reports tracking their developments, requirements, specifications, schedules, conversations, planning, meeting agendas, and action plans. The information is secured, requiring password entr, and is immediately published in any format onto the Web.

Quality

Many pundits believe that the quality movement is just for manufacturing and has nothing, or little to do, with intranet development. In the infoworld, which slowly, but surely is marking the end of the industrial revolution, quality has never been more important.

On the Internet, and in your organization's intranet, the quality of information is the difference between success and failure. The manufacturing of knowledge products that are reliable, valid, and usable has many lessons to learn from its predecessor, industrial manufacturing. The quality guru's words still ring true on the intranet—improve quality, which decreases costs. Costs decrease because of less rework. Fewer mistakes and fewer delays make better use of machine time and materials. Productivity improves and you cap the market with better quality and lower prices. You stay in business and provide jobs and more jobs.

Bottom Line: On the intranet the quality of information is known as truth. Are you ready to use it?

Tim Berners-Lee, father of the World Wide Web model, says that quality on the intranet will drive quality partnering. A link from a quality source will generally be only to other quality documents. A link to a low-quality document reduces the effective quality of the source document. The lesson for people who create web documents is that quality links are just as important as quality content. When users can rely on your information, they grow to trust you and seek your services when in need.

Providing quality information on the intranet is a big win. Executives rely on business analysts, who rely on data gatherers, who rely on the source to provide the best information available to assist in making world-class decisions. Within an organization, quality of information is what makes you succeed. Building an intranet web site that hosts the best information, the best researched content, the best delivery of that quality information builds reputations, builds organizations, and builds careers.

Intranet Quality   Quality is quality. Quality issues are the same for knowledge-ware manufacturing as they are for material goods and services. Quality products are the basis for transforming the organization into a quality company. In Table 4–3 below, we highlight key intranet enablers that instill quality in knowledge production.

Table 4-3 Quality and the Intranet

Intranet Quality Enablers
Putting the Wood behind One Arrow   Executive management uses the intranet to articulate purpose, encourage innovation and research, and educate to support that purpose. Make this very clear!
Intranet Computing Model   There is an intranet computing model where everything moves to the Web. Provide tools and demonstrate how it works.

Table 4-3 Quality and the Intranet *(Continued)*

Intranet Quality Enablers
Depend on Collaboration for Quality Processes are identified on-line, and rapid collaborative prototyping reveals the quality of a web site (a process, service, product) to all observing eyes long before the product is released.
Quality Links, Quality Vendors Your links on-line are only as good as the supplier's highest level of quality. Link to quality sites, ones that have a reputation and a hands-on maintenance strategy.
Promote Self-Paced Learning Realize the intranet is organic, developing as an entire live system. Constantly review and study design, content, navigation, and experience. Record your methods for achieving results, and post them on-line for future use or future planning.
Provide On-Line Resources Embed training into every web site on the intranet, even if it is only procedural help, how to fill out a form, how to order a product. Go beyond and provide training on how to sell a product, how to conduct a needs analysis.
Provide Clear Intranet Leadership Webmasters, gatekeepers, web architects, and experts on-line represent the leadership functions on the intranet. Executive management must reward and recognize effective leadership.
Empower Users with Two-Way Communication Open feedback mechanisms, e-mail, discussion groups. Chatting with the leaders provides a mechanism for getting your word out and eliminating fear. Consider anonymity in feedback mechanisms.
Intranet Cross-Functionality Break down barriers between cross-functional areas. Cross-functional web pages identify the processes, needs, and efficiencies of different staff areas. Barriers will only exist with nonparticipation.
Natural Attrition Let the web site on the intranet either improve the process in a cross-functional environment, or let the web site naturally fall off. Let each function maintain their own website, instead of developing targets for the entire workforce.
Performance Is the Evaluator Quotas don't improve web sites, process improvement does. Web sites represent processes. If the web site is working for internal customers, the system improves.

Table 4-3 Quality and the Intranet *(Continued)*

Intranet Quality Enablers
Pride of Workmanship Allow individuals to put their names at the bottom of their web sites. In fact, ownership of a web site encourages pride of workmanship and also provides contact with the owner for clarification or link partnering.
Vigorous Educational Environment Create a virtual university on-line, where training schedules are available, training on demand is instituted, and an orientation training program exists that prepares employees for the new intranet model of doing internal business.
Create a Global Village Put a workstation on every desk, provide everyone with a home page, and let the magic happen.

Competitive Advantage

Businesses are co-evolving organisms. They are unpredictable and exist within a constantly shifting international environment that has no controls. Learning how to survive in this environment is what creates competitive advantage.

Intranets provide businesses with the ability to co-evolve. Because intranets are organic, representing the "shifting business ecosystems," they develop awareness and action-oriented thinking regarding the competition and the customer. Because the organization is contributing to the collective knowledge of the intranet, the end result is a model of the future. The employees are constantly emerging as innovation solution providers, geniuses of assimilation, and harbingers of process and product improvement. The corporation is in a constant state of becoming a product or a service, of becoming a partner with others, of becoming one with the customer's needs and loyalty.

Companies need to learn how to cooperate and resolve conflicts and differences very quickly. The slightest appearance of dissension in an organization can turn a customer away instantly. There are so many competitive solutions for customers who have evolved into well-informed, intelligent consumers. As we've said before, it takes generating and sharing visions to make an organization work efficiently. The workforce must know how to manage complex relationships and to gain fresh insights from new knowledge construction. The full implications of intranets and competitive advantage are as yet unknown, but at the very least, this strategic form of thinking enables the rapid response capabilities of the organization.

Competitive Advantages Are Short Lived

Your intranet is not a panacea to all the woes of your company. However, you can transform your organization and prepare it for international on-line e-commerce if you have your own internal mechanisms and people in place. What you are inside is a reflection of what you are outside. Your intranet has to be robust, healthy, and strongly customer focused. Once you attain a level of competitive advantage, your intranet will be obsolete.

Continue to build, to streamline, to automate processes, to involve the customer's needs, to acquaint yourself with your customer's customers, and to align all the internal processes that plan, design, develop, and deliver products. When you're created a synergistic body like this, you've got your next move for the future.

Branding Turf

This is a new area of branding turf, where the enterprises who are used to hogging all the territory are discovering that they do not know how to exactly move on-line in a way that will create new markets and provide a venue for competitive advantage. Others who seem to intuitively understand the intranet technology are building empires so quickly it feels like an invasion. You can see the companies, the organizations, the networks, and the universities that are getting smarter and smarter at this. Some have 40,000 employees, some have 40. No matter what the size of your company, an intranet that ties together people, processes, and procedures has a strong advantage over an organization that is still trying to calculate ROI (Return on Investment) before they make an intranet investment.

Intranets and Sales—the True Advantage

Although sales seems like a function for the Internet, it is the information that the organization provides to the salesperson in the field that truly matters. Certainly many individuals will prequalify themselves on the Internet even before allowing "face to fact" contact with a salesperson. But, when it gets to the bottom line— how is this really going to help me with my business, reduce costs, and improve my productivity—an intelligent knowledge working salesperson must act as a single point of contact to the customer and use the intranet as the entire organization of help.

In order for the salesperson to act solely as a single point of contact to a customer, they need access to plenty of solid information, solid processes, demos, explanations, technical assistance, systems explanations, executive buy-in. If this wealth is on-line and internet accessible in an easy search-oriented web tool, the salesperson is seen as the most connected, tuned-in, representative of the organization. This reflects on the product as the most connected, tuned-in product on the market, and closing the sale remains in the hands of a single point of contact. The sales person develops a web site maintaining all interaction with the client and links the client to service, support, troubleshooting, extended products, and so forth, always escorting the client through needed decision making.

Examples of Intranet Sales Use   One use is as simple as using an internal customer tracking database or discussion group to do some preliminary work on what the customer is looking for, or what questions they'll ask, or who has seen this customer before, and what benchmarks to use when in the middle of the sales cycle. A viewable sales environment, with constant live, competitive information fed to a web site that any salesperson can access worldwide is the truest use of an internal intranet.

Education and Demos On-Line. Get the intranet folks building educational sites and exquisite demos that are not only used for training internal employees how the enterprise works but can also be extended into the open Internet so salespeople can point to their resources and training. The customer feels integrated.

Communications Resellers. Use the web for communicating vital information on the reseller: password-protected information; information on new products, product changes, specials, discounts; link pages for the different sales groups. Fix a top level page and link to the various sales offices. Incorporate any shared transactions in an extranet.

Showcase Successes. Show special perks and discounts; pipeline of products and availability; sales tips and training; product information; product launches; channel preparation. Show customers how to use the enterprise. Show context of products in systems and solutions; feedback from the field on problems and solutions, what they need and like and dislike.

On-line Partnering—the Intranet Evolves

Key to competitive advantage on an intranet is really the extended intranet's capabilities of on-line partnering. Subcontractors or clients can use passwords and gain entrance into your intranet as well, sharing information previously provided by memos, reports, faxes, FedEx packages, voice mail, meetings, and corporate lunches.

Before the advent of security over an intranet, extended by the Internet and the World Wide Web, it was nearly impossible to allow external people into the network. Intranet technology manages electronic escorting within firewall security. Established internet standards for accurately securing a server are employed. Intranets protect private information behind firewalls and fire ridges to keep out everyone but employees and selected outsiders.

In Figure 4–6, vendors, clients, and partners communicate with your intranet through your browser, which passes information through your firewall security area and checks it for appropriate clearance. If the clearance is acceptable, then entrance is permitted. Otherwise, a message is sent back via the browser to politely discuss further options.

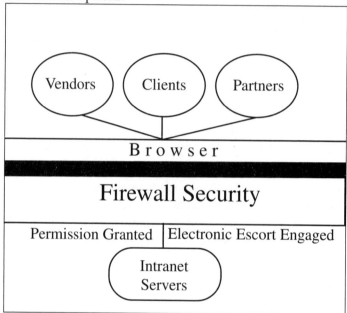

Figure 4–6 Firewall Security between You and the Outside

Competitive advantage is a moving target as soon as you have it in your sights, some other company will see something on the horizon, investing time and effort in it, and suddenly you see the competition in your sights, not your competitive advantage. No wonder on-line partnering is becoming the next great wave in intranet evolution. Its advantages are multiple. But the security issues will be a nightmare. One thing is certain, maturing your intranet for readiness into the open world of e-commerce is a competitive advantage of this decade.

Critical Success Factors for Competitive Advantage

Some areas identified as competitive advantage because of deploying a full service intranet have been

- Developing an intranet that puts the force back into salesforce
- Creating a more high-touch marketing to sales to distribution flow web site

- Designing a customer-focused intranet by integrating efficient feedback mechanisms onto the web site

- Quickly and intelligently adapting to new situations by pushing everything on-line to expedite administration, development, and research

- Linking on-line goals to individual performance, on-line web site

- Benchmarking, using web site statistics, against the competition

- Closing quality, cost, and cycle time gap

Because you can implement change and break down barriers between departments faster, you gain a competitive edge. Also, because you measure results and measure how you achieve those results, you have a clearer path to evaluating how you do business. Knowledge like this undoubtedly reduces production life cycles and speeds up time to market.

Expert Knowledge Workers

If you create knowledge workers who understand how to acquire knowledge, who know how to become autonomous, self-paced learners, you have a critically thinking distributed body of human potential to focus on any problem, customer need, or troubleshooting solution.

In an industrial era, we created workers who were capable of following instruction. Industrial manufacturing required workers to carry out a set of procedures that were proven to work flawlessly. There are only so many ways to build a car, to manufacture a textile, to build a house. The individuals dedicated to moving beyond the limits of manufacturing were few in number. The great intelligence created from improved university systems produced a generation of capable manufacturers.

Managers became intermediaries to move information around the organization. Among the intermediate managers, quality circles popped up, automated processing arrived in the industrial era, and suddenly there was a smarter, more intelligent way of doing business. In order to think like a system, you had to study the system. In order to study the system, you needed to know how to study, how to examine facts, data, and information and reconstruct it to explain how business was being done and how well a process was automated, given the benchmarks that the managers were able to derive.

Enter the knowledge worker of the 21st century, who must understand how to take knowledge and turn it back into a knowledge product. Enter the knowledge worker, capable of teaming with large groups of individuals, partnering with companies all over the globe, communicating over fiber-optic power, and responding to every change, or fluctuation that occurs in the market. These knowledge workers have no managers, really. Nobody can manage an individual creating a knowledge domain, except the knowledge worker.

Never in history has there been a time where learning and learning how to learn have reached a pinnacle. In order to forge a new on-line world, our communication capabilities must improve. Our ability to process information must improve. In order for us to compete in a world where access to international knowledge, methodology, and tools is available, we need to get smarter, and work less. We need to free up our administrativia, our repeating process, and our ineffectual redeveloping, reengineering, reorganization, and allow ourselves to grow as big as the intranet we're creating to live on.

We use the tools of the intranet to collect the magical elements of knowledge, information, analysis, intuition. We create our culture on-line with our pervasive influx of knowledge, processes, and principles. We improve the quality of our lives and of our society as a result of growing on-line together, improving our intelligence, and developing uncanny ways to utilize what we learn. And in doing so, we make some money as well.

Distributed Computing or the Collective Consciousness

Whatever you want to call it, it's the same thing with respect to the intranet.

The intranet has been called the answer to distributed computing. This simply means that computers are connected to servers that are connected to hubs, routers, and gateways. These in turn are connected to servers, or other clients, and everyone can pass data around to any of the servers of clients. The point is we have a large international, global network where everyone can talk to each other or e-mail each other, or do business with each other.

One Large Collective Unit

But it means more than that. All of sudden at the dawn of the 21st century, we have connected ourselves, through technology, as one single collective unit. We have strung together copper wire and fiber optics and computer terminals that can store vast arrays of human knowledge. We are growing together as one large collective consciousness in which a discrete body of intelligence can be connected, referred to, or assimilated by someone else.

From a safe, anonymous distance, we can peer into the hearts and minds of others and explore the dimensions of what we think and how we think as a combined unit. As we seek to be understood and to understand, we continue feedback cycles for increasing our experience until sooner or later we reflect back on ourselves just to see who we are, what we do, and how we add value to the whole. "Perhaps the technological and market forces driving us forward can be tempered by deeper nonmarket human values" (Tapscott, Don. *The Digital Economy: Promise and Peril in the Age of Networked Intelligence.* McGraw Hill, 1996).

Defining Your True Self

Intranets are great for communication and collaboration. That point is clear. Intranets are excellent for improving business processes, streamlining workflow, and reducing production life cycles. That's clear too. The intranet saves time and money, undoubtedly. But, what does the intranet do for you? What will the collective consciousness provide you once you become assimilated?

You may be sitting at a computer putting in information, adding to the collective consciousness. You are doing your job. But, what are you? What are you going to produce on the intranet that represents your true self, your true capability, and your true competence. And who's going to know it? Who's going to care? You are part of the collective one.

How do you define your true self? The answer of course is to develop your own home page. There is nothing like a web home page to truly understand what this technology means. It is only when you see how the words, the pictures, the transactions, and experiences interact with your own self-perception that you understand the organic nature of this technology. It is then that you become a responsible contributor, or a Netizen.

Assimilated in the Blink of an Eye

Never before have we been interconnected like this where a huge audit trail of our thinking, our meanderings, our guesses and hunches, our cyber-self is available in a single location for scrutiny and libel, for praise and fame. For better or worse. Once we dare to admit participation in such a risky, untested global human knowledge experiment, we might reflect differently on exactly how we're going to use the intranet beyond our simple tasks for the enterprise. Will it be a toy, a tool, an extension of our work, or an extension of ourselves that will be measured, modified, evolved, and cut and pasted under other domains with the blink of an eye?

Preservation of the self in a world so huge, so connected, so unordained by anyone but by our folly is the greatest challenge our race faces. In working with each other in our future, we must remember to ally ourselves with the basic principles of humanness in order to continue to contribute to the large collective body of memory, body of experience, body of connectivity of the intranet.

The principles that make up our humanness

- fairness

- integrity and honesty

- human dignity

- service

- quality

- excellence

- patience

- nurturance and encouragement

We mention principles to stress that fundamental communication between international citizens at deeper levels is taking place. On an intranet, you extend yourself like an artifact and thus expose some raw truths about yourself. The best way to survive in this environment is to create an empowering center of interconnected web sites which you can rely on to effectively solve problems, maximize opportunities, and continually learn and integrate with the basic principles of humanness and the technology of the collective consciousness.

The intranet stores all the information from telephone calls, meetings, white papers, letters, memos, e-mails, mind maps, opinions, arguments, education, competency, skills, strategies, and even more. Designed well, it becomes a strong voice, a leading voice. As people link to your expertise, to you, you evolve the knowledge into a working memory, used in intelligent decision making in a split second.

When you extend into the social environment of e-commerce and begin global communication, you have to evolve your culture into a new convergent culture, where cyberlaws take place. The cyberlaw is still unwritten, being written to those who possess split-second decision-making skills that allows them to architect the future.

Increasing intelligence is imperative in your enterprise. You must find a way to make your people learn how to access the right knowledge bases and develop their critical thinking skills. You've got to concentrate on innovation and creativity, no matter what face it takes in its nascent stages of development. Most importantly, you need to figure out how to deal with truth, trust, sharing of information, economics of reliability, serviceability, availability, and ultimately social responsibility.

Individuals are responsible for their own actions and can learn to regulate and continually improve their behavior through goal setting, self-reflection, and self-evaluation. The intranet is all about goal setting and aligning goals across the enterprise. When you place yourself on a web site, you reflect and self-evaluate every time your hourglass stops spinning, and you see yourself summed up in one part of the intranet. From here you grow and integrate with others who are growing equally fast, because judgments and actions are partly self-determined, and people can affect change in themselves and their situations through their own efforts.

As we become one on the intranet, joining in a great collective stamp of human communication, we can do best to ensure that the intranet we create embodies the principles of human life. It is hoped that intranet history synthesizes our intercultural social fabric and leads us into a world where all human knowledge turns itself inward, inward like an intranet, to work its processes, its workflow, its communication, its cybergentics of human improvement to improve the quality of our experience and habits.

The experience is individual, personal, solitary. Yet, there are fundamental practices that make up successful integrative work as you can see in Table 4–4. These principles may be fundamental in building your intranet community.

Table 4-4 Intranet Practices for Successful Intranets

Intranet Practices to Live by	Intranet Enables
Do it now	Get on-line and work on-line. E-mail is for newbies. Publishing is for intermediates. And, interactive experiences with your customers and users are for the advanced.
Plan the future	Write mission statements that ultimately explain where you see everyone in let's say five years. Identify your enterprise's principles and make them available at all times to the user.

Table 4-4   Intranet Practices for Successful Intranets *(Continued)*

Intranet Practices to Live by	Intranet Enables
Prioritize, then do it again	Design your intranet to chunk information into the top five to seven things that are the key, critical factors of your organization. The design communicates what's important to each employee.
Partner and co-source	Partner by linking. Ensure that the link is placed appropriately in each web site so the user understands the equal value of the link.
Customerize, then personalize	Get involved with your customer. Collaborate by linking, by e-mail, by newsgroups, by chatting. Collect information in forms; examine web statistics to see where your user is going within your web space.
Webicize	Get everyone involved by promoting home pages, group pages, project pages, top pages, etc. Keep your eye on the extranet and partner between enterprises.
Cybercize	Constantly communicate with your audience on-line, in person, in usability testing. Extend out to the Internet and assimilate all integrative, communication technology. Seek to interact and find ways to connect your intranet to keep continuously improving processes. Plan a backup when all fails.

Belonging to a movement that sweeps you up like a great tidal wave is intimidating to say the least. The resistance to going on-line is understandable. Yet, to preserve a good place for you in the real estate gardens of the intranet is getting harder and harder, unless you bring a quality, an edge on information, a creative solution, or way to reduce time, development, or dollar cycles. You can't get caught living off the intranet and not feeding back what truly belongs to the collective intranet, your memory. But, once you contribute genuinely to the intranet, the rewards are unimaginable.

Intranets Build Character

They build

- **Trustworthiness** because they provide e-mail communication promoting task efficiency, authenticity of information, honesty, facts, and collaboration with various interrelated participants.

- **Interpersonal trust** because people feel they all have the same rights and access to information. Inability to access information becomes a reason for distrust and disorientation. Exposure to all information affecting the company creates an ability to contribute and protect the core of that information.

- **Empowerment** is enabled on intranets, because people can make things happen if they are informed. Open conversation and instant feedback to the corporate marketing groups, to the sales people who live in the field, and to quality production encourage individuals to improve their processes, regard others' requirements, and see how they are affecting the company.

- **Organizational Alignment** occurs easily when one department knows why the other department needs timely, accurate information, and when that department can expedite the delivery of that information. With a common culture, organizational alignment comes easily.

Web Space for the Future

> Constant change at a rapidly increasing rate is what doing business in the '90s is all about. You can learn to manage change, to embrace it, and use it to your advantage. But you have to start by taking charge of the way you think and the images in your mind. Then you can significantly improve the way you run your business or your life.[1]—*Lou Tice*

Self-Actualization, Enterprise of One

Because the intranet is more than a filing cabinet to manage your documents, you can use it as a personal tool for self-actualization. That means how you truly become the best at what you do, so that when you contribute back to the intranet, you are contributing quality. The enterprise is attempting to self-actualize, as well. Once you have developed a solid understanding of the self, refined it to a single pure entity, then you join more freely with the rest of the world in socializing and doing business. Only when you are truly defined as an automated set of processes

---

1.   The Pacific Institute (http://www.pac-inst.com/).

and a valued system that has a proven method for doing business on-line, then you are placed in a position of authority on your intranet. You are a web that works.

Interactive Human Experience

It is because the intranet goes beyond simply publishing static pages on the intranet, beyond e-mail and newsgroups chatting, and right into the heart of interactive human experience that you see the intranet affecting our thinking, our millennium synthesis of what we have become, and where we're going next. If you have any interests in being in the web space in the future, it is imperative to learn how to interact on-line. In order to increase your human experience, the intranet will provide mechanisms for talking, thinking, socializing, investigating, guessing, playing, investing.

The Digital Economy

Don Tapscott[2] sums up business and leadership for the new digital economy.

> The digital economy requires a new kind of businessperson: one who has the curiosity and confidence to let go of old mental models and old paradigms; who tempers the needs for business growth and profit with the requirements of employees, customers, and society for privacy, fairness, and a share in the wealth they create; one who has the vision to think socially, the courage to act, and the strength to lead in the face of coolness or even ridicule. The digital economy requires yesterday's managers to become tomorrow's leaders. As we enter the new age, the future won't just happen. It will be created. And if we all get involved, our values, aspirations, and growing expectations will shape and drive the transformation of our businesses and our world.

> Past technological paradigms—the broadcast media and the old model of the computer—were hierarchical, immutable, and centralized. As such, they carried the values of their powerful owners. The new media are interactive, malleable, and distributed in control. As such, they cherish an awesome neutrality. Ultimately, they will be what we want them to be. They will do what we command of them.

> This fact should give us not only great hope but determination to shape the future for the common good—to create a new social consciousness and conscience. If we act, rather than passively observe, we can seize the time. And the Age of Networked Intelligence will be an age of promise fulfilled.

---

2. *The Digital Economy: Promise and Peril in the Age of Networked Intelligence,* McGraw Hill, 1996.

Bottom Line: What does the intranet buy you? It buys you a place in the 21st century economy.

Summary of Key Points

- WEALTH CREATION

  In this section, you studied how to create wealth by aligning your internal processes, putting all the wood behind one arrow, and focusing your resources behind the knowledge worker. Wealth is created with each iteration of the intranet.

- ORGANIZATIONAL TRANSFORMATION

  In this section, you saw how every business theory in the last 20 years has been looking for the model to run a company that manages a constant state of change, in a global market that just won't stand still. The intranet provides a home base for these business models.

- PRODUCTIVITY

  This section highlighted how to increase productivity: accelerated communication, rapid collaborative prototyping, enabling effective teams, reduced development cycles, data warehouses, streamlined processes, increased customer satisfaction, reengineered organizations, ISO 9000 Certification. Need I say more?

- COMPETITIVE ADVANTAGE

  This section discussed your survival! Business is a system. It is organic and comprised of diverse evolving cultures. The intranet is your global system. Leveraging your knowledge workers, accelerating access to future markets, and co-evolving with stellar partners on-line gives you the needed advantage.

- DISTRIBUTED COMPUTING OR THE COLLECTIVE CONSCIOUSNESS

  This section examined what are the ramifications of being totally wired? Every individual, potentially a global partner, empowers the whole as a knowledge architect. Distributed computing changes the way we do business because we build interenterprise relationships.

CHAPTER

5

What's It Going to Cost Me?

Worldwide corporate spending on internet technologies and services more than tripled between 1994 and 1995 reaching $12 billion. Leading analysts in the business estimate that total worldwide spending on the intranet will hit $2 billion by the year 2000. *You will be the buyer.* But, how much it is going to cost depends on how you're going to use the technology. Are you building full-service, large-scale intranets? Or, are you prototyping a small intranet in one area of the company to quantify the ROI (Return on Investment)? Or are you somewhere in between?

Cost is dependent on many factors. The most obvious is the size of the company. Naturally larger companies are going to build larger intranets that interconnect people in more places around the globe. Another salient factor is the level of performance you need. Some companies need high-end workstations for clients, because they work with animation, video, and high-end graphics. The type of intranet you're going to build depends on what you are going to do with your intranet.

The technology investment (hardware, software, and administrative resources currently in your business) is fairly much the same as the IS (Information Systems) investment you've expended on your existing infrastructure. The reason for that is because your existing infrastructure is half an intranet already if you have a TCP/IP LAN in place. How you add on to extend the functionality creates the costs.

Finally, how these costs are incurred depends on the path of intranet management chosen. You can outsource your intranet completely—you can use subcontractors and partners to develop while you do the administration, or you can do everything yourself.

Costs, Costs, and More Costs

Study the costs in these pages as you build your awareness of intranet use and subsequent development. The costs will depend on how you intend to put your intranet to work for you. All of the variables have been identified here, but they may not necessarily fall within your budgeting concerns.

Look at what you've got in place, build yourself a plan to know how to proceed, and start plugging in costs one by one. Weigh them heavily against what it means to have open standards, open platforms, global communication, automated, streamlined processes, training on demand, and high transaction processing. Your competition is doing business in the cyberworld of intranet computing. Will you be ready to do business intranet to intranet? Will you have a competitive advantage?

Cost Factors

The largest cost factors affecting the development of an intranet are shown below. Use them to work with your MIS group, an Internet Service Provider (ISP), and/or a knowledgeable web consultant to develop a plan and budget for your intranet.

- *connectivity (bandwidth) options*—What applications do you want to run and how do they relate to bandwidth? The number of transactions and users affect your connectivity options. Most intranets do not have to suffer with 14.4 or 28.8 modems to communicate on-line. For graphic-intensive users, doing business publishing, T1 lines at 1.54 Mps might be your first consideration. You could start with T3 lines at 45 Mbps, but you're probably a very large organization if you're thinking along those lines. Bandwidth will be the major growing cost.

- *web server platform*—For individual access running just e-mail and news-groups, a $2,000 Pentium with a monthly connect charge of $50 is probably sufficient. For a small business access, consider a $6,000 server. Add setup and monthly connect charges to an ISP if you're a smaller business. Multiply this by the number of servers you'll need. Remember there are many different functions that servers provide, and the size of your organization determines the overall cost.

- *business publishing*—You'll need at the bare minimum $13,000 for servers, with $3,000 for setup fees, and $2,000 for monthly connect fees. Think in terms of main servers and staging servers. And, multiply by the number of servers you think you'll need. This would be dependent on the amount of information you're planning and serving. Then, examine the amount of transactions you'll be processing. Look at the server information in Chapter 3 to help decide which servers you'll need.

- *security of the network*—If you're building Internet access by allowing your employees to use international e-mail, send files and software through the Internet, and move proprietary information over the intranet, a firewall solution should be considered mandatory. It is highly recommended for an Internet gateway server. Placing the externally available web server outside your network and separating it from the corporate network with a firewall is strongly recommended. Price Range: $5,000–$25,000.

- *full annual cost of operating an intranet client*—In an enterprise environment this will be less than $2,500 per seat. Operating desktop-centric clients, WindowsNT, Win95, UNIX, and so forth, is estimated to cost between $10,000-$15,000.

- *building interactive applications*—This requires specialized programming in Java, ActiveX, VRML and Shockwave, not to mention application programming interfaces from both Netscape and Microsoft. Time is the driver and the extended or automated development tools at $1,000–2,000 per tool per developer will increase the cost. Common development $60,000–$100,000.

- *maintenance and updating of content and design*—Either off-site or on-site these costs continually rise to maintain the essence of the intranet.

- *people*—Resources are needed to plan, implement, and maintain your intranet. Start with contractors to build infrastructure. Build the foundation early. Start with a cross-functional team of people to create excitement, provide content, seek out applications, write the HTML, provide legal assistance, keep quality, and provide network support. Then develop your staff. Webmasters range between $80,000–$200,000

Types of Costs

Some costs can be somewhat predictive such as hardware, software, and administration. And, those costs are certainly driven by the size of the intranet, the quality of the performance desired, and the need to integrate your legacy network and applications. These direct costs may be the easy part of your intranet cost analysis. However, soft costs and hidden costs also need to be examined, as they may or may not impact your buying decisions.

Direct costs include outlays for hardware (servers, clients, hubs, routers, LAN/WAN technology, telephony), software, and those administrative tasks generally associated with outlays, for example, training and configuring and communications setup. Hardware costs include the network (if not installed), the servers, and the clients. Software costs include server software, client browsers, mail technologies, search engines, firewall software for security, and additional software depending on application. Some representative costs would be

- Client and server platforms

- Client browser and server software

- Application software to enhance capabilities, like replication and Web integration

- Application tools, development, and integration

- Directory administration, maintenance, document conversion, and replication

- Management and support personnel

- Gateway and management technology

- Security

- Search tools

- Gateway integration

Human resources are also necessary cost outlays. You need to supply resources for training, web planning and design, content providers, programmers, graphic artists, consultants, legal review, web testing, e-mail management, MIS support, and quality assurance.

Administrative costs include implementation, management, development, and ongoing support for the intranet, including e-mail and wide-area messaging networks, and technical administration of the central server. These costs include directory, gateway, Web management, and other activities that require personnel. Administrative costs involve the time investment of administrators that is both an organizational expenditure and an activity that creates value.

However, expense reduction can offset some of these costs, and are usually measurable. We see examples in software distribution and licensing. We see reduction in internal support calls by posting frequently asked questions or new-hire web sites in high web real estate areas. We see the reduction in printing and copying costs. Internal mail and communications experience similar cost reductions. Job postings on the intranet reduces the amount of administration and paper printing. And, the reduced use of processing, storage, and network resources occur as intranets eliminate duplication on-line.

Soft Costs/Savings

Some of the soft costs and savings are demonstrated in productivity fluctuations. Because employees have remote access to information, they can get their jobs done more efficiently. The intranet allows them to do company research and to grab information off personal home pages or find quick answers to frequently asked questions. The accuracy of their work is increased as well as the timeliness.

But, the loss of productivity due to document conversion, legacy system to intranet deployment, and distributed technological transformation procedures and policies can affect your bottom line. Intranet-related people and processes will incrementally require budgeting as you migrate to a full intranet environment. Also, because "surfing" on the web is a fun activity, many hours will be lost to surfing rather than working. This can result in a discovery learning organization in which individuals are adding to their collective knowledge, which in turn benefits the company. But, the other side of the coin suggests that corporate time is being wasted by personal searching.

Another increase in productivity is due to the emergence of a unified corporate culture. The intranet community develops on-line relationships and partners in processes and leverages off work in progress. The intranet presence builds cultural image and awareness of how the company does business, reflected in improved employee morale. Sharing of work and interests with co-workers expands, and the ability for self-expression invigorates your staff's creative potential.

Yet, customer support needs may rise. Unless you have an advanced on-line help desk to handle customer support (internal customers), then you'll have a loss in productivity because users will be spending time looking for answers and solutions themselves.

Publishing and templates must be provided to accelerate publishing on the intranet. Again, if these are nonexistent, the organization must suffer the learning curve required for employees to learn how to publish, maintain pages and servers, and build robust, interconnected intranet sites.

Security leaks may drain corporate knowledge right through the e-mail wires. The increase in security will prevent this from happening, but the loss of corporate memory and methodology might also cost your organization. The fear and uncertainty factor will have its toll on implementation, losing precious development hours.

Being aware of potential productivity fluctuations enables you to prepare for budgeting and planning. Developing a full-service intranet from the start will certainly get you over the hurdles more quickly.

Hidden Costs

Legal issues arising from information misuse may stand out as one of the prominent hidden costs. Loss of proprietary information through e-mail to the competition also causes serious delays and setbacks in scheduled production. Content provider maintenance, especially if the employee leaves the company, is among the largest hidden costs on the intranet. What happens to the information, or the maintenance and growth of a web site when the employee leaves? Often the responsibilities may be picked up by a successor. At other times, the web site goes down, breaking links all over the intranet.

These costs ebb and flow, wax and wane, but keep in mind that there are various levels of cost affecting your intranet bottom line. When the integration of the intranet meets directly with your existing IS initiatives or goals, you can count on increasing costs, especially in

- Intranet infrastructure (people, process, procedure)
- Programming time (Java, database, application development)
- Management (workflow, collaboration, interactivity)

Some of the more advanced intranets we've reviewed report hidden or unanticipated growth costs that provide necessary, unforeseen functionality for the company. Among them are

- World Wide Web integration if necessary
- Agents for profiling internal customers
- Extended abilities like faxing from the desktop, multimedia presentations
- Project management software that is intranet ready
- Forms and workflow development
- Calendars and scheduling

Try to keep these "potential costs" in line when planning your intranet.

Generational Costs

Naturally big companies are going to build bigger intranets. They are going to integrate intranets with existing LANs and WANs that connect their corporate offices with their international field offices. They're going to integrate databases and begin internal audience customer profiling with intranet agents. The costs will reflect the endeavor.

But, all companies are not grandiose in their intranet plans. In fact, their rationale suggests building small generations of intranets, gaining momentum, and encouraging innovation. Costs then depend significantly on which generation of intranet development you are in. Many small companies have all the intranet components in place. They need to focus on policies and procedures that conduct company business.

Go deeper? OK, do you have an interconnected, globally distributed communication and collaborative infostructure that any authorized mobile user can securely log in to and access well-structured, meaningful information pages created by your empowered workforce that you click on to access different departments within the organization around the world in a split second?

In most companies the answer is no.

But, what about the companies with computers on every desk, with software distributed on local area networks, perhaps even a wide area network, with a data warehouse stored in huge database files that business analysts and outside consultants use for trending and strategic planning? These companies even have standardized products, standardized reports, processes in place, quality circles meeting often.

In these companies, the answer is "kind of."

They don't have the interconnected, globally distributed, communication and collaborative infostructure that any authorized mobile user can securely log in to and access well-structured, meaningful information pages created by your empowered workforce that you click on to access different departments within the organization around the world in a split second? At least not yet.

No matter which size of a company you are, or what level of technology you've matured to, it is apparent that the company benefits if everyone goes on-line. How you go on-line, what processes you move onto the intranet, and how you use them to profile your internal and external customers to assist in making better products and information drive the costs for your intranet development. This is what deploying an intranet is all about, company involvement and shared intelligence.

If you are starting out small, making just one department grow, you won't need a full-service suite of programs and hardware to coordinate the next Space Shuttle flight. You'll scale to your needs obviously. You need to determine how many user transactions will take place. Netscape boasts over 1,000,000 transactions a day on their enterprisewide server. To determine the number of transactions, take a quick look at five variations of intranet evolution. Each type increases the number of transactions and the amount of security you need.

- Basic intranets—costs of communication

- Publishing/library intranets—costs of project management

- Collaborative Intranets—costs of product/service development

- Transactional intranet—costs of the infostructure

- Extranets—costs of e-commerce

Basic Intranets—Costs of Communication   When many companies set up basic intranets, it allows them to communicate on-line around the company. This is actually fairly new in global business. You can e-mail anybody at any time within the company and get a response back fairly quickly. You also set up simple HTTP servers with HTML web pages. Now you can electronically store and share global data, messages, and software all linked through visual hypermedia.

Attaching documents to e-mail extends the basic intranet into even a more powerful intranet where participation is dramatically increased, information is shared in more elegant documents, and decisions are made quickly and interactively.

In many people's minds, e-mail is the soul of the intranet. It certainly is the simplest intranet of all. And you can see how powerful it is already in transforming an organization into a more intelligent and open enterprise.

To build this level of intranet is very inexpensive. You need a basic LAN running TCP/IP, a centralized server, a mail server, access to a computer for each recipient, some software, and an administrator.

It doesn't take long before users want e-mails stored in different directories for retrieval. E-mail usage accelerates quickly once it is in place. Transactions can start out as low as 10 percent of your workforce creating 20 e-mail messages a day in the first few months of operation, to nearly 90 percent creating 40 messages a day within the first year. E-mail messages are subsumed shortly by access to web pages. The number of transactions per day at each server can increase from 50 hits per day to hundreds of thousands per day.

Soon directory management and historical access to intranets with a common database are desirable. The basic intranet naturally evolves into the publishing library intranet.

Publishing Library Intranet—Costs of Project Management   Soon you evolve past the e-mail and web page phase of intranets and start creating a larger publishing library. You introduce more advanced intranet skills such as CGI (Common Gateway Interface) programming, and search engine technology and create a centralized intranet web site that acts as a publisher's clearinghouse for all the web sites and web groups that begin to form on the intranet.

Instead of e-mail and personalized web pages to manage projects, users publish centralized web sites that store vast specialized libraries of information to help employees with projects.

Publishing library intranet costs include document management, version control, document conversion, improved multimedia and hypermedia scripting environments, and specialized servers for storing and managing data libraries (including text, graphics, animation, and video). Resource costs increase due to personnel for maintaining additional servers, managing resources, content, and process.

You invest money in creating a common look and feel and introducing polices and procedures for operating in a publishing library intranet. Training costs, or help desk support systems, introduce their needs into the cost picture. Bandwidth costs soar because of the increased bandwidth requirements for high-end software helper applications.

The soft costs affect you more at this level. Some groups are project oriented and cross functional. They only last for a short period of time, building a product, planning a strategy, storing valuable information, creating new opportunities. Then they disengage. If they build on the intranet, their legacy information is not maintained by the group and disappears.

Intact groups, on the other hand, are more cohesive and maintain their legacy information on their individual servers. CGI scripts tie together processes and relational data. Intact workgroups (sales, marketing, operations, training) set up publishing library intranet sites to help leverage organizational memory.

Since intact groups form and the intranet begins to form at a systemic level, the costs of creating and maintaining the intranet are dispersed throughout the various functional organizations. Naturally the heavy users end up footing the bill. This usually means marketing communications, sales, engineering, and human resources.

The need to centralize communication and intranet architecture control pushes the costs into the information technology group (MIS). The intranet begins to evolve into a vehicle for collaborating, combining skills, resources, and human effort and the costs begin to blur into the cost of doing business. Revenue increases are not seen because no commodity artifact is created by the intranet. And nothing can potentially be attributed to the bottom line.

Collaborative Intranets—Costs of Product/Service Development Collaborative intranet costs include increased forms-based programming to capture business process and events into a form-oriented interactivity site on-line. CGI scripting and integration of collaboration software is labor intensive. Forms-based software and existing CGI libraries reduce the collaborative intranet costs somewhat. But costs occur in extending these capabilities to integrate robust application software interfaces with the intranet, such as Lotus Domino, Netscape's Collabra, or Microsoft's NetMeeting products.

The main purpose of a collaborative intranet is to enhance product development, especially if product development results in a software or knowledge product. Because collaboration integrates existing knowledge products into datamarts (small stores of business objects which can be used or purchased for integration into the development of a product), they incur the increased costs of storage, administration, maintenance, support, and distribution. Organizations develop few products that do not include knowledge products to accompany their products (marketing collateral, manuals, procedures, processes, training, communication, or support).

If an organization has already integrated a collaborative or work group solution into their information infrastructure, the costs of migration (or integration) and potential retraining costs need to be figured into the cost-benefit analysis.

Collaborative intranets allow different parts of the organization to integrate their functions across groups. The organizational structures that evolve out of collaborative intranets create reusable on-line processes, or business objects. Other organizations that might want to develop similar software solutions might want to leverage some of these collaborative intranet artifacts, or datamarts.

Transactional Intranets—Costs of the Infostructure As your organization builds its intranet acumen, it sees that many of the processes that you use to build products, provide service, and distribute information around the company could be radically improved. Collaborative intranets provide a usability testing ground to evaluate the product development or service effectiveness within your organization.

With refined business objects stored in datamarts, the organization must integrate all of its processes together now in order to move to a fully integrated on-line transaction processing intranet. The data warehouse, the juxtaposition of all relational databases and web sites, allows you to incorporate lessons learned with commodity enterprisewide transactional environments on-line.

The enterprise intranet migrates the on-line network experience to a full-service transaction environment, where classical organizational transactions move the intranet onto common desktop web pages and fully integrate with relationship databases in the background. The full integration of automated business process, including finance, purchasing, accounting, sales, marketing, engineering, operations, and certified learning comes into full deployment.

The implementation, training, and on-going support costs associated with an intranet are very small in comparison to the way you've been doing business over mainframes and proprietary client/server systems. Intranets make an ideal foundation for

- Engineering Change Order (ECO)
- Staff and end-user training
- Distributing technical information
- Enterprise software licensing
- Purchase requisitioning
- On-line expense reporting
- Customer tracking through support
- Financial reporting
- Posting patches and FAQs (Frequently Asked Questions)

This fully integrated environment cannot come into existence without going through the evolution of the intranet. So many of the costs that were incurred during the development of your basic intranet into a collaborative intranet are already outlaid. And at this stage, many of the costs of doing business are drastically reduced. The processes have been automated in back-office applications and pulled by the user whenever needed.

When you move all your internal processes on-line, you require full service intranet connections. You need a messaging system (e-mail); you need servers for multiple distributed purposes, especially security, caching, staging and proxy servers, you need thin clients (fast machines without hard drive consuming operating systems) with TCP/IP on every machine. You need a strong Web administrative staff with every application interface programming skills; you need database integrators and research in Java, ActiveX, Shockwave, VRML.

The costs of developing internal network-centric applications and maintaining an infostructure within the organization begin to integrate with the existing network and information technology costs. To defray some of the impact on the information technology group, some of the costs are distributed to the user who manages cost in development, content, maintenance, support, training, and so forth.

Instead of calculating each of these costs separately, you may easily be entering the realm of the cost of doing business as the intranet becomes your main critical information and communication device in the organization. You've restaffed, or reorganized your organization to focus solely on the intranet. Your costs simply support the intranet as operational costs.

Consider reduced manufacturing rework and lead times. Consider shorter manufacturing and sales cycles, lower overhead, and minimal support! Intranets are simple to use and allow access from almost any workstation anywhere. Each access or each transaction becomes an activity that you can quantify in some way. Up to 1 million transactions can occur a day for mature intranets. The manufacturing of the knowledge products and the delivery of the full intranet services can be statistically measured and repartnered for superior expert quality.

We'll look at the metrics for examining costs in Chapter 7.

Extranets—Costs of E-Commerce   Most companies are not yet ready for inter-enterprise computing (extranets), that is, partnering or integrating with other intranets outside the organization. The internal intranet is the first step. Develop a strong, internal business model that knows how to evaluate customer needs (feedback on web sites), turn customer needs into actions (streamlined human information processing), which in turn become products and services delivered to the customer on-time, on-budget, on-demand. Then, you can integrate with other fine-tuned intranets to excel in partner relations.

You need to convert your company into a living, organic intranet that focuses all its attention, processes, business, and potential on the customer. The costs are again immeasurable as few companies have succeeded in attaining this level of intranet development. But a strong, well managed, focused intranet can be leveraged when partnering with interenterprises intranets outside your domain.

The costs of doing business to external partners reside in security enhancement to your intranet and payment software for Electronic Funds Transfers. Additionally, staff resources will increase due to the need for new competency. Add to that the cost of more robust search engines and additional software.

Summary of Costs

Table 5–1 provides an overview of potential costs for intranets based on size. In Table 5–2, Sun Microsystems, Inc. provides a table for intranet components. I've also inlcuded e-commerce costs for those planning on developing extranets from the beginning.

Table 5-1 Summary of Intranet Costs Based on Size

	Basic	Mid-Size	Large
Overall costs	50–100K/year	200–300K/year	300K+1.SM/year
Value	Server, ISP, design, consulting	Interactive sales, catalogs, publish-ing environment	Full-scale enterprise, intranet applications, internet e-commerce

Table 5-2 Itemized Cost Items

Item	Appropriate Cost in Dollars (1 Year)
Server	$20,000
Web server software	$5,000–$20,000
ISP fee (if chosen)	$10,000–$50,000
Application development costs	$60,000
Webmaster	$80,000–$200,000
Other support staff	$80,000–$200,000
FOR EXTRANETS	
Internet circuit	$6,000–$10,000
Payment software for EFT (Electronic Funds)	$5,000–$20,000
Customer service staff	$60,000
Additional software, such as catalog or search engine	$6,000–$20,000

Data courtesy of Sun Microsystems, Inc.

Cost Savings

Chief Information Officers (CIOs) face very specific problems. Infrastructure costs are very high and getting higher. The non-intranet strategy load a complex operating system—hundreds of applications and corresponding data on each desktop. Configure it and support it. When you have 25,000 workstations and 400 applications, that makes 1,000,000 individual network connections. It is impossible to manage.

A simple change in technology is capable of restructuring the costs of intranet deployment dramatically. For example, the Java friendly web top where the OS (Operating System), the applications, and the data are all kept on the web, not on the client, could eliminate huge overhead costs for client maintenance. The client, or Web top, is "thin." That means that the processing is done on the server, leaving the client to display vital information at rapid speeds. Administration is free, because everything comes off the Net. You have a big win that is really dramatic. In a large organization, you could save nearly millions of dollars a year.

Examples of Cost Savings

As we continue to approach the potential of the intranet as a secure data and applications server, we also move closer to realizing its range of benefits to companies. For many businesses, the use of corporate intranets can greatly reduce hardware investments and maintenance costs as well as administrative support burdens. Companies that recognize this potential and are first to develop practical applications for organizational intranet computing will be on the leading edge of providing this important new technology.

To gain maximum benefits from new technologies, corporate IT (Information Technology) plans must aggressively consider how intranets will affect corporate resources. Following are some examples of how intranets have affected the bottom line.

Sun   Sun has some incredible cost savings stories. One such area is in internal communication. Table 5–3 provides some examples of familiar internal communications that have traditionally been done using paper and print media. Once your company provides electronic access to all or most of the company employees, newsletters, job postings, and benefits information can be communicated over the intranet. At Sun, newsletters and updates to employee communications are delivered over the e-mail system, worldwide, and interested employees are encouraged to download and print only what they need.

The cost savings per unit is based on the cost to copy and distribute via traditional interoffice mail envelopes. Benefits information involves two-way electronic communications. Employees can make changes in their benefits program via the intranet, saving the cost of face-to-face meetings for routine changes. Sun estimates this could save at least $8.00 per transaction as the face-to-face meeting or phone call is no longer needed.

Marketing product information is disseminated in the same fashion. Sun has 9,000+ products, so updates are constant. By communicating changes and publishing updated documents via the intranet, Sun achieves substantial savings versus traditional paper interoffice mail.

You can find similar activities in your organization and determine estimated unit costs as Sun did. The hard savings in paper, printing, and handling help justify and fund your intranet investment. Improved communication is just an extra benefit!

Table 5-3 Sun's Internal Communications Savings *

	Units	Units Cost	Savings
Internal newsletters	28,000	$0.74	$21,000
Job listings	52,000	$.074	$41,000
Employee benefits	14,000	$8.00	$112,000
Marketing updates	235,000	$0.66	$115,000

*per month.
Courtesy of Jerry Neece, Internet Marketing Manager, Sun Microsystems

These figures look great. It would seem from the very cost savings that the organization could afford to purchase more web technology, thus continuously improving both the hardware and tools budget.

Another area where Sun has seen costs savings is in the reduced use of corporate processing/storage/networking resources. Figures from Sun indicate that an average 500K printed document roughly costs $500 to transmit globally. To store the same document, $3,250 was needed to manage the document the old distributed way. When you move production and distribution on-line, expending 2K of resources to notify everyone of the URL, the transmission costs you $2.00 and the storage costs $13.25. This is a total savings of $3,734.75. Of course, you'll need to subtract 10 percent more to account for those who still print the documents.

FedEx[1]   Federal Express has already discovered the benefits of their intranet, including the affordability and speed of setting it up because the hardware and networking were already in place. Most importantly, however, Federal Express has found that a platform which enables them to deliver up-to-date information to their employees and allow easy, universal information access is the best way to maintain their edge in the time-sensitive business of package delivery.

Sandia National Labs[2]   Government agencies are always at risk of budget cuts and often look to technology to find ways to cut internal costs. Sandia National Laboratories has harnessed the power of the World Wide Web inside the laboratory to increase employee productivity and reduce computing expenses.

Sandia's intranet provides enterprisewide access to all corporate information— databases, financial data, policies, engineering and manufacturing data, newsletters, bulletins, and administrative information. Every major department has a home page on the web. In addition, corporate applications are loaded into HTML from SQL and other UNIX applications.

The labs' intranet helps it cut costs in several ways, including better management of mainframe resources, lower application development costs, reduced printing and distribution costs, and more productive employees who have direct access to the information they need to do their jobs.

Sandia wanted to get better access to financial and corporate data on its mainframe. The mainframe was difficult to use and was getting bogged down because it was used by employees throughout the company to access and view data. Their intranet allows them to develop one forms-based interface for an application. They can implement it on a server one time and all employees can download the application themselves. This cuts down greatly on development and distribution costs.

Cost Tips

Before you start costing out all the expenses and determining the potential cost savings, we've included a few cost tips that the experts swear by. The main idea is don't skimp on hardware servers and leverage internal resources when you can. When you can't train your internal resources, the skills are usually quite easy to acquire. And, only use consultants when you have to. It's hard to find one who really understands your business and the technology at the same time. The effort of automating your organization will do best in your own hands with the experts developing the processes.

Hardware Platform Costs   When it comes to hardware servers, reliable TCP/IP connectivity, and increased bandwidth, you don't want to save money and then lose reliability and availability. You simply don't want to skimp. You want to get the best equipment you can, from the sources who know what the intranet is.

---

2.   Copyright 1996, Netscape Communications Corp. All rights reserved. This page may be not be reprinted or copied without the express written permission of Netscape.

For multiple users supported by Netscape Navigator, or Microsoft Internet Explorer, a shared intranet server is recommended. The high-end intranet-ready servers offer a complete solution with easy to administer intranet software and support. Remember you need a gateway access server to provide electronic mail, FTP support, and other Internet services. Prices range from $3,000–6,000.

For mounting a web server, a higher capacity machine with large disc capacity and fast I/O is recommended, except for small sites. A web server should have a minimum disk size of 1 Gb and 32 M memory, and upgrade potential should be considered. Prices start around $10,000. A machine in this category can handle as many as 400,000 transactions per day when the average transaction size is 10K. It can easily support a T1 connection.

For large companies and very active web sites, multiple web servers should be considered to provide redundancy, parallel processing, and to service international locations where local Web "mirrored" servers will provide improved response time.

Make sure your server supports any of these connections: Ethernet; Token Ring; ISDN (Integrated Services Digital Network); high-speed serial/PPP, which is a protocol that allows computers to use TCP/IP to connect to other computers over a standard phone line using high-speed modems; and direct T1 connections. Can it be upgraded to multiple processors? Can you add memory, disks, multiple network segment connections, enhanced security features?

Bandwidth. In choosing your connection strategy, it is important to consider the amount of graphics and sound to be downloaded and the number of concurrent transactions anticipated. It is important to ensure that if you're using an ISP (Internet Service Provider) that they have the capacity to increase your bandwidth as your intranet activity grows. For 50 concurrent users (simultaneous access) T1 (1.54 Mbps) is recommended. But remember, bandwidth is your most valuable resource.

Leverage Internal Resources. Use your existing internal staff, equipment, and resources within the organization to reduce potential costs. You have a healthy group of information knowledge workers who have never had the tools in their hands before to create an infostructure. They know what work needs to be done, they know which tools they wish they had, they know which things have to change in the organization, given an opportunity.

Training Internal Staff. If you have the internal resources, use them, but if you don't think they've got the necessary skill set, consider training them before you outsource immediately. The reality is that there are no real experts out there yet in your field and the intranet. You need to develop them. It is quite possible that retraining knowledge workers in a couple of areas could result in some significant savings.The payoff is better when you keep intellectual property stored in the organization. The idea of consultants moving from company to company, moving intellectual property from one laboratory to another can be quite debilitating to an enterprise.

Training costs can be reduced by creating on-line training and by maintaining all training materials on-line. Further interactive environments, with apprenticeships on-line, are additional ways to reducing the heavy learning load and sufferable long waits to get into a class that seats only 20. The best advise is that current internal staff learns best by doing.

Use Consultants Only When Necessary. Don't spin your wheels trying to develop something that could be easily handled by an outside consultant who has designed, installed, and administered intranets innumerable times. This is a new field, and you won't find a lot of consultants who have the full picture. Some of the consultants will be technical and can give you a considerable leg up. However, when it comes to internal business processes, or streamlining workflow, you might run into huge deficits. With consultants, you get what you pay for. Look for consultants that come from large internet companies, or large system integrator companies. Go with the well-rounded consultants who have as much business acumen as they do technical acumen.

Costs of Going Outside the Intranet

With the information in Chapter 3, you can measure the hardware and software pieces that you need to build a sophisticated intranet. Once you build your super-intranet architecture, start examining which business processes you want to focus on to prepare you for doing business with the customers, partners, and vendors directly outside your intranet.

In Table 5–4, you can see that business processes are tied directly to costs. Depending on whether you're automating business processes on the Intranet or building extranet processes on the Internet, you must consider the architecture and intrastructure needed to support them.

We've repeated several times that what you're going to do with your intranet will drive development and maintenance costs. You can count on that building your intranet will be only 25 percent of your budget, while managing, administering, and creating content will be the other 75 percent.

Table 5-4 Business Processes Identify Intranet Development

Business Process	Internet or Intranet Development	Architecture and Infrastructure
Finding Customers	INTERNET Educate and prequalify your potential customers on your outside internet pages.	Server outside the firewall, and proxy server to run firewall software. Webmaster and a development team to program interactive, market-driven forms.
Gathering Customer Requirements and Interaction	INTRANET and INTERNET Create a sales and marketing web on the Intranet that allows sales staff to profile customers and manage their requirements on-line. Make requirements available to others in the intranet for input. Develop an outside mechanism for customer to view this profile.	Full enterprisewide intranet connecting everyone in the organization. This is the bulk of your development efforts. See Chapter 6 for templates and guidance on construction.
Adjusting to Strategic Markets	INTRANET Use your centralized intranet home page to keep the entire company aware of changes in markets, customers, and requirements.	Web publisher and a staff of producers, editors, writers, and graphic artists. The need here is to maintain the absorption level of current knowledge.
Partnering with Outside Vendors, Suppliers, Resellers, and Customers	INTERNET and INTRANET Use secured electronic escorts to bring partners into various stages of product development, especially in development and distribution.	Full-Service intranet with e-commerce secured servers. Firewall software, staff to manage internal entry into the network.
Celebrate Success	INTERNET and INTRANET Announce your customer success stories prominently on both outside/inside pages for future customers and future process improvements.	Bottle of champagne and catered dinner.

Customer Costs

To conduct business with any customer, internal or external, you need to build a communication intranet that delivers—24 hours a day, 7 days a week—information services to anyone within your organization and directly into the heart of the customer. The model is to build a data repository. Tell the story of your company, your products, and how your products fit into the needs of the customer. You can interact with the customer as much as possible, and develop a profile of the customer. For that you'll need connection to the Internet, a server outside the firewall, a proxy server to run firewall software, and a Webmaster and a development team to program interactive, market-driven forms.

Customer Requirements and Interaction Costs

Next you'll need to model how to conduct sales and marketing over the intranet. Your internal employees all need to know how their processes feed into sales and marketing, so that when there is contact directly with the customer, both the customer's story and the one being told by the salesperson are identical.

This calls for the building of a sales marketing web. The sales and marketing webs are a pivotal achievement on any successful intranet and consequently can be the most expensive. The salesperson in the field has got to be able to access company databases for information, pricing, quotes, demos, and so forth. The sales group has got to have a place where they can learn, configure, assess competitive strengths, and integrate strategies with the customer by using the shared corporate memory. The internal sales and marketing web has got to be as robust as the reseller's web, the vendor web, and the customer transaction web.

This may need a dedicated server, and possible servers across the various regional areas. Consider a sales and marketing gatekeeper and a pool of content providers. Existing sales infrastructure and processes can be automated. Create a reseller extended intranet.

High-Performance Development Teams

Once the sales and transaction environment is set up, then the next web area has to be developed for the engineering, manufacturing, operations, design, and development folks. The intranet connects project schedules, project management, sharing of prototypes, and all forms of documentation. The collaborative processing model has been discussed already. Hard costs are always hardware, software, and resources. The soft costs are redesigning processes between departments and retraining staff. The hidden costs are suffered from individuals not being able to compete or perform in this technologically demanding environment and excellent resources and processes fail from inexperience.

Full enterprisewide intranet connecting everyone in the organization is needed. This is the bulk of your development efforts. See Chapter 6 for templates and guidance on construction.

Strategy Costs

The intranet needs to keep the employees in a constant state of progressive flux. Why? Because everything is changing so fast. Whenever something changes in the strategy between the customer and the organization, the entire intranet audience must be kept aware of that change. Awareness occurs on the central intranet home page designed to inform the entire organization of highly mission-critical strategic information. Supplemental e-mail sent to every machine, or an announcement flashing on the screen when you log in, are all incremental assurance to strategically align everyone in the company. The level of communication has to be designed and factored into the costs of administration.

Budget for a Web publisher and a staff of producers, editors, writers, and graphic artists. The Web publisher can work from the existing intranet structure without any special requirements. The need is to maintain the employee's absorption level of current knowledge.

Partnering Costs

You can't build it all and you can't maintain it all. Subcontracting, partnering, and outsourcing are all going to occur. You need to identify two things:

1. Which partners are going to be allowed access into your intranet to help build key components and maintain them?
2. Which partners are going to provide you fixed, services to speed up your development time?

When you bring in outside partners, you must accommodate for security risks, and recovery of lost processes. A full service intranet with e-commerce secured servers, firewall software, staff to manage internal entry into the network, webmasters, gatekeepers, and content providers are all needed. This area will blossom the most and will take the biggest pull on your network.

Cost of Success

For every great merger, ideal partnership, or delighted customer satisfaction, the sound of success is sweet. The stories you can tell about a successful deal are valuable to future customers and to your internal employees. Celebrate with a live event on your intranet, where everyone participates and either views, listens to, or dazzles in a Shockwave-like announcement that you've hit the big one again. The information you provide on-line to tell these success stories become global databases of what works well, weaving a visual story of the best groups, departments, or companies to do business with—a library of excellence.

A word of warning. Success can easily cave in on you. You can have too much success raising expectations. Your users may begin to require more bandwidth, ore performance, more storage space that you planned to provide. Once knowledge access and measurable knowledge use become productivity issues, you may discover you have many unforeseen costs hitting your books. Make sure you fully understand the success that information availability has on your organization. Done well intranets will reduce costs.

Cost Samplings

We've examined a lot of scenarios for building an intranet. We all know that variables are different in each business infostructure development plan. The ownership and responsibility of the intranet is yours. You know your business, your employees know their tools and processes, the customer knows your quality. When costing this out, look first inside your company to answer how you'll use the intranet. Then, renew your relationship with the MIS department so they can estimate the best cost value for your information needs. Turning to consultants with cross-industry intranet experience is an alternative.

Bottom Line: Prices and services vary widely worldwide and change rapidly. Three different price quotes will serve you well.

Intranet Systems and Components

In order to understand costs ranges, you'll first need to look at the intranet systems and their components. You have to understand the range of the components that you need for the tasks that you wish to complete on your intranet.

Table 5–5 reviews the intranet systems and components needed. The range of components and tasks for your intranet solution again vary on what you're going to do with the intranet, or what type of intranet you wish to develop.

Numbers are not used in this table because of the enormous fluctuation in pricing structures in the intranet industry. Consider these as evaluative categories of individual costs. Continue researching intranet usage in your company, so you can calculate the costs more efficiently for your organization.

Table 5-5 Intranet Systems and Scale of Components and Tasks

Intranet System	Scale of Components and Tasks
Server platform, including software	News server, mail server, directory server, enterprisewide server, proxy server, certificate server, name server, and server software for each configuration
Client platform, including software	Webtops, PCs, workstations TCP/IP, browser software, e-mail, productivity software
Product capability Software	Agents, search engines, plug-ins (audio/video and multimedia presentation enhancements), Shockwave, VRML programming. Administrative position for support and mgmt.
RDMBS access	Vendor intranet/RDMBS connectivity software, light CGI programming, Java, Active X or other application development interfaces
Security, firewalls	Firewall software and server, security audits requirements analysis, network topology, hardware, operating system, user applications
Application development	CGI programming, Java/ActiveX programming, JB Scipting, Lotus Script, and Visual Basic Scripting API tools and forms development software
Intranet administration	Adherence to procedures for publishing. Directory maintenance, directory synchronization, link management, web statistical analysis.
Intranet management	Controlling information on the web server Webmasters, gatekeepers, content providers, technical staff web planning and design Legal review, e-mail management, IS support, quality assurance

Gartner Group Estimate

The Gartner Group estimates the total cost per seat of PC platforms to be $11,900 per year.[3] Client configuration annual full cost per year heterogeneous, highly customized fat clients and servers (Wintel, UNIX, OS/2, Mac, MVS, etc.) with primarily local applications and local data file storage cost between $10,000–$15,000 per seat per year.

Homogeneous, standardized fat clients and servers (i.e., clients and servers are desktop-centric and binary-compatible—Solaris clients and Solaris servers, for example) will cost you between $9,000–$12,000 per seat per year. X-terminal clients backed up by very high bandwidth network infrastructures and high-performance servers run between $7,000–$8,000 per seat per year.

Diskless clients backed up by very high bandwidth network infrastructures and high-performance file servers cost $6,000–$7,000 per seat per year. Homogeneous dataless clients with all applications and data files stored on servers of the same architecture, for example, Solaris servers dataless Solaris clients that have a local hard disk only for virtual memory run between $4,000–$5,000 per seat per year.

These data are based upon the experience at Sun of moving to a homogeneous dataless network architecture for its 35,000 internal-use network nodes. The savings of moving from fat to dataless clients has already been captured internally by Sun. Projected cost of dataless thin clients with all applications and data files stored on servers and generally executed on clients that include a hard disk for virtual memory (i.e., Java devices): less than $2,500 per seat per year.

This estimate is based on an analysis and extension of the cost elements of the homogeneous dataless environment that has already been implemented internally by Sun.

Forrester Research Cost Estimate

Forrester's analysis concludes that Web site costs vary by business objectives and vary from about $300,000 for promotional sites, to $1.3 million for content sites, and to nearly $3.4 million for transaction sites. These costs will rise 52 percent to 231 percent between now and the year 2000 because of increasing staff costs and new web security and interactive technologies.

---

3.   Gartner Group, Strategic Planning Research Note SPA-140-22, April 26, 1996.

Table 5–6[4] provides a breakdown of the 12-month costs (all figures in thousands). These figures are for external sites; however, they can be used to estimate internal sites, as well.

Table 5-6 Cost Estimates for Promotion, Content, and Transaction Sites

Item	Promotion Site (the Internet)	Content Site	Transaction Site
Platform	$52K	$252K	$675K
Service	$237K	$813K	$1,910K
Marketing	$15K	$247K	$783K
Total	$305K	$1,312K	$3,368K

The main reasons for increasing costs in the future, Forrester cites, are new technologies, rapid and unpredictable growth, lack of loyalty to vendors, and labor demand outstrips supply.

Market Expectations

One last piece of information to consider in planning and budgeting for your intranet is that the external markets are gearing up to help you spend your money. The figures in Table 5–7 estimate that the global internet market is expected to soar to $12 billion. Although these figures are for the internet market segments, they explain the revenue goals of companies who will be building your intranets. From this table, you can anticipate spending hard dollars in these segments.

Table 5-7 Forecast by Market Segment by CyberAtlas

Forecast by Market Segment	Year 1995 ($M)	Year 2000 ($M)
Network services (ISPs)	$300	$5,000
Hardware (routers, modems, computer hardware)	500	2,500
Software (server, applications)	300	4,000

4.   Source: Forrester Research, Inc., Cambridge, MA.

Table 5-7 Forecast by Market Segment by CyberAtlas *(Continued)*

Forecast by Market Segment	Year 1995 ($M)	Year 2000 ($M)
Enabling services (electronic commerce, directory services, web tracking)	20	1,000
Expertise (system integrators, business consultants)	50	700
Content and activity (on-line entertainment, information, shopping)	500	10,000
Total Market	$1,170	$23,200
Reprinted with permission from CyberAtlas from I/PRO, owners of CyberAtlas at http://www.cyberatlas.com/market.html.		

ROI versus Human Performance Improvement

With the technology changing as rapidly as it is, we seriously doubt if network designers are mapping out five year plans and implementing them with periodic measurements of ROI. Initially, companies bought what they could afford, like a PC on every desktop. After a couple of years of upgrades, backup disasters, software incompatibility nightmares, and so forth, someone in the organization wises up to open network computing and begins to leverage upward compatible approaches to scaling their network computing needs.

That's when the company bites the bullet and shells out the money to install a real production network. That's the point when it's possible to look at longer-term ROI and managed growth and productivity.

Cost Savings and ROI

Keep in mind that your first sign of recouping your investment comes in the form of cost savings. Publishing costs and human resource administration seem to be the first areas to save you money. However, the "intangible" benefits are the real drivers of the return on investment. There are some cues from the past to consider when looking at ROI.

- Large systems don't get ROI'd.
- Telephone systems don't get ROI'd.

- Training doesn't get ROI'd.
- Human performance doesn't get ROI'd.

Nonetheless, because we are integrating technology so seamlessly, we look at ROI only to determine the "usability" of information with other business processes and business transactions.

Productivity Gains

End-user productivity gains created by improved functionality of the intranet's feature set returns dollars back to the organization, sometimes in an "intangible" or in an "indirect" manner. The openness of intranet architecture enables increases in productivity or communication among employees. Work is done faster, more efficiently in less cycle time.

The shareability of information is another factor that improves productivity. Collaboration improves project management and development cycles are reduced, again gaining in productivity and most definitely returning to the bottom line. Also, applications can be developed on the server and distributed globally simply by e-mailing users. Again, a cost savings in time, and an increase in productivity.

Finally, the additional time users are not involved in training because the Intranet's ease of use is another productivity gain. The hours or days spent in training can result in additional sales profits or increased time on task. Certainly, these costs or cost savings can be somewhat soft. Who has ever really been able to quantify the effects associated with "lost opportunities" or "gained productivity." Even more so, who has effectively measured increased human performance? Most human performance technologists are hard pressed to come up with significant studies leaving the "real" ROI to be elusive.

Bottom Line: Human performance has not really been measured effectively.

Although these ROI figures are generated from cost savings and additional revenues of improved processes, such high ROI figures indicate that intranets are certainly a low-risk implementation in an organization. Although many large systems like this are not ROI'd, there is significant evidence that suggests that some significant ROI is being realized.

Imagine the scene—a shift in thinking makes the staff act differently. When they act differently, they perform differently. Determining what those variables are that affect "a shift in thinking" will always be difficult to capture in an organization.

Many different models are used in organizations to determine performance. However, little ever results in hard numbers. This is where risk assessment comes into play. And, this is where you have to look at the stockholders and say "faith is the determinant factor."

In Chapter 7 we'll examine some new research that suggests certain human performances may be observable over intranets.

In a preliminary report entitled *The Intranet: Slashing the Cost of Business* published by IDCs Providers of market information industry analysis, and strategic and tactical guiders to builders, providers, and user of information technology, at http://www.netscape.com/comprod/announce/roi.html

> Return on investment studies of Netscape intranets found the typical ROI well over 1000%—far higher than usually found with any technology investment. Adding to the benefit, with payback periods ranging from six to twelve weeks, the cost of an Intranet is quickly recovered—making the risk associated with an Intranet project low.

> The results to date clearly show that for any company, not just those already contemplating an Intranet, the best strategy is to begin an intranet deployment today. The sooner an intranet becomes a core component of the corporate technology infrastructure, the sooner the company can reap the benefits. Some reports indicate a 1000% ROI in Cost Savings.

Trends that Will Evolve Cost

Perhaps because internet investments remain notoriously difficult to justify, consultants are proclaiming with glee that intranet ROI is both measurable and impressive. However, these studies are somewhat beside the point. Intranets don't need ROI justification any more than telephone or training systems, because they are becoming a fundamental part of companies' core infrastructures. Building, managing, and maintaining them is simply a cost of doing business.

The demands for more diverse applications and strengthened networks will grow significantly in the society of the early 21st century. Requirements for the info-communications system are set out below. The way in which infocommunications is used will also evolve.

Making Business On-Line More Real

As we explore the depths of doing business over the intranets, we will want to extend our ability to express ourselves more as we do in real life. We'll want to interconnect telephones with the full intranet experience; we'll want to create on-line environments that will enable us to have the same advantages we get from face-to-face meetings, or casual lunches or time on the golf course. Somehow we'll need to integrate our social environment with our on-line environment to benefit from all the ways of doing business.

Many forms of expression today combine images, audio, and video. These systems are exciting in their innovation but slow in their increasing bandwidth demands. Demand for simulated experiences on-line using these multimedia will create a demand for pushing technology. Perhaps it will drive us into inventions that don't exist yet. We've got core technology, but we certainly haven't explored all the variations of using it to create more real experiences for us while we move to e-commerce and intranets.

Multiparticipant Interactivity

User interactivity means making choices and having influence on the outcomes of your decisions. The need to develop interactivity will increase and affect the way we do business on-line. This will promote a shift from one-way information to multiparticipant interactivity. The two-way media solutions will drive our intranets to improve, and the needs of individuals to transmit information will also increase.

Getting immediate feedback will become a priority. This doesn't mean a response in e-mail either. It means something like an immediate video link to an expert, or a group of experts, to share in your decision-making process. You will be able to get consulting on demand with industry leaders and visionaries simply by asking for it over the intranet. The development of these environments will affect the increasing costs of the intranet.

More User Profiling and Agent Technology

Users come in so many different packages—some like aural or audio information, some are visual, preferring video, and some like to slowly look at the juxtapositions between text and graphics to gather needed information for improved performance. The user will need to see the technology to understand their needs more adequately in order not to waste time.

Agent technology and user profiling databases will affect the intranet's evolution. Users will want recognition of natural language and vaguely uttered keywords to be understood by the researching mechanisms of the intranet. They'll want web crawlers or agent technologies to crawl over the intranet to determine what information may be important and will diagnose and prescribe follow-up by each user. Agent technology will learn functions which enable action to be taken on the user's behalf. This technology may replace existing search engines, changing the costs only marginally.

Temporal and Geographic Expansion

Thanks to mobile communications systems, individuals need never be cut off from access to information in any aspect of their lives. The need for a global communications capacity, regardless of time or place, will inevitably arise. Users will be able to enter their intranet with increased security from anywhere in the world, either working with a wireless connection or accessing intranets over satellites or cellular connections.

The cost of security will be affected most dramatically. The costs of losing information to hackers will also increase.

Sharing Information

Functions which allow people to access information on ideas, knowledge, and social events whenever they want will assume greater salience. This will require creation of a database of past and present events, and people will have to have free access to that database in terms of time and place. Individuals will be able to exchange information readily. This will promote the creation of "information-oriented communities," which will gradually replace traditional communities.

Economies of Scale

Many successful intranets now consider their intranets as mission-critical resources. Consequently, streamlining the network architecture and infrastructure to accommodate for intranet development will occur in various economies of scale. The larger the organization, the more quickly you'll see the emergence of a full-service intranet.

The usual evolution starts with the organization offering departments the option of setting up dedicated sites on shared "home page servers." Additionally, they set up caching and proxy servers at strategic points around the company in order to bring mission-critical servers into a controlled environment. There's a cost benefit, because people don't administer their own web site if they're truly focused on creating content. Larger companies can afford to distribute the responsibilities. By helping to reduce the sheer number of web servers in the company, the shared systems decrease network load and improve end-user performance.

In smaller companies that might not even have a full information technology management group, you can expect to see more technical and strategic skills in your intranet developers. These people will not be easy to find, so anticipate paying for them if you want someone good. Naturally, the size of the organization will prohibit you from formalizing the development of the intranet, as you'll read about in Chapter 6.

Cost Abatement

In order to keep maintenance costs down, heed the advice of good web page design. Ensure consistency in page design, that is, adopt a common look and feel and make templates available for development, so common elements will change across the company when the linked templates change at a centralized location.

Also, use a centralized intranet home page that everyone in the company links up to. This central "voice" provides a consistent message and enables you to enforce quality standards. Also, make sure there is an approval process for posting something on the intranet home page, or any of the group pages.

Distribute the responsibility for content to the information owners. For instance, engineering directly edits and updates design specifications on their own site. They do not need to get the Webmaster involved in the make up of the pages. Instead, engineering sends announcement to the webmaster when the pages are ready for inclusion in the intranet home page site. Content is approved through an on-line workflow process in engineering. Approvers are predefined and web pages cannot be published without their approval. Also, include mechanisms to ensure that approvals do not "stall."

Building an intranet will not be a project with a specific end in mind. Nor will you be able to identify all the costs. We've talked about the intranet being an organic entity that grows with your ability to use it as a modern communication tool. Can the intranet break ahead of the pack? Now that the tools are in the hands of the users, the answer is yes.

Summary of Key Points

- COSTS, COSTS, AND MORE COSTS

    This section discussed cost drivers, types of costs that affect the cost drivers, and generational costs that determine the maturity of the intranet needed.

- COST SAVINGS

    This section asked the question, who is saving what? Internal communications and publishing cost savings seem to be the winners.

- COSTS OF GOING OUTSIDE THE INTRANET

    In this section, you looked at what happens if you're going to extend your intranet out into the interenterprise. You need to pay attention to customer costs, partner costs, and increased security.

- COST SAMPLINGS

  This section provided cost samplings. Everyone has got a cost analysis story, or a cost saving story. Here we highlight Sun Microsystems, Sandia National Labs, FedEx, and others.

- ROI VERSUS HUMAN PERFORMANCE IMPROVEMENT

  This section underscored that you can't determine ROI on a communication and collaboration tool without evaluating human performance. You must determine your ROI based on improving the infostructure that transforms human performance capabilities into revenue drivers. You also discovered that ROI may not be as important as intranets fall into the category of doing business rather than return on investment.

- TRENDS THAT WILL EVOLVE COST

  This section identified what trends are going to affect intranet costs. Interactivity, simulated reality, geographic expansion, economies of scale, and entry to e-commerce are among the most popular.

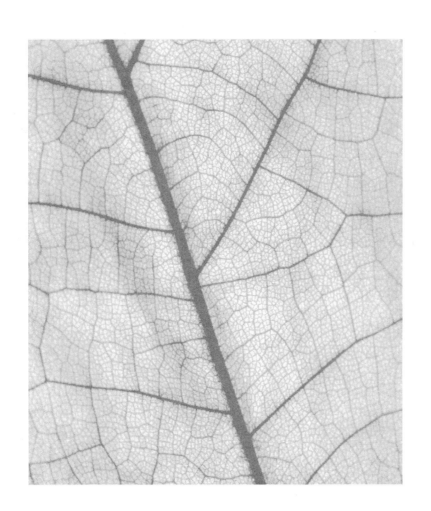

CHAPTER

6

How Do I Make
It Work?

By now you should know what an intranet is. At a minimum, you know it's a technology based on the shared Internet standards. You know it is made up of a network, routers, hubs, servers, browsers. You know that you can look at information on any computer platform—mainframe, PC, UNIX workstation, Apple MacIntosh. You understand the key benefits are cross-functional communication and integration with your legacy data. You understand the costs are relatively low, and that maintenance and content are where you'll be spending your dollars. You know that security is the key risk, and that the greatest limitation is the investment you've made in legacy systems already.

You should know that the most important point deals not with setting up an intranet technically but figuring out what to do with your intranet to help work-flow, to streamline business processes, to accelerate development cycles, to improve corporate culture, and to communicate in highly interactive experiences. As you know, urgency is the primary factor for success, because your competitors are planning or have already implemented a similar intranet strategy. Any organization capable of responding quickly to customers' changing needs and a spiraling market knows the value of an intranet. You also know inter-enterprise transaction will occur only between robust intranets. We called these extranets.

This chapter is dedicated to helping you with a process for getting your intranet up and running as quickly as possible. It is a synthesis of the success stories of several intranet development efforts in several different industries. Although there are several ways to approach the development of a communication environment in each industry, there are several repeating variables that can be attributed to the successful deployment of an intranet.

Naturally, some of you may already have deployed the technical requirements for building an intranet, that is, the setting up of the network, the servers, the software. For those of you who haven't, there is guidance here. However, this chapter is designed to assist you in building the intranet environment, including the technical development, the infrastructure, the people, the processes, the procedures, the roles, and responsibilities.

Managers can use this chapter to understand what the cost factors are, what the action plans need to include, and what the cultural mind-set of the organization must evolve to in order to build robust, useful, collective, collaborative communication environments. Your intranet will fortify your organization mission and liberate the individual creativity to achieve the mission.

Like all recommendations for deployment, these templates must be modified to fit the development of your intranet. They are guidelines and best practices of successful intranet deployment. Depending on how you wish to proceed, you can alter the steps to fit your purposes. Feel free to develop your own plan, use a more general technical solution, and take a wait-and-see attitude about any organizational change.

First Things First

Identify Why You Are Doing This

What is the purpose of establishing an intranet? Do you want it for internal and external communications? Are you connecting small groups within your organization? Are you going to connect to your corporate databases? Are you creating a collaborative environment when information is shared across several departments for rapid development?

The better you define your purpose, the better you'll be at pulling together the right tools for the right job. In this book, we'll tackle the larger site setup as it is the most challenging. If you want to set up a small group intranet, you have little to do but dedicate a workstation or PC on the network as your intranet server. Load the server software that you download directly off the Internet (specifically at microsoft.com or netscape.com), configure the browser on all the machines that will be accessing your server, and start writing HTML pages. Setting up a small project intranet site is fairly simple; setting up an effective communication and collaboration tool is quite another feat.

Note: For the purposes of this discussion, we'll assume the technical aspects of setting up an intranet will be handled by your information systems group. You can review these steps in the section "Designing the Intranet" later in this chapter.

Articulate a Guiding Principle

Once you have defined why you're setting up the intranet, it is imperative to articulate what this guiding principle is. You must clearly define and communicate your intranet principle throughout the organization. The principle must include the organization's core goal for information sharing, communicating, and collaborating throughout the enterprise. Without a guiding principle, you do not share the simplicity of getting the job done right the first time. Instead, you're constantly changing, revising, or amending.

To help you define the principles that will drive the intranet, you must look to the leaders in your organization who are responsible for communication, workflow, business simplification, education, leadership, and moving the organization forward. You must also connect with the individuals in the organization in order to understand their needs, their expectations, and their capability to move into a connected on-line environment. This is the age of eager technologists and terrified technophobes. Finding the right principle to motivate the technologists and secure the technophobes is your first challenge.

Think Organic

If you think of the intranet as anarchistic and chaotic, you're wrong. The intranet is organic. It is made up of systematically interrelated parts. No part of it completely controls the other parts. The individual components must develop on their own, leveraging their best components and accommodating their environment effectively. Intranets will only work if you let them grow naturally. Let the intranet evolve as the people who use it and develop it evolve.

For the intranet, organic means think decentralized and distributed. Each function, each group, each unique part of the intranet develops on its own server, maintained by its content providers and used by its niche audiences. This includes functions like financial operations on a unique server, legal operations on a unique server, educational operations on a unique server. Even managing security and log-in access is dedicated to a single server, all interconnected with web technology over the network.

An analogy that clarifies the intranet's decentralized and distributed requirements in the intranet is like the human body. It has a central knowledge repository or data warehouse (the brain) that stores security information for the rest of the system. It has different functional parts (the appendages, the organs, the nervoussystem), each with their own unique functionality and use. Each subsystem of the human body works independently within the human body to improve experience and produce responses to its environment.

The intranet's appendages are its functional web groups, the organs are the internal filters for information quality. The nervous system is the network, the Web itself. The more data each group receives, the more able or functional the part becomes. As the intranet assembles human knowledge and integrates with workers' knowledge bases, it becomes an integral part of the organization's infrastructure.

Human interaction underlies the intranet. When people talk to each other, interact in unprecedented ways, track information accurately, and use critical thinking skills in real-time situations, they are more involved in the process of developing the organization. They contribute more. They learn faster. They adapt to change more readily. Their investment grows crucial to sustaining their position in the company. And, their contributions equalize across the organization.

When users communicate and store their knowledge on-line, they develop a collective mindshare. Thinking and analysis become a group process, where consensus and expertise rule, where innovation and "out-of -the-box" thinking predominate, where creativity and innovation are valued highly. Focusing multiple users' attention on a problem is a mighty tool.

As everyone becomes involved in continuous business improvement, an atmosphere of learning emerges. When a learning community predominates, the organization matures quickly into an entity that develops itself and knows its capabilities for performing at maximum potential.

See Figure 6–1 to review the components of an organic intranet. Human interaction accelerates business process development. A learning community is created and collective mindshare unleashes the maximum potential and the systematic evolution of the organization.

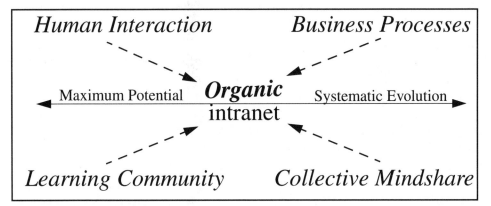

Figure 6–1 The Organic Intranet

Invite Everyone to Participate

Communicate and invite everyone to get involved up-front. You'll probably find a few of your employees have already created something on the Internet and are already using external resources like Microsoft Network or America On-Line. There are already 50 million web pages on the external Internet. Now is the time for convergence and for leveraging gained expertise on your intranet. This is a new environment and creative solutions can be gleaned from almost anyone in the organization.

Simplify working together and building intranet pieces together by making sure the people who need to be involved are invited to participate. Build a first-class intranet by participating, sharing, discussing, and trying out different points of view. Then promote the idea of a unified body of knowledge, a community of practice.

Grow Now, Prune Later

We do not totally understand the effects or the evolution of the intranet yet. We only know that it's changing everything about the enterprise. In order for it to be healthy, you must let it grow on its own. You need to manage its growth in some ways, but let it grow quickly, wildly, almost unhampered. In short, encourage everyone to think critically about how to innovate and integrate the intranet into their workflow. Allow the intranet to grow in stages, realizing there is a time for unbridled free flow, and a time for creating a single, solid organizational voice.

Bottom Line: Allow the unpredictable and the unknown. Creation is occurring.

This methodology of grow now, prune later is very important. Too many intranets get killed because the company viewed it as "experimental" technology or tried to impose the same old rules and regulations on its command and control. The result was an intranet that no one liked or wanted to maintain.

Allow the control of information to flow freely and naturally. Breed trust and sharing through access and analysis that is shared on a wide scale. Make everything you can available to all people in the organization. You never know what piece of information, large or small, will create the genius your organization is capable of. Think of flat organizations with direct contact between the consumer and the producer of the information you are providing.

Bottom Line: Allow your intranet to grow in every conceivable direction. You can prune later.

Planning the Intranet

Now that you've got some basic principles working for you, you need to build an environment in your organization that will allow organic growth to happen. For the intranet to work, you must align your executive management with the potential of the intranet. Then, you must empower the content providers and allow the magic to happen. A successful intranet requires innovative, converging solutions, so maintain a focus, a central theme, a centralized web page that will pull together all of the individual efforts in the organization.

Step 1—Determine Scope

Determine if you are planning a large-scale intranet, or if you are taking a small group within your organization and building a modest intranet. It doesn't matter which size you build, as the parts are interconnecting at any point. Many grassroots movements started this way. Each group developed their own site and then shared its cross-functional group meetings. As one group views the successes and false starts of other groups and working relationships and interdependencies with others' groups, a natural partnering occurs. In essence, the scope of the project identifies itself, and a snowball effect occurs. Each group leverages the experiences of the others.

Groups link together in the framework of natural evolution and improved workflow. If you think of motivating each group to create their own version of the intranet, the development becomes modular, the scope becomes manageable. The great intranet successes come from groups sharing process and tasks on-line. The minute someone sees what another group has done on-line, the easier it is to align the various groups. Starting small has its merits.

Step 2—Determine Executive Commitment and Resources

Every technology that has survived the test of the early adopters acquired executive commitment first. Naturally some parts of this technology are growing in the basements and garages of the new entrepreneurs. However, sooner or later, the effort is one of economies of scale. The more you're connected to the organization's communication strategy, the more likely the intranet will have the breadth and depth to be truly successful.

Deming, the great quality guru, would not see anyone in a corporation for the first interview but the CEO and his staff. Why bother unless the corporation's leaders are fully supportive and involved in the full deployment of a method and tool for improving the organization. It's even better when the executives are heading up the effort. Later in this book, you'll read interviews with CIOs who provide leadership and vision in the development of their internal intranets. The CEO must make a statement, define a mission, and publicize that commitment on-line in a very central and highly visible place on the intranet. See Figure 6–2 for an example of Netscape's commitment.

Resources   Every project takes money and people. Once executive management has embraced the development of an intranet, budgets need to be determined. You cannot work without resources. Most often, you'll reallocate some of your MIS budget to intranet development. People either volunteer or are appointed to focus on planning, designing, implementing, and testing the intranet.

Appointing people will be a challenge. You cannot strictly rely on your information technology group to get the ball rolling. You can focus this group to build the technical components of the intranet. They do understand the network, the configurations required, and other technical details. They can act as internal consultants to help the various groups set up their machines. But, the people who need to

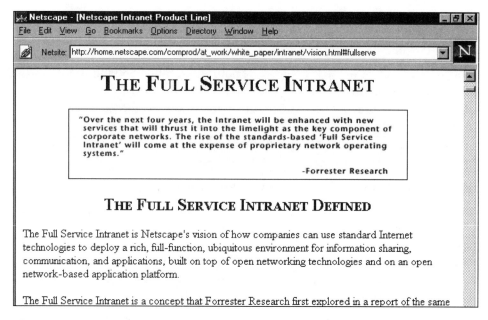

Figure 6–2 Netscape Communication's Commitment to the Intranet

be focused on developing the intranet are the information managers and the actual content providers. Most often, most organizations simply add the responsibility to individuals already concerned with information dissemination.

Step 3—Mandate an Open Technological Environment

Executive management must mandate a technological environment based on internet standards (especially TCP/IP and HTML) in order to achieve an open technological environment. Mandating standards may seem rigid to some in the organization, as other client/server solutions or legacy systems may already be fully functional in the organization. However, these standards allow open platform communication and must be in place to create one of the most versatile communication systems.

The win is project planning, project tracking, subcontractor management, configuration management, requirements management, integrated/distributed software management, and effective measures for continuous process improvement.

Another decision is whether to standardize on a browser or plug-ins. Many companies have done this with unsuccessful results. Since intranet implementation has occurred, different browsers have entranced everyone with more features. There are pros and cons for standardizing on browsers. The key benefit is support and shared functionality.

Step 4—Identify Key Players and Teams

Gather Key Players   Before you go much further, you have to get the key individuals involved: executive management, the information technology group, marketing, sales, engineering, operations, human resources, research, and the various product lines. Include other key positions that are unique to your operation. Identify overall strategies, risks, and limitations. Buy-in is very important to making the overall intranet work. You need to assure the key individuals what the intranet buys them. Consequently, a few key meetings will take place.

Identify an Executive Sponsor   Once the executive leader has established a strategic intranet position, identify the tactical owner. Depending on the structure of your organization, you'll need to appoint an executive sponsor—Chief Information Technologist (CIO), Chief Technology Officer (CTO)—or a technical chief Webmaster reporting to the executive sponsor. The sponsor is responsible for making sure the overall intranet structure is strategic with the critical mission of the organization, while at the same time advocating organic, bottom-up development. The technical chief Webmaster integrates the existing Information Technology (IT) structure with the intranet.

Identify Intranet Positions   There are many terms to describe the new opportunities on the intranet. Webmaster, gatekeeper, content provider, producer, publisher, editor. The terms are simply used as a way to divide up the tasks of the intranet. We'll discuss more of the human resource requirements later on in the chapter. At this stage, you need to identify strategic positions with key areas of accountability in order to get the intranet moving quickly. See Table 6-1.

Table 6-1 Key Areas of Accountability

Accountability	Title	Alternate Titles
Responsible for the overall intranet	Chief Webmaster	CIO, MIS Director, Producer, Publisher, Marketing Director, Communications Director, Director of Information
Responsible for the technical aspects of the intranet	Webmaster	Technical Webmaster, MIS Director, Engineer
Responsible for the development and maintenance of a large section of corporate knowledge, i.e., sales, HR, operations, product line	Gatekeeper	Editor, Knowledge Architect, Site Architect, Webmasters, Site Coordinator
Responsible for providing content, or ensuring content is publishable.	Content Provider	Editors, Authors, Contributor, User

Form a Cross-functional Intranet Team or Web Council   A cross-functional team with a central moderator, whose primary focus is to run the council, is a necessary ingredient to a successful intranet. These groups, or steering committees, tend to be enterprisewide, objective, cross-functional, and creative. The purpose of such a group is to collect all the rapid development occurring in the organization and to enable others to leverage it. Intranet web sites multiply very quickly, so a central steering committee can help channel the rapid growth.

Schedule a weekly meeting place in a room with intranet connection and large screen projection whenever possible. Invite demonstrations of existing sites. Collaborate in focus groups for standards, templates, human resources, policies, and so forth. Invite anyone to attend. Use focus groups to determine requirements.

Web Council Responsibilities

- Alignment of executive goals with web sites
- Agreement on group/department representation on the intranet
- Collect and distribute best practices
- Coordinate legal, security, and HR requirements on the intranet
- Avoid bureaucracy and rigidity

Intranet Review Committee

Whenever top decisions are being made such as goal alignment, tool requirements, creativity integration, and policies, make sure you have organizationwide consensus. The following is a list of the individuals who should be involved in review:

- Chief Webmaster
- Marketing Communications
- Public Relations
- Legal Advisor
- Information Technology Group
- Key Content Providers
- Technical Architecture Group
- Design, Human Ergonomics, and Education People
- Human Resources

Step 5—Learn the Information Needs of the Users

A starting point to learn about the audience is to realize two fundamental uses of the web technology. In Figure 6–3, you see a breakdown of two main process categories: informing and transacting. When you're informing, you are pushing information one way. You put information on the Web for access. When you're transacting, information is going both ways; it communicates information and waits for a response in order to carry out the transaction.

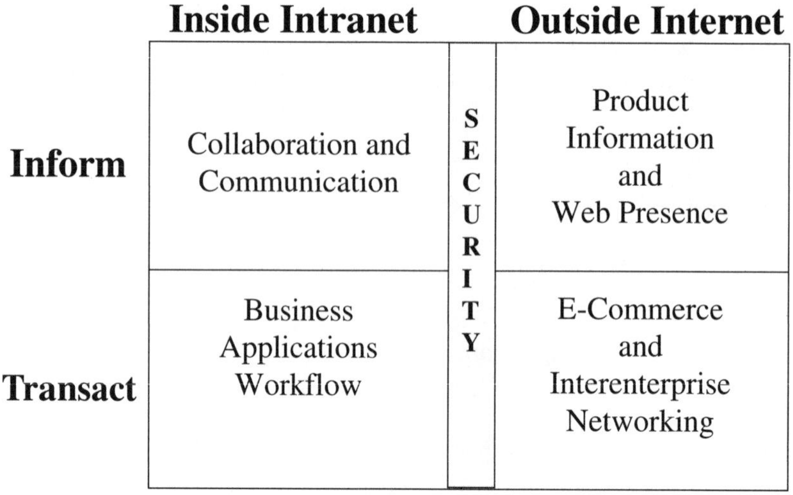

	Inside Intranet		Outside Internet
Inform	Collaboration and Communication	S E C U R I T Y	Product Information and Web Presence
Transact	Business Applications Workflow		E-Commerce and Interenterprise Networking

Courtesy of Sun Professional Services

Figure 6–3 How Are You Using the Intranet—to Inform or Transact?

Audience Intranet Needs   How you use the intranet depends on where your users sit in the process of transacting or communicating. Consider the following.

- Are users inside the firewall (intranet), outside the firewall (Internet), or both?

- Are you informing your users by sending text, messages, graphics, e-mail, and presentations to your clients (collaboration and communication)?

- Are you transacting with your clients, partners, and suppliers? Buying, selling, exchanging (business applications and workflow) on the intranet? e-commerce and interenterprise networking (on the Internet)?

- Are your customers internal customers, external customers, or both?

- Do you have human intelligent agents (people) transacting directly with your audience, or will you automate human processes and transact by machine only (like an ATM machine)?

- Will your data be real time, or it will be delayed?

Audience Considerations

What is the skill level and technology level of the users? Using computers all day long to transact and communicate is not everyone's favorite way to pass the time. How can you make your intranet simple enough to be useful and useful enough to be simple? What prior knowledge do your users already have with software?

Are they Microsoft Office oriented, or are they Framemaker and UNIX oriented, or are they Apple or mainframe oriented? You'll need to design to make the intranet desirable.

What kind of security is necessary? Security becomes a top priority for many groups. Find out what security needs the intranet users require. Then look at the limitations of the security issues to determine whether you can develop in this environment or not. If so, test your security and continually monitor it for the utmost in safety. If you're going to transact from intranet to intranet, you'll need to study security issues. It is important to communicate security procedures and policies to users and developers.

Critical Thinking Skills. Determine the critical thinking skills of your audience. Will they draw the same conclusions you have when you create a web site and identify it as expert, reliable content? If you're communicating, do your users understand your message? If you're transacting, do your users understand their participation in the transaction? Will your audience be able to use the information, or perform the transaction in a way that matches their expectations?

Process Flow. Does the audience understand process flow and how they can leverage the intranet to both streamline and profit from linking with various web sites? Can your audience figure out how to integrate their web sites into the process flow within an organization? It is key that an individual, or individual group, understands how to integrate with the process of their work. If they can't identify where they are, then some realignment, or education is required.

The web council or cross-functional web group that you form as a users group, or a policy-making body, will align itself according to the audience's needs and expectations. This step is crucial to making sure you build the right tool for the right purpose. If you want your needs to be heard, attend the web council and get your issues addressed.

Step 6—Determine the Intranet Business Model

Centralized   Most CIOs and Webmasters interviewed for this book identified that administration of the intranet needs to be centralized. The main intranet web page represents that centralization. From a centralized web server many security and architecture controls can be managed. Among them are user access, authorization, software currency, security, and integrity of top-level information. The centralized group can set up or automate procedures for joining the intranet together. They can provide comprehensive tools for developing on-line. Search tools and databases for accessing the large company data warehouses are maintained by this centralized activity.

Decentralized   The decentralized intranet is made up of the rest of the organization. Each group is encouraged to have their own web servers, publish their own pages, and categorize information as well as they can, from their own perspective. They try to maintain the common look and feel of the central web site but cannot be restricted by it.

Content is decentralized. This means that the individual groups are responsible for the quality and quantity of their information. They create it, manage it, maintain it, and submit it to the centralized web site for organizational placement. If they seek not to be placed in the organizational framework, they can operate independently for the sake of the group they are representing.

Certain recommendations are made by the central group in order to create a corporatewide common look and feel and to streamline adding the information to their top page. Use it if it builds your web site faster and if it enables you to integrate with corporatewide pages. While in your world of intranet design, you are free to develop the information, analyze it, and link according to your needs and expectations. Then, you subscribe to the home page, getting yourself placed on it according to the overall design of the master home page.

Step 7—Determine Usability Tests and Metrics

If you're going to build it, they will come. If they come to your intranet and start using it, you'll need to know whether or not it works. You'll need to establish usability tests in order to determine whether your audience is having their needs met. You'll also have to establish other metrics for evaluating the effectiveness and the costs of deploying an intranet.

Identify the metrics and usability tests you'll undertake to ensure that your intranet is serving the audience's needs. See Chapter 7 for some ideas on metrics. Experiment with what you can learn from metrics. Marketing demographics are just the beginning. You can tell who is hitting your site, how long they stayed there, where they came from, and where they're going. You may be able to understand the choices of your users and can create more compelling business processes and transactions on-line to speed up productivity.

Bottom Line: Find a way to talk to the customer directly to measure the usefulness of the intranet.

Step 8—Determine the Training and Communication Plan

Quality intranet use and development depend on some training and communication. If you are using WYSIWYG tools to create HTML, and it leverages a tool that your group already knows, then you're ahead. For those less fortunate, provide as many tools, and as much on-line training as possible. Training must take on a new face in the coming years. It is imperative to use the technology to teach the technology. This means embedded learning on demand in your training plans.

You can provide procedural skills on your intranet for quick access. You can use animation, video, and audio for teaching concepts or processes on-line. Java and ActiveX enable you to capture information from the user, so you can develop excellent feedback mechanisms for fine-tuning student learning. And, you can use web conferencing tools, electronic whiteboards, and virtual-reality experiences to provide both face-to-face contact and telepresence.

Create a training plan that emphasizes self-paced learning, tracks knowledge transfer back to the job, and involves users in both discovery and anticipatory learning techniques.

The Communication Plan   Publish a good communication plan on the intranet so your entire organization can clearly see the vision and understand the results of customer needs. Communicate the business plans so you're all working from the same model. Inform all team members what resources, people, or money are available to them. Communicate where the goals and processes are. And make known how you know when you've achieved success. What works, what doesn't. Announce best practices and learn from mistakes. Communicate the next steps. The intranet is an organic cycle of information evolution and organic solutions.

Intranet Learning Tools   Remember that many of your employees will know nothing about the intranet. They'll be confounded by its enormous rise to popularity and will be daunted by the amount of information. Make sure you have some learning tools available such as tutorials, guided self-help, computer-assisted instruction, computer-based training materials, and on-line guides or experts who can get involved one-on-one as mentors, or consultants, to your internal customers. Below are some topics to consider.

Intranet Basics (browser usage, searching, navigating, passwords, research, forms)

- Web publishing for beginners and advanced
- Design issues
- Conversion lessons
- Forms development

- Intranet standards/protocol knowledge (optional)
- Policies/procedures/code of ethics.

Intermediate skills

- Stylesheets
- Plug-in scripting, i.e., Shockwave, audio streaming, video streaming
- Java, JavaScript development
- Visual Basic, JScript
- SQL for integrating with databases
- Search engine and agent technology

Learning to Build Network-Centric Business Applications   You'll need tools to build applications that go beyond the capabilities of HTML, the language of the intranet. You don't them at first, but once your intranet becomes the center of the technology, you'll want to consider building internal business applications. Various vendors exist that offer products for integrating your environment with the capability of business applications. Using features of Java and ActiveX, developers can increase the functionality of your website. Their tools provide solutions in various industries—manufacturing, finance, retail, health care, etc. Development can be rapid and cost effective when built into your intranet.

Table 6-2, identifies the emerging technologies that increase the functionality of your intranet sites. With HTML by itself, you get basic information exchange, but with the increased functionality of CGI, you obtain forms capability on your intranet. If you add Java or ActiveX to your intranet site, you're able to perform business transactions.

Table 6-2 Increasing Your Intranet Functionality

	HTML Only	HTML w/CGI	HTML w/ Helper Apps	HTML w/Java, JavaScript, LiveWire Pro, ActiveX
Primary use	Linked hyperdocuments	Forms	Real live audio	Web business applications
Interactivity	Select various hyperlinks	Autoresponders once the form is submitted	Full multimedia presentation	On-line transactions
Navigation	Menus and frames	Clickable buttons, scroll bars	Interactive chatting	Customized selection of content with profiling
Challenges	Interactivity	Cannot handle multiple transactions per connection	Requires download of vendor software	Secured electronic commerce
Risks	Inert or dead linked hypermedia	Security risk	Compatibility with operating system	Cost of encryption and secured servers
Highest Memory Use	Clickable in-line graphics	Repeated access to databases	Real live video	Web events

Step 9—Determine Maintenance and Security Plan

How are you going to manage the intranet? Build a plan, so you are aware of the components for maintaining and supporting your intranet.

Maintenance

- *Backups.* Make sure that you have a mirror server somewhere on the network that replicates the main server. Also, rely on staging servers.

- *Subdirectory maintenance.* Subdirectory maintenance is a key issue. Clean out used files.

- *Control file permissions and access.* Your plan will determine who has access to top-level documents and administrative areas within the intranet. In order to secure information and manage the intranet, you'll need a centralized individual or group to manage this area.

- *Develop an approval process for putting files on the Web.* At the same time, identify the process for whom and how to post information on the web site. You can use open access—anyone can put anything on the server. You can use an approval through a gatekeeper. Or you can have several points of approval in a distributed approval process.

- *Develop a review cycle* of the web pages, to include new information, to streamline information, and to delete old information.

Security   Create the security policy, distribute it, and train with rigor. Determine information access levels and write permissions for groups sharing common web sites. Install firewall software and monitor it. Determine encryption methodology if necessary. Be aware of U. S. export laws on encrypting software and selling it abroad. Plan different levels of security, encrypting and login, for example.

Determine how you'll use routers to screen traffic on different port numbers. Develop a policy on downloading software from the Internet, for fear of viruses. Make this policy well understood. Funnel outside information through a proxy server, or a firewall, to prevent external intrusion. Set up procedures for encrypting secure data.

Support   Provide 24-hour, 7-day, x365 on-call problem resolution. Develop a support structure for managing technical issues, publishing issues, and new orientation issues. Produce FAQs (Frequently Asked Questions). Rely on training courses to support the use of all the web tools that you make available in the web toolbox.

Organize user support. Issues will center around browser setup, using the browser, connecting to the web server, printing, navigation, setting up accounts, using passwords and permissions. Issues will center around connecting to Web server, user accounts and permissions, publishing, server status, and response time. Track user response. Consider telepresence solutions like Microsoft's Net Meeting.

Create a Help Desk

Create a help desk environment for

- *technical support*—server, network connections, peripherals, modems, third-party equipment

- *database support*—software, utilities, Operating System Database (OS/DB) requirements, resolve DB failure, provide disaster recovery procedures

- *publishing support*—procedures, authorization, authentication of information, strategic alignment with corporate goals, tool support

- *development support*—software help, libraries, best practices database, procedures, tips, and troubleshooting, frequently asked questions, analysis of development tools

- *new orientation support*—where do I start first, what is this company all about? Provide a checklist if a departmental checklist doesn't already exist

Plan for additional calls when implementing new systems. Coordinate training for a help desk team on new systems and identify any new escalation procedures. In Figure 6–4, Netscape uses a menu, a reference to articles model, and a hot list, for the most frequently accessed pages to their internal intranet Help Desk.

Designing the Intranet

Now that you have defined your plan, you are ready to start the design phase of the intranet. Quite often these activities occur at the same time, as getting your intranet deployed quickly is a competitive advantage for your organization.

Your information technology group may have already designed or implemented the architecture for your intranet, so you may quickly read through some of these beginning design steps to be aware of what they needed to accomplish. These decisions could share budgetary dependencies with you.

Step 1—Review Your Network

Make every attempt to find out how your intranet will impact the network. Get the network administration staff involved with your architecture immediately. Clearly, this is not a technical guide, and you'll have to rely on the network administrative staff for your answers. Nonetheless, an understanding of bandwidth consumption (how many lanes you're taking on the superinformation highway) and an understanding of mission-critical applications need to be discussed.

You'll also have to understand that the clients must be configured with TCP/IP and a browser. This may or may not be done already. If you're going to maintain your own server(s) within your group, you'll need to understand the procedures for managing the server(s) and how it works with the network.

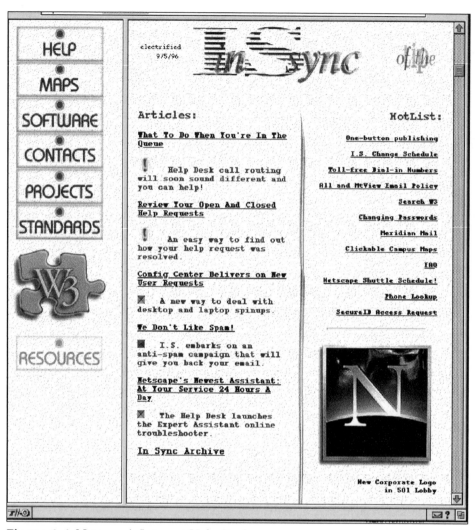

Figure 6–4 Netscape's Intranet Help Desk

You'll also want a clean understanding of both legal and security issues pertaining to storing and serving confidential information, including login access and document flow throughout the organization.

Step 2—Install Servers/Browsers

Install Servers/Browsers Choose your hardware servers and install the server software. The installations are usually quite simple because web page interactions guide you through the easy steps to follow. You'll need to think about how to set up directories, backups, archives, permissions/security, searching, purging scripts, and procedures. This may be handled exclusively by your information technology group. However, your developers will certainly want to get involved in the naming and configuration of the subdirectories.

Choose and install the browsers on the clients. Make sure to standardize on a browser for easy support and maintenance but allow use of other browsers. Find out how to fine-tune for performance.

Dial-In Accounts Consider how you'll handle dial-in accounts as well. Choose between SLIP, PPP, and TCP/IP-based e-mail protocols, (ARA for Appletalk-based protocols). And choose modem speed of 28.8, 33, or 56Kps. Faster is better, but find out if the telco (telecommunications infrastructure) is supportive of the higher speeds. Research the feasibility of using ISDN or even cable modems. Calculate the impact on bandwidth, and architect the server environment for optimal efficiency. Again, these may be information technology issues, but as a manager you need to know what it takes to get telecommuting up and running on your intranet.

Automate Installation Provide an automatic solution if you can. Sun's Enterprise Network Services group has developed such an automatic solution where the entire process for setting up an intranet is managed from a form. See Figure 6–5. You can see this screen enables users to add themselves to the Enterprise Network Services group that centrally controls the intranet from the technical point of view. Basic service, extended service, and deluxe service are all available through an easy form like this to help users set up an intranet site without having to go through the technical learning curve.

Forms like this are found in many intranet sites to speed up the various processes within organizations. A centralized service like this removes the technical barriers from setting yourself up on the intranet and enables the information technology group to manage the intranet more effectively.

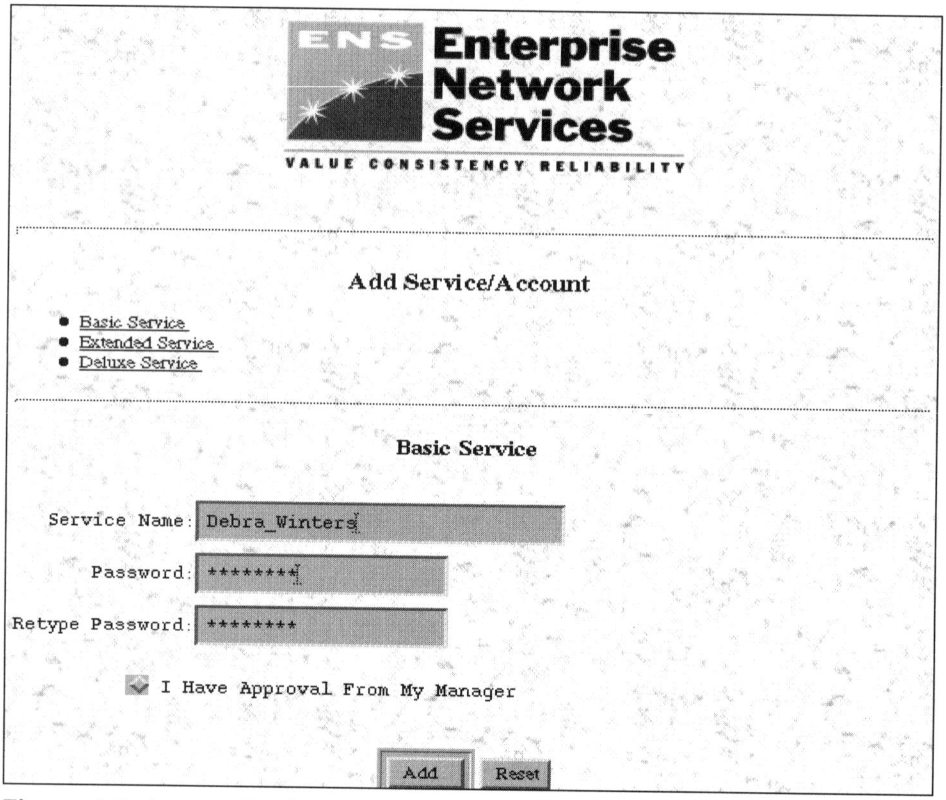

Figure 6–5 Automating Intranet Setup

Step 3—Choose Your Intranet Services

This may have been taken care of by the information technology group again. There are many additional services to the intranet, including e-mail, news servers, FTP (File Transfer Protocol), Telnet (logging into another computer), chatting, web conferencing, and video capability. Talk with the information technology group in order to determine what capabilities are available, and which can be added upon demand.

Step 4—Choose Mail Platform and News Server

Make sure your e-mail systems are Internet capable. You'll want to use the standard SMTP protocol, the latest POP protocol (mostly in use), and the emerging IMAP protocol which is moving us into a new era of hyperlinking and graphical e-mail. Choose an integrated mail system like Netscape Mail, Microsoft Outlook Mail, ccMail, Eudora, or integrate with network mail if it is compatible with the internet protocols.

If you do use network mail, make sure that it uses the standard internet mail protocols (SMTP, POP, or IMAP). SMTP is the "internet" mail protocol used to deliver mail between multiuser systems but is limited to mail transfers that are initiated by the sender and limited by the information you get about the mail transfer. POP and IMAP protocols are more interactive and can be used on central web servers. Features you're looking for include

- identifying the user by user name and password

- transfer ability between server and desktop

- deleting or saving choice on the server after delivery

- capable of reading encrypted passwords passed over the network

- performs string searches through mail that still resides on the server

- understands the MIME-structure of a message

FTP, Gopher, Telnet, IRC   Decide among FTP (transferring files between computers), telnet (logging in remotely to another computer), gopher (libraries of information), or IRC (chatting on line), or any of the other standard intranet services. These services have security issues because they reach outside of your intranet. However, working without them can be limiting.

Step 5—Choose Your Search Engine

You still have a lot of information to search through. Some information is stored one way, some stored intuitively, some not. Since content comes from the individual providers you can expect multiple, ingenious ways of preparing information for use. Dedicate a section of the intranet to catalog all of the various topics of information that are created. Typically you use indexes, tables of contents, library catalogs, and subdirectories as classical ways of storing information. These data catalogs are only good if you can find them.

Using metatags and search engines, you can have immediate access to data catalogs anywhere, on any server. Metatags are high-level description words or phrases embedded in HTML documents associated with each document that you store on the server. Search tools locate these special metatags throughout your intranet quickly and provide instant access to excellent data catalogs.

Search tools should contain

- enterprisewide searching, full-text indexing

- retrieving, organizing, caching, and replicating capability
- relevance ranking (prioritizing)
- automatic/dynamic concept searching
- interoperability and scalability
- conversion on the fly
- elimination of redundancies
- inferencing searching

Evaluate and select a way to index so the search tools you select will be robust and powerful. Make sure your search tool is capable of text-based and concept-based searching. Many of the search technologies you'll find on the Internet use the same technology for intranet searching. Look at Inference at http://www.inference.com, Verity at http://www.verity.com, and Fulcrum at http://www.fulcrum.com.

Step 6—Choose Your Filtering Agents

Although optional, you might want to prosper from the web technology that filters and customizes information for you automatically. You may want to invest in web crawlers, spiders, robots, or agents. Users may or may not report that a web server has been set up on the network, so you'll need tools that go out and constantly examine the site for various information.

Agents are developing quickly to help you identify what you're looking for on the intranet. These agents are capable of profiling your search requirements over a time period and identifying the "kinds" of information you're looking for. As various forms of information are sent to you through e-mail, newsgroups, and search tools, you might want a tool for managing all this data for you. You simply need to know that the data are being collected for you, filtered, and available for quick search and retrieval.

Traditionally, agents have looked for information based on a set of internal rules (an artificial intelligence feature). However, these kinds of agents are limited by the computing power of the server and tend to produce irrelevant information. Agent technology is growing in importance on the intranet.

Step 7—Choose Your Tools

In order to understand the environment you'll be designing in, it is important to choose your tools at this stage. Publishing or producing on the intranet requires a wide set of tools. Choose these tools from the many vendors that are providing intranet solutions. As in all software selection, the features you need depend on your preferences and your organization's standards.

We've provided you here with the various groups of tools that you'll find useful in designing and developing your organization's intranet. We've purposefully avoided making too many tool recommendations with the fierce competition for web tools today. However, the best tools are compatible with the platforms you're using and the tools that you already invested in.

- Web Authoring

- Creating Clickable Graphics

- Converting Documents

- Viewing Documents

- Collaborative Sites, Groupware, and Videoconferencing

- Plug-ins or Add-ons

- Database Integration

You can find further information at the Intranet Journal's Toolshed
http://www.intranetjournal.com/toolshed.html

Web Authoring   HTML was the first web authoring tool. It was created in text editors using tags to create text, establish links between documents and graphics, and to perform simple formatting. Some people can write in the mark-up language called HTML. It is not necessary. However, it can be useful for trouble-shooting pages sometimes.

WYSIWYG Web authoring tools are required. These include web authoring suites like Netscape Gold or Microsoft's Front Page. You'll want tools that allow you to create text, import graphics, link files, and manage the pages. You want to be able to create tables and frames and apply style sheets for quick page development.

You'll also need tools for creating graphics, audio, and video (when the time comes). The market changes with the talent and creativity of the users of such tools. Shop for tool, talent, and support.

You can leverage your existing word processors at times. Many of today's word processors provide HTML conversion or creation. Contact your word processor manufacturer and find out if you can easily write HTML documents. The answer is usually yes. Some of them are actually integrating web creation tools directly into their programs. It is imperative to put web authoring tools in the hands of your users. As it is, only those being provided with the tools are authoring the content. This skews the flow of information throughout the organization.

Site Enhancement Creating graphics you can click on makes an intranet site more appealing and faster to use. Frames, tables, and forms can also contain clickable items. Search for graphical tools that help you create clickable graphics, clickable maps, clickable items on the screen. See Sun's example in Figure 6–6.

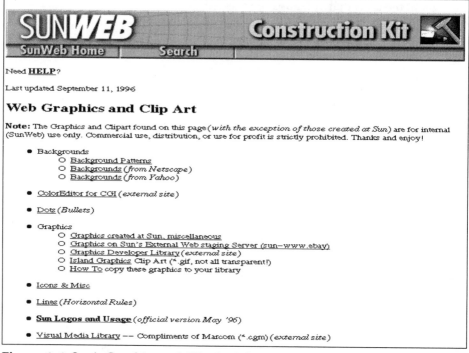

Figure 6–6 Sun's Graphics and Clip Art Library

You'll want to know about animation tools and cgi scripts on-line that will enhance the features on your site. You can include small forms to interact with the user. You can capture counters to determine how many people are hitting your site. You can use various backgrounds and graphic art found at various library sites on your intranet. See http://www.isecure.com/Webmaster/hotsites.htm on the Internet for examples.

Converting Documents The tool you choose to convert documents depends on the application you want to convert from. You must research which sets of tools will convert your documents from the original to HTML. Remember everything doesn't have to be converted. But, convert the critical items first. Get key documents that are used frequently on-line first. Start creating your documents in HTML as soon as you can, however. The hyperlinking capability with multimedia integration make more dynamic documents that users will find more useful.

Viewing Documents   So many great tools are available for representing data. There are spreadsheets, databases, presentation software packages, full multimedia packages. The list goes on and on. You may prefer your tools for representing information. Some of these tools do not have conversion directly into the HTML format on the intranet. You'll have to acquire viewer tools in order to see some of these documents. Look at Adobe's Acrobat products, Microsoft Viewer for Excel, Word, and Powerpoint. Also, look at Shockwave for multimedia presentations.

Other kinds of viewing tools include those that can take a chunk of the intranet site and make it available when you are disconnected from the intranet. These are useful to allow viewers to examine their HTML files anytime, anywhere. These tools usually support most tags and typical HTML features, plus bookmark management and directory buttons.

Collaborative Sites, Groupware, and Videoconferencing Tools   In order to maintain the effectiveness of collaborative processing on your intranet, you need tools that allow for highly coordinated collaborative workflow. Integrating with Lotus Notes for example is highly desirable. Since Lotus is preparing for a full integration with the intranet, you'll be able to leverage the excellent groupware functionality of Notes.

Videoconferencing, discussion/conferencing groupware will maintain the mind share of the Internet at this point. Videoconferencing tools are needed for electronic meetings. Examples are Attachmate Open Mind, Netscape/Collabra Share, Microsoft's NetMeeting.

Plug-Ins or Add-Ons   You must realize that your intranet site is sure to grow. You will be improving the site continually. You will want to make it more powerful and have more functionality as web tools become available. You need to know about helper applications or plug-ins. Browser companies have in-line plug-in centers for you to learn about what functionality you might need. See Figure 6–7. These are software programs that increase the functionality of your web site.

A plug-in might

- Spellcheck for e-mail
- Provide virus protection from downloads and e-mail attachments
- Organize bookmark for on- or off-line searching
- Provide interactive internet chat sessions
- Improve animation, video, sound, and 3D

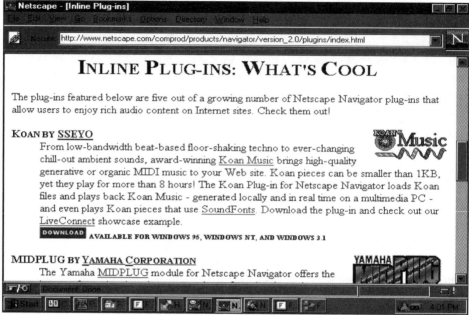

Figure 6–7 In-Line Plug-Ins from Netscape

Web Cartography   What does an entire site look like? Whatever the graphical representations on your site, the entire site plan, or knowledge network that you're attempting to display, defines who you are. What your user or customer sees throughout the entire web site is crucial to understanding what you offer and how your products or services fit in with their needs.

Your intranet site reflects the vision and goals of your system thinking. It is key to how the intranet site integrates with the rest of the organization. If something changes at one web site, there are consequences, rippling effects, to other information producers throughout the organization. These need to be reflected and studied for strategic knowledge representation.

Your internet web site equally reflects both your capability and your competitiveness in understanding how your products integrate with the customer's procedures and processes. An individual examining a web site on the Internet must understand what your product and services are, how they work technically, what your support agreement looks like, and what your future plans are for developing and integrating with affinity.

Bottom Line: The site, either intranet or Internet, reflects your strategic thinking.

On the Web, it's a basic task to develop a content map and to use a program that includes tools for managing the vast content on the site. Web cartography enables strategic information distribution. Coupled with a focus on innovative technology, your positioning strategy, your business plan, and your direction, you can produce potent web sites that improve productivity, reduce work cycles, distribute workload evenly, and enable effective e-commerce on the Internet.

WebMapper from Microsoft maps any site on your intranet or the Internet and presents the site in a familiar outline or tree view by providing a visual guide of the structural relationships among the resources in your site. Version 2.0 includes the company's unique Cyberbolic™ interface, a visually dynamic view of the structural relationships among the resources in a web site. See Figure 6–8 for an example.

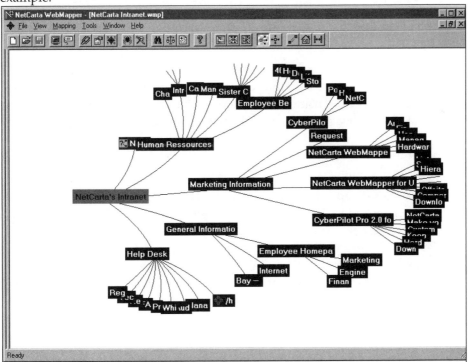

Figure 6–8 Web Cartography Shows Your Overall Strategic Structure

Database Integration Tools   Because you have an investment in database technology, you'll need tools to help you convert your database information into intranet-ready data. You'll need flexible software tools that dynamically publish database files on the Web or intranet. Look for tools that provide the flexibility to make calls to MDB or SQL servers if needed. Other database companies have unique tools for their unique environments. This is an era of open systems with many legacy systems. Make sure your intranet database connections are reliable. The strength of the intranet is developing business applications around robust database systems.

You'll certainly need to consider tools that connect your legacy systems with the intranet. Some of the more common legacy systems already have intranet solutions. You'll have to contact your vendor to determine the best way to integrate database applications with the intranet.

Application Building Tools   You'll need a visual tool set to easily build and maintain live, data-driven Web applications. You'll want to create interactive catalogs, classifieds, discussion forums, questionnaires, and so forth, or build web interfaces to existing client/server database applications. Look for productivity-boosting visual tools and standard database support. Java and ActiveX provide the kind of network functionality and application building capability you are looking for.

Creating On-line Tools for Building Web Sites   You can create an on-line environment for building web sites quickly. You can create walkthrough procedures for creating web sites by using a form-based web page. Such on-line tools are excellent for creating a site using templates or style sheets. It is a bit more difficult to customize these sites for your particular need, however. Such assistance is reserved for those involved in low-end web page development like personal Web pages, or small group web pages.

In Figure 6–9, Netscape offers "Creating Net Sites" which provides advice and assistance on creating a Net site. In the true spirit of the Internet, they also offer links to many different vendors on all platforms to help you develop your Net site. These tools are equally good for internet and intranet development. The site breaks down the Net creation activity into adding functionality and developer's tools. Start at Netscape's Page Start Site for an overview. This is on the Internet and provides you with a good foundation of what development entails.

Figure 6–9 Netscape Primer for Developers

Step 8—Create a Central Intranet Web Page

At some point, you need to develop a centralized intranet web page which represents the overall growth and development of the intranet site. This is usually referred to as the home page.

You can brainstorm the design on paper in what is traditionally known as a storyboard. Or you can create a sketch outline on a whiteboard in a meeting with the key players. You need to designate one page as the single point of contact for the organization (and for each individual group as well). If you prototype this page on-line, you will get quick results and an incredible amount of useful feedback from everyone in the organization who is accessing it. This is rapid collaborative prototyping. You'll also weed out useless information quickly.

What you want to accomplish is to create a single point of communication during design and development. You may end up using this page as the core of your intranet once it is substantially developed. The central web page acts as a community bulletin board. It identifies key contacts, the definition of the project, the potential common look and feel, navigational devices, and so forth. It serves as a project management center, providing schedules, milestones, and deadlines. Once you create the prototype of the centralized web page, you can move it over to the electronic version very easily.

Remember how these pages are modular. You can take large sections and move them around just by changing a link. You can redesign the front graphic and still maintain all the original functionality of the page. You can drop off features that are not useful.

In Figure 6–10, you see a bare minimum centralized web page. It identifies the key elements that a typical project would include. Notice how this is a centralized starting point, designed to link to other areas immediately within the web site.

The links work well on a startup page. You'll be able to fit any of the pieces you build here in your more formal design that you'll develop later. In the starter kit, you can place a small orientating tutorial of how the site works. You add definitions, glossaries, step-by-step procedures, or anything that a new person would need to begin the design and development of their own pages.

The other buttons speak for themselves. You can preselect tools and make them available. You can maintain a news section to focus the group on the key issues affecting the project or the group. The key people will include telephone numbers, e-mail addresses, group identifiers, and personal web pages. The projects section can contain action items, problems, schedules, milestones, project definitions, specifications, and so forth. This page will evolve. Perhaps you'll keep these buttons, perhaps not. The point is to get something together to prepare for the intranet's debut.

These pages can act as a prototype to demonstrate the intranet to executive management and others from whom you need support.

Step 9—Design a Master Intranet Blueprint

You cannot build a building without a blueprint. It's a simple concept. Builders cannot build without a master plan. The central intranet web page you designed in the previous step is a concept piece to get you up and running on the intranet. It also acts as a project management center or community bulletin board.

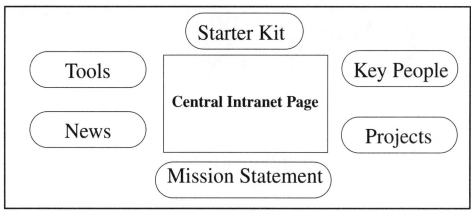

Figure 6–10 A Startup Central Intranet Web Page

This master plan you are designing here is different from your centralized web page in that it graphically represents the superstructure of your organization. You must assemble those affected by the intranet infrastructure to begin a series of brainstorming sessions, process analysis meetings, and architectural reviews in order to determine the best possible intranet blueprint. Everyone must be involved as the identification and flow of information in an organization affects everyone. But you must decide quickly.

Take a stance and design a top-level picture of how you're going to represent the organization as a series of Web impressions. Review the top design with sales, marketing, training, executives, engineering, research and development, support and service, operations, maintenance, human resources. Get everyone involved and make sure that they understand how their part of the organization will be represented.

Understand the importance of intranet real estate. Where do you want the most important information? What are the navigational paths to the most important supportive information? Promote competition. This is healthy. Encourage it. It is within these exercises that you get to a deeper level of your organization and determine high-level strategies.

Create the Site Map in Tiers   Build the site map on a foundation. For a foundation, consider four tiers to an intranet site map: the main intranet page tier, the indexes and search engine tier, the content tier, and the data warehouse tier. See Figure 6–11. These tiers represent the structure of your intranet.

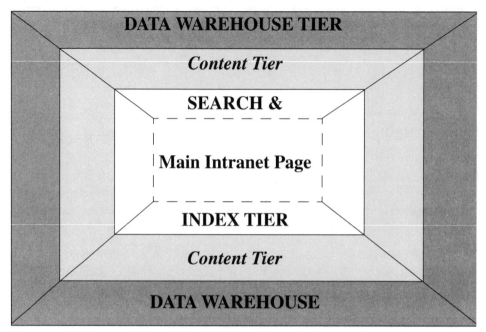

Figure 6–11 Intranet Tiers: Main, Index and Search, Content, Data Warehouse

The main intranet page represents your community center and business center. This is the centralized web page you designed in the previous step. It is prime real estate for emphasizing top-level information and navigation on your intranet. Keep it as clean and simple as possible. This tier points users to the other three tiers. Either a user needs to search an index or a table of contents, or they want to move directly to a content tier, for example, the sales site or the library site. Or, they want to access the legacy data warehouses for cross-functional analysis.

The index and search tier houses all the index pages and logically defines the structure of the various functions of your organization. These are both functional and cross-functional indices. The search tool is standardized for the intranet. You can set up this site as a table of contents or as a topical site. See Yahoo's example in Figure 6–12 for an example.[1]

The content tier represents what is known as datamarts. A datamart is a specialized web site, managed by a gatekeeper (publisher) that acts as a specialized site for specific information. It's like shopping in an information mall and entering

1. Text and artwork copyright © 1996 by YAHOO!, Inc. All rights reserved.

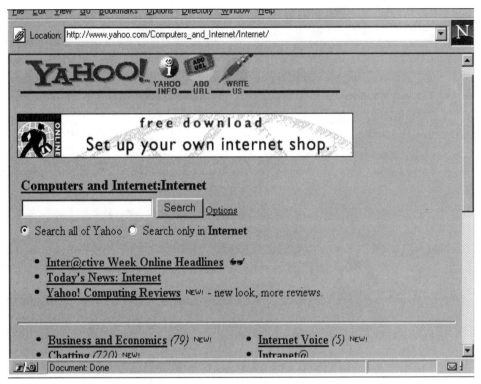

Figure 6–12 Yahoo's Index Tier

into a specialty shop that provides specialized information. For example, you can find a salesmart, a librarymart, a financialmart, and so forth. This tier is designed and maintained by the individual functional groups in the organization. This tier contains personal pages, group pages, department pages. It is the distributed, localized area of the intranet. See Microsoft's ITG site in Figure 6–13, for an example.[2] The "Dog Food" button is ITG's testimonial that they use their own products and services too.

The data warehouse tier encompasses all tiers as it ties together all network, legacy, and web data and makes itself available for decision support and historical analysis of the organization, its processes, and its project accomplishments. This is the tier of the intranet that manages all the data in the entire organization.

---

2.   Screen shot reprinted with permission from Microsoft Corporation.

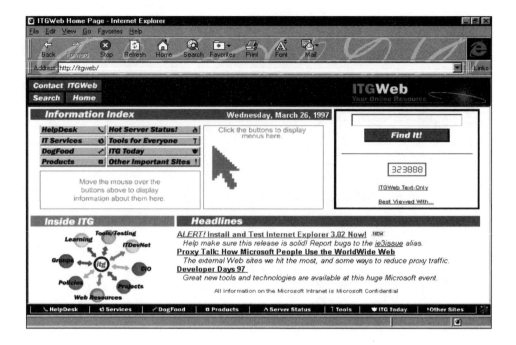

Figure 6–13 Microsoft's ITG Web—A Content Tier

A Method for Site Mapping

- *Brainstorm.* In a group, on 5 x 7 cards brainstorm how your business works. Once you've exhausted all the possibilities, arrange the 5 x 7 idea cards into related groupings. Write headers over each grouping. Use consensus to agree on the groupings and headings.

- *Prioritize the groupings.* Which items are chaotic, complex, critical to the organization? What needs to be identified in detail? What needs to be kept broad? Which of these processes are business critical? Imagine each grouping turning into a web page.

- *Identify all interrelationships and interdependencies.* What crucial information or activities occur that need to be communicated? Look at causes/effects. Identify the actual tasks, concepts, procedures, or processes that interrelate. Consider these the subordinate web pages. Speak in global terms. You can craft the right words later.

- *Prioritize the critical relationships and dependencies.* Which relationships need attention first? Attend to the dependencies in the critical path first.

- *Select the top priorities.* Weed them out again to between seven to nine. If you have too many items, go back a step and reevaluate. Choose a small number of top items. We recommend no more than five to seven total items. This is your <u>main intranet page</u>.

- *Maintain an index of top categories.* When going through these exercises, many ideas, suggestions, recommendations, systems views, and other categories will emerge. Do not delete them, categorize them whenever you see a grouping and start indexing in any way you see fit. This is your <u>index tier.</u> If you've got so much information, you need to be working on your search engine and a metatag strategy for all your documents.

- *Map out the subordinate content pages.* This is the level where you'll find the group pages, departmental pages, personal pages, and so forth. This is the <u>content tier</u>. Including representatives from key groups, or using a web council as a forum for identifying these individuals will help accommodate every project, product, and service page that needs to be available. Web pages with too much information kill comprehension.

- *Identify interrelationships as links.* And create links to all pages.

- *Map out the first two tiers of your intranet site.* First tier is the intranet home page. The second tier is the search tools and sets of easy-to-read, easy-to-navigate indexes. Let the third tier be the working ground of the content providers doing what they do best. Get everyone to look at it and agree to it.

- *Create your data warehouse.* Create a connection to your legacy data. This is the <u>data warehouse tier</u>. Discussing the methods for creating data warehouses can be found in other books focused specifically on data warehouse techniques. This is fundamental for web evolution at your site.

MindMaps or Categorizing Information   MindMaps are fascinating planning tools to help you plan your intranet site. They are easy to create and can assist you greatly in setting up an entire intranet, or a departmental intranet. To create them:

1. Draw a circle.

2. In the inner circle, write a key word or phrase that represents your web site on the intranet, such as "intranet products," "intranet publishing," "pharmaceuticals." Be as specific as possible.

3. Draw some lines away from the circle, lines that look like sun rays coming away from the sun. Draw no more than 7–9 lines (you may eliminate, or collapse headings, but avoid more than 7–9. This is based on short-term memory studies which suggest that most adults can process only 7–9 items in their short-term memory at one time).

4. At the end of each line, write the *one word* that best represents a body of information. For "intranet products," one of those words might be "servers," another "browsers," a third one "policies."

5. Consider these words for several hours or days to make sure they best represent the word in your main circle. In this case, "intranet products." You're beginning the design of your web site.

6. Once you come up with the words, use those 7–9 *words* as centers of 7–9 additional inner circles all emanating from that initial circle. See Figure 6–14, which takes the word "polices" and develops its top headings.

7. Repeat the same activity 7–9 times, until you run out of words. Soon you will have exhausted all of the reasons, causes, goals, concepts, functions, and so forth, that your organization has in mind for communicating, collaborating, and transacting on-line.

8. You essentially have performed a top-level system overview of your intranet site.

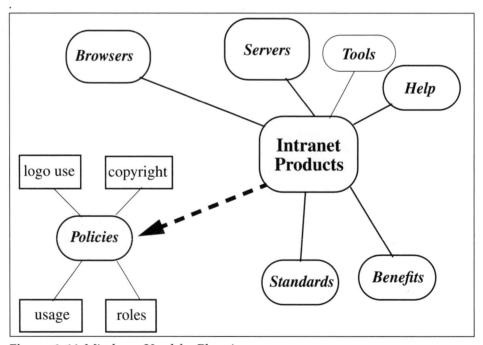

Figure 6–14 Mindmap Used for Planning

Notice how the one node "intranet products" is a central core topic. Around it lie only 7 high-level concepts. "Policies," one node, has its own high-level concepts that focus on information specifics. These are mind maps that describe the structure of our knowledge.

Step 10—Staff the Intranet Infrastructure

In order to get everyone in the organization involved in contributing to the intranet you need to get human resources involved in identifying intranet tasks, skills, and competencies to plan, design, develop, and maintain the intranet. You need visionaries, business people, finance, hypermedia experts, intranet technologists, instructional designers, human interaction experts, HTML programmers, and representatives from every major function in your enterprise—sales, training, marketing, human resources, partners, clients, operations, and so forth.

The Key Issue   You need talented, sophisticated people with business savvy and technical acumen. You need people who will take the intranet beyond the wires and cables, beyond static web pages, and information overload. You want a staff to craft an infostructure that makes your organization competitive and reliable.

Typical Job Descriptions   Below are some typical job descriptions of intranet-related jobs. This list is not comprehensive, but rather an awareness of the new skills and competencies that are required to create an intranet. They are only examples:

Chief Webmaster. The Chief Webmaster is responsible for the planning, implementing, and support of all the physical web site infrastructure for the company. This includes all hardware, software, network, and full environmental support, with full budgetary and resource responsibilities. This is either an information executive position, or someone who reports directly to the information officer. The Chief Webmaster is the final control point for the intranet.

Webmaster. Also known as producers in some organizations, Webmasters have similar responsibilities as movie producers. They are responsible for an entire intranet production. They foster and maintain working relationships within the organization, expediting production, and resolving problems. Webmasters assure quality, integrity, and usability of all mission-critical web site data and systems. They determine policy, procedure, and compliance with legal and security. They act as arbitrators and internal consultants for helping to set up and maintain web sites. They manage their decentralized intranet web site and scout out resources when appropriate.

Webmasters install and manage site capital equipment as required. They oversee the creation of tools and business processes for Web content development staff to stage content for the site and monitor quality. They ensure statistics are gathered for usability and audience evaluation purposes. Webmasters ensure integrity, availability, and maintenance of all mission-critical web site data and systems.

Webmasters maintain site-specific database infrastructures to meet interface needs of e-commerce partners (if using extranet). They manage web site customer registration and tracking and database-generated site content.

Webmasters are responsible for consultation with senior management on intranet operations and sufficiency and carry out planning and forecasting for all intranet infrastructure. Webmasters are the drivers for much of the technical innovation and information workflow in the organization.

The following are some major responsibilities of some Webmasters.

- Chairs or is an active member of the Web Council
- Establishes the technical working environment
- Appropriates authority to cross-functional groups
- Develops policy and procedures for site development
- Spearheads organizational intranet design
- Adjudicates on links and content when necessary
- Establishes and manages security and access
- Works with cross-functional groups to maintain a smooth process for managing the intranet web information
- Advises on educational needs for groups
- Speaks, evangelizes, consults, and promotes new uses and research efforts

Technical Webmaster. Although optional, a web site should establish a technical Webmaster position to be responsible for the daily operation of the web site. Operating includes installing, configuring, supporting, maintaining, updating, backing up, and administering the intranet. This individual understands the technical issues: bandwidth, size, capacity, availability, reliability, and growth of the intranet. This individual also reviews and selects tools to enable users to accomplish their tasks on the intranet. These people must be technical enough to troubleshoot when something goes wrong.

There are many technical matters that a qualified networking, World Wide Webber with the ability to see beyond one solution needs to attend to. Bandwidth issues, caching servers, proxy servers, authorized log-ins, attempted break-ins, general bug fixes. These professionals are network/intranet/client server gurus, with an answer or work around for everything. They must understand business and know the corporate information goals. Key is to have good programming skills (network, database, UNIX or NT, Java). Also, these people must maintain state-of-the-art knowledge of technological trends and opportunities.

Gatekeepers. Information management requires a thorough know-how of publishing. The publishing model uses an editor-in-chief as the coordinator of a publication. A hierarchy of editors, graphic artists, layout artists, writers, and reporters are required to run a publication. A web site, an intranet site, runs much like a magazine. Its principle commodity is words and graphics. The key skill is to understand how to write in a hypermedia world. Few do it well.

Gatekeepers are also known as publishers in some organizations. They are information experts who manage a strategic function of the intranet. Their key responsibility is the upper-level content requirements at various strategic organizational units in the organization. Usually you'll see a sales gatekeeper, a marketing gatekeeper, a legal gatekeeper. These positions are functional in nature. They focus on providing the best infostructure possible to satisfy the needs of the group they represent. Gatekeepers are site architects and usually report to the operating manager of the entire department or division they represent.

Gatekeepers design and manage the functional web site (i.e., sales). They define a web site's strategy and vision. They understand internet technologies and evaluate configuration management needs. Gatekeepers identify tools requirements. They drive promotion of the web site, maintain strategic relationships with vendor/partners/key customers. These people evangelize and act as the general spokesperson for the Web site. They manage editorial, creative, and production functions; common look and feel and usability; customer profiles, needs, and feedback mechanisms.

Gatekeepers or publishers are individual departmental representatives or ambassadors. Each has individual responsibilities within their group. As a group they establish and follow guidelines on style and content organization at the top level. Their major purpose is to ensure group participants, content providers, and strategic executives are buying into the content and strategy. Gatekeepers provide a checkpoint for legal and security issues coming from their group.

Gatekeepers define, design, and at times even develop intranet content. They also align content development and content management with strategic intranet corporate goals. They act as primary liaison with product groups, sales, and marketing content providers to obtain input and enforce standards. Gatekeepers architect and manage a key web site that others feed into, much like a publisher.

Their position provides a single point of contact for anyone in the organization wishing to get the best, expert, most updated information in the gatekeeper's domain. These individuals define web site strategy and vision.

Site Architect. Site architects define, design, and develop functional web site content (infostructure), including prototypes, organization, and implementation. They establish content management processes and design templates for content providers. Site architects act as the primary liaison with content providers to obtain input and enforce standards. They conduct focus groups and feedback programs to identify and incorporate customer requirements. They manage contractors as required. Good site architects must be customer-focused business thinkers with excellent written and verbal communication skills. They must have marketing and communication experience, knowledge of HTTP, CGI, Java, ActiveX, and authoring tools, including multimedia content. They must have excellent interpersonal skills.

Web Gardner. Web gardeners or editors ensure all information is updated and validated. They are involved in hands-on integration of material into the larger site, including pruning, organization, and cross-product references. They perform competitive analyses and recommend changes to the web site. They analyze and distribute state reports. They either take care of or dispatch web e-mail inquiries. Web gardeners run feed back mechanisms/databases. They engage in routine daily contact with content providers. They work with site architects on nonowner content pages, creating documents such as FAQs (Frequently Asked Questions). They must have knowledge of HTTP, CGI, authoring tools, stats, and database tools.

Web Designer. Web designers are recognized as experts on web site design, including stylistic and information architecture issues. They design web sites to hold content. They perform navigation design, cognitive design, graphics design, multimedia design, and human interaction design. They must understand interactive web relationships between people. Their abilities to elucidate a clear content design and stylistic strategy for the site, to create stunning, out-of-the-box solutions to web site business problems is crucial. They synthesize solutions from a wide range of sources, both from within company and from elsewhere in the industry.

Content Providers. Content providers are the foundation of the web site. Also, called editors and authors at different levels of content, they submit the documents to be posted on the intranet to the gatekeeper, editor, or publisher, or they publish it themselves. They are responsible for the integrity of their data, the accuracy of the posted information, and assuring that the information they post is compliant with security, legal, and management's standards.

They determine initial content, focusing on facts, concepts, procedures, and processes. They add value to data, turning it into information, and often into analytical, strategic statements that others can rely on for quick decision making.

These are the people who provide the content that makes the intranet work. If you give these people as much freedom, creativity, and innovation license as possible, they will create the most brilliantly linked human networks of knowledge about your organization.

At the same time, this group needs templates, tools, a common look and feel, design guidelines, navigational aids, network support, a clear mission, on-line procedures and training, and an artistic or political forum for expressing their needs for improvement. These are the creators of original content. They understand the presentation better than anyone. They are knowledge workers. Knowledge workers are becoming invaluable company assets. They are experts. Their inventory is either in their heads, in their PCs, or on their intranet web site.

Intranet Statistician (Web Evaluator). In some capacity on your intranet team, it is vital to have someone who can interpret intranet statistics, access counts, and clickstreams (histories of any given employee). Someone has to be able to know how to set up situations to gather good statistics, gather them, and analyze their importance and effect on human behavior. Human performance can be tracked for the knowledge worker. Expert knowledge workers can be observed and behaviors repeated by on-line agents or tutors. Quality is properly worked at this level to ensure understanding of customer needs and satisfaction.

Web Consultant. A true web consultant would be able to explain to the management what the technical staff already knows. They also know when to bring the technical management in to explain their data needs to management. Similarly, they're familiar with what PR companies are useful for and what can be done in-house. Consultants provide company structure and organization architecture decisions or models. They help design information flow. And, they can identify in-house artists and copywriters, the network manager, and so forth. They can also help write job descriptions, determine salaries, and review applicants.

Subcontractors. You may need to identify subcontractors to help you do some of the initial work. Perhaps you'll want to pull in a graphic artist to design the common look and feel. You may need someone to do the layout, the HTML, and CGI programming. Perhaps you'll subcontract the creation of your entire intranet.

A word of caution. If you do subcontract, pull the content development back into the hands of the users. And, if possible, pull back the server and directory maintenance as well. The individual groups or departments are quite capable of maintaining their environments and leaving overall intranet administration to the central web group, usually MIS.

Minimum Skills Required   One person may be building your intranet. Or a team may be building it. Here are a set of minimum skills required to put an intranet together.

- Creation of HTML files, CGI scripts, JavaScript, or VB Script
- External database configuration
- Development of user interfaces
- Usability testing

Competencies for an Intranet Staff   When a large staff is working to develop an intranet, a careful blend of skills, competencies, and experience is important to ensure success. We've selected a few here to provide you with the kinds of people needed to build your intranet. The names in the Position column in Table 6-3 are titles that were commonly found during the research of this book.

Table 6-3 Skills, Competencies, and Experience of Intranet Staff

Position	Skills (concrete ability)	Competencies (abstract ability)	Unique Experience
Webmaster	Program management Performance analysis skills Programming skills (Perl, python, C, C++, Java, JavaScript) DMBS management and programming	Strategist, risk assessment, capacity planning, configuration management, subcontractor management, visionary, thrive in chaos, sense of humor, creativity, and fun	Supporting 1M+ daily hit web site with multiple hosts and network feeds Managing and maintaining large-scale, high-availability installations 24 x 7 site management
Gatekeeper	Program management Navigation design Content design On-line publishing processes	Strategist Acting on feedback Risk assessment Conflict management Communication and evangelizing	Software product development Intergroup/cross-functional team management Web management expertise (if possible)

Table 6-3 Skills, Competencies, and Experience of Intranet Staff *(Continued)*

Position	Skills (concrete ability)	Competencies (abstract ability)	Unique Experience
Web Designer	Graphic design Hypertext design Layout Navigation design Content design Cognitive design HTML, CGI, Java, ActiveX	Software development process Human factors Interactivity Feedback mechanisms Subcontractor management	Large scale site design Hypermedia design Multimedia design Library Science Broadcasting
Intranet Departmental Technical Manager	Web Server and browser installation and configuration Network configuration, access control, firewall and security implementation, Internet connectivity Cataloguing directories	Capacity planning Knowledge of HTTP, TCP/IP, and other internet protocols Content and structure management Library and index management	Education and evangelizing skills to help motivate staff to use the intranet effectively Broadcasting

Table 6-3 Skills, Competencies, and Experience of Intranet Staff *(Continued)*

Position	Skills (concrete ability)	Competencies (abstract ability)	Unique Experience
Content Provider	Content development Writing Subject matter expertise	Quality control Currency of topic Market Perception	Expertise in subject, at least 2+ years Writing for multimedia
Web Statitician or Web Marketing Analyst	Statistics Web statistics Audience and marketing analysis Usability testing User requirements and task analysis Developing and tracking customer satisfaction metrics	Human factors Subcontractor management Designing user interface prototypes	Product development Customer packaged goods market research and usability testing 10+ years in human factors design Psychographic dynamics of researching fielding in multiple ethnogeographies

Departmental Responsibilities   Each department is responsible for establishing their own information format and structuring their company knowledge in such a way as to make it useful and linkable to interdependent web sites. Also, the department maintains and updates all information for their group. Usually this group has a gatekeeper. However, most of the content providers are found here.

It requires everyone in the organization to be involved at some level of decision making about what goes onto the intranet and what doesn't. At the most fundamental level, a knowledge worker must make the call to publish her facts, concepts, and procedures. These processes integrate with knowledge managers, who charter and streamline processes. In turn, those decisions support the overarching goals and principles of the intranet site, which are clearly articulated and updated by executive visionaries.

Bottom Line: It takes a global community all contributing their best to build an intranet.

Step 11—Building It In-House or Outsourcing

Either you're going to build your own intranet, support it, and maintain it, or you're going to outsource most of the work. If you're going to outsource everything, try an organization like http://www.association.org for a comprehensive list of outsourcers. This group can help in-house people hone their expertise; they are much more than just a body shop.

Or you can try outsourcing organizations like Internet Media, Inc. http://www.yourcompanyhere.com shown in Figure 6–15. They have a one-stop shop where they provide access, service, maintenance, design, and management of your intranet. They are focused on the smaller business.

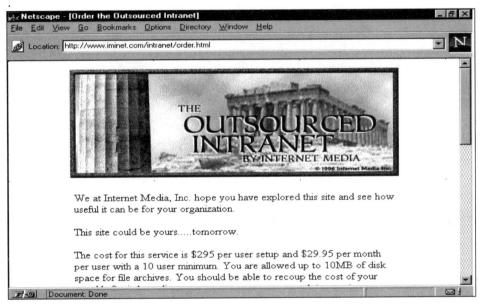

Figure 6–15 Outsourcing Your Intranet

Outsourcing organizations are specifically designed to help companies unleash the power of the Web by developing an intranet strategy and by identifying the people, process, and technology requirements for implementing a focused intranet solution. Their special skills include

- identifying system topology, scalability, and integrating leading third-party products
- web processes and skills development
- security and firewalls

- legacy data integration

- network and systems management

- project management expertise in creating and deploying a pilot intranet project

- security and disaster recovery processes, capacity, and performance tuning

- asset, problem, and change management procedures

- establish, maintain, and support infrastructure

Developing the Intranet

You've got your plan, you've got a design, you've got a prototype, and you've got the people. Now it's time to develop the intranet. The developer of the major part of the intranet lies in the hands of the content provider. If you provide templates, style sheets, tools, guidelines, and automated web pages for the content provider, you will have an intranet up and running much faster than you've ever dreamed. The job of the intranet staff is to create the environment. The job of the content provider is to provide the content.

Your intranet will develop as the intranet community develops. Some of it will be planned and executed with diplomacy and laser striking accuracy, while other products, services, processes, uses, and future pushes will emanate from the ingenious, unguided employee looking to make their own job easier.

Step 1—Empower the Content Provider

Ultimately, the implementation of an intranet is driven by balancing two strongly opposing forces: autonomy and control. Content providers need autonomy in order to participate and to respond rapidly without being slowed down by bureaucracy. Webmasters, on the other hand, need to control the management of the network and to contain costs. Gatekeepers also need to be responsible for content alignment without becoming bottlenecks. Autonomy and control are handled well in the distributed computing model of the intranet.

Much of the management and original content creation need to come from the source. Similarly, the content needs to be managed and kept up to date at the source. Usually this occurs with a content owner adding fresh content, checking live links, ensuring the reliability of the information, and supporting any inquiries behind each level of content that they're responsible for. The distributed computing model of the intranet allows for autonomy of the content provider.

Development occurs in the centralized administration, decentralized content model that we've discussed previously. Fundamental to a quality intranet is to empower the content providers. In Figure 6–16, the large dark circle represents the entire intranet as managed by the Webmaster and the information technology group. Remember this group manages only the physical intranet, the network, and the maintenance of the network.

The rest of the intranet architecture is built on top of and distributed across the entire organization. Gatekeepers manage content at the departmental level and ensure that the proper content is supplied. Content providers create the majority of the web site pages and are held accountable for validity, accuracy, and currency.

In this model control is managed from an architecture position while site creation is autonomous, belonging to each individual provider. This is reminiscent of the publisher's model. Content providers, authors, or contributors submit their information to publishers (gatekeepers), who in turn position the resource on the web site.

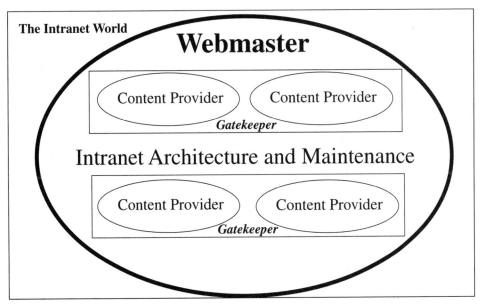

Figure 6–16 Content Providers Have Autonomy, While Intranet Management Has Control

A similar explanation is the country analogy as seen in Figure 6–17. Canada represents one intranet, while the United States represents a second, unique intranet. Security exists in each country to protect proprietary information. Each province and each state represent gatekeeper domains. They are individual and independent, yet integrated with the country they make up. The cities represent the content providers, again independent from other content providers, some in the same state, some not. This model is no surprise, when you consider how intranets democratize enterprise information and transactions.

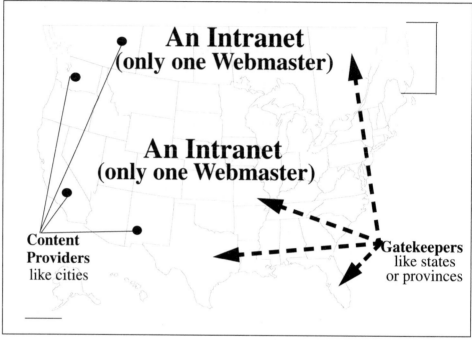

Figure 6–17 The Country/Intranet Analogy

So what do you do to help content providers develop web sites that are integral to the organization and not isolated silos of self-supplying data?

- *Promote early adoption.* Content providers are closer to the information than anyone. Promote an environment for sharing and exchanging what they know and do best. Provide a link strategy that always checks with enterprise goals. Get them moving especially on mission-critical or strategic goals.

- *Promote analysis and creative solutions* at the content provider level. The people responsible for the processes at their level analyze best why something isn't working or repeat what works well based on their shared experience. Intranet-connected teams solve problems more quickly and respect change more rapidly. Promote creativity and "time to think." Reward innovative or excellent solutions.

- *Provide a tool kit.* As soon as you discover them, place tools, open standards, templates, libraries, graphics, audio sounds, plug-ins, and innovative support at their fingertips. Provide a central source of resources and let them create! Tools, helpful procedures, and templates need to be accessible at the top level of the intranet.

- *Allow grass-roots, organic development, "web anarchy," and managed chaos.* There is already a strong sense of an internet "community" around your company. How could anyone possibly have missed the internet explosion? Internet development did not come through careful speculation and planning. Rather, it came from grass-roots groups just getting out there and doing it. Teach this lesson internally. Then mature to a balanced centralized-decentralized model.

- *Promote accelerated growth.* Plan for immediate implementation of an intranet. Provide the strategic platform framework required for success. Although web servers will multiply, network traffic will jam, and no central information architecture will exist. The beauty of an intranet is being able to tie it all together in a short period of time for a small cost.

Step 2—Develop and Post Policies, Procedures, and Templates

Publishing Process   You need a process for pushing out pages to the server. You can stage their creation on individual workstations, or work off staging servers. Figure out the process for publishing documents officially onto your intranet site. You need method for authorizing the placement of information on a web site (unless it is a personal web site). Group web sites, departmental web sites, and the major intranet web page all need more documental control management, so automating the process is in your best interests.

Publish on-line support regarding how to create hypermedia content. Define the procedures for submitting content for approval by department. Instill editing and approval for submission. Identify ways for the information to appear in other web sites. Advertising may come to mind. And, some of the lessons learned from placing banners on pages to indicate to others about the availability of information on a web site are very helpful.

Involve the publisher or the Webmaster for issues of decency, legality, security, and urgency of information dissemination.

Procedures for publishing on the intranet might include the following:

- e-mail to Gatekeeper@yourcompany.com

- Request to put info on Web

- Request to put feedback capability on pages or links

- Review for conformance to page format, appropriate content, and accuracy, and so forth.

- Determine placement in structure.

- Create announcement service (subscription service)

Bottom Line: Provide standards and processes for publication, but generally speaking, remain ultimately flexible.

Legal   Have legal articulate clear, brief, and unambiguous language on permissible behavior such as language, prohibited use, trademark, confidential information, permissible external links. At Intel for example,

> Our new policy restricted outbound Internet access to specific systems. Inbound access was limited to certain protocols going to dedicated servers. The outbound systems, controlled by site administrators, would be tightly controlled. Applications for Internet access systems would have to be signed by site network managers, the system administrator's manager, and our internal Information Security group. Applicants promised to read and obey our policy, which was circulated with the application forms. ftp://ftp.intel.com/pub/papers/horses.txt

Publish Style Guides   Publish a style guide with a collection of templates showing standard page layouts, graphic locations and size recommendations, link strategies, standard navigation buttons, scripts, required textual information online, and so forth. In Figure 6–18 you can see an example from Sun Microsystem's style guide.

Linking procedure   You must have a strategy or a procedure for linking sites to one another. At first, it seems there is no problem when you link to a site. Sure you know each other, you're working on a project together. But, the site must be reliable and accurate in order to link up to your site. In fact, you will grow dependent on the validity of the sites you are linking to. They represent expert content, and you need it to complement your site.

The links must include a transaction so each of the parties concerned understands the commitment and responsibilities expected of their linking partnership. Someone ultimately must be responsible for the link. So, an intranet form that includes

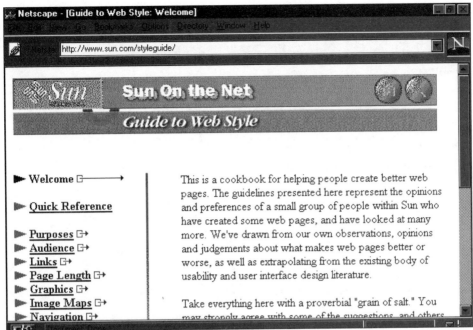

Figure 6–18 Sun Microsystems Design Page

everyone in the linking procedure can be built to manage the linking and qualify a linking partnership. In Figure 6–19, a link request form is used at Sun Microsystems to capture the linking procedure.

Step 3—Create Feedback Loops

The beauty of the intranet is getting internal feedback about your site content and method of presenting it to users. You need to make sure the employees can contact you for questions, for clearing up misunderstandings, for partnering with you, for sharing common processes, and especially for linking up and creating wealth creating interdependencies. Use forms. Use e-mail. Use on-line discussions. Use videoconferencing. Use interactive games. Just create feedback mechanisms that go both ways openly.

Sun Microsystems, Inc. had a clever idea on using feedback in the form of reward and recognition for the best web site design, the best content, and so forth, in their What's New section as a way of getting users to identify the criteria for a good

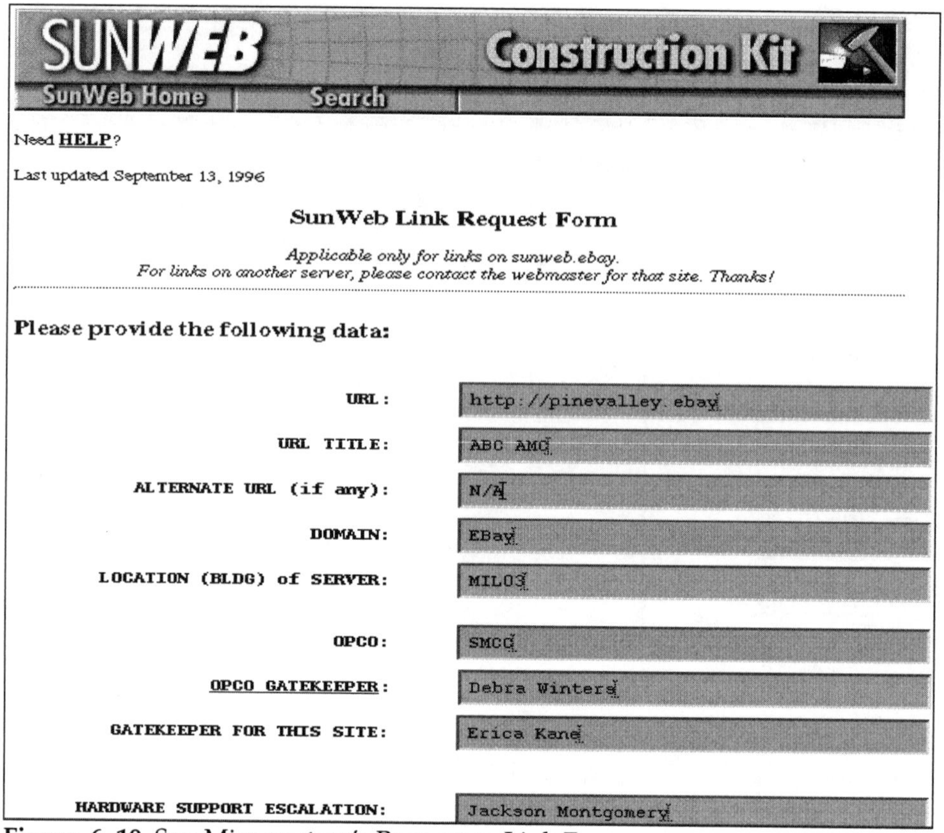

SUNWEB Construction Kit

SunWeb Home | Search

Need **HELP**?

Last updated September 13, 1996

SunWeb Link Request Form

Applicable only for links on sunweb.ebay.
For links on another server, please contact the webmaster for that site. Thanks!

Please provide the following data:

URL:	http://pinevalley.ebay
URL TITLE:	ABC AMG
ALTERNATE URL (if any):	N/A
DOMAIN:	EBay
LOCATION (BLDG) of SERVER:	MIL03
OPCO:	SMCC
OPCO GATEKEEPER:	Debra Winters
GATEKEEPER FOR THIS SITE:	Erica Kane
HARDWARE SUPPORT ESCALATION:	Jackson Montgomery

Figure 6–19 Sun Microsystem's Request to Link Form

site. Naturally, everyone is welcome to participate, to vote, and to comment on the results. Feedback is essential to self-efficacy and self-improvement on the Web. See Figure 6–20.

Step 4—Create Departmental Sites

Create access to key corporate information. Develop a centralized clearinghouse page, where new items are posted, where every web page passes, that is the center of your intranet culture—a community hall. This is your strategic 30,000-mile view. Critical pages are indexed here, and appropriate links are managed. The common look and feel is showcased here. Embed appropriate design items: navi-

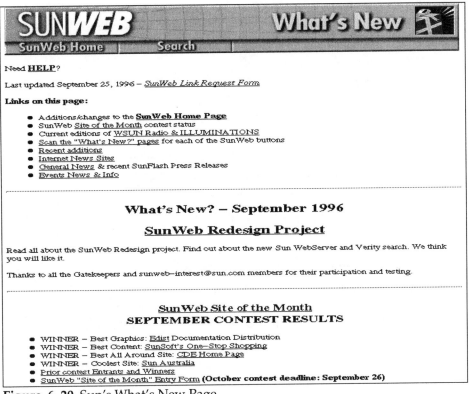

Figure 6–20 Sun's What's New Page

gation, layout, content design, cognitive design, human interaction design, and graphics. Publicize a central home page URL. Some common approaches are summarized in this list.

1. ***Start with an Organizational View.*** Provide access into key areas (marketing, sales, human resources, executive, PR, customer relations, investor relations, etc.). Appoint an owner. Define responsibilities of ownership. Produce and provide process for linking to this level

2. ***Provide an A–Z Department Directory.*** This is by far the most popular feature of an intranet. A lot of us have been trained to use alphabetized telephone books. It's encouraging to know that some of the old resources are still available.

3. ***Provide International Presence*** (if appropriate for your organization). Provide complete lists of international web sites, services, and directory information. Plus whatever is unique to each site. Provide language and design the culture into the site.

4. *What's New!* Provide late breaking news area. Update this area frequently. Announce new intranet sites. Announce business streamlining processes. Reward and recognize intranet sites that are making a difference. Show by example.

5. *Provide Entertainment.* Create things like news tickers written in Java, international news, CEO responds to Dilbert tips, and stock quotes. Offer games that demo products, or teach concepts about the company. Provide chat areas with the CEO, and so forth.

6. *Self-Improvement Area.* Create action lists, post what needs to happen. Make the continuous process improvement of the site obvious and interactive. Invite participation and evaluation.

7. *Intranet Architecture and Policy.* Again, this models the way you want your employees to build on the intranet. Provide architectural designs and all the help and tools you can to produce intranets at their own level, linking to the central administrative, organizational site, your home page.

8. *Financial Information.* This needs to include historical financial information, access to legacy database and tools for extracting data from data warehouses. Revenue, performance, cost models, budgetary roll-ups, and so forth.

9. *HR Button.* Intranets have to have access to medical information, personal information, benefits information, and other HR services. This is a legal requirement, as certain HR information must be available to employees 24 hours a day, 7 days a week. So HR needs their own presence at the top of any intranet home page. Similarly employees need information to common questions, such as, How do I move my desk? How do I get my room temperature adjusted?

10. *Management Information.* Implement security around sensitive management information. Payroll can certainly be moved on-line, but not everyone needs access to it. Salary planning, employee changes, software quality index, and production schedules need to be centrally located for managers.

Step 5—Design and Develop Database Integration

Intranet Database Connectivity   Establish a dedicated and centrally managed database server infrastructure, based on a reduced variety of hardware platforms, to be accessed in a client/server approach. Such an infrastructure should be dedicated to databases and not be mixed with other services. Offer partitions to each major database community and provide full support for operations, systems, and database software, as well as central database administration.

Choose a preferred server configuration, with a database running on a server with a reliable Operating System (OS). You may want to consider grouping your servers to cover your main needs. Most likely, you'll need

- *an administrative support server* to manage logging and control of your DB-based applications. These include purchasing, accounting, receivables, document management, import/export of goods, human resources, and so forth.

- *a technical support server* to manage your project planning, cataloging, installation, operation, maintenance, testing, and backups

Each server group has different service definitions and different base user populations, although, in practice, a distributed database model is becoming more and more apparent.

The character-mode tools will generally be maintained on these servers to allow existing applications to run in client mode. Users, however, are strongly advised to prepare for migration to tools that offer general-purpose interactive services.

The centralized acquisition, distribution, and installation of basic, general-purpose database software and documentation should be maintained in the IT division, as well as a centralized first-line support team.

OBDC and JDBC   OBDC or JDBC tool compliance (an SQL database access interface) presents a split in the way databases are accessed for the intranet. The OBDC differences are noted in Figure 6-4.

Table 6-4 OBDC vs. JDBC

ODBC	JDBC
Microsoft standard for PCs and LANs	Sun/Netscape/Oracle superset of ODBC
Server application	Rides with the client
CGI oriented	Java oriented
HTTP driven	Tracks user name, tracks passwords, can maintain a single database connection, and perform multiple transactions

Access popular ODBC databases such as Microsoft SQL Server, Access, dBase IV, Foxpro, Paradox, and Excel with Cold Fusion, available at http://www.allaire.com/.

Host Access   Today's web environments must interact with, or at least extract data from, key applications on a variety of host platforms. Integrate existing host data and applications with web/internet/intranet capabilities to increase the availability and value of host-based information. Use 3270/5250-to-HTML converters. Provide server-based 3270/5250 development tools with Visual Basic®

and ActiveX™ custom controls. Replicate host data on SQL Server and access via Internet Information Server (IIS). Provide a direct connection with host via Microsoft's IIS. Use Java™ as an add-on.

Step 6—Usability Test Your Designs

Create a staging server, so you can attempt to administrate the intranet before releasing to your employees. Usability test it with various groups. Get as much cross-functional input regarding the architecture and design as possible. Ensure navigation works the way you designed it. Examine how well users can use the index and search tier of your intranet. Time test to understand how long it's taking for an average user to find what they're looking for.

Determine if the site is laid out logically for the average user. Get them to speak out loud when they're surfing around the intranet. Observe them in their working environment if possible. You can never stop usability testing either, because your intranet will continue to grow. Keys are performance, reliability, availability and serviceability.

Step 7—Publish Your Intranet

Taking the intranet site from pilot to live system is a fairly easy process. Once you have completed usability testing and made changes to design, especially navigational design, you are ready to test all the links to make sure they are active. Server software provides this functionality for you. Develop a process for determining a ready, set, go policy for publishing.

- Ensure that all contributors understand the cutoff time and get their content processed before that deadline

- Get approvals from each gatekeeper that all content is ready to go

- Get approvals from legal that all issues have been resolved

- Get approvals from the information technology group that all outstanding bandwidth issues have been resolved

- Get approval from security people that all security issues have been resolved

- Webmaster makes final word "go"

Communicate across the Organization   As you become more intranet oriented, communicating new information on the intranet will be as simple as subscribing to the central intranet page. Banners are useful, as mentioned previously, much as they're used in advertising on the Internet. Also, you'll use e-mail to distribute information about the web site's new release.

Also, it is advised to advertise the intranet presence and highlights throughout the organization using traditional channels. You can advertise in common lunching areas, send out flyers, add the information in the newsletter. You can also do a mailing when Human Resources sends out its frequent mailings.

The process for announcing web information on the intranet will grow more likely on the intranet as people begin using it more frequently. Undoubtedly, you must build a process within your intranet for subscribing to the intranet, and posting new information. Again, this is done successfully on the Internet, so get your examples from there. Once this process is in place, it can be easily automated in a Web environment. The outlook is hopeful, for the future holds a place for each individual employee, where customized information will be sent to you on a continuous basis, while you provide feedback for updates and improved profiling.

Manage the Intranet

In many ways, the intranet will manage itself. Much like the post office system, where mail and information flow freely with the price of a stamp, the intranet will allow the free flowing of information among people, both on a personal level and on a collaborative level.

However, the intranet still needs to be managed from the point of view of coordinating a vast resource of knowledge and designing it with an architecture that makes it highly valuable for employees, and ultimately customers. Certainly there is network management, server management, and administrative management. These constitute the greatest amount of management.

Push as much management down to the client as possible. Get the content providers to manage their documentation, the metatags, and the directory structures where they will be posting. Centralize upgrades, database access, network management on the centralized, or enterprisewide servers. Constantly review and update goals to make sure they're aligned with each web site in some way. Collect metrics—innovative ways to model and capture expert human performance behavior.

Make sure you can remotely administer all the critical intranets from any site. You don't want your administrative web server sitting in a restricted area, unless you can access it from afar. Also, make sure that you can make changes to the server's configuration easily. Sometimes your technical Webmaster will need to apply operating system updates or other patches that won't always be obvious from the start. Make sure you can add or increase processor, memory, and disk components when your intranet project explodes.

Step 1—Choose Software for Web Management

There are many tasks a web staff is responsible for at the administrative level.
You'll need good administration or server site administration tools. Major corporations are including administration in their full-service solutions. They essentially are all the same. Some user interfaces are more intuitive than others, but this is dependent upon the tools you are accustomed to.

Intranet Administration Required Tasks

- Link Management, both deadlinks and orphans
- Multiple Webmaster access
- Server management (caching, mirror, proxy, administrative)
- Database support
- File and directory management
- File age control
- Access control
- Authentication
- Version control
- Template, library, design, look-and-feel management
- Server side or client side support

Key Features of Administration Tools

- Identify and fix broken links, notify link changes
- Maintain integrity of document collections
- Track changes
- Support on-line real-time user and group administration
- Ensure the validity of a single source of accurate up-to-date information for user analysis
- Manage internal and external IP addresses
- Build templates and wizards for intranet sites
- Remote access and support
- Automatic full-text search capability, page archiving, version control
- On-line support, training, report generators, and security features

Link and URL Management Links between pages and content can easily be broken. Why? Because someone stops managing a site. They leave the company. They change departments. The web site rots like an overripe fruit. The atrophying of links must be managed. Once you set and publish a link, don't change it because users and other pages rely on it.

Similarly, Universal Resource Locators (URLs) can be changed without the Webmaster's knowledge. Netscape has developed LiveWire Site Manager, a visual site management tool allowing web sites to be modified with "drag-and-drop" ease. Microsoft has FrontPage. Adobe has PageMill. NetCarta has WebMapper. Search the market for what suits you best.

Access Control and Server Configuration Management The Webmaster sets up access control. Who gets in? Who and what gets out? How are individual groups protected on the intranet? Password protection and password management need to be set up. Manage lock features on proxy configurations, default home pages, customized help menus, and customized directory buttons.

Manage directories and catalogues Directory servers manage your large directory structures, especially because they expand at enormous rates. Cataloging needs to occur. Find the appropriate software to facilitate this effort.

Step 2—Use Document Management Software

Document Management You'll be dealing with large libraries of documents. You need to index them, categorize them, integrate them, manage their reliability and availability. You need to spellcheck and automatically create databases based on common hyperlinks to alert new developers of potential links or partnerships. As sites become larger and more complex, the issues of internal consistency and structure have taken on new dimensions.

Features of Document Management Software

- Manage your web site as a single document
- Resolve links
- Version control
- Automatically generate navigation buttons and dynamic table of contents
- Ensure valid HMTL

Step 3—Manage the Network

Indexing   Index pages so that users can easily search through the organization's knowledge. This is usually accomplished by software that automatically runs on the server. Provide indexing to look for something specific, to widen the search, to focus the search on a function or department. Searching should support multiple file types and subdirectories.

Purging   If you don't use it, lose it. Retire pages from the web site, archive them, and provide FTP to the archives if you think it's important to maintain the data for future trending or analysis.

Security/Access   Maintain user accounts and passwords. Set up general access for everyone. Teach people how to secure their information on their site.

Maintaining Directories   Directories need to be created, deleted, and renamed. Organize the directories according to the higher-level groupings from your home page. Try to use the same names or words for directories as you're using as titles for your pages.

Manage Network   Monitor disk space usage closely. If disk space usage approaches capacity, you'll have to add more. You may want to consider redesigning or reorganizing. Monitor system throughput. Establish minimum acceptable levels for response times. Upgrade frequently. Always be reading about new development tools, search engines, and operating system. Back up and restore server regularly.

Step 4—Manage Your Multimedia Files

Bundle multimedia editors for images, sound, video, and other multimedia types, and tighten integration with industry-leading multimedia tools from Adobe, Corel, Macromedia, and others.

You'll need to also manage your graphics files, your video files, your audio files, and your multimedia files. You'll need tools to create these files, edit them, store them, and present them to all of the users on your intranet. Also, you'll need a tool to create templates for your users to use. Make these templates standardized documents. Try to create as many objects as possible. You may easily replicate objects across web sites, since many templates use repeating multimedia elements. Jave applets and ActiveX controls provide this kind of functionality.

Step 5—Manage E-Mail

Look for point-and-click administration of e-mail and newsgroups. Look for software that supports multiple domains per server and addresses per user. Develop a policy regarding the saving of e-mail and ensure that it is clear to all employees which e-mail needs to be saved for auditing purposes. Integrate e-mail with your data warehouse. A lot of e-mail is useful information to others within the organization. Keep aware of the changes in e-mail protocols, especially those evolving from SMTP, to POP, to IMAP. Each version provides increased functionality.

User Management Features   Several aspects of e-mail management may be passed down to users, including automatic replies and user profile information. Administrators will be able to arbitrarily set limits on user resource consumption, including mailbox sizes, total disk space usage, incoming and outgoing message size limits, and shared folder usage. Infinite mail loops will be automatically detected and prevented.

Step 6—Manage the Security

Look for security standard Secure Socket Layer (SSL) 3.0. It enables secure remote administration and prevents network-based attacks. Additional security enhancements support multiple levels of password security. Benefits include greater access flexibility, minimally privileged process, restricted access, storage of users in a separate database, and S/KEY single-session key-encrypting client-server communications, including passwords.

Step 7—Manage the News Server

Administrators will also gain more flexibility in setting management policies for discussion groups and the overall server environment, including limitations on discussion group and messages sizes, as well as expiration, purging, archiving, and backup policies.

Step 8—Manage the Database Servers

Dynamic index configuration will allow database indexes to be created or removed by the administrator on the fly. Robustness will be improved with automatic detection and repair of errors. Look for tools for analyzing and tuning the database, including an easy-to-use interface for optimizing the directory server's performance.

Step 9—Manage the Proxy Server

You can manage a network of proxy servers with Netscape's simple, remote administration and SNMP v1 or v2 and route web traffic using Proxy Scripting and Navigator's Automatic Proxy Configuration feature.

Look for the ability to perform configuration rollback, enabling administrators to tune configurations without major planning efforts or high-risk implementations. Encrypted communication remote administration is made possible using SSL.

Additionally, proxy server management requires transaction logging and analysis logging of all HTTP, FTP, and Gopher transactions in common or extended log formats, including referrer field, user agent, and transaction completion status.

Step 10—*Manage Intellectual Assets, Intranet Problems, and Change*

In order for an intranet to be built truly for its users, by its users, and of its users, you need to manage three essential areas: intellectual assets, intranet problems, and change within the enterprise.

Intellectual Assets   Intellectual assets are strategic procedures and processes that your group knows how to do best. This information can be valuable to people, if available at the right time. If you're offering your services or products for free, then place your intellectual assets at the top of your web site. If you are charging for them (which many will), then create a marketing page that extols your service and product and advertise it on your intranet.

Problem Management   Make sure all information has owners. Create action lists of what kinds of problems you need to manage: cost avoidances, traps, legal issues, and so forth, that will occur and make that information available to all Webmasters and gatekeepers to promote at their individual sites.

Change Management   Your organization will change faster than anyone can keep up. Define the top-level organization structure and make it available for the rest of the enterprise to know what you represent. But, remember, many people want a functional perspective, others want a business perspective, still others are interested in a contact perspective. Make your design flexible enough, however, to accommodate for the many restructurings, reorganizations, and growths of your enterprise.

Bridge to the 21st Century

No matter how you build your intranet today, the need for it will be larger, more sophisticated, and faster in a few short years. Bandwidth is for sale, and you'll see plenty of companies (including telecommunication companies) scrambling for your bandwidth dollars. Your intranet, today, is a small feat to express how your corporation and community transform into the digital economy. Networked intelligence will only improve itself. To support those efforts, government has taken groundbreaking action for improving the international development of intranets worldwide. In doing so, you'll see that getting an intranet to work right, and work now, is imperative for economic global participation.

Summary of Key Points

- **FIRST THINGS FIRST**

  These are the first things you need to do if you're going to set up an intranet. They include defining a purpose, articulating a guiding principle, communicating and inviting participation, and a shift in thinking about organizations as organic.

- **PLANNING THE INTRANET**

  The section provides a step-by-step planning guide to prepare you and your organization for setting up an intranet plan. Align management, mandate an open technological environment, create a cross-functional web group, determine information needs and intranet use, and write a mission statement.

- **DESIGNING THE INTRANET**

  Here we provide a step-by-step management template for setting up intranet in your organization. We discuss technical setup from the management perspective. We include information about intranet services including FTP, chatting, search tools, agents, and filters. We introduce the array of tools you need to decide on, avoiding brand names and focusing on functionality. We explain the need to create both a centralized web site and an intranet blueprint. Finally, we identify the human resources required.

- **DEVELOPING THE INTRANET**

  This is a short and easy guide for setting up templates, procedures, and policies for developing your intranet components. It focuses on empowering the content provider as the key developer of the intranet. It advocates legacy design setup as well. These are the steps to consider as managers of intranet development.

- **MANAGING THE INTRANET**

  In large part, the intranet will manage itself if you've decentralized your intranet. There are some issues in network management, server management, administrative management that require you to centralize the physical administration of the intranet for reliability and security.

CHAPTER 7

How Do I Know
It's Working?

Most web sites take a lot of time and effort to create and successfully launch. But after this extensive work, many people are left asking the question: Is it doing the job? The way to find out, of course, is through web metrics. Ouch. Don't let the word metrics scare you. Web metrics are simply numbers and graphs that describe technical and human performance.

Corporate executive teams readily admit that they maintain two sets of measures: the ones they are required to disclose to shareholders (financials) and the strategic ones they actually use to manage the business (performance and outcomes). With your business on an intranet, you can observe and track knowledge processes or the strategies employees use to solve problems or handle processes. Like the brain, all on-line transactions (experiences) between departments (parts of the body and the outside environment) are recorded. The interactions make up intelligence.

Expertise is gained as we solve problems and gain further knowledge of our performance over time. We enrich the intranet data warehouses with practical skills that make up intelligence. We use all metacognitive skills to utilize the intelligence on-line—we plan on-line; we select from knowledge on-line; we connect to other sites to enhance our knowledge base; we tune our web sites to more accurately portray the concept, process, procedure or principle we're trying to establish; and we monitor value and effectiveness through web metrics.

When your intranet site gets developed quickly, you will know it's working merely by the rapid growth and activity that you'll see. Employees will find ways to get work done faster and smarter, and you'll be able to observe the effects on your network, and the workflow and process streamlining due to the intranet.

Three Types of Web Metrics

In order to understand how the intranet site is working, you need to examine three levels of measurement:

- Web traffic analysis for technical tuning

- Workflow measurement

- Human performance measurement

Web traffic analysis is empirical in providing hard facts to help with technical tuning. Interpretation is bound to human analysis and carries with it both the objective and subjective responses of the Web analyst. Other forms of measurement for analyzing workflow are emerging: clickstreaming (studying the series of clicks any one user follows), search word analysis (looking at the words that users use to search for information), and cookies (interactive cues on web pages that are designed to identify the user's interests and choices). Cookies are emerging as a standard for profiling employees usage behavior and are investigative in determining user workflow.

Bottom Line: Aligning goals to human performance improvement may prove the intranet to be the champion computer science discovery of the 21st century.

Organizations of every kind have increased their use of computers and networks to perform work. In doing so, they have left a trail of worker behavior that is very revealing. Many completed projects in an organization leave behind memos, project-managed PERT charts, presentations, spreadsheets, desktop publishing documentation, e-mail, discussion group threads, policies, and notes stored in every format. Weaved together, this information is a treasure map of how to get work done in your organization.

Many organizations used to, or are still, keeping databases of best practices. The concept of a data warehouse is similar in maintaining large bodies of data and storing them for various kinds of access on demand.

On an intranet, these gems of process can be synchronized and visually designed to provide an accurate picture of work behavior, or learning behavior. Once visually designed, such processes can be accessed by anyone and can be used to solve problems, answer questions, negotiate business transactions, show process flaws, and identify organizational goals. The intranet is yet to unfold.

Reasons for Observing Web Metrics

The first reason to observe web information is to design sites that improve performance and enable the user's ability to navigate quickly through the intranet site. Users aren't going to rely very much on your intranet if it is not interesting, logical, or technically demanding. You already know that navigation design is key to making a good site. With web metrics, you can continuously evaluate your users and make sure that the design efforts pay off.

Another key reason is to identify broken or dead links that don't provide any information to the user. Dead links occur when directories or files have been moved to another location. This occurs because of the constant maintenance on servers to streamline the way files are stored. It's inevitable that something will be eliminated or changed without someone's knowledge and you'll have dead links. Link dead links and identify orphans as well. Orphans are pages which rely upon other pages but become orphaned when their parents are removed from the click-through traffic.

The most compelling reason to observe web metrics is to improve human performance. The study of Human Performance Technology (HPT) is not a new one. In fact, it has quite a following in cognitive science, learning psychology, systems engineering, artificial intelligence, information technology, ergonomics and human factors, psychometrics, feedback systems, organizational development and change, intervention systems, and psycholinguistics.

Bottom Line: Web metrics improve human performance on your intranet.

These disciplines have dissected how humans perform, how they learn to improve their performance, and how they develop new technologies to enhance their performance. The methods are in place. It is only now that the tool has arrived to harness all this creative discovery into action.

Not until now have the methods for analyzing human performance and designing solutions to improve human performance been integrated with a globally distributed system of the intranet and equally tied to the global consciousness of the Internet. The *catalyst* **is the user's ability to integrate their work processes in a universal, viewable environment dedicated to managing an integrated whole system**. The intranet is the perfect performance measurement tool that culminates in an organization conducting business in an electronic environment—a new business, a transformed business, a continuously improving business.

Web Metrics Benefits

Web metrics have many capabilities that seem technical or mechanical at first. As you see in Table 7-1, you can gather all sorts of information about the web site and the user. Webmasters use this information to fine-tune their servers. Web designers analyze data for usability. Business simplification analysts examine web metrics to identify business processes and improve workflow.

Gathering the information is one thing. Knowing what to do with it to help your web site, your intranet, and your organization is something that you'll take seriously once you get started. Learning how to utilize the information may require a bit of study on web metric interpretation. Most of the information that has been collected so far is outside Internet marketing data. Engaging a competent web statistician is not a bad idea in a large organization. In a small organization, you may not have the luxury of adding to the staff, so much of the responsibility will fall on the Webmaster.

Table 7-1 Web Metrics and Their Benefits

Web Metric	Benefit
Analyze top web site hits.	Plan the server load of the responsible web site.
Determine the top users or departments of a site.	Identify who your internal customers are, so you can streamline processes or gather user requirements more effectively.
Determine graphical location of hits.	Distribute additional servers across the geographic locations for faster access and localization.
Show top files, grouped by directory.	Determine the effectiveness of directory architecture. Are some directories plump, or starving?
Show usage by time.	Determine peak loads and prepare other network activities accordingly.

Table 7-1 Web Metrics and Their Benefits *(Continued)*

Web Metric	Benefit
Look at multimedia files, audio, video, graphics.	Discover the web pages that are requiring the most memory.
Examine the various errors that occur when users fail to connect	Highlights broken links and signals which servers are stressed.
Identify what a user is looking at the most.	Monitor usage policy and track security issues.
Analyze how people are finding the site.	Assists in navigational design.
Which pages are linking to mine?	Uncover internal customers that find value-added in the work I create. Possible links.
Which words are people searching for to find my site?	Used to contribute to the search terminology and metatags used to identify a web site.
Are people using images from my site without permission?	Legal issues can be tracked more easily, with intermediate solutions being applied.
Who has bookmarked my page?	Can provide spontaneous associations with other sites, organically evolving your site into something even bigger than your mission.
Which types of errors are occurring?	Retrain staff in order to eliminate common errors.
How many times have people requested something that returned an error?	Evaluate the effectiveness of the training.

Certainly this table does not reflect all of the possibilities of web measures and their benefits. What's amazing is the ability to look at human performance using Web technology. Needless to say, the right variables are in place to make this a serious study in the immediate future.

Web Site Traffic Analysis for Technical Tuning

What we've learned from internet site metrics can be equally applied to an intranet for analyzing how the network is handling increased web site traffic. You need to review web traffic measurements in order to perform capacity planning. You have two basic responsibilities: Do you have enough bandwidth? Are your servers configured to handle your network activity?

Some of the departments in your organization can be quite the bandwidth consumer hogs, so it's important to know who is using what resources, how they are using the resources, and how this is affecting everyone else around them. This kind of vigilance is required of all network activities, nothing out of the ordinary here, really.

Each time a user interacts with your intranet site, your server software records information about the interaction. This is commonly known as a "hit." It is recorded in a special file called a *log file*, which can be viewed easily by anyone wishing to look. Web statisticians, or web metric software, filter through log files and examine what is known as a *clickstream*. A *clickstream* is a series of URLs and IP addresses that a person passes through from their point of entry on your web site to the point of departure.

Some software programs make reading log files very user-friendly. Software exists to make log files readable in tables, charts, and live formats where you can see the changes on a real-time basis. Your needs will determine the kinds of metric software you invest in. See Figure 7–1.

With this information you can examine peak load times on the server, geographically locate your users, and size your configuration based on the volume of electronic transfers. This is the brilliance of the intranet.

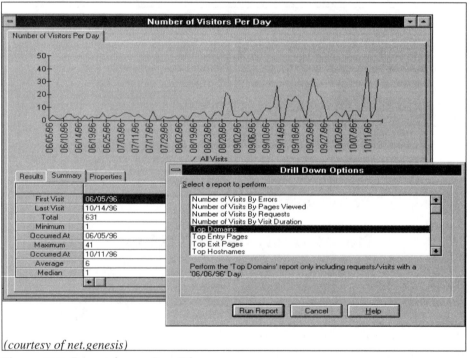

(courtesy of net.genesis)

Figure 7–1 Report from a Log File

You can see which documents are accessed more frequently, when the busiest hours on the network are, who is using most of the storage space, and whose pages are drawing the most attention. You are able to see a series of reports that focus on web site content and traffic. You can observe trends in overall usage of your intranet site. You can observe the most commonly viewed pages by directory level and browser type. You can examine the number of visitors from different geographic locations. How many are from the United States? How many are international organizations?

Web Metrics Software

You don't have to get technical and learn how to read these log files. Instead various companies have developed software to measure web traffic statistics. The programs produce textual or graphical reports that read access logs like a database and allow you to query them for analysis.

Textual reports, like the one **wwwstats** produced in Figure 7–2 provide data in a table format, written in HTML. Information is broken down by different queries. Here, we're looking at total transfers per date and per hour.

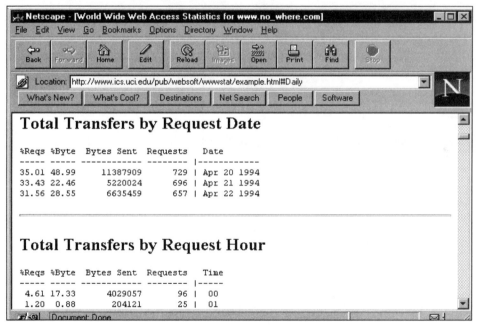

Figure 7–2 Graphical Usage Log—Number of Visitors Per Day

The graphical reports are certainly easier to view and provide quick analysis of web site behavior. However, both reports provide powerful information to help determine web site performance. Take a look at Interse, Microsoft's latest web metric acquisition for another example of excellent graphical output.

Web Metrics Software Companies

There are several web metrics companies. Some of them originated as programming projects of college students who wrote brilliant Perl scripts to slice and dice the metrics for your analysis. Others, like *net.Genesis* partnered with *the Webmasters Guild*, are graphical interactive databases that help you drill down in the data.

Instead of naming all the software companies in business, it would be best to direct your attention to *WebMaster Magazine's* web site of metric companies that they've screened for you. They call this section "WebSite Counters and Trackers" (their name for web metrics tools). It will keep you current on the best and the breakthroughs in metrics software. See http://www.cio.com/WebMaster/wm_notes.html#Trackers/.

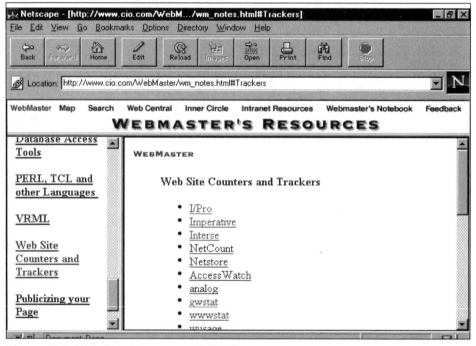

Figure 7–3 Web Site Counters and Trackers

Key Features for Analytical Tools

Software must be able to understand intranet "log files." They need to work well with large log files and perform automatic handling of log files generated by info-system daemons (ftp, gopher, http). They must be able to report graphical trends, as well as provide tabular and readable data. They must be searchable. Web metrics software requires excellent support and innovative thinking. The company must understand both the technical and the human performance side of web metrics.

Web metrics software must be evolutionary in nature. In large intranets, your best bet is to start looking for a web statistician and provide a dedicated resource to finding the right tool and keeping it finely tuned. Web statisticians can provide quantifiable results to your web site's traffic performance and help you evolve into the next generation of human performance measurement on your intranet.

Web Statistician

Web statisticians support the development, assessment, and refinement of an intranet site. They focus on calibrating and understanding the web site audience and on the human factors of the displays, interactive features, and software functions that are supportive of and are relevant to the site audience. It is expected that this individual will contribute substantially to the creative design of the site.

Web Statistician Audience/Market Research

- Plan and execute web-site-specific market and audience research to provide a thorough, ongoing understanding of the audience for the web site.

- Responsible for audience and market analysis which underlays all business and investment decisions for the web site.

- Drive planning, design, and implementation of all systems and processes related to measuring and understanding the web site audience.

Web Statistician Responsibilities

- Develop a database which contains customer profile information captured off the intranet.

- Use assessment tools and profile existing usage patterns.

- Create and define customer satisfaction measures.

- Conduct field studies, user analysis, task analysis, and task profiling.

- Create processes to yield monthly customer satisfaction data.

- Manage/create internal test facilities as required.

Web statisticians will have some intriguing jobs. They'll bring back the interests seen in artificial intelligence research and some of the higher order cognitive studies in the 1960s. They will attempt to use fuzzy logic, inferential thinking, information processing analysis, and other psychological studies to determine human performance factors on-line.

They take activity records and define the complex human actions required to create those activity records and associate motivations and thought processes to these complex human actions. They develop tests to refine their understanding and test the accuracy of the thought processes and motivations that they believe they have seen or expect to see. In some ways, they'll be web psychologists analyzing the integration of intranets and human performance.

Workflow Measurements

If we go beyond the mere analysis of web site traffic statistics and examine other data collecting methods like clickstreaming or search word streaming, we begin to observe insights into the mental models of a user. With clickstreaming and search word streaming we can observe linguistic patterns, based on metatags or search words. If we can create mental models through sophisticated data collection on the intranet, we may have a fair chance of providing direction for improving the way knowledge is managed and created on the intranet.

Click Streaming

Clickstreaming studies the individual clicks a user makes from entry to departure in a web site. This means following the user's path and information flow. In essence, we are simply following URLs or links. These links may or may not have related information in the URL. But, we can identify Web pages visited and design a navigational map that may provide a language frame for how the user makes decisions.

Unfortunately, we cannot access any more than the URL, so we're not certain why the individual is accessing a particular page. If we use metatags in our documents and access the metatags as well in the header, then we may use linguistic analysis to determine some meaning. Clickstream data can be compared to caching data to identify certain congruities between what are the most popular URLs and what methods of getting to them can be observed.

Clickstreaming can provide significant data; however, interpretation remains subjective. Over time evaluating historical clickstreams, we can develop a cogent understanding of a user's clicking behavior. Undoubtedly, users continue using the same strategies for searching and utilizing information. Whether the clicking behavior translates into human knowledge representation is a matter for careful study.

Search Word Streaming

Search word streaming is similar to clickstream analysis and provides much more linguistic information to determine what kinds of information an individual is searching for. The information comes from the search engine databases that you use to provide search capability on your intranet.

In search word streaming, we analyze the words the user chooses in a search tool. Then we examine jump-off points to specific URLs the person went to, and whether or not they returned to the search tool to refine their search. We can parse the metalanguage of search word streaming and perform discourse analysis to determine how the user(s) is interacting with the intranet to dig deeper into the intranet's knowledge warehouses.

Feedback mechanisms can be put in place to send information back to the user regarding our analyses of their search patterns. We are attempting to understand how to evoke the same thought patterns. With search word streaming, the choices of the user must be processed by human analytical effort, thus slowing down the interaction.

Again this is pioneering researching in identifying human thought processes over the intranet. However, with the enormous sums of data being collected regarding human interactions with the intranet, we will soon have some substantial data to support some of the claims of these more advanced Web analysis measurements.

Using Cookies to Measure Workflow

Cookies are another web metric that we use to measure user behavior and workflow on the intranet. A *cookie* is a technical term for a nugget of information that's sent by a web server to a browser and then back again from the browser to the web server. This establishes an interactive transaction between the user and the intranet. This state of interaction is new for internet technology. It means information is two way; it means feedback is immediate, and it means that measurement can occur simultaneously, causing the quality of information flow between you and the intranet to improve with each transaction.

Cookies are stored temporarily on the hard drive and are used as identifiers between the user and the server for the next time they have an interaction. The server can access the cookie on your client, process what it knows about you, and send you back more customized information or feedback. How this is going to work on a Webtop where there is no hard drive is to be uncovered by Java technology.

Bottom Line: The method for accelerating the interaction between the user and the server is a technique called cookies.

Profiling Databases   Cookies are used to maintain a personal ID in a database, or a collection of preferences and information "types" you are looking for. This is used in a cross-reference table that pulls out relevant information and sends it back to you. A cookie sets up a relationship between you and the server that attempts to define your needs and expectations. In marketing, this is called profiling. You interact with the user/customer, ask questions, interview, provide focus groups—whatever it takes to learn more about the knowledge needs of the user. Carried further, cookies can help you manage a project, improve a process, or accelerate your workflow.

Cookie technology was originated for observing user behavior on the Internet. It was designed to observe consumer tastes when a user surfed through web pages that hosted advertising banners. Advertising banners are electronic ads. If the user clicks on the ad, a database records that information and the server begins to identify a clickstream that identifies the user's navigation patterns. The next pages that are sent back to the user interpret the cookie and the clickstream pattern and create a web page on the fly that contains more relevant information.

Banners haven't been used on intranets yet, but, they hold potential in getting users to communicate relationships with each other. An intranet site can easily use the concept of banners to advertise processes or methods, or services that can be offered to any taker in the company. When someone responds to the banner, a relationship is established, and the originator can watch the individual's behavior, trying to develop a more successful inforelationship.

Cookie technology performs user profiling on the intranet to anticipate how a user is getting their work done. If we can observe how a user moves through information, how they choose to access processes or procedures, then we can identify methods of working behavior. If that can be done, then we can prescribe process improvements and redesign information flow to facilitate getting the job done more efficiently.

Cookies Measure Workflow   Measuring cookies as individual items in a process helps us to measure workflow. If engineering, for example, has a web page dedicated to reporting software bugs, and we observe through traffic analysis that one particular department is hitting the page, we want to know why that department is hitting the page. If we find out why, perhaps we can integrate and automate the part of the process we uncovered.

Bottom Line: Process improvement accelerates workflow.

The cookie sent by the server is private and cannot be viewed by anyone else except you and the appropriate Webmaster. Information is stored on your system. No one else can see it or write to it. It's there as a kind of tag for the original web site you visited.

More Cookies, Please   For additional resources, including standards, magazine articles, discussions on security, and examples of cookies in use at web sites on the Internet, visit the following pages. The IETF Proposed Standard which includes the current and past internet drafts on cookies—http://portal.research.bell-labs.com/~dmk/cookie.html. Netscape's home page on persistent client state HTTP cookies is at http://home.netscape.com/newsref/std/cookie_spec.html. You can also find Malcolm's Guide to Persistent Cookies resources at http://www.emf.net/~mal/cook-iesinfo.html, one of the most talked about resources for cookies.

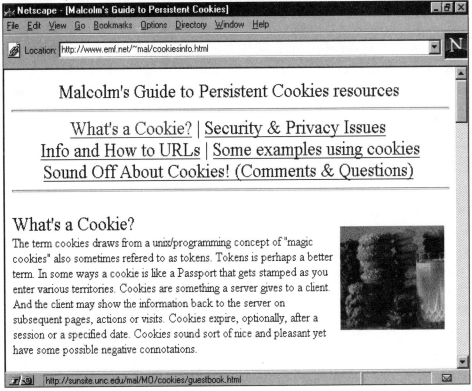

Figure 7–4 Malcolm's Cookie Page

Human Performance Measurement

The goals of informational technologists and knowledge architects are born from success stories, lessons learned, goals and objectives, observable human behavior, and data analysis. Measurement in this area is an intriguing subject for those envisioning the intranet as a mechanism for capturing and changing human behavior. Behaviors change, performance improves. Much of that performance occurs on-line for the knowledge worker. The intranet may serve as the greatest tool of the 21st century for capturing human performance for the knowledge worker.

Start with a Framework of Goals

In order to improve human performance in an organization, a web site needs a framework that allows analysts to understand the variables that affect a person's performance. The intranet is such a framework. Many of the virtual groups in an organization unite in a single sector of the intranet with the goal of developing on-line knowledge products using the organization's information technology. The intranet captures their lessons in unique ways, messaging, scheduling, publishing, project managing, budgeting, and so forth. The way users perform on-line becomes a part of the vast data warehouses within the organization and can be evaluated for future performance given similar behaviors.

In Table 7-2, we identify the common goals of the information technologist and recommend possible Web metrics to measure them within the framework of the intranet.

Bottom Line: When intranets measure organizational goals against actual performance, your intranet is worth its weight in gold.

The intranet provides a common framework to identify goals and measurements for contributing to the healthy growth of the organization. Once clearly identified, a good goal permeates the business community and becomes a standard for doing business. If we can perceive an effective way to measure the outcomes of our goals using the intranet, we will be able to accelerate our growth potential, development cycles, and productivity gains.

Table 7-2 Information Technologist's Goals and Intranet Measurements

Common Information Technologist's Goals	Intranet Measurement
Demonstrate flexibility and adaptability	Measure hits to the central intranet page and to the help desk, using the central intranet page to communicate the changing needs of the organization.
Manage complexity and continuous change	Measure individual group managers' goals' to the development of departmental intranets. How many users within their domain are accessing their goal-oriented pages?
Use process as a key capability to enable dynamic product development	Once you've identified a "stable" product development process, use cookies to measure Web user's access to internal processes that are already in place.
Understand human behavior vs. organizational structure as the key IS organizational enabler	Measure word search streams to identify human behaviors for building mental structures instead of web hits to functional pages.
Move to more flexible, "federated" organizational structure to leverage internal and external resources	Use cookies to customize web site for internal resources and to profile external resources. Match them up.
Show business foresight and strategic thinking as key competencies.	Develop web sites that demonstrate business foresight and strategic thinking and count access to the pages. Also examine e-mail directed to the Webmaster for anecdotal data
Courtesy of CIO Communications, who contributed the Common IT Goals.	

Measure Architecture and Technology Environment

Metrics are key to understanding how to align information technology strategy with business strategy. Financial explanations of the organization's performance have been fundamental in identifying processes and balancing the utilization of resources in an organization. It is now time for the organization's infrastructure and technology environment to supply us with ample numerical information to help us determine the effectiveness of our intranet. Undoubtedly, the study of speeds and feeds to measure architecture is a classic.

But, now we want to go beyond the architecture and evaluate the use of the architecture, or the technology environment. Managers have to understand how to manage distributed computing environments like the intranet to use its technological solutions to accomplish tasks, to communicate progress, and to calculate and report analysis regarding the effectiveness of the technology environment. By creating an information intranet architecture as discussed in this book, benchmarking it, and capturing and analyzing information technology metrics, the technology environment will become more easily identified.

If we identify the technology environment, we are able to single out the variables that contribute to the health of the organization. We can identify those variables that erode the technology environment and those variables that fertilize the environment. Our accomplishment provides us with the surety needed for moving into the new Digital Age.

Two additional technological environments that must be understood as well in order to develop a metrics systems that is effectively building the corporation are data warehousing and workgroup/groupware. Without understanding how to set up a data warehouse or use workgroup/groupware software, you will have a difficult time building and measuring an intranet that works for you. You will find it difficult to gather enough data to analyze how your organization is doing business.

Once the architecture and the technological environment have been put in place based on the alignment of the strategic goals, you can build a communication system on the intranet that groups your processes by function. You can simultaneously allow serendipity to occur and populate your intranet with bright, innovative solutions.

The central processes reach out and link with other intranet web sites across the organization to create a networked process environment. The intranet will grow by itself (if you leave it alone) and will provide continuous feedback for its requirements and support needs.

Processes to Measure an Intranet

In order to effectively evaluate human performance, it is imperative to evaluate what an employee does, and how the employee's skills fit into the overall organization. A formal process for doing this can provide insight into how web metrics help align goals with performance. Some of the processes to put into place to fortify the web metrics against organizational goals include

* *Provide an overarching mission statement* about the organization, so that any metric can look directly at the mission statement and say, "yes, we are fulfilling our mission."

- *Clearly define how the intranet is designed* to carry out the individual goals and objectives set by each department to fulfill the mission statement. This needs to be available across the organization. The real estate must be Park Place on your intranet.

- *Make sure each web site on the intranet clearly articulates the desired performance* the web site is to achieve. For example, a software try-and-buy web site would like to see at least 40 users download software per month, with a monthly increase of sales by 20 percent. Post this again, so the departmental group understands how to contribute to that goal.

- *Express the desired path you'd like a user to take* when they come to your web page. Then use navigational metrics to determine if they are taking the expected route. Expedite your knowledge transfer by creating paths to conclusive information that work!

- *Provide a working action plan,* one that identifies what to do to reach the goal, who is responsible for doing it, and a path to lead people to make necessary changes to their related web sites. Also, provide inhibitors to successful completion.

- *Keep the action plan in place* and check progress against it continuously.

- *Gather more data on performance* making modifications continuously.

If you can establish this kind of strategically aligned intranet, you will stimulate interactivity and codevelopment. Transactions will move on-line to improve workflow and to visualize processes. Learning will occur on-line and your data warehouses will fill to the brim. It's then when you can observe employee behavior and provide interventions to improve human performance.

Once you understand the framework, you can begin to wrap your arms around how to distribute information in an organization so that its use can be observed, measured, and improved.

Capture the User in Action

Some ideas for capturing what the user is doing.

- Identify accomplishments (create home pages that link up to the group, the department, and ultimately to the top goals of the organization).

- Identify requirements (encourage action plans to be posted by intranet groups, and keep the project plans on-line for constantly viewing and interaction).

- Identify exemplary performance (when a web site identifies a perfect process, push it up to a higher level so it can be used by more people and exemplify how to improve performance).

- Measure exemplary performance (get reaction to exemplary processes that you push up to the central intranet site. Keep all of your users involved in feedback mechanisms. Use usability tests, and cookies).

- Measure typical performance (identify good examples of web sites to other users. This can be done by rating top sites. Set up some kind of standard against which other web sites on your intranet can interact and strive for improvement. Benchmark design, navigating, interaction, experience, usability, speed).

- Compute the potential for improving performance (discusses the discrepancies and differences between exemplary web sites on-line and typical ones).

- Translate this potential into stakes (identify the savings or improvement that can be expected from improvement to exemplary performance).

Bottom Line: The organization that can analyze its performance can develop interventions for improving them.

How Can Web Metrics Improve Human Performance?

Measurements of success include organizational results from executive clarity to goal consistency across all units of the organization. The satisfaction of stakeholders is key to improving workflow as well. You have to include as much feedback and as many motivation sources and cues as possible. The frequency of updating information and the timing you use to present information updates to your employees are key elements of tying human performance to success.

Processes must be put in place in order to evaluate how the entire system is working. It is critical to develop the processes on-line. Everything that requires knowledge transfer can be represented visually. You must keep the processes aligned with your model of centralization/decentralization, so users have an understanding of consistency of operation, flexibility in evolving processes, appropriate links/interactions. Also, they must understand what their performance requirements are, and how their skills are adding to the knowledge base of the organization.

Make sure that your intranet allows users to input to the strategy, mission/vision, and strategic direction of the organization. There are always external needs, driving forces, and competitive advantages that need to be expressed in the culture. If you provide consistency of values across the organization, measuring between stated values and actual behavior, demands/objectives, time requirements/objectives, predictability/cycles, workload and management expectations, then you're using the intranet as the tool it is—a great universal mirror. Measure yourself against your own vision. The benefits you reap will be unimaginable.

Web Metrics Future

Some of the newest usage analysis products allow users to perform very advanced visit analysis inquiries, which quickly highlight how users find resources, where users leave a site (end pages), and correlations between different types of users and the pages they visit. By being able to "ask the right questions," the Webmaster can gain real insight into their user's behavior, interests, and degree of sophistication.

Moving forward, the ability to perform real-time visit analysis will allow sites to dynamically target content to end users. Some very basic attempts at this functionality exist today, but they are a long way from where the technology will allow us to go. The push technology popularized by PointCast and Microsoft's MSN will provide great strides in understanding user requirements and consumption behavior.

These "user responsive" sites, while incredibly complex from a systems perspective, will serve information, interactive media, and promotions/incentives based on user preferences, history, technical capability, and real-time bandwidth availability. The end result is akin to the "teacher interception" process that occurs so effectively and is so effective in the classroom. The teacher intercepts student thinking and poses questions or introduces new information to cause a clarification in thinking. This is much like the function of true dialogue. This area will blossom. Understanding the audience is key to engaging the audience in truly interactive experiences.

Research Directions

- Quality indexing incorporating new metrics using large databases

- Improved granularity

- Refined IP address mapping

- City databases

- Demographic data mining

- HTTP extensions
- Distributed query analysis
- Java and VRML

More Resources

Netscape Analysis

> http://help.netscape.com/kb/server/960513-122.html.

This URL discusses generating statistics about the access log with the analyze program.

Log Analysis Tools

> http://www.yahoo.com/Computers_and_Internet/Internet/World_Wide_Web/Servers/Log_Analysis_Tools/

Yahoo features access to many of the vendors developing log analysis tools.

External Analysis of Web Sites

> http://www.ipro.com/about.html

As this large market grows in demand and improved Internet savvy, greater demand is put on the need for interoffice connectivity. This is where the intranet meets the rubber of the road. CyberAtlas™, the Internet Research Guide published by I/PRO, providers of services and software for independent measurement and analysis of web site usage, sums up the various study results on how many people are using the Internet.

Web Metrics Tutorial

> http://www.idg.com/ice/conference/tutorials.html

This tutorial will demonstrate an easy-to-use analysis tool for extracting trend and usage data from Web sites. In addition, probabilistic models of bandwidth utilization and current and future trends will be developed from the resulting data. These models are critical for designing and maintaining a productive web site, and they supply reliable measurements of the web site's traffic, providing invaluable sales, marketing, and PR feedback on the existing web message.

This allows an organization to evaluate the overall effectiveness of individual web pages and determine the most dynamic content and presentation strategy. Interactive analysis of diverse log files will be included from which we will derive models describing the clickstream. In addition, the practical applications of the models developed and how these can best be leveraged as competitive decision-making tools will be discussed.

Summary of Key Points

- **THREE TYPES OF WEB METRICS**

  This section identifies three types of web metrics for evaluating your web site's behavior and how workflow and human performance can be measured.

- **REASONS FOR OBSERVING WEB METRICS**

  This section synthesizes the user's ability to integrate their work processes in a viewable environment that fits into the whole system.

- **WEB METRICS BENEFITS**

  This section reviews the basic benefits that web metrics provide for an organization. Provides examples of various metrics and identifies a key benefit as the observation and ability to react to human processes on-line.

- **WEB SITE TRAFFIC ANALYSIS FOR TECHNICAL TUNING**

  This section provides information on web metrics software and software companies. Identifies key features for analytical tools and requirements for web statistician, key analyst of web metrics.

- **WORKFLOW MEASUREMENTS**

  This section covers other forms of web metrics, namely clickstream analysis and search word analysis, and concludes that the cookie technology is capable of identifying and helping to improve business processes that make up workflow.

- ## HUMAN PERFORMANCE MEASUREMENT

  This section suggests that the third method of web measurement is to align goals to human performance using the uniqueness of the intranet.

- ## WEB METRICS FUTURE

  This section guides you into real-time visit analysis that allows you to dynamically target the end user. Push technology is the driver of the future in metrics.

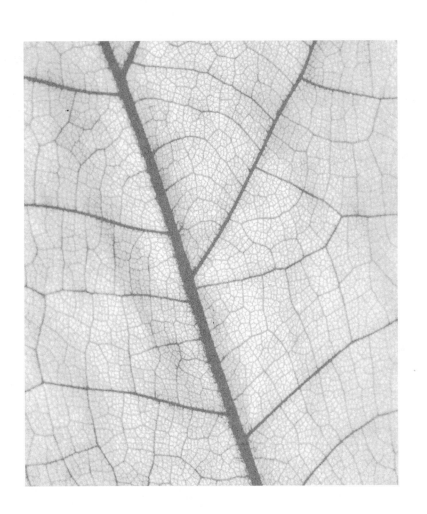

CHAPTER

8

What Do Other People Say about Intranets?

Key Industry Strategies

A lot of key technology companies are strategizing for the great information architecture of the 21st century. The whole idea here is to create open standards for developers, make operating systems invisible to the end user, and make hardware technology configurations interchangeable. The bottom line is to improve the way your company does business in an environment where technology has become a single, elegant commodity, and knowledge and information have become products.

Let's take a look at some of the key industry strategies for bringing intranets into your office and homes. Many of these strategies offer web server solutions, web tool publishing and management software, and consulting services to help you strategize your intranet environment. Their greatest contribution is their vision. Collectively their message is powerful.

Bottom Line: Key industry analysts focus on the best architecture, the best infrastructure, and the best resources for the customers.

Sun Microsystems

Strategy   Introduce web technology throughout the enterprise. Use SunSparc stations as the servers, coupled with Netscape's server solutions, Sun's firewall solutions, and Java, Sun's new interactive, web savvy programming language. Sun's focus is on open systems and maintaining robust solutions.

Products   Netra Server, Java Programming Language, Solstice FireWall-1, Solaris network operating system, and Joe, an extended development environment for working with legacy systems. *Sun focuses on architecture.*

Netscape

Strategy   Netscape has provided mass distribution of its servers and key browser for setting up intranets. Their full-service intranet service provides four major user services: information sharing and management, communication and collaboration, navigation, and application access. Their servers also provide four major network services: directory, replication, security, and management. Replication is the technology that updates the same document across all the network servers. Netscape does not presently own an operating systems so they must build their solutions for both UNIX and NT.

Products   Netscape Navigator, Netscape SuiteSpot (integrated server software for building and running an intranet). *Netscape focuses on Webcentric solutions.*

Microsoft

Strategy   MS's strategy is to incorporate the intranet into the operating system as an infrastructure for interoperability. This means all Windows 95 and Windows NT environments will see full integration of Internet and intranet services in their OS. Microsoft's ingenious wizards make setting up the intranet environment seemingly flawless. Microsoft is betting on managing the enormous mindshare they have behind users who are familiar with Microsoft and Microsoft products. They're also strategizing on a Zero Administration environment which will create very easy to use intranets.

Products   BackOffice, a family of server applications; Microsoft Internet Explorer (a browser); Office 97; FrontPage and Internet Studio, software designed specifically to publish content and manage web sites. ActiveX^{TM}, Microsoft's development framework friendly with OLE, Visual Basic controls, and Java applets. *Microsoft focuses on integration.*

Lotus

Strategy   Integrate Lotus Notes into the intranet/web environment. Migrate Lotus applications onto the World Wide Web, enabling users who are familiar with Lotus to integrate seamlessly with intranet technology. Lotus is aggressively bringing their advanced workgroup solutions to the intranet. Lotus struggles with a proprietarylike environment making their transition to the intranet substantially challenging.

Products   Domino server and Lotus Notes. *Lotus focuses on collaboration.*

IBM

Strategy   IBM's interests are met by its being able to provide Java-enabled systems based on non-Microsoft operating systems, such as AIX, OS/390, and OS/2. Domino is behind IBM's intranet strategy. It bridges the open standards environment of the Web with the power of the Notes object-oriented database, replication, mail, security, collaboration, content management, and rapid application development environment to deliver the most complete and powerful intranet solution available today.

Products   Lotus Notes, Domino. *IBM focuses on legacy solutions.*

Oracle

Strategy   Oracle intends to utilize their expertise in relational database management systems, which will be widely required by any organization managing the entirety of corporate knowledge. The intranet enables users to access databases on a much larger scale. Low-cost devices for accessing the intranet/Internet are being strategized by Oracle called NCS or Network Computers. Whether users are ready to give up their personalized hard drives and their ability to add indefinite functionality to their computers is still to be seen.

Products   Oracle WebServer, Oracle applications for the Web to integrate Oracle databases with the intranet. *Oracle focuses on future web database solutions.*

Novell

Strategy   Novell pretty much invented the Network Operating System (NOS). Whether you describe the software used to define the network as "NOS" or an "intranet" is fundamentally irrelevant to Novell. What's important to them is that the NOS as we have known it is no longer adequate to meet customer needs. The set of internet standards which created the intranet significantly expands the baseline requirements of what constitutes a usable network. So, Novell is retrofitting for internet standards. With renowned Sun's chief technology officer, Eric Schmidt's move to Novell as CEO, Novell will be a formidable contender to this list of key players.

Products   IntranetWare™ is Novell's platform for a full-service intranet. Built on the foundation of Novell's industry-leading NetWare 4™ network operating system (NOS), IntranetWare provides both IP and IPX™ access to intranet resources such as web servers, FTP servers, and WAN connections to the Internet. It lets you use your existing network infrastructure to make your networks do more for your business. *Novell focuses on web customer integration.*

There are many other players in the field, all with software and hardware offerings. Some companies strategize acquiring them; others consider partnering them. Some companies, like Cisco, Pointcast, MCI, and others, are capable of turning the tide.

Intranet Facts by Key Industry Analysts

What are key business groups, consultants, and advocacy groups saying about the intranet? What do they recommend? Where are things leading from their vantage point? Critical success factors make your company soar. These leading groups provide you with detailed market information about the use of intranets, the future of intranet development, and key technologies to watch.

The Burton Group

http://www.tbg.com

As the intranet market rapidly matures, web-enabled software will allow organizations to build effective collaboration and communications systems using intranet technologies. Netscape's SuiteSpot is a leading intranet contender that will enable such systems. Customers who prefer to build a homogenous server operating system environment may well prefer Microsoft's intranet products and their tight coupling with NT Server.

Microsoft is taking an operating system-centric approach to intranets, while Netscape is taking the cross-platform approach. Customers looking to establish a common set of services across multiple operating system platforms will clearly find Netscape's approach more to their liking. While the cross-platform nature of Netscape's products remains a constant, two other decision factors come into sharper focus—directory-enabled intranets and application development in a distributed environment.

First, the directory-enabled nature of the Netscape product line gives Netscape some significant advantages. Netscape has shipped its Lightweight Directory Access Protocol (LDAP)-based Directory Server, and SuiteSpot 3.0 will follow through on the company's promise to ship upgrades to key server products that are integrated with the Directory Server. That integration will allow the SuiteSpot server products that support the directory (Enterprise Server, Messaging Server, and Collabra Server) to be centrally managed from the LDAP directory.

There are some caveats, however. Netscape has transcended many of the basic issues that have blocked directory deployment for Novell, such as using the directory only for administrative purposes. Netscape's directory is also platform independent, while Novell has only recently begun to deploy NDS across operating systems. Yet Netscape Directory Server is a first-generation product, lacking many important capabilities. (Jamie, I'd like you to name the top three here).

Second is the application development issue. With Enterprise Server 3.0, Netscape is one of the first vendors to demonstrate the value of the directory beyond its capabilities as an administrative tool. By making directory services a core component of the application development framework of its products, Netscape has done a great deal to accelerate the move to distributed applications. The degree to which you can turn the directory-enabled applications into a competitive advantage will be determined by how ready your organization is to build those applications. Directory services make distributed application development and deployment much easier, but organizations must be directory-enabled through solid planning and training before that advantage can be fully leveraged.

However, it's also clear that Microsoft's intranet server products offer significant advantages that should not be ignored. With the introduction of Internet Information Server 3.0, which includes the Active Server Pages scripting engine, Microsoft has begun to deliver on the promise of ActiveX. Active Server Pages allows developers to script server-based application solutions with reusable ActiveX components. Active Server Pages is also integrated with Microsoft Transaction Server, which provides object broker and transaction monitoring capabilities, giving those server applications added reliability and performance. As Microsoft integrates all of its BackOffice products with Active Server Pages and the ActiveX object model, NT Server will be an attractive intranet solution for many corporate customers.

Forrester Research

http://www.forrester.com/hp_mar96nsr.htm

Forrester Research analyzes and predicts the course of technology change and provides unique and valuable insight into the impact of emerging technologies on businesses, consumers, and society. A survey by Forrester Research, Inc. of 50 major corporations found that 16 percent have an intranet in place and 50 percent either plan to or are considering building one.

A new report from Forrester's Network Strategy Service predicts the emergence of a next-generation intranet, enhanced by five standards-based services: directory, e-mail, file, print, and network management. This full service intranet will displace today's proprietary NOS—like Novell's NetWare, Microsoft's NT, and Banyan's Vines. Companies will migrate to Full Service intranets for (1) easy connections with the outside world, (2) multiple competing suppliers, and (3) lower costs. Directories are the cornerstone of the full-service intranet. The vendor with the first credible intranet directory will have easy entree to corporate buyers.

Forrester sees Netscape as having key market advantage. "Netscape has several structural advantages (in servers) . . . dominant browser market share . . . better relationships with content developers and Web ISVs . . . able to compete on both the NT and Unix fronts. Content developers should favor Netscape." You'll find that each analyst has their favorite company. The technology changes rapidly so these analysts tend to follow an organization.

Bottom Line: Look at many analyst's views. The customer counts as much as the company.

Business Research Group

http://www.brgresearch.com/

Business Research Group (BRG), a leading research group in Newton, Massachusetts, reports that "the corporate intranet implementation rate will double again in the next six months. Manufacturing, Publishing, and Entertainment lead the pack in implementing intranet applications, with 30 percent to 40 percent in these verticals taking the intranet path. Retail, Finance, and Healthcare are significant yet far less enthusiastic intranet application implementors at this time."

BRG continues to report that the **major business driver** for implementing intranets is "increased effectiveness of business processes." Clearly, with the need in organizations to reengineer and reach levels of quality set by International Standards Organization (ISO), the Web server methodology is a natural for identifying business processes, communicating vision and process to interested departments, and streamlining the department to satisfy the needs of all internal customers.

C++ and Java are the most popular languages for developing web applications, at 43 percent and 42 percent , respectively. Only 26 percent say Visual Basic is their language of choice. C trails, with only 19 percent choosing it as their web development language. Users will require excellent Web-to-legacy system integration to achieve their intranet application goals . . . A very high level of database integration is required according to BRG. The most popular databases used to interface with the Web are Oracle (24 percent of respondents), Microsoft Access (22 percent), Sybase (14 percent), and IBM DB2 (8 percent).

The BRG is a good source for statistical averages. They conduct indepth inquiries into the customer base providing key consumer usable trends.

Gartner Group

http://www.gartner.com/newsltrs/cis.html#page1

Gartner Group, Inc., is the world's leading independent advisor of research and analysis to businesses worldwide.

Gartner defines an Internet- or intranet-enabled application as one in which clients or servers exploit internet technology such as HTML, TCP/IP, internet e-mail, or web browsers. Such applications involve no new programming principles *but often require developers to operate with new data types or communications protocols.* When considering internet applications, it is useful to identify two separate issues: creation of logic and creation of content. In this context, the term "content" refers to both the information presented to the internet user and the interface by which the user may interact with it.

Gartner Group analyzes trends very well. They interpret their results and provide vision and insight into the overall market. They are quoted heavily in the industry, providing excellent financial support data.

Zona Research

http://www.zonaresearch.com/Pubs/inet2.html

Market researcher Zona Research, Inc. in Redwood City, Calif., predicts that sales of software to run intranet servers will shoot to more than $4 billion in 1997, from $476 million last year. In 1998, Zona says the figure will hit $8 billion, four times the size of the internet server business. See Figure 8–1. And that doesn't include all the applications packages, programming tools, and other pieces that go into intranets. No wonder Netscape, Sun Microsystems, Microsoft, IBM, Oracle, Computer Associates, and nearly everybody in the software business is rushing out intranet products. "Intranets are huge," says Sun CEO Scott G. McNealy.

Internet and intranet: 1996 is the second edition of Zona Research's *Internet vs. intranet: Markets, Opportunities and Trends* which can be found at their URL. It examines the internet and intranet industries from the perspective of the supplier. Zona defines the Internet as "connectivity potential" and the intranet as "the use of Internet technologies within the enterprise to enhance user productivity." The

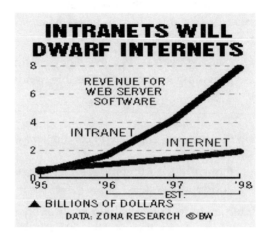

Figure 8–1 Zona's Intranet Revenue Predictions

report introduces several new definitions, including the "extended intranet," while offering more depth on intranet applications. Their estimates for the market for internet and intranet products during 1995 are offered, as are updated forecasts through 1999.

Zona Research charges to get a glimpse of this information from this report. However, it may be well worth it. Major topics covered in the document include

- Definition of the Internet, intranet, and extended intranet

- Segmentation of internet technologies and products

- Web servers

- Browser technology

- Authoring technology

- Search and retrieval technology

- Key vendor profiles

- Presentation of primary research on intranet applications and planned expenditure levels

- Discussion of key issues and trends, including Microsoft and Internet use outside of North America

Zona Research has identified key issues facing internet/intranet decision makers:

- The paradigm shift—intranet organizations

- Integrating the legacy environment with the intranet
- Development and deployment of business critical applications
- Network computers, thin clients, and the Internet
- Multimedia and telephony on the intranet
- Role of outsourcing web sites
- Security and the intranet
- Collaborative computing issues—notes, intranet, and beyond
- Role of indirect channel in selling intranet products

Statistics Support Growth   Zona Research's on the *growth of intranets through 1998* indicates intranet growth will spurt in the electronic marketplaces. They report, "The worldwide market for Internet and intranet technologies and products will exceed $4 billion during 1995. The number of users with Internet potential will jump from approximately 16 million to more than 42 million by 1998. See the following table.

Growth of Web Servers

	1995	1996	1997	1998
Internet	64,350	155,160	294,200	495,385
Intranet	49,250	207,280	643,550	1,167,350

Courtesy of Zona Research.

What Users Think According to Zona

- Nearly all corporate computer users use e-mail.
- The most common intranet applications relate to document creation and distribution (information publishing).
- Intranet use within the sample base is expected to increase dramatically.
- Vertical intranet applications represent the primary need going forward, yet there are few of these applications today.
- Within the intranet sample base, HTML is currently considered the key technology.
- Into the future, Visual Basic and ActiveX^{TM} (Microsoft) and Java (Sun Microsystems, Inc.) are considered the key technologies.
- Windows applications availability is viewed as more critical than that of Visual Basic, ActiveX^{TM}, or Java.

- Purchasers expect to pay little or nothing for a browser.

- The average sites expect to spend more than $7,000 for search/retrieval technology, and $4,000 for content authoring tools.

Gilder Technology Report

http://www.gildertech.com

Gilder Technology Group Incorporated (GTG) was formed in April 1996 to provide research, consulting, and publication of the Gilder Paradigm. The Gilder Technology Report will be published regularly (12 issues), with occasional special bulletins. The *Report* will have a basis of timely data and indices developed specifically for each issue. A research staff is totally committed to obtaining the available information and in some instances previously unavailable information. George Gilder oversees the research and writes the report.

The *Report* will cover on a regular basis the following:

- A summary of the major trends dominating the industry

- Roles of individual companies in shaping the technology evolution

- Statistical summary of key indicators

- Commentary on the most recent significant events affecting the telecommunication industry.

CyberAtlas Sums Up Internet Usage

http://www.cyberatlas.com/market.htm

Just so you can see how much your intranet will be growing and merging with the intranet, take a look at CyberAtlas Internet Usage Statistics. The numbers for Internet usage continue to swell as can be seen in Table 8-1. Clearly business and information processing is being conducted on the Internet.

As this large market grows in demand and Internet savvy improves, greater demand is put on the need for interoffice connectivity. This is where the intranet meets the rubber of the road. *CyberAtlas,* the *Internet Research Guide* published by I/PRO (http://www.ipro.com/about.html), providers of services and software for independent measurement and analysis of web site usage, sums up the various study results on how many people are using the Internet.

Table 8-1 Internet Usage: Composite Index

Source	Date	Definition	Users
International Data Corp. (IDC)	Oct. 31, 96	Web users	31.4M
Computer Intelligence Infocorp	May 96	U.S. Internet users	15.0M
Hoffman/Novak	April 96	U.S. Internet users	16.4M
Wall Street Journal	March 96	North American home/office users	17.6M
Morgan Stanley	February 96	1995 Net/Web users	9.0M
Mediamark Research Inc.	October 96	Any cyberspace usage	27.0M
Matrix	February 96	1995 Worldwide Internet users	26.4M
FIND/SVP	October 96	U.S. users who use any internet service except e-mail	27.0M
Nielsen	October 95	North Americans (16+) who used Web in past 3 months	23.0M
O'Reilly & Assoc.	July 95	U.S. users with direct net access	5.8M
Reprinted with permission from CyberAtlas from I/PRO, owners of CyberAtlas at http://www.cyberatlas.com/market.html. June 26, 1996.			

Intranet Resources

The best place, besides this book of course, to look for intranet resources is on the Internet. Because this field was born in cyberspace, it has grown up almost in its entirety on the World Wide Web.

CIO Magazine Intranet Page

http://www.cio.com/WebMaster/wm_irc.html

CIO Magazine does an incredibly good job of bringing the concept of intranets to your desktop. Read this link to get a good comprehensive overview of one of the leading concepts in corporate America today: case studies, web reports, web on-line seminars, Webmaster's notebook, related sites, calendar of web events, web central, web technology notes, Webmaster magazine, talk to us . . . management.

Intranet Journal

http://www.intranetjournal.com

One of the most complete sites on the Web regarding intranets, it features a live threaded conversation/chat session with key web developers regarding intranet design and development. A must read! Considered by critics to be the first choice for everything intranet.

Netscape's Intranet Vision

http://www.netscape.com/
comprod/at_work/white_paper/intranet/vision.html

Written by Marc Andreessen, Chief Technology Officer (CTO), and the Netscape product team, this paper presents the IT professional with Netscape's vision of the full-service intranet. The paper also provides a road map for Netscape's existing and planned intranet product line, including Galileo, a next-generation version of Netscape Navigator, and Orion, a next-generation version of Netscape SuiteSpot.

Intranet Resource Centre

http://www.infoWeb.com.au/intralnk.htm

The Intranet Resource Centre provides standards: architecture, document handling, remote access, tools, multimedia, groupware, viewers, authoring; conversion tools, newsgroups, database products, articles, publications, and Java.

The Complete Intranet Resource

http://www.intrack.com/intranet/

Complete with Frequently Asked Questions (FAQs), Intranet Q&A, this site introduces you to intranets, case studies, conferencing software, intranet vs. groupware solutions, statistics, case studies, conferences, seminars, presentations, training classes, vendors, software and hardware, white papers, firewall resources, books, jobs.

Beyond the Horizon, Intranet Video

http://www.corpchange.com/intranet.htm

A professional two-hour video captures the Transition Management Advisor's intranet seminar in an easy-to-understand, easy-to-follow format. The information is introductory and allows beginning users to understand how intranets work. Use this video to learn about intranets and to educate your team and end-user community on how to implement this productivity tool.

Summary of Key Points

- KEY INDUSTRY STRATEGIES

    This area highlights Sun Microsystems, Microsoft, Netscape, Novell, Oracle, and Lotus as key players in the development of strategies and products. It is meant to introduce you to the builders of intranet hardware, software, and solutions. The approach is very high.

- INTRANET FACTS

    Looks at leading industry analysts' views on intranets: the Burton Group, the Gartner group, Business Research Group, Cyber-Atlas statistics, Forrester Research, and Zona Research, and the debut of *George Gilder's Technology Report.*

- INTRANET RESOURCES

    This section introduces you to on-line resources covering intranet issues, discussion groups, and training with commentary. It's always difficult to find reliable resources on the Internet because of the wide availability. This section reduces your choices to the key intranet sites.

CHAPTER

9

Interviews with CIOs, Webmasters, and Other Visionaries

CIOs

Bill Raduchel, CIO, Sun Microsystems

Bill Raduchel has been working in information technology for most of his life. His current role mixes strategic direction with practical implementation. He has a broad understanding of corporations and organizations, having also been both the chief financial officer and acting vice president of human resources at Sun. Although his early roles vary from academic and administrative positions at Harvard through senior executive roles at McGraw-Hill and Xerox, information technology and planning have been consistent themes through them all. Right now, he is leading the effort to make Sun a showcase implementation of Java computing.

Randy: So where are intranets going?

Bill: Simply put, TCP gets larger, all the stuff blurs. In our own case, MCI runs or shares the backbone and it's all just a large private network. We are really running on the Internet; there are just a few common pipes connecting network addresses and people. An intranet is a portal into this cloud. It's a lot like the public switch telephone network. One seamless cloud with people going in and out of it at will.

Randy: What intranet feature do you find the most valuable?

Bill: E-mail, believe it or not. E-mail has allowed Sun to do something which is very valuable. It has allowed us be participative in a decision and do it fast. You can be asynchronous and instantly communicative. You can be both participative and quick to act. Sun's culture has built itself on these processes to build rapid response capability.

Randy: Isn't the intranet more than e-mail?

Bill: Sure. It's e-mail with web pages, pictures, and video.

Randy: How has it helped business process improvement?

Bill: Business process improvement is something that happens at a lower plane. Web pages are an extension of our culture. We use the network as a fundamental place to conduct business and provide benefits to employees. Place didn't matter anymore in working together, so a lot has improved there. We can get global involvement in a decision and keep everyone fairly well informed. People use e-mail to tell me what's happening every week; all the time then I can visit project web pages and perceive issues that I can work back into the network. This is just the way we do business.

Randy: E-mail aside, so, how do you see Java evolving the intranet?

Bill: PCs opened up computing power to the individual. Java opened the network to the masses. Java lets huge audiences build value-added applications that are local. Java, like DOS, makes it possible for users to engineer software. DOS was a huge win for Microsoft, letting lots of people go and innovate on a PC. Java lets you innovate in a distributed networked environment. Everyone can build on the intranet using Java, even if you don't know how to program. The graphical interfaces written for Java programming will democratize technology. The Web subsumes everything.

Randy: What do you mean by the Web subsumes everything?

Bill: All applications have web front ends, and you unleash the power of the network. This fundamental advantage of the Web is also a double-blind strategy, though. Corporate CIOs, in theory, have to worry about M applications talking to N desktops. In theory, the CIO has to worry about $M \times N$ interfaces. It gets mind boggling like, 400 applications on 25,000 desktops, that equals 1,000,000 interconnects. One million is very difficult to manage, imagine 10 times this number. The intranet lets me reduce that to 1+1, which is great, and shifts the burden. I build my Web and I shift my burden. Shifting the burden here is good because shifting the burden dramatically lowers cost and complexity for the network while putting little onto the users and providers of content.

Randy: Can you talk about costs, hard, soft, and hidden?

Bill: CIOs face certain problems; infrastructure costs are very high and getting higher. Current ideas are to load a complex Operating Systems (OS) and data on each desktop, configure it, and support it. It costs an awful lot of money. Java Webtops, that run only Java, are inherently administration free because everything comes off the Net. You have a big win in cost, that is really dramatic, or just phenomenal from a viewpoint of a corporation. Java moves state to the Web, cutting the cost from a factor of 2 to a factor of 6 and 7 or roughly 1 million dollars a year.

The hard costs are the costs of maintaining state. "Maintaining state" means maintaining what applications you can access, file and printer locations, passwords, network locations, etc. These are the mass of details that defines who you are on the network. If nothing changes then state maintenance costs you nothing. That is why the costs are forgotten. In practice, change occurs constantly, and making these changes is a large part of the total cost of ownership. In the mainframe world and in a PC world, state is maintained on a single device. State is bound to the piece of hardware. Whatever it costs to maintain state is where you'll find the hard costs.

The soft costs are the value of participation and acting quickly. Soft costs and soft benefits are gained from having an efficient operating Internet. If you don't, then you're not acting as fast as you should. All of your costs then end up in administration. The costs that drive people crazy are the costs of administration.

There are the costs of lost data. Then the cost of not finding a better way to automate, test, and check state. State maintenance has its hidden costs. State is ultimately the hidden thing that they don't see.

Bottom Line: Hardware, software, bandwidth, and state—those are your costs.

Randy: With state on the intranet, interactive transactions will accelerate. What killer apps do you see coming out of this?

Bill: People are making the same mistake on the intranet on this as they did on the Internet. The killer apps are local, not global. The press is missing it by not understanding that all politics are local, all activity is local. The power is in local applications. Two thousand web sites of 2-3-6 people who create from the bottom up are creating the intranet. The applications are created by users, who build what they need locally.

The intranet will demonstrate that the power is local innovation, as opposed to global. Project web pages are a great example. If I want to go see what is going on, I go to the project page. This is sophisticated e-mail, instantaneously updated each time I visit. I can see where I need to go next; I can redefine the way work is done. This has become the norm at Sun. The killer app that will drive more social change than any will be e-mail between parents and teachers.

Randy: Communication between business and customer is crucial indeed, even if those customers are parents. This sounds like an interconnected world of local users. So will intranets interconnect with other corporate intranets?

Bill: No. Intranets will not be interlinked because the simplification for assuming a closed world is very high. But I'll allow third-party access into my intranets, secured, of course. Very few corporations let people walk around unescorted. The intranet has electronic escorts, gateways, or firewall software monitoring—what you do to make sure you stay within bounds. With this kind of electronic escort capability, we can interlink some of the processes in other intranets. But, when you're done doing business, you are electronically escorted out of the building.

Randy: Security, guest access, confidential data. What else can you say about intranet security?

Bill: All the bad things that everyone has done on the network in the last years have trained me well. Everyone has a risk on the intranet, especially with quite a large number of internal employees. The risk is overblown in the sense that it is not some new issue. No matter what information systems you have, be they paper or electronic, you've got a security risk. Hackers are a problem, kids or serious criminals. They're thinking of new ways to commit crimes, not verify their stories.

Electronic extortion may be the biggest risk. Every corporation has to worry about that. But, the answer doesn't come from shutting yourself off the Internet, but by using it to manage those risks everyday.

Randy: In order to reduce the risk, do you see the intranet as a centralized or decentralized infrastructure?

Bill: Infrastructure gets centralized, content gets decentralized. Look at the voice telephone. It's run highly centralized. But the content is highly decentralized.

Randy: I take it you can manage security more effectively with infrastructure centralized. How would you extend the definition for an intranet computing model?

Bill: The key phrase that would extend the definition of the intranet is "content-neutral." The telephone network is content-neutral, so are copiers, television, radio, CD-ROMs, print media, etc. Computer networks were not content-neutral. Indeed, step one in traditional development is to specify the application and then design the infrastructure. The reason the intranet dominates is because it is content-neutral while supporting a very broad range of applications and information. You do not need to know what you are going to use the Web for to build one. This is very different from traditional computing.

Randy: If you change the infrastructure, you'll need a measurement for evaluating your success factors. What kinds of measurements do you use for the intranet?

Bill: I look at business metrics: revenue per employee, gross margin per employee, gross margin growth, cycle times, measuring internal processes. It's a simple equation of more orders and more profits. What else matters?

Randy: What about measuring human performance?

Bill: Cycle times are human performance times. People can process more information, great. Information is valuable only if it leads to better decisions.

Randy: The intranet has been equated to an effective decision support environment for quite a while. We've also talked about it as a collaborative and transactional system. Bill, from your vantage point, what's the future of the intranet look like?

Bill: Basically, the public switched telephone network. The intranet has to evolve toward that model; it's the only mass technology we use today that is universal. Whatever it looks like, it will be more like a telephone and less like a computer. We've got something that can give us more, and that goes further; it's the features and the applications. Fax, modem, voice, video, telephone, web phones, they're communication and transaction devices.

Larry Geisel, CIO, Netscape Communications

After reaching the position of CIO with a Fortune 50 company, Larry worked in several startups. In the late 1970s he worked with banking automation on minicomputers. In the mid 1980s, his second startup was working with information processing using expert systems, neural networks, and natural language processing. The third startup involved an early client/server solution for salesforce automation based on PC, UNIX, and Relational Database Systems (RDBS) for nomadic sales people. He sold those companies in succession, then did a stint at Xerox.

Randy: What did you learn from all your years of high tech experiences?

Larry: How to deal with frustrations. How to make systems behave.

Randy: What do you think of the intranet as a system?

Larry: Well think about the momentum of intranets being adapted by corporations. InfoWorld's statistics say two-thirds of U. S. companies in the Fortune 1000 are planning on deploying intranets. That has radically jumped in the last three months. 51 percent of corporations are implementing intranets now, maybe 39 percent three months ago. Forty-four percent planning to implement within the next few months. These facts should tell you that the intranet is a significant system. The key to the system: browser and web server interface software as the primary development platform. Ground swell of moving to the intranet is a testimony.

Randy: What is the momentum due to, do you think?

Larry: High expectations. People feel good things are going to happen to them. They're seeing that an intranet can be brought up quickly and that it reduces the cost of operations. They see productivity in their Information Systems (IS) groups, delivering rapid applications, and they see their individual business entities interacting as a result of intranet. This is good for them.

Many of the corporations had just about given up on client/server solutions. The results were disastrous: (1) Applications turned out be complex; (2) it took a long time to develop them; (3) they were difficult to deploy; (4) they were expensive to support over their life cycle. The economics of traditional client /server was eating their lunch. They discovered that it was even more expensive than host-based computing. Now they're looking for a silver bullet to recover. The good news is that there is more fire than smoke. Intranets can do it for them.

Randy: How easy is it going to be to convert?

Larry: There are two classes of companies: (1) Systems Network Architecture (SNA)-oriented networks; simply put, they're in deep trouble. They have expensive infrastructures to get out of. The good news for them is that there are some emerging software products to support TCP/IP over SNA. (2) Then, there's those that support traditional client/server. They have little to do to convert. They can use the same equipment. They can repurpose their hardware as web servers. The network elements are the same. The software purchased in volume is no more than $25.00/seat. HP is an example, 51,000 seats in a weekend. They can make their switch, from pseudo-proprietary to open protocol messaging backbone.

And, what is going to be the messaging backbone? It has to be TCP/IP which uses the open standards of the Internet. Basically, there are three fundamental choices here for them. (1) You pick a messaging architecture built around an application (like Lotus Notes); (2) or, built around an operating system (Microsoft Exchange); (3) or, built around the open standards of the Internet (e.g., Netscape products). Whichever you choose, you make the choice and have to live with the consequences. You can't build an enterprise around Notes. The Microsoft approach only works if you have a homogenous Wintel platform.

Most corporations don't have a homogenous platform. Now if I deploy an intranet, based on Internet open standards, and expand it to my customers and link upstream to suppliers and partners, then I've got a great solution that works. Make sure that your backbone message system is based on open internet standards, and the rest is an exercise.

Randy: How does an intranet affect the way a corporation does business?

Larry: Look at the transition from the Internet to the intranet. The corporation says, "Internet. Okay, we'll build an application to allow the customer to reach our site. They'll be able to download some marketing stuff and perhaps buy from us. We'll do some demographics and exceed our customer's needs. Once that is all in place, we'll have to build our internal environment, so we can get the work done smarter and faster.

So, we build an application largely for our own internal operations and interface with our customers for feedback. This is BPR (Business Process Reengineering) coming to life. This is rightsizing. We can service our customers, and they can service others better too. This is all so easy to use; it doesn't require training or instructions. The bright customers will use it first, others will catch up later on.

Randy: Whenever I hear BPR or rightsizing, I think about cost. BPR always has its share of cost. Talk about the costs of doing business. Hard, soft, and hidden costs?

Larry: Cost reduction is a big win, here. Intranets let you build top-line revenues, while decreasing bottom-line costs. If you have the right architecture in place like I said, you easily maintain a cross-platform, cross-network, cross-database environment. The intranet makes this a seamless expandable environment. So your hard costs are minimized. The big costs are going to be bandwidth. As our demands grow for running e-commerce businesses and building intranets to support e-commerce, we'll need to purchase access. We'll want faster speed; we'll want bandwidth, and lots of it.

The soft costs are all centered around BPR. I've got some painful memories from other companies that couldn't find an answer to their business processing woes. They understood the problems; they just didn't have any methods for solving them. Finally, the answer came to them. Get the right tools in place, like an open standards, TCP/IP-distributed networked environment, and then implement your BPR methods. If you keep hashing over the same company problems, without using a tool to provide a solution, you just spend a lot of money. Empowerment and communication reduce costs, and that is exactly what the intranet builds in your company.

Corporations aren't ready to hear that there are solutions. They've invested 50–60M in two years. It's amazing to see how people react when they can design their own notes, share ideas, collaborate on component designs. They've never done that before. It's always required IS to do it for them. But, now, when people are solving problems and getting their work done faster, you can't stop them. They're all learning how to enable themselves. You give them access to the Internet, and they experiment on it after hours, at home, anyway they can, building whatever works for them.

Randy: What are they building? And with what tools?

Larry: They're building a multitiered data architecture for one based on the concept of a data warehouse. They regularly pull down live data, suitably aggregated into a RDBM data warehouse, with enough metadata to figure out what that stuff is. Once in the data warehouse, you can do all kinds of things. You can look at all the legacy data you want. The only thing you're competing with is your fellow web citizens.

There is no impact on operational systems this way. You have active data warehouse programs with access privileges. You can't do business anymore unless you have a good data warehouse and easy access into it. With Navigator 3.0, you have that easy access and easy publication capability at the same time. LiveWire Pro helps connect databases to web pages and creates dynamic data. A few clever people have started to access live data as well. You can actually see live production schedules and performance on live apps. Some potential lies there today. Each user builds their own applications to access the data warehouse, using their tools of choice.

There are some really cool tools out there to help you. NetObjects Fusion product is a clever way to manage web pages. Webified Decision Support System (DSS) and On-line Analytical Processing (OLAP) tools from companies like Arbor are also very cool. People can buy these applications for a few dollars and have a lot of power on-line. The tools work out of the browser, with incredibly rich plug-ins right off the Web. They're creating some very sophisticated environments for being their own publishers.

Randy: What does this multitiered data warehouse look like?

Larry: It's a three-tiered data architecture (maybe a four-tier).

The first tier is a transaction repository. All transactions flow to and from live systems. This provides a common point to connect best of breed apps and allows you to see transactions at the lowest level of detail. It is used to get communication between apps and bring data from diverse data sources into the system.

The second tier is the actual data warehouse. In here, you constantly clean and purge, eliminate dups, record and fix errors, aggregate when possible. You've got to organize your data warehouse by subject area, so people have a chance to find what they're looking for.

The third tier is made up of datamarts. These are departmental level databases separate from the data warehouse and organized for reporting performance. Data are typically downloaded from the warehouse in an unnormalized form. Departmental users manage the timing of the update downloads to occur when they want current data.

The fourth tier, where necessary, involves live data generated within the department. No one accesses it directly but the transaction repository. IS writes the scripts which pick the transactions and ultimately put this data into one of the read-only databases.

Randy: What metrics do you use to ensure that the four tiers are working?

Larry: Let me put on my business hat. Ultimately, the goal is to try to gain and sustain customer relationships. I guess the basic metric is customer satisfaction. But we like to refer to it more as customer loyalty. Let's see, metrics. The reduced cost of operations is another metric to determine if your intranet is working or not. Look at the average cost per seat and total cost of ownership of applications over their life cycle. You can also look at the classical speed metrics like increased business productivity, time to market, and introduction of new products.

One of the speed measurements is IS productivity, frequently measured in terms of lines of code. But, at Netscape we feel these metrics are almost worthless. They're too easy to game. Plus you can drive up productivity metrics by doing the wrong thing. Effectiveness is the ultimate measure, not efficiency. The most basic measurement is how successful you are in reaching your customer base. For many companies, there is more vanity in that than reality.

We take pride in the fact that we surpassed America OnLine (AOL) in customer visits per day. Our web site has the most customer visits, over 100 million hits/day and converging on 1 billion hits/week. We take pride in having more users of Netscape Navigator than any other application in history. We download more than 1 million copies of products to customers every month and sell even more shipped products. Zero to 40 million users in 18 months. Now there's a measurement of effectiveness.

Randy: As a competitor, what are your thoughts on Microsoft?

Larry: Well, my son works there, and it'd be better if we could talk about our jobs over dinner, but we can't. Microsoft is a formidable competitor. Microsoft is probably the greatest thing that happened to Netscape, and vice versa. It got us both off our butts and stopped us from being so self-satisfied and made us realize that we're just in the beginning of this and that the customer is in the middle.

The pace and frequency are actually scary, though, for both companies. We're replanning every other week. We have to keep our strategies brilliant and concentrate on blending the internet interface with the current desktops to come up with a common Graphical User Interfaces (GUI). The principle flaw and limitation Microsoft suffers from is that they are too Wintel-centric. Microsoft believes that anything worth doing can be put into the OS. This doesn't allow customers to have a choice of which platform to buy.

Netscape believes that the functionality should be laid on top of the OS, so customers can have any platform they want, any OS they want. MS has to go back to the board with OLE. OLE was not the best platform to base their strategy on. They have to rework that idea. OLE was not written to be a network-based application architecture for a distributed application development environment. One of the key differences is the ability to build dynamic applications on the network.

Randy: Your opinion of Java as a competitive strategy?

Larry: Sun now realizes that it screwed up when it wrote its Java deal with Microsoft. It immediately empowered Microsoft to create its own Java engine, faster and better than Sun's. Sun is now catching up again, but it has learned its lesson. Secondly, if Sun isn't careful, Java will be the next UNIX. They can not afford to let it get out of the box before anyone could make money with it. Until the recent anti-Microsoft coalition, it had no home, no driver, and it was languishing. It lacked an economic model that would permit anyone to make Java big. Oracle, IBM, Sun, and Netscape will beat Microsoft (MS) at the intranet. MS, you've got the last bit of technology from these firms—no more free innovation for you.

Randy: With this "anything but Microsoft" coalition, what can you tell the customer about the future?

Larry: People should learn about publishing and merchant systems and integrate that technology. The areas of big development will be in telcom, pharmaceutical, manufacturing, on-line banks (on-line statements, move money, make investments). Wells Fargo is already there. Financial service corporations will grow around the world, once we can use internet wire-based transfer services for large sums of money.

Also, you'll see entire private networks and mergers occurring between Internet Protocol (IP) companies and telephony. IP over fiber will carry much more of the traffic in the future. It's the only way to avoid a complete standstill in traffic. The telcos do not have the necessary infrastructure. We've only tapped a small percentage of fiber networks, in 45 cities around the U. S., 50–60 sites internationally. When we have fiber quality cable across the Atlantic, the whole European continent will bloom. They've never had anything like this before. Heads are going to roll.

Randy: Who will keep their heads and prosper from these changes?

Larry: The network architect (NA). Smart network architects are worth their weight in gold. They've got great ideas, like dual fiber rings running through the entire operation. Triangulated. This requires a lot of clever thinking. Architecting for redundancy is another. Imagine a total network outage of less than 15 minutes. That is excellent by today's standards, but it is unacceptable to the business. It is possible to architect around these problems, so the NA will reign.

Randy: What does an effective architecture look like today?

Larry: Multiple connections to multiple points. One web presence equals 12 web sites around the world. Australia is the second busiest web site we've got internationally. We brought up Paris recently. We've located key web servers around the world. One is in Washington D.C., connected to two other locations.

We're installing web sites in London, Munich, Stockholm, Singapore, Japan, and they will all link together. No matter where you are, you can reach our web presence. The least numbers of hops is the goal. The content is fully mirrored, with localized advertisers. We've got servers that do nothing but serve advertising. These servers are dedicated to changing out banners, managing the web hits, and interactively customizing the screens that international customers are going to see. Centralized information, with localized content.

Randy: You've certainly got an effective architecture. You've actually got several success factors. What's Netscape's secret to success?

Larry: We are assembling the best and brightest people at a time when we are the vortex of the computing universe. Finding people is easy, working hard together is our secret.

Jim Barksdale is the action-oriented and hands-on kind of leader. You know, Mel Gibson leading the browser wars. When you start up a company with high-caliber leaders, and high-caliber workers, you succeed. Under Barksdale, everyone is primo. For example, Mike Homer, a brilliant senior VP of marketing, was surprised when our competitor formally announced a bundled deal with the *Wall Street Journal.* He hadn't seen that one coming. So, he rallied his team, and within one week, delivered a personalized content area, via e-mail, that partnered with 20 key publishers to deliver content. That was fast.

Randy: Larry, where is the hubris in all this?

Larry: (laughing). Ask the Fortune 500. They've made hugh investments in old crusty applications that will literally make them fall to their knees in the year 2000. Every COBOL application is going to crash when 2000 occurs. These organizations invested huge dollars in SNA networks. Their legacy applications are functional stovepipes. They believe you cannot retire smokestacks, so their money goes into patching up their infrastructures. That is the hubris, to believe they can survive with SNA.

With intranets, you keep your legacy applications until new processes are in place. Then, build your migration strategy on sophisticated intranet applications, using your legacy apps and legacy databases. Unless they start thinking differently, the established corporations will get passed by, this could even include the PAC Bells and the AT&Ts, if they are not careful.

Randy: With large companies like the PAC Bells and AT&Ts challenged by visionary thinking of the 20th century innovation, who do you consider visionary in thinking about technology.

Larry: Chris Locke comes to mind. He is an absolute brilliant visionary trying to push boulders up hills in corporations. He helped initialize the shopping mall at MCI, plus he was the brains behind MecklerWeb. He's worth another interview for another viewpoint.

John Connors, Vice President, CIO, Microsoft Corporation

As CIO, Connors is responsible for Microsoft's worldwide internal technology infrastructure, corporate information, and implementing key internal systems. During his tenure at Microsoft, Connors has held a variety of positions across the company. Most recently Connors served as Corporate Controller where he was responsible for Microsoft's worldwide accounting, forecasting, and fiscal planning processes and organizations. Prior to his role as Corporate Controller, Connors served as General Manager of Worldwide Financial Operations, Director of Business Operations, European Headquarters, Paris, and Director of Business Operations, Worldwide Sales and Support Strategy Group. Prior to joining Microsoft, Connors was Corporate Controller for PIP Printing and has held financial positions at Safeco Corporation and Deloitte, Haskins & Sells. Connors is a CPA and graduated from the University of Montana in 1984 with a B.A. degree.

Randy: John, you've just assumed the CIO position with Microsoft in July 1996. What is your mission?

John: The migration of fairly large transaction environments onto the intranet. I'm aligning the highly centralized sales system with the information architecture that we now have, which is a financial intranet that replaced our legacy systems.

Randy: What did you build your architecture on?

John: We are using full service client/server systems using web technology and open internet standards?

Randy: What is Microsoft's intranet strategy?

John: Let me differentiate between the internet strategy and the intranet strategy. We have an internet strategy in which we are planning on connecting our thousands of partners together either in a sales, distributor, or support role. We want to create the one-to-many communication medium that is sought after so badly in this industry. I am talking mostly about end users.

Randy: And the intranet strategy?

John: In terms of the intranet, we are focusing every part of the organization in every country on building intranet applications to communicate shared ideas, product plans, and to run the administrative part of the company more effectively. Already we have about a 90 percent intranet-focused organization dedicated to the internal perspective of developing the organization.

Randy: What is your bottom line conclusion regarding your business reengineering capability over the intranet?

John: If you have a good vision for where you want to go and have smart, young passionate people who are empowered to take you there, then you're off to a good start. If you focus on removing obstacles, it doesn't take many resources to transform the resources into a strong system. It's really the people who do the transformation, not the technology.

Randy: What is your formula for selecting the people for building your intranet team?

John: Well we first looked internally and found many good people who just needed obstacles removed from their paths to restructure the business processes that they're used to working with. Once those obstacles were gone, they were empowered to get the job done right. We also brought on some very strong senior managers from Andersen Consulting, who were skilled in the planning process and Systems and Applications Products (SAP). When you put a strong team of senior managers together with young, passionate technical people who know both their technology and their subject areas, you get results.

Randy: It sounds like you've got a great formula for putting together the right teams.

John: Yes, skilled managers with passionate employees in a wonderful environment like Microsoft is a good formula. This is a good place to work if you are passionate about technology. When you have skilled managers, you quickly can empower your staff to use their skills and passions to create innovate and creative solutions to run a business.

Randy: How are they empowered to build the intranet?

John: We ask the younger people where the technology should go and what makes sense. We listen. We provide executive sponsorship and support. And, they make it happen.

Randy: What exactly do you mean by young?

John: Under the age of 30. Of the younger group working on the financial intranet, we had four very bright accountants and two people with IT backgrounds. In fact, the strongest technologist was also an accountant. When people have double skill sets like this, they are incredible.

For example the accountant/technologist created a 10,000-line Visual Basic application to manage the group sales processes. He streamlined the way they were extracting data from the legacy system. He did this on his own time. That's incredible. We now call this MS Report, and its the principle user interface for this group.

Randy: That is ambitious. Are your application solutions created specifically with Microsoft products?

John: Yes, we eat our own dog food if that's what you're asking. Visual Basic used broadly with all the VB extensions, of course. Front Page, whom we recently acquired from Vermeer Technology, is used in certain situations and now with the release of Microsoft Office 97 and its internet capabilities we're seeing more and more groups creating Microsoft intranet solutions.

Randy: Define an intranet solution.

John: This is a good one, really. The best way to describe it is internetworked computing applications. And what I mean by that is the whole power of an intranet is the ability to connect users through the network, instead of working on an individual client site base. It's the difference between network-centric computing and PC-centric computing.

Randy: What problems do intranets solve?

John: Probably the most tremendous thing about web computing, whether it's an intranet or the Internet, is that companies are being forced to work toward a common set of standards. There are already an unprecedented level of standards to work from.

There is a lot of leverage from that. A web-based model is being broadly adopted in business, education, commerce, government, and so on. In the last two months, I've been to Asia and Europe, and although they're not in the same place as the United States, the rate at which they are adopting these standards is accelerating. Especially in Japan. Some countries are at an advantage actually. They have no installed base, no mainframe or mid-range technology, so their move into the current generation of web-based technology is fairly short.

Randy: Meaning that they'll be up and running, competing in an electronic global market, sooner than we anticipate.

John: Precisely.

Randy: What about the cost of bandwidth in the international scene? Won't it prohibit that growth?

John: Yes, it's true that the cost of bandwidth is more prohibitive internationally than it is in the United States. But if you look at what's happening with deregulation geared for 1998, you'll see the international market align quickly with telecommunications bandwidth and international internet standards. Also, mergers like the one between MCI and British Telecom (BTT) will drop prices and even commoditize international bandwidth. Some of the carriers in Asia are working with this goal in mind as well.

Randy: Once bandwidth is more readily available, what do you see are the key benefits, risks, and limitations of intranets, from your vantage point?

John: The greatest benefit of the intranet is that it is a very efficient communication and distribution medium. Its potential has barely been uncovered. The risks are overcoming the security issues that exist, especially as universal security standards get adopted. The most salient limitation is that people have already invested a fair amount of money in their legacy systems that they haven't even expensed yet. You just don't turn off your legacy systems one day. The decisions to migrate must be weighed accordingly. It's not as difficult for a software company to move quickly to an intranet, but it's completely another for a manufacturing company heavily invested in mainframe solutions.

Randy: Do you find this to be the typical situation with most companies?

John: Yes, this limitation is pretty standard throughout our client base. Many customers are still kind of waiting to see and sort out who the technology leaders are, plus the rate of change is so great that they're just waiting to see how it turns out. Once they do decide though, getting up to speed so their IT needs are integrated with their business processes moves a lot smoother for them than they originally thought.

For me, any organization has to have three things in place for a large successful technology project, like deploying an intranet. You must have effective strong sponsorship from executive management. They provide the vision for getting where you're going and support for the business processes for getting there. Second, you need competent business process people, and third, you need strong IT professionals. Without the first two, the third almost always fails. Without quality from the first two groups, the third always fails.

Bottom Line: Successful companies are clearly disciplined with effective management and well thought-out business processes.

Randy: One of the biggest questions in most organizations wanting to convert to intranets is how do you ensure security, reliability, and performance?

John: The amount of research and development (R&D) investment going into security is phenomenal. Microsoft has a broad range of security in their intranet solutions. We have something called Authenticode, in which the browser checks the download of controls, using digital certificates, and ensures that security standards are happening.

Actually, this is an area where a lot of companies see big opportunities. If people see big opportunities, they invest a fair amount of money in it. In this case it's security. Visa, Mastercard, American Express are all investing in secured commerce. However, I don't think the security issues are as profound as people think. But, until you see a broad base of billions of dollars of transactions with limited security issues, you simply won't gather the mindshare that the Internet is fully secure.

Randy: And what about intranet security?

John: The intranet controls seem to be more of a function of the company. Naturally, there is information in the intranet that needs to be protected. Payroll and Human Resources (HR) are always secured. Most of our intranet security issues are handled with operating level security and NT domain password levels, and also with security within applications.

For example with the sale systems, we have a standard policy that if salespeople want to see any secured information, they need to do so under the management of their departments. This doesn't mean that management approval must be gotten every time a transaction occurs, but that the sales management is aware of their staff's use of the sales systems and resolves problems, misconduct, or abuses accordingly. You see security is more of a management issue than an issue of encryption.

Randy: And how do you maintain availability of information for your end users?

John: Availability is going to be a function of your LAN or WAN bandwidth. We have a trial going on today, where we're looking at four sites: Portland, Oregon, Denver, Colorado, Neuss, Germany, and Amsterdam in the Netherlands. We're experimenting with bandwidth. We've turned off our public networks to these locations and are using leased lines through Independent Service Providers (ISPs) to manage the data traffic. At three of the sites, performance is better and with less cost. These ISPs provide favorable prices for bandwidth, so our conclusions are leading us to believe that we can use leased lines to maintain availability and performance of our intranet sites. The fourth site is an anomaly, we haven't figured it out yet.

Randy: What is the intranet computing model at Microsoft?

John: We distribute servers to a large extent, but we use data centers with a highly centralized model. We have our large data centers in Redmond, Australia, Japan, and Ireland, where manufacturing in Europe occurs, and we also have sites in the Nordic region, France, Germany, and the United Kingdom. We have a centralized architecture and a centralized physical location server model.

To date our intranet site is globalized at Redmond, then distributed or mirrored out to the various data centers for localization. However, presently, everything that is done on the data centers passes through Redmond, then is propagated throughout the world.

We're evaluating a couple different models, where we're creating web server farms when the data centers are enormous. When the traffic is excessive, we create data ranches, which are much larger server configurations in selected locations. Basically, when the intranet was started, 85–90 percent of the traffic originated in the United States. As the overall traffic grew internationally, it gets harder and harder to come through the Northwest Net connection. So, we're looking at intranet-based Post Office Protocol (POP) to move our traffic out to the server farms in Europe and Japan.

Randy: Will the server farms be self-regulating.

John: That's a great question. The server farms presently get localized from the subsidiaries, then are mirrored back to the server farm. Presently, they're not self-regulating. But should they be? Yes, I'll address that.

Randy: What is your position on OS/browser integration?

John: It's simply a great value for customers. Microsoft will move forward in that direction. The competition will likely do what they think is best for their future customers. We do not want to see proprietary solutions. Netscape's browser must work with our OS. The standards for browser technology are really becoming commonplace however. The browser battleground is really overstated. A lot more of the long-time business is ending up on the server side.

We have a host of internet-based servers coming out under the Normandy code name, the Catapult proxy server, the Internet Information server, the Merchant server, the Chat server, just to name a few. And they'll all work seamlessly with Windows NT.

Randy: What's your take on Java and ActiveX?

John: There is a lot of enthusiasm around both environments. The work with Java in the ISV community is pretty amazing stuff, and the ActiveX work we've done to embrace and extend Java will be a heck of a lot of value to customers. And the work you'll see coming out of the development tools group will be excellent—a lot of the server side scripting will be very good. It's a very big market and both of the technologies will be important.

Randy: What is your position on the ABMS (Anything But Microsoft) frenzy coming out of Sun, Oracle, and Netscape?

John: They're good companies and the bottom line is that there's a lot of customers that'll decide what the future is. We're spending $2 billion on research and development and we're just not going to stand still.

Randy: What multimedia do you see converging with the intranet? And why?

John: Probably the thing we're excited about with internet technology and transport technology, particularly Asynchronous Transfer Mode (ATM), will be the merger of video, voice, and data in a single-switched environment at high bandwidth speeds. People will get high multimedia applications, especially in on-line games, stock trading, interactive education, and training. There is going to be a heck of a lot of good stuff that comes out in the multimedia arena.

The network technology that is coming in the next two to three years will change a lot of the way we're doing business, and how we're socializing and entertaining ourselves. Asymmetric Digital Subscriber Line (ADSL) technology with speeds 10 times faster than what we're working with now over the same wires will have a lot of promise. Internet and cable transmissions will also add some dimension. There is a lot of money and time that are going to be spent, and an equal amount that is going to be generated.

Randy: How has an intranet improved your organizational effectiveness?

John: Right now it is the Internet with its distribution and sharing of information with our partners that has had the strongest organizational effect. The single best thing that the intranet gives us is one-to-many communications. The intranet extends e-mail. With e-mail you need a targeted address and you need to know whom you're sending information to. With the pull model, you can access whatever you want, whenever you want. That's a new way of doing things, which changes the creativity IQ of a company.

Randy: Some of that creativity is appearing in collaborative and transactional uses of the intranet.

John: Yes it is. We are moving toward building collaborative and transactional intranets. The MSN (Microsoft Network) business has moved from a proprietary to an internet model, where business collaboration and transactions will become a standard way of doing business. We do not, however, consider selling software over the Internet.

Presently, we are giving away a lot of free software, but we're not selling it. We already have a distribution model in place for distributed software. We believe in preserving our distribution channels because of what additional services they provide as well, that is, promotions, networking, increased business demand, and so on.

Randy: John, in this book, I've identified the intranet as the tool that will enable many of the key business models identified in the last 15 years, such as streamlining business processes, rightsizing, creating learning organizations, quality circles, and so on. What's your opinion of the intranet as that tool?

John: Well, Randy, I see the intranet as an enabling tool, right. I'd also add that any effective organization must have strong leadership and management to drive the organization forward. In Microsoft, you can point to Bill Gates or Steve Ballmer and a host of other great managers who have formed the organization with strong leadership and great partnering. No tool will provide this capability.

Randy: I heard it put another way recently. "No tool, no web application, no intranet, or any amount of technology will ever be able to run a day-care center."

John: (Laughing). That's exactly it. Leadership.

Randy: Talk about intranet costs. Anything special, any hidden costs?

John: The initial costs are low in that you can get HTML content created pretty quickly and inexpensively. You can buy servers at reasonable prices, the software is either inexpensive or free. The initial costs are low. The hidden costs to pay attention to are maintaining and running the servers and keeping content refreshed. People can get a web site up quickly, but it needs professional content people to keep sites up and running the content. These fixed costs are missed by many planners.

Randy: How do you explain Return On Investment (ROI) for intranets?

John: The ROI question with Information Technology (IT) is always a difficult one because there are so many qualitative things to measure. For example, how fast do people learn, how much sharing of information didn't happen before the intranet. For those companies that do an effective job with their intranet, they know that the ROI is pretty profound, especially with respect to productivity gains.

Randy: What standards have been put in place for things like publishing, content management, user administration, and links to legacy systems?

John: The standards revolve around what the purpose of your publication is. What is the function of the information that you're going to publish? Is the user more likely to gain benefit from the information or publication than from the traditional publishing mechanism? The departmental managers make these decisions.

At Microsoft, one of the key groups who manage intranet standards is the library. They have a key role, because they are a strong organization that uses their expertise to research articles, index, and look at the cross-group administrative function for diplomatic discussions.

Randy: Is there a Web Council?

John: Yes there definitely is. The Web Council is a great way of getting cross-functional teams together, and to share standards.

Randy: Do you head up the Web Council?

John: No, I don't. I delegate it to the Webmaster position in my group. The council is great; it's made up of people from different operating groups and library.

Randy: I want to talk about how you know the intranet is working for you. Or intranet metrics.

John: Clearly you'll see an incredible ability over time to identify users, what information they retrieve, how they use your products, what kind of customer web-built pages you can send back, based on their behaviors. Cookies or banners are an interesting way of doing that.

Randy: How are you measuring quality business processes with the intranet?

John: To date we have not done a lot of business process measurement. Because we are the incubation stage of the human intranet, we haven't isolated the variables yet for effective evaluation.

Randy: What's on the horizon for intranets from Microsoft?

John: You'll see a broad host of continued expansion in one-to-many communications with a broad range of customers and users, and a whole host of chats and live meetings with customers and end users as the fundamental business model for our technology.

Webmasters

Bill Prouty, Chief Webmaster, Sun Microsystems, Inc.

Bill has 16 years of software engineering and program management intelligence community work at GTE. Then, he worked at SunFed as a program manager on various intelligence agency and NASA projects and took the position as the Solaris transition manager for Sun. Bill was the senior team leader to transfer Sun from SunOS to Solaris 2. This moved him from engineering to informations resources. Bill become the chief after a stint as the hypertext architect. Bill became the chief Webmaster to marry the roles of architecture, technology, and operations.

Randy: I read that Sun was building intranets, when most people thought that was a typo, thinking Internets, not intranets.

Bill: Sun has always been an intranet company. As soon as server software and client browsers came to be, Sun found itself with 1,200 web servers, mostly located on people's workstations. From my point of view, they were extremely hard to manage, placing the onus on the person to back up their systems, and take care of other administrative details. Sun prefers that the employees spend time doing their work, instead of administering a web server on their desktop. So, SunIntraWeb, Sun's centralized internal web site, was born to provide full technical setup and maintenance for internal users.

Randy: Describe that centralized model.

Bill: The idea is to move as many of the web servers into groups as possible, so you can centralize the administration. We created a sort of internal Internet Service Provider (ISP), in this case intranet service providers to do just that. We then strategically placed very large web servers into key separate geographies. We built in an accounting function so the servers can be self-servicing. We automated procedures to prompt the user to set up their account with no administrative intervention so it is technically correct.

Randy: How does that automated process work?

Bill: The SunIntraWeb site sets you up technically as you follow through interactive forms. The way to set up the service is automated as well. Fill out the form in Figure 9–1, and it sets you up with an account name, permissions for security, a common look and feel, and recommendations for links to the SunIntraWeb Home Page. Even better, a manager's approval process comes with the form and through e-mail, your manager is integrated into the process.

Then, all administration, restoring, backups are handled by SunIntraWeb, so technical maintenance is not ever seen by the user. The subscriber to this service does their own authoring of web sites and FTPs them to their specific account on the intranet web server. And yes, there is a charge for the service. But the service is unbeatable.

Randy: I see from the form that there are different levels of service. Can you explain that?

Bill: Yes, there are three levels of service:

- Basic level—small amount of disk space, single account, single user, single external URL.

- Second group level—single account with additional disk space but multiple URLs.

- Third golden account—more disk space, have multiple accounts, and multiple URLs.

Randy: So, you only provide technical support for the intranet?

Bill: Wait a second. The Webmasters under IR (Internal Resources), are also in the content side of the house as well. Not only do they manage the technical aspects of the intranet, but they provide consulting to enhance the user's experience as well. They utilize web interaction on the internal SunIntraWeb page to communicate appropriate tools and processes for success.

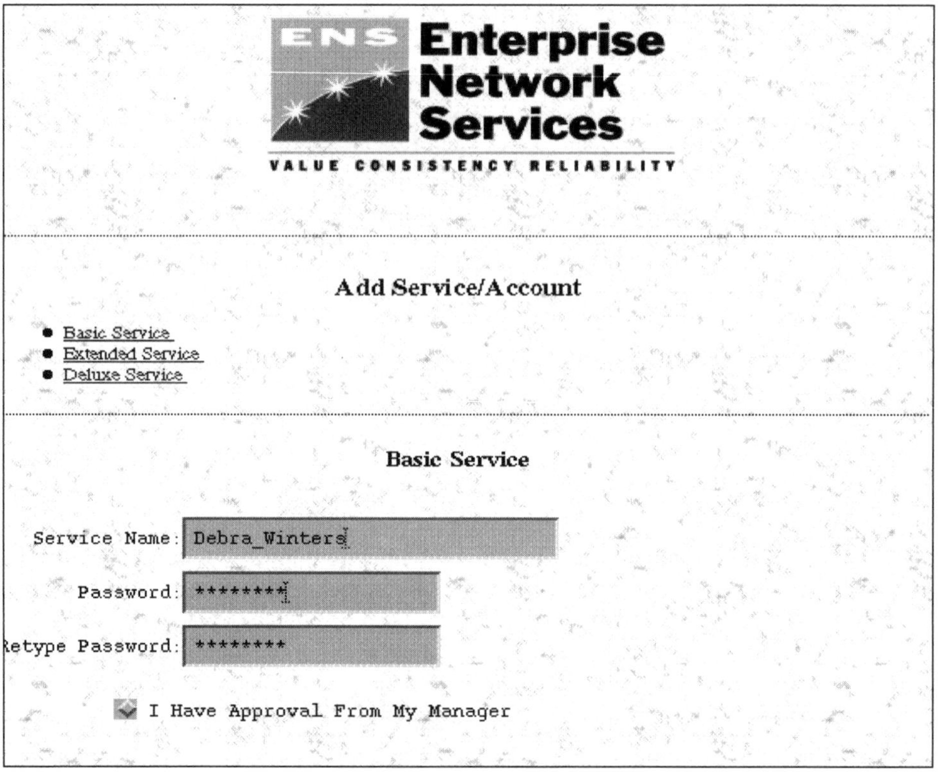

Figure 9–1 Sun Automates Setting Up a Web Server

1. They put out approved graphic libraries, tools for content creation, and procedures for using them. They provide tailored cgi-script libraries, which provide web sites with more features than the average content provider would use, that is, page counters, calendars, send e-mail comments type functions.

2. They help integrate cgi-bin scripts, so there are no clashes. If they have more than a cgi-bin script, then they have to write it and integrate it into the web server for them. The idea is to eliminate bottlenecks to the cgi-bin directory.

3. We are planning on a Java applet library. We try to library-i-tize as much as possible. We have an area called the Construction Kit (see Figure 9–2), which is the great repository of all the excellent efforts of developers throughout the company. The Java applets will be very successful.

4. Sun IR controls the look and feel of the intranet. The perspective is to keep up with the latest technology, so the individual business units can concentrate on content. The OpCos (or individual business units) have an

approval matrix, where each OpCo president has anointed a head Gate-keeper. Their responsibilities are to manage the content that makes it to the SunIntraWeb.

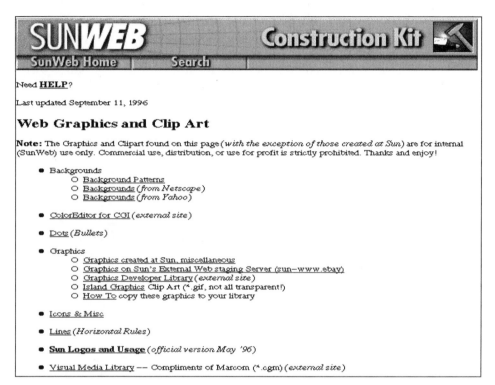

Figure 9–2 Construction Kit for Best of Breed at Sun

Randy: How do you define the term Webmaster?

Bill: Webmasters must be in the Information Resources (IR) organization. From Sun's policy, the company definition of the Webmasters handles the technology and operations of the web servers. We do have two Webmaster groups that are operations oriented. The Webmaster for Sun's web site, and the Webmaster for SunIntraWeb—these Webmasters are not responsible for the content. They don't actually create the content, they are more concerned about the operations end of providing content that is legal, correct, and that use the best technology for presentation. We also have a Webmaster in Europe and a Webmaster in Japan. These people are responsible for the mirrors or clone sites in those locations. They are operations oriented, managing technological upgrades and operating web servers in our international locations.

Randy: Webmasters and gatekeepers, top to bottom. This seems like a pyramidal infrastructure.

Bill: How is a Webmaster or a gatekeeper any different than a product manager who is responsible for everything until the product is released? You have different components rolling up to the product manager (or in this case, the gatekeeper) and all of those individual pieces need to be managed from a single point of view. So, the paradigm is already in place for managing the development of a product. These are just knowledge products that the Webmasters and gatekeepers are responsible for.

Randy: What would you say is your biggest value-add to the way you have this all set up?

Bill: The added value for the authors are the templates, processes, and standards that are tried and true. Everyone who has built a web site in the organization has got a success story. We have captured them. We recommend the standards, such as what HTML standards to use, what HTTP standards, and we provide canned templates whenever possible. The idea is to improve workflow. With our automation, there is less one-on-one consulting between our Webmasters and our authors. So, Webmasters can put their attention on Frequently Asked Questions (FAQs), recommendations for software, conversions, guidance of authors both new and old to become Web authors, critiquing and aiding SunU in their HTML and intranet courses. Authors can put their emphasis on what they do best and add their value as content providers.

Randy: What is the strategy behind the intranet?

Bill: The real strategy is data navigation. What's the easiest way for a Sun employee to get to the right information, at the right time. Secondly, the strategy of properly linking to facilitate navigation. Work processes are analyzed, and as much of the process is automated through the intranet. The part that can't be automated is linked to experts' sites, so the investigator can get to the source to help make decisions.

Randy: How do you get tactical with your intranet strategy?

Bill: We use the methodology of focus groups to select major things like button titles, the look and feel, the contents of the library, whatever. We do that so we can tailor these processes from these original sources for improving the various services that we provide.

Randy: How do you know you're doing it right? What performance metrics do you have in place?

Bill: They're not as good as they could be. In an enterprise, the metrics need to be enterprisewide, and there aren't any metrics packages for a local web server to measure such complexity. We naturally do localized performance monitors: disk utilization, system load, internally and externally. We do that as a load smoothing type of method so that we know when to deploy cache servers in an optimum configuration around the intranet. We've tried to look at performance monitoring packages and couldn't find anything. So, we've written a set of requirements of our own.

Randy: What are the benefits of the intranet in your organization?

Bill: Well, you've got a client/server network where the center is Sun-IntraWeb, which is an information distribution mechanism. In some sort of way, it's an internal electronic commerce center. The Web turns it into a center like this because of the web page. It becomes your first navigation point. From here you launch applications, communicate through e-mail, look at information, keep up on web information, examine workflow, all centered off of various focused web pages. The benefit is the ability to enter at one single entry point. And, if you can come to it at this point, you have one location to vector from the client/server to the intranet. This is home base.

Randy: Talk about security.

Bill: We use the "moat principle at Sun." But, nobody's got passed the alligators yet. Naturally, we have firewalls around SWAN (Sun's Wide Area Network). And, we have secure intranets within intranets. Commerce servers on the client/server network are a great idea.

Randy: Sun's been doing this for a long time. What's their secret?

Bill: We keep everything in the customer perspective. We try to be very customer focused, with internal and external customers alike. We take pains inside of Sun to make sure that the customer's perspective drives our decisions and strategies.

Ken Trant, SGI Webmaster

Randy: How'd the intranet get started at SGI?

Ken: SGI has always used the network as an integral part of our business practices, the Web gave us a higher level structure to organize the chaos into something useful. The FAQs, engineers handbook, and other documents were always available on-line but finding them was always a painful process for new hires.

The concept of an intranet was thought of by some engineers who wanted to streamline the way they were passing information back and forth. The first web server was set up, we downloaded a browser, and put out some HTML so other engineers could find papers, bug reports, e-mail, discussion threads, FAQs. We just wanted to be as productive as possible. Then, this thing grew enormously. Everyone started putting up servers and pages all over the place.

The culture is unique, everyone is computer literate, and we enjoy very open free exchange of information. Everything started to pop up on the intranet, engineering handbooks, installation tools, instructions on setting up

Domain Name System (DNS), things they needed to know about the company. It hardly took more than two to three weeks for someone to get their web pages up on a server. By even my optimistic estimate, I'd say we created a random data warehouse fairly quickly, where people could go and get information quickly. Everything recent was available. It was a great state of informational chaos.

Randy: Did you develop an infrastructure to manage the chaos?

Ken: It developed by itself actually. People could create a home page on their own server, or they'd get more efficient and start grouping web pages on one server. Then groups or division servers started to grow, with information linking up. The overhead was very low, so it was easy to reconfigure into groups. But, you're right, we didn't want to have an administrative nightmare, so we formed a cross-functional centralized group. That took off fairly well.

We started creating some centralized areas, the Engineer's Handbook, the FAQ Server, where to go for HR, campus maps on-line that kind of necessary stuff. Slowly the company was being assimilated into one server. We started to suffer from success. So I had an idea what to do. I went to executive management, and explained an intranet strategy. I didn't have to sell the concept.

Bottom Line: The executives bottom line—it's really easy to put your information out there, so do it now.

Within six months, management said they had to make it a universal, real service for the entire company. We defined a mission statement, put some resources behind it, and then built the present day architecture and infrastructure. That was the worse part though, trying to decide how this thing should be put together.

Randy: So how did you put it together?

Ken: Well our initial thoughts were to create a kind of clearing house, not so much as a content creator, but a magnet for content. You could advertise your service there. We thought about creating a main campus, one that would only have two levels, or two tiers. One would be a general pointer to information, and a second level would by a UNIX file system with a root, and major directories below. Standard UNIX stuff, really. The top page would have pointers to major services, HR, manufacturing, engineering. From there down, it would be somebody else's information.

But trying to figure out what should go on the top pages was very difficult. We hired a contractor to design the top page. They did a fine job, but it wasn't good enough, it didn't mesh with who we were or what we wanted. The second contractor provided some quality images, good looking pages, but they just didn't match either. So, we put together an in-house team (few technical people, some mid-level managers, and members from the staff). We ended up with more dynamic top and second levels.

We call the main page, the Junction.

The Junction, Figure 9–3, is a data warehouse. The company made a commitment. Money and resources were thrown at it. A manager was brought in from Europe. We hired three to four engineers for content creation. They created the tools for displaying the content (WebForce), and they helped individual departments move their legacy data off of paper, or any other system, into a web-based format. We've had good luck in converting information, phone books, HR information, processes for updating medical information or changing your 401K. Anything in HR you can basically do on the Net. All the information is constantly there to be built on. We are only limited by the tools that run on the server to determine the content.

Figure 9–3 SGI's Intranet Home Page—the Junction

Randy: Do your executives use the Junction?

Ken: Every one has signed up to use it. As soon as some of the departments found out you could secure your information, the number of web servers increased dramatically. The top page is very dynamic. It is used like a television station, or a broadcasting station. If you want other people in the organization to know what information or services you have available, you advertise it on the top pages. The company president makes general announcements at the Junction or all-hands meetings on the top level. But, you don't have to plug into the Junction at all. The idea is to advertise on it when you have something to say. We do keep robot tools, sniffers to scan the intranet though for information that we think would go on these pages. The main idea though is to use the Junction to search for what you want, or advertise what you think others might want.

Randy: You haven't said a whole lot about the content providers?

Ken: It's all about providing information, not so much about creating content. The bottom line with content creation is, who owns the content? Companies are in flux all of the time, so the only answer is the intranet owns the content. The intranet server is designed to get you to the information as soon as possible. If people keep that in mind, they'll see how access is key, not so much as who is providing the information.

Randy: How do you define Webmaster?

Ken: A Webmaster is like a headmaster. The Webmaster manages the overall processes. The Webmaster puts up the web server. You organize a team for coding a web site. The team is set up as a response team with the Webmaster delegating the types of things they need to do. Webmasters, in essence, debug problems. Anyone who is responsible for a server, is essentially a Webmaster at SGI. A bunch of techies rally around a Webmaster. The Webmaster is an evangelist for a server.

Randy: Do you have another structure below Webmasters, people or gatekeepers, who manage content?

Ken: Not really. Content is pushed down to the person who would normally create the content anyway. They aren't necessarily web people. They're people who, given WYSIWYG, can produce their own content. Three-fourths of the sites are run by people who are significantly less conversant with setting up or maintaining a server. Instead, they use these cool desktop tools.

Randy: How do they learn to use the tools?

Ken: While software is mostly free, since SGI is the creator of a good deal of it, some software has associated license costs. We use the Web to generate licenses, and to submit the PR to the appropriate manager for approval.

We have also started training support and sales engineers via the Web. We recently held a three-day course for our worldwide sales and support personnel over the Web. It used a live audio feed and a central web server. The benefits were that we were able to use the engineers who created the new products to teach the courses so questions were answered real-time instead of the classic "I'll find out and get back to you" type of training.

In three days the entire worldwide field sales and support staff was trained, something that used to take weeks and dozens of trainers flying around the world. We also created a set of tools that recorded the live training and now those training courses are available on-line for anyone to take. The web pages are keyed to the audio feed so the pages change the same as they did during the live broadcast. It was all very cool and a huge success.

Randy: This is great stuff. It sounds like you've revolutionized distributed training. I especially like the expert trainers, and the knowledge trail the training leaves behind. Do you let everyone have access to all information like this?

Ken: No. There is a lot of engineering information that should not be shared, mostly because it sometimes makes it to the customers, and it could be purely experimental. Customers have expectations; when they see something that comes out of SGI, they want it, no matter what shape or form it's in. So, we have to build secure servers inside the intranet as well. Another reason not to let everyone have access to all information is because of copyright problems. Disney protects their images seriously, and if one of them appears on one of our pages, the user needs to know about copyright infringement. There is also some information that needs to be protected. But, we don't put up all the copyright information for people to follow to the letter, because the copyright laws on the internal intranet are not exactly the same, are they? After all, the company owns all of the information inside.

As far as we're concerned, the web community handles what belongs out there. They considered themselves web warriors. They do what they have to in order to get the message across. Still you'll get e-mail that asks for permissions to link. It all works, somehow.

Randy: What are your greatest challenges you face in deploying an intranet?

Ken: Getting the machine configured for everyone. This is where the bread and butter lies. Performance, tuning, and design have always been critical issues. When you have everyone in the corporation hitting the servers all day long, you really need to perform some serious load balancing. Either you have to get a bigger machine, or you design innovative solutions. Like round robin or DNS load balancing to duplicate your service. Netscape uses round robin with their million hits an hour, or whatever it is now.

Randy: What are round robin and DNS load balancing?

Ken: Using round robin load balancing is very straightforward. Let's say you have four machines; the first request is handled by #1, the second is handled by #2, and so forth. DNS load balancing uses a DNS to tell the client what the IP number of the system they want to talk to is. The answer provided by DNS is determined by a script that runs every N interval. The script checks all four machines (using the same four systems as the example above) and whichever system has the lowest load is the answer DNS will return to all requests until the next test period. These are esoteric issues though for this discussion, you wouldn't need them until you have heavy duty use on your intranet.

Randy: What kind of heavy duty use?

Ken: Well, a chatroom would do it. We have something called Silicon Studios which was created by the users. It's so easy to use, but it takes up a lot of bandwidth. It's like a custom-design newspaper, where everyone spends a lot of time learning about how things work here. They talk a lot between each other, solving problems, learning about things they didn't know about.

The multimedia advertising that we do inside is another big one. Things have gotten so competitive inside SGI that everything is a grand multimedia intranet production or competition. We have things like brown bag discussions that are video taped, with Q&A, that you can watch while you're eating your lunch at your desk. Advertising is just as important inside as it is on our outside Web. But it takes its toll. Chat rooms are great for talking over what you're going to do for one of these panel discussions, what kind of info they might want.

SGI has new tool called COSMO. It allows people to create these tools using Java and JavaScript, videos, and everything. You'll want to leverage knowledge and information. It'll do overheads for executive board meetings, and slides using whatever tools you have on your desktop. The conference rooms are wired for intranet presentations. SGI has a whole range of tools for content creating. Can you see what I mean by heavy use?

Randy: Yes. What I'm wondering is how you fund all these internal productions?

Ken: Each group pays a fixed amount of money to the corporate coffers for their phone and facilities services. We're trying to decide if that should be done with the intranet or not. They're all utilities, used for communication. So far, we've shied away from that, but at some point, intranets will have to do something like charging back for services they provide. I'm sure corporate IS would agree strongly. But, at the same time, each IS department has their own web server and Webmaster, too, so they understand the dilemma.

If one server gets 50K hits an hour, how do you figure out their utilization? An individual page can have five hits, or have five gets, so a page could have just one real hit. It sounds confusing, and it is. The stats show how many pieces of data were pulled from your server. But it's hard to determine what to charge for, data, hits, people. We haven't figured that one out yet. The problem is trying to figure out how to manage it fairly.

Randy: What's the future of the intranet?

Ken: You'd think I would say Java or Shockwave. But these technologies won't move into the market fast enough. Users will like to see this stuff, but I don't think they're going to see it on their desktops or their individual user pages for quite some time. It's just too difficult to use for the average user. Not everyone even has access to browsers, or network connections that will allow them to be viewed easily.

This was a problem for Silicon Surf, the outside web site. How far do you reach for the Least Common Denominator (LCD)? Do you worry about the people who have low-speed connections? Do you assume the LCD is a 14.4, 56K, or T1? The future will be bandwidth and content.

Tim Horgan, WebMaster Magazine Webmaster, CIO Communications

Tim Horgan is the Webmaster for both *Webmaster Magazine* and CIO Communications.

Randy: What would be your first message to corporations developing intranets?

Tim: Get started today. Now. There is a lot to learn and more is being added daily. If you wait too long, catching up will be very difficult. Senior management support will be a key success factor. Strategize how to get it. It is critical to develop an overall strategy for where you want to go, a vision thing. Actually, this, to me, is the most important thing.

Bottom Line: If you don't have a clear idea where you're headed, and what the pieces are that will need to be filled in over time, you'll wander.

Randy: How would you recommend to develop a strategy that works?

Tim: Start with a vision. Then, figure out where you want to get from there. Make sure you design your vision to meet your business needs. Don't try to follow the latest technical fads. Find the key areas in your business that will benefit from intranet information flow and develop these key areas. Track your progress. Small steps work best, so work one step at a time. Do it, test it, redo it, move on. Communicate, evangelize, and train. You've got to manage evolution. Anticipate the flood!

One of the challenges is to think ahead to what the problems will be when there are thousands of servers and users. So I'd start with the business goals, figure out your guiding principles around information access and sharing, then work through what will need to be there to support large-scale use. This provides the road map, from which small-step plans (three to four month chunks, no bigger) can be deduced. Then you come back and sanity check this in three to four months.

Randy: Do you see the intranet as a real business tool?

Tim: Yes. The benefits and cost savings are real. There are companies using it now, with many more starting to. And the tools are enabling more sophisticated and wider applications. In the end, the deciding factor will be how we use it to get business done. Significant changes will not come from applications, but from changes in how we do work.

The capability to deliver information to every desktop is revolutionizing how we use, find, share information . . . but revolutions need direction and leadership!

Randy: What technology do you see that will move us faster along in revolutionizing the way we do business?

Tim: Netscape Application Programming Interface (NSAPI), Internet Server Application Programming Interface (ISAPI), and other programming interfaces will provide us faster access, reduce overheads, and provide persistent database connections. These are key. Conferencing technology with threaded discussions and work group forums will have a great impact. Transaction-oriented computing, the mission-critical applications, will be faster to develop and cheaper to deploy. Also, agents and personalized views of information will move us faster along the continuum of improved workflow. Already search engines are improving so fast, they can scale enterprisewide information well. And, the database access (Web to database) software is making this all a very exciting time to live in.

Randy: How will this all affect workflow?

Tim: Well first of all, document management will help with the chaos of the Web. As applications connect work processes, or automate tasks, we will be able to more effectively measure and improve workflow. Already it is easier to share information across wide areas. If we can move to the dream of paperless office, standardize the sequence of tasks (with help desks), define tasks, track status, and application use, we can again measure how work is flowing through the organization. I'm not even mentioning all the collaboration applications out there that improve workflow, like Lotus Notes, and Collabra.

Realize, that many companies have been working on workflow for some time now but have been prevented from effecting large-scale solutions because it was so hard to connect systems and people—the very thing the Web now enables. So, we've been working on making this happen, and now it can really be done!

Randy: What are the tools that you like?

Tim: Well authoring tools of course. They reduce the need to know HTML to publish. HTML isn't all that hard, but the graphical software for publishing is extremely good. Some companies are smart and using native formats to create web pages. Doing something like this accelerates production and reduces the overhead of training. If they already know the software, their production rates will improve significantly.

I like this class of tools because it allows the people with the information, the business people, to become publishers—the Webmaster should be concentrating on innovative Web products, which stretch the technology and escort you through the evolution of communication!

I also like tools like NetObjects Fusion which simplified web site development overall, at least for smaller sites. Great stuff for internal groups.

Randy: What about application development tools?

Tim: Well, initial web application development is tedious at this point. We need better tools to develop production-quality applications. We have Java WebObjects which enable custom pages on the fly in response to user input and database content. These tools accommodate for typical applications like order entry, scheduling, and real-time information such as stock quotations. But, the real application development tools will be object oriented and integrate seamlessly with all other enterprise tools.

The three areas of concern here are getting the skilled Webmasters and information designers who know how to build these applications, ongoing maintenance of the environments when they're created, and scale to the future. Intranets will not grow by themselves. Another concern is getting the client/server, production quality developers to get doing web stuff—they know the issues that need to be focused on when we scale up.

Randy: How would you characterize concerns, challenges, and benefits?

Tim: Wow, that's a big question. The benefits are pretty obvious. You can search, find, browse, and retrieve all kinds of information: research, products, libraries, services, vendors, and so forth. The platforms are independent, so you can use access multiple platforms. You get just-in-time information and training. It's a distributed access to a wide range of information and services. We haven't had that before. Increased platform independence is the one the press has picked up on the most.

Enterprise information sharing and information provided in context are what impress me. Easier interaction with experts and who knows what's coming up next is resourceful. The challenges include dealing with hundreds of thousands of users, and understanding their requirements for information and ease of use. Where do they start? What do they use? What do they know already? You've got to know your audience.

And as these audiences swell, the number of internal servers expands as well. How do you keep up with that maintenance challenge? Some of the biggest challenges are security, bandwidth, scalability, manageability, measuring payback, maintenance, and as I've said before getting and keeping skilled Webmasters and information designers.

And today we use the Web as a communication vehicle where we talk to people geographically separated, but whom we expect are viewing our material now, or in the near future. One of the hidden major benefits of the Web will be that of information access across time. The Web is the stuff that we can start weaving our corporate memories on top of—who did what, what different projects were about, and what they gave us (analyses, ideas, reports, products)—the stuff that we have been losing for years! If we can preserve this (a big assumption), and if we can recall it, we will see significant increases in productivity, decreases in time to market.

But this assumes that we have been good historians, that we have created web sites that would be of use to history (which could mean someone 12–18 months from now, or 12–18 years from now), that we have included contextual information, have preserved a rich set of artifacts, and so forth. For this to happen will require advances in how we design information, which may take years to happen. Our understanding of the ways in which people use and reuse information is fairly primitive, at least in the corporate world— because we've never really had the richness of information that we're about to have!

Randy: How have you seen the intranet evolve in companies?

Tim: Well, they've moved way beyond document exchange to complex uses. The document access is still there: newsletters, reports, maps, price lists, product information, directories. But when functional group pages began to appear, you saw a change. Scheduling, project management, and project tracking. You saw collaboration and collaborative development. Software distribution grew as a big user, and of course e-mail and discussion threads. But now, you see database access, virtual conferences, workflow improvements, agents helping with personalized searches.

Companies are shutting off legacy delivery systems. They're insisting the new applications are web-enabled, and they're creating web teams to look at how to develop the organization.

Randy: Do you have some examples?

Tim: Lots. Boeing has hundreds of intranets. NASA uses the intranet for planning large projects; they say the intranet enables distributed team collaboration. Federal Express is the company everyone refers to, but they have customer package tracking on-line both inside and outside of their intranet. They are saving an estimated $2 million a year with this intranet service. Visa connects members' banks to an intranet of their own, and has reduced 2 million pieces of paper received daily.

Sandia National Laboratories uses conference-room scheduling, financial-management queries, knowledge preservation, official airline guides, subscription services, and technical reports on their intranet. The examples are endless—MCI, Booz-Allen, Sun Microsystems, Digital, Ford, National Semiconductor, SGI, Eli Lily.

Randy: What do you think the core competencies are for building an intranet?

Tim: Well, the first would be a reference capability. You must be able to identify and present yourself exactly as you are. If you understand who you are, and what you do, then you can build the infrastructure to support it. Another competency is to have a deployment strategy. Do you understand the user's needs well enough to put an intranet out there that will be helpful, and set up an environment in which they're providing open and honest feedback to improve the system? In deploying an intranet, you are building the shared knowledge of the corporation.

Which brings us to the third competency, information strategies. You have to know which information your user needs. You have to supply them with information they don't even know they needed. And finally, you have to have business acumen; this means that your intranet needs to reflect your values, your access to information policy, your publishing skills, and how you plan on handling security. These must be made clear to all employees; they must have this competency to succeed.

Randy: What do you need to get an intranet going?

Tim: There is a range of things, depending upon your level of commitment. You definitely need a common, maintained set of complete enterprisewide references pages, so everyone knows what's going on. Legal issues, HR policies related to web use, user tool sets (including browsers, viewers, licensing, testing, and support), developer tool sets, and training aimed at various levels of expertise. Naturally, you'll need search and navigation tools, plus the strategies that go with using them.

One thing I'm hearing a lot these days is to have a complete publishing system, including icons, or reusable graphics, tools, guidelines, templates, process guides. In order for people to get their information on-line, they need to know how to publish. Plus, they'll need information strategies. They always ask, "how do you present information in the best possible way?" This goes with knowing how to technically link up to legacy systems, and the gateways for moving data easily across the network.

You'll also need a consulting service, either inside or outside of the organization, that can help with policies, guidelines, standards, interfaces, access, security, and all the other issues burgeoning from this expansive field.

Randy: Can you discuss real cost savings?

Tim: People are starting to believe that the benefits, while "soft," are critical, and should be viewed on par with "administrative costs," or the costs of doing business. But there are other measurable costs that show how intranets are cost-effective. The cost savings in paper costs is well documented. Software distribution and development is another. It is easy to quickly prototype and test ideas. It also saves work time by reducing the time to process and consolidate work processes in automated Web pages.

Visionaries

Christopher Locke

Locke was founding editor of *Internet Business Report* and has written extensively on net-related themes for *Internet World, Information Week, Byte, Network Computing* and the Internet Society's magazine, *OnTheInternet.* He has held positions with Mecklermedia, MCI, and IBM, and his Internet work has been reported on by publications such as *The New York Times, The Financial Times,* the *Wall Street Journal, Forbes, Fortune, Business Week,* the *Economist, Advertising Age, Inter@ctive Week,* and NBC Nightly News. Locke is also editor of a highly irreverent Webzine called Entropy Gradient Reversals. If you want to know what that means, visit Chris' web site at http://www.panix.com/~clocke/EGR/.

Randy: You have an interesting background that shapes your vision. You were editor and publisher of internet MCI's Net Editors Web pages, you were the guy behind MecklerWeb, you were founding editor of the *Internet Business Report* at CMP Publications. Larry Geisel, CIO at Netscape, calls you an Internet visionary. So what's the vision?

Chris: It's more of an open issue, than a vision really. I've got this nagging question in the back of my mind. Are audiences as stupid as many seem to believe? Or have they just been waiting for something like the Net to come along? I'm not suggesting this is a conscious thing necessarily. There has been so much conditioning by previous media models in which people were simply information consumers that, at this point, I think they're not sure what they want. But when most people I've talked to first encountered the

Net, they sort of went crazy—and I mean that in a very positive sense. It's so open and free compared to traditional media, and invites participation as broadcast never could—nor usually wanted to.

It's genuinely empowering, well beyond the cliché that word has become. This whole constellation of questions also applies to employees—and since we're talking about intranets here, that's critical.

Bottom Line: The old industrial-era mandate to "check your brain at the door" is utterly dysfunctional in an economy driven by knowledge and innovation.

That doesn't mean this mentality is dead by any means; just that it's more suicidal than ever. Intranets invite participation in the same way the Internet does.

But businesses, especially large ones, have been subject to a lot of denial with respect to this radical shift in the capabilities and desires of both external markets and internal workforces. If I have a vision, I've built it around confronting that denial wherever I encountered it, and believe me, I've had no lack of opportunities.

Randy: One shift, two results—with the technology supplying the motive force. That's saying you see significant parallels between the desires of the market and the needs of employees?

Chris: Well, I'm not convinced technology is the primary driver here, but it certainly potentiates other trends that were in motion well before networks or even computers came on the scene. That's a long street to go down, though. As to significant parallels, yes indeed, these do constitute the two sides of the network coin: Let's say obverse is the market-oriented Internet and reverse is the workforce-focused intranet. Each relies on the other in fundamental and highly complimentary ways. Without strong market objectives and connections, you have no viable focus for the work of the intranet; without a strong intranet, your market objectives and connections might remain wishful thinking.

Randy: That seems pretty easy to accept. So where does the denial come in?

Chris: There were tremendous economies of scale in the old-school broadcast-advertising alliance—and there still are in some traditional media. Many companies don't want to relinquish that. It's what they know. It's where they made their fortunes. But trying to keep things in that old familiar rut is to deny that the ability of markets to respond and interact—and this is what the Internet has brought to the party—makes any real or lasting difference. But in fact, it does.

Randy: Are you suggesting that companies are afraid that intranets will actually make people smarter?

Chris: Yeah, actually I am saying precisely that. The single greatest difference the Net has made to market realities is that—because networks enable people to share relevant knowledge with those having like interests—the lowest common denominator of informed awareness tends to be much higher online than in broadcast media.

And it also tends to get higher a lot faster. This raising of "informed awareness" obviously applies to intranets as well—I'd say it's where their primary value lies. Notice I said networks had this "potential" though. A lot can get in the way of that before it's realized—like the denial we just mentioned.

Randy: So what would you say is the greatest danger for a company seeking to create a viable intranet?

Chris: That's easy: the command-and-control mentality.

Randy: Can you give an example of how that might work against an intranet effort?

Chris: Well, I'm reminded of an excellent cover story on intranets that *Business Week* ran a while back—this was just around the time the buzzwords were emerging into general parlance. Several CIOs were quoted as saying they had so many thousand web pages behind the firewalls. And they were kind of crowing about it. But my take was that this content didn't get created top-down by the IS organization. Instead, these pages sprang up overnight like a crop of magic mushrooms on a rich motherlode of corporate horseshit.

Randy: That's certainly an amusing turn of phrase, but what does it mean in practical terms?

Chris: Well, look, when all this got started—all of what? maybe 12–18 months ago at best?—you had thousands of workers with easy access to free web browsers and a smaller set of folks who had figured out how to set up servers whose only cost was download and tinkering time. These people soon figured out that HTML wasn't rocket science—and the rest is history! Suddenly there was nothing in the way of their own ideas and creativity. Skunk works wanted to build broader support for their projects, individuals wanted to be noticed for their technical savvy or penetrating wit or business insight.

Randy: And then the corporate types stepped in . . .

Chris: Exactly. To be fair, a certain type of corporate types, because there are people out there—a handful anyway—who truly understand the dynamics of how all this stuff works. And by dynamics, I mean more the cultural aspect of networking. For the technology, you can buy a book. Aside from this handful, though, most corporate managers are clueless in the extreme.

For one thing, far too many have never spent any serious time on-line. Then the first thing they think about is who will report to whom and where everybody sits in some abstract organization chart. But command-and-control thinking throws cold water onto all that magic-mushroom enthusiasm. You know, directives saying "Your pages must be formally approved by the Department of Business Prevention." That sort of thing. But it's quite often the people at the lower levels of the organization that have the most valuable knowledge—not the managers and corporate control freaks.

So if you kill off this enthusiasm, you can have a large, professional looking, very expensive intranet that nobody uses or cares much about. The question companies should be asking themselves is, "What if we built an intranet and nobody came?"

Bottom Line: If control is what you're really after, you might as well go back to mainframes.

Randy: But don't you need top management support to make it really work?

Chris: Yeah sure, but mostly that support needs to come in the form of facilitation and enough brains to get out of the way. It's gotta be more like rock and roll than strait-laced traditional business—and that puts the command-and-control crowd right over the top. This is the exact corporate analogy of the broadcasters not wanting to relinquish their mass markets. It's stonewall denial.

Randy: But come on. Are you seriously suggesting that you can run a company by improvising all the time?

Chris: Companies run that way whether anybody wants them to or not. Nobody runs them, nobody writes the score. If you plan to serve these companies—which means making money of course—you'd better have a clue about what's going on out there in the marketspace. And what's going on is the intranet, or the extended intranet.

The Net was a novelty when I was first preaching all this stuff, but market expectations are totally welded to Net-speed performance today. Your software product isn't available for downloading? You don't have secure transaction processing so I can buy it when I need it? Hey, I'm gone! And so is a big chunk of your market share. Your company doesn't have access to a high volume of corporate data, or you aren't doing process transactions on-line, I'm looking for another company.

Randy: This doesn't just apply strictly to software companies—nor to product marketing, I assume.

Chris: That's right. It applies across the board to information of every stripe. It applies to ideas—how to acquire them within the company and from the market, move them around, get peer feedback, sort them, slice them, dice them, move them back out into the market as new products, get customer feedback—then iterate, getting better at it as you go. Make mistakes. Debug on the fly. It's fast, it's furious. It's fun! You get the picture. If you want a rock-and-roll company, which is more important, knowing how to dance or adhering to procedure?

Randy: Well, yes, but how does all this get coordinated? Doesn't this turn into anarchy?

Chris: Yeah, it does, and you start instigating it. It's bizarre. What I've always been really interested in is revolution. A real one, not some bogus "revolutionary" flavor of the month management obsession like "downsizing" where everybody gets screwed but the top dogs. Where do you think the fervor came from to produce that first wild-oats crop of intranets? It surely wasn't from the CIOs who got quoted in *Business Week.* Look, workers at every level have had it with repressive organizations. Markets have had it with hyperbole-laden corporate rhetoric that's 99 percent hot air. Why not put them both together and kick some serious butt? About time, don't you think?

Randy: And you say you worked for IBM?

Chris: It was a short marriage.

Randy: But I have to ask the question again. How does this get coordinated? It can't just be a bunch of individuals doing their own thing.

Chris: Well, I'd say that's already the case in too many corporations that only think they're in control. People largely do what they feel like anyway and give as little as possible to the company. It's adversarial as hell, yes. But if you look into it, the company almost invariably has set things up that way by not trusting people to be motivated, intelligent, creative, innovative . . . the list goes on.

Randy: So would you say that intranet initiatives represent an opportunity to turn this situation around?

Chris: Absolutely. But only if there's genuine awareness of what's on the table. Remember Deming? Was he just whistling in the wind or was he pointing out real problems in organizations that can't just be swept under the rug? I'd say the latter. However, too much of the juice that's gone into intranet development is focused on whiz-bang technology and not nearly enough on the cultural revolution all this implies—in fact demands.

The answer to your question about coordination—finally—is cooperation and negotiation among peers and colleagues. But these have to be executed very fast, not in committee meetings. This is why people need power in organizations—not to lord it over others but to make intelligent decisions on the fly and not see them get overturned two days later by managers who don't know the territory.

Without getting into the politics of it, do you remember the biggest complaint of the armed forces in Vietnam? It was that the war was being fought from Washington. Again without getting into the politics of it: We lost. This is a big clue as to how many intranet initiatives could play out.

Randy: So is there some kind of infrastructure that would better fit this new mode of operation?

Chris: I'm not so sure any imposed infrastructure would help. Most "empowerment" programs are embarrassingly paternalistic, to the point of backfiring entirely. Real authority is based on knowledge and the two are inherently intertwined. Also, both grow bottom up. When arbitrary "management" takes over what was initially a "hand-rolled" intranet—the individuals who championed and created it often feel betrayed and disenfranchised. If you look back into the history of craft and what happened in the Industrial Revolution, you see the same thing. We are making some very old mistakes here.

Take another example much closer to the present. The autonomous PC challenged the hegemony of mainframe information systems and enabled the development of quick solutions that could end-run the infamous MIS-bottleneck. Then IS management discovered the LAN, which did deliver another layer of utility. However, instead of leveraging this new resource for the benefit of "users"—even that word is an artifact of the mentality—they largely used the LAN to reestablish control over information access and work environments.

Now, many companies are doing the same thing again with the intranet. You get this rule-book mentality—the corporation's common look and feel, logo placement, legal number of words on each web page. Whatever. It's all so cramped and constipated and uninviting. Dead. The people who actually built the intranet—created the content that makes it valuable—will bail, looking for yet another open system. And today they're sure to find one.

Randy: Where?

Chris: Well, remember the context for all this. Twenty years ago, or even five, only corporations could provide the kind of resources needed to process even modest volumes of information. The cost of such systems was a significant barrier to entry for new businesses that might become competitors. But today individuals have this kind of power in their rec rooms! And they can get all the Internet they can eat for 20 bucks a month. If the company doesn't come through with the kind of information (and delivery) that turns them on—provides learning, advances careers, and nurtures the unbridled joy of creation—well, hey, they'll just do it elsewhere. Maybe in the garage. You can laugh, but it's happening right now.

Randy: I assume the results of all this are showing up somewhere on the World Wide Web?

Chris: Yeah, but you've got to get down to the underbelly of the thing—way down below the hype and hoopla, there's something very different brewing. It has to do with living, with livelihood, with connection and community. This isn't some smarmy New Age mysticism either. It's tough and gritty and it's just beginning to find its voice, its own direction. This is hard to communicate—you have to see it for yourself. You have to live in the net for a while.

At the risk of sounding self-serving—a dirty job but someone's gotta do it—you could take my own Webzine, *Entropy Gradient Reversals* as an example. This might be shocking stuff to some corporate denizens, but they'd probably be even more shocked by the subscriber list. It includes some of the best minds in the on-line business.

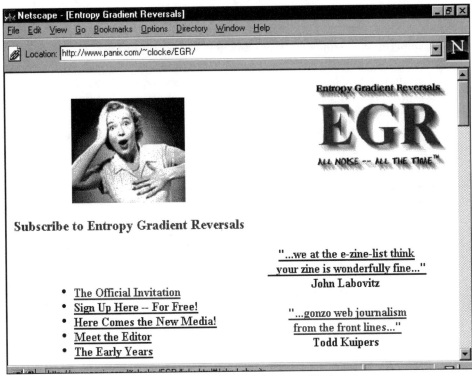

Figure 9–4 Entrop Gradient Reversals—a Visionary E-zine

Randy: You've mentioned several cases where things are radically other than they appear, almost as if a new kind of logic is emerging, or needs to.

Chris: Yeah, I call it gonzo business management—paradox become paradigm. We're not in Kansas anymore, Toto, and we might as well get used to it. The opportunity here is to keep your day job but at the same time to indulge your human creativity and self-expression.

Companies that try to prevent this sort of thing within their firewalls—as many do—need to have their collective heads examined. Conversely, companies that foster and encourage it will win big.

The best software, design, graphics, writing—elegant, artistic, fantastically interesting and valuable content—are coming out of places where people feel their creativity is valued. Places where inspiration is king. No arrogance, no pretense, just like grunge rock coming out of Seattle garages. Here's another clue: Unless your industry is very "mature"—which means ready for the bone yard—your market isn't wearing pinstripe suits anymore, either. In many cases, your workers are your market. Come out of the bunker once in a while, see what they're up to—it could be your future.

Randy: And what would this innovative creativity do for a corporation?

Chris: Well, the last few sentences in fact described exactly where intranets came from in most cases—not from the boardrooms, but from the corporate basements. After *Business Week* blessed them as "Significant Developments," everybody jumped aboard. But how do you know where the next big thing is going to come from? You need great radar today, and that means a wide-awake workforce that's constantly tinkering, exploring, figuring out new ways to have fun.

If that sounds too frivolous, this kind of creativity also tends to jump-start real knowledge exchange.

Bottom Line: Intranets could blow corporations out of their counterproductive stove pipes and get people charged up to bring new knowledge into the company.

But for that to really happen, you've to get outside the firewall to a very real extent.

Randy: You just went from intranet to Internet to what Zona Research calls extended intranet.

Chris: If that's not just another empty buzzword, it could point to a much needed dimension of all this. I'm bothered by the Internet/intranet dichotomy. It reinforces the "not invented here syndrome" that has seriously damaged so many companies. I think the businesses that are going to make it will not only have to tear down their internal walls, they're also going to have to tear down their external walls. The survivors will be left standing naked—in the middle of a thriving marketplace. That's actually a very promising paradox, but it's the stuff of nightmares for many companies.

"Drive out fear," Deming said and he was right. But it's not easy for the Old Guard. It goes very deep.

Randy: Fear of what exactly?

Chris: Well, we were just talking about mistrust a while ago, between managers and the managed. Do you follow Dilbert? Mike Hammer, the god of reengineering himself, said it wasn't a comic strip but a documentary. There is a long history of adversarial worker-management relations in America. And it's not because of Karl Marx or the AFL-CIO as much as it is the fallout from people like Frederick Taylor and Henry Ford, ideas like "scientific management" and Theory X—it's a long story.

The basic fear is that employees are pilfering your time, collecting a pay-check while hanging out on the Net or playing Solitaire all day. Let me tell you, though, the people who built the first internet sites in the organizations I worked with put in 17-hour days. They worked like soldiers rebuilding a bridge. You had to be there to believe it.

But many now managing internet or intranet projects were not there and they don't believe it. It all goes back to a fear of losing control. Whatever the cause, it has to go. Right now these fear-driven corporations are spending millions on market research, the whole point of which is to find out whom they're selling to. They don't know anymore. They've barricaded them-selves in their executive suites, and now they want to erect firewalls on top of that.

Randy: This goes back to your belief that you have to live on the Net to work with the Net. That is why data security is so necessary.

Chris: Yes, yes, it's necessary. Data security is no joke and it needs to be done well. But many of the outfits I'm talking about here are desperate for fire-walls because they don't want the market to see they have nothing worth stealing inside them! That's not security, it's paranoia. You can't identify best practices without sticking your neck out—but if you don't, you risk prema-ture death. You can't invite customers to contribute design ideas and requirements by holding them at bay.

In contrast, companies that are in touch with their markets have got the doors flung wide open. They're constantly searching for solid information—we're not talking advertising here—that they can share with customers and prospects via Web and FTP sites, personal e-mail and phone calls, whatever it takes. They're not half as concerned with protecting their data—with cer-tain critical exceptions of course—as with how much of it they can manage to give away. That's how they stay in touch, stay competitive, keep market attention from drifting to competitors.

Randy: It's as if the kind of companies you're talking about here are creating a whole new kind of corporate identity, not based so much on brand aware-ness and the repetitive advertising needed to create that, as on substantive, personalized communications.

Chris: Yes yes! The question is whether, as a company, can you afford to have more than an advertising-jingle persona? Can you put yourself out there—say what you really think, present who you really are, what you really care about, what really turns you on? Do you have any genuine passion to share? Can you deal with such honesty? Such exposure? Human beings are often magnificent in this regard, while companies, frankly, tend to suck.

You asked where the fear was coming from. I think it's fairly obvious. For most large corporations, even considering these questions—and they're being forced to by both Internet and intranet—is about as exciting as the prospect of an experimental brain transplant.

Randy: You predicted that the Internet was going to be a very big deal in a 1992 *Byte* cover story. So what do you see happening by the end of the decade? You're painting a pretty dismal picture here.

Chris: Well, yes and no. It's only dismal if you're spooked by the prospect of coming in out of the cold. The companies at highest risk are not wonderful places to be working in—at any level. Their prospects could be very bright if they'd just decide to stop being prisons with nasty wardens.

And if they choose not to . . . well, I don't have much pity for them. Companies that are harming themselves out of genuine ignorance can, with a little humility and a lot of hard work, begin to learn and change. I've seen it happen and it's an impressive thing. On the other hand, companies that are harming the people who work for them out of cowardice, greed, and willful stupidity richly deserve whatever fate may have in store. Passion is a two-way street, you know. It doesn't always refer to love.

As to predictions, I predicted in a 1992 *Byte* cover story that the Internet was going to be "A Very Big Deal"—and everyone thought I was completely nuts. So I've tried to stop saying those sorts of things. However, I strongly suspect that unless Fortune 1000 companies wake up with respect to the issues surfaced here, half will be gone by the year 2000. These giant companies tend to look only over the tops of the trees at the other giants they consider worthy competitors. Few bother to look down at their feet. If they did, I think more than a few would see their foundations being nibbled away by competitors many times smaller, yet fiercely committed to do battle for even a tiny slice of this new territory. Some guy in a garage can only take away, say, .001 percent of market share from one of these monster companies. However, a million guys—or gals—in garages can take it all. And given the new business dynamics that the Internet brings to bear, this can happen overnight. There will certainly be some radical discontinuity. Some catastrophic breaks.

Believe it: There really are people out there who know what to do with this stuff. But again, I don't think it's necessarily a dismal picture. Let's just say companies currently have a lot of motivation to get serious. And to get really serious, they first have to get a sense of humor and relax.

Randy: Whoa. You suggest that maybe half of the Fortune 1000 may soon evaporate, and then you say these same companies should relax?

Chris: Yeah, yet another pretzel-logic paradox. They need to relax to break that obsessive-compulsive control habit. They need to trust their people to do the work better than they ever could themselves—Jack Welch said that several years ago in a GE annual report, so it's not just more of my own mad-dog opinion.

Corporate intranets, if implemented along the lines we've been talking about, could unleash the potential energy of the corporation. But in order to nourish and grow that potential, you first have to let go of it. The Zen master Suzuki Roshi said "to control your cow, give it a bigger pasture." That is the true essence of the intranet, oh Grasshopper.

Patricia Seybold, Patricia Seybold Consulting

Patricia Seybold is president of the Patricia Seybold Consulting group based in Boston, Massachusetts. She has been a technology visionary for nearly 20 years. She is working on a book called *Customers.com*, in which she synthesizes the best practices in e-commerce, especially those that have developed a mature intranet/extranet customer focus. Her web site is at http://www.psgroup.com

Randy: Patricia, you've carefully watched the development of organizations using modern technology for some time. What is your take on intranets?

Patty: I believe that most vendors and the press are much too inwardly focused on how to use an intranet. They are focused on information sharing and streamlining internal business processes. They need to be more focused on improving the relationships with their customers. They can use the intranet as a tool to maximize customer loyalty.

Randy: What you're suggesting is that companies developing intranets need to focus on steamlining the internal business processes that extend out to the customer?

Patty: Precisely. Focus on any internal business process that requires a transaction with a customer, especially those processes which provide high touch between the corporation and the customer. American Airlines, for example, saves money by providing travel services over the Web. The users make their plans directly with American Airline's internal systems, reducing the cost of overhead. This works well for a transportation company like American Airlines because a recent survey indicated that 85 percent of their most frequent travelers had PCs at home and would prefer to do their own travel planning.

Randy: Do you think every company should start their intranet efforts by focusing on an extended intranet?

Patty: There are certain classes of customers. The web savvy companies that use web technology to conduct business with their partners over the Internet fit into one class of customers. They use web technology to communicate and share information within the corporation. Sun is a great example of this.

Many of their processes are already on-line. And, if you want to do business with them, you partner over the Internet to streamline the touch with their customer.

Then, there is a middle class of users. They are toying with marketing over the Internet and are developing internal intranets within their organizations. They are engulfed in capturing internal information and making it available for decision making. Their efforts are incomplete, and they are working on the build now, pay later method. They are ripe for focusing their efforts on the extended intranet.

And, there are classes of companies that don't use technology much at all. Their ability to use information, or visualize their business processes on-line are minimal. They are either in the information gathering stage, or simply in denial that the technology will not affect them. This is another group ready to listen and to be convinced by demos.

Randy: Would you still focus on deploying intranets in their organization for the other reasons, like Business Process Reengineering (BPR) and workflow?

Patty: I certainly would. Once they understand how this technology helps them access valuable information, they learn to share ideas, to produce better information for anyone in the company. Accelerated decision making can turn their companies around fairly rapidly.

Randy: When you talk to your clients about intranets, what pieces of the intranet do you emphasize, given what you've said about different classes?

Patty: Customers want to be able to get at information from their different systems. They may wish to integrate information from their billing system, their provisioning system, their repair system, their service tracking system, whatever. They've got many systems that don't talk to each other. They want to pass information from one system to the other.

The way to make this happen easily and cost-effectively is with an intranet. The key is to find which of these systems is their mission-critical one and talk about the pieces then.

Randy: You're suggesting that a user can take a critical-mission application and simply move it over to the intranet?

Patty: Well, intranets use web technology to set up web front ends to manipulate the data in the different data structures that have evolved over the past 20 years. Applications today are designed to integrate all these different business applications together in order to touch the customer. An intranet makes it easier for you to have all your data in just one place and to cross-link information in different ways.

Randy: You refer to the customer constantly. That is super. Are you using the term to refer to customers on the outside, buying goods and services, and customers on the inside, building and testing same?

Patty: The primary focus should be on external, end customers. But, again the revenue producers will be the intranets that cause the internal and external customer to interact more directly. The intranet is a tool for customer focus, customer loyalty, and customer measurement.

Randy: What kinds of intranet tools are we talking about for building sites that respond to customer focus, loyalty, and measurement?

Patty: The tools are there already, from various vendors, Netscape, Microsoft obviously. They're building the middleware to work with the Internet's open standards. You'll need middleware to link applications together, workflow to streamline business processes, and data warehousing to gather, measure, and mine customer information.

Randy: When you're discussing intranet benefits to a client, how do you identify the costs and the returns on investment?

Patty: Costs are simple because the biggest cost is going to be in application integration and middleware. The data engine layers increase costs with increased functionality. Once customers begin with the simple intranet benefits, they want to start taking a firm foothold in fortifying their position as a competitive company in an e-commerce world.

Many clients say they want to develop their intranets over time, but after a bit of web screen scraping, their need to have a more developed architecture increases rapidly. It takes very little time to see ROI. Within a short time frame, they want application servers, rules engines, and database engines that sit between their browser and their front ends. This is when you really start spending money. If you architect it right, though, you can save significantly.

Randy: What methods do you use to build an infrastructure with the right architecture?

Patty: We separate out business objects, business rules, and business events. We use business objects to model the business and to present information both to end users and to application development at the level of abstraction that maps closest to the business. It's important to ensure that the results are understood by the business and by the customer. Without a systemic model of business, you struggle to build the right infrastructure.

Next you use business events as the way to integrate your applications. Business events are things like "order received," "credit check," product shipped." These events let you integrate the billing system, the accounts payable system, the ordering system, and so forth. Each application publishes the events it handles to all the other applications that need to know about them. These other applications "subscribe" to the events they need to know about.

Business rules should not be integrated into the application logic, but, they should be separated into a business rules engine and maintained by the business users, the policymakers, the lines of business. This methodology does not include the customer in the interaction, however, weakening the currency of the business rules. On the other hand, if customers download a profile, then set up the rules on how to do business, then the customer can maintain his own preferences about how he wants to do business with the company.

It is within the interactive processes that the business rules are kept vital, and current in real time. In this model, the customer is taking care of their own business needs, while integrating tightly with the suppliers of information to more adequately represent the customer's needs and expectations.

Randy: What recommendations, Patty, do you give to clients regarding measuring the effectiveness of their intranets?

Patty: The interactive use of intranet technology provides the best model of capturing measurements over the intranet. E-commerce servers and customer-driven applications will capture preferences. Preferences are an effective measurement for profiling the customer. But preferences are one thing, action taken is another.

You can measure which top-level pages were accessed most frequently. But this data only indicates how newbies are utilizing the intranet. It does not present a comprehensive picture of the more advanced user. You can do configuration management for example, like *PC Order*, where you can configure your PCs and laptops from a variety of vendors, tracking who placed the order, how many items they bought, and other tracking information.

Randy: I can see that you're very customer focused in recommending intranets. Many corporations see the intranet as an inward process much as you recognized in the beginning of the interview. For those inwardly focused companies, then, what do you say the intranet buys them?

Patty: Much more streamlined business processes and information sharing. But, again if you can off-load business processes to the customer, you'll make them happier and yourself more streamlined as a result. For example, in our case, we provide information reports either in mail, or over the Web. A customer orders a piece of research over our extranet.

They download it; there are no printing costs, no delivery costs, no billing costs. We save a huge amount of internal work. The costs of the research piece are the same no matter what venue we deliver with. It's just that our profit margins are higher using the Web.

Randy: And what about information sharing?

Patty: What I have found is that information sharing inside the same company does not automatically result from making it available. People hoard information; it is a remnant from the mainframe/MIS department mentality. Silos of information still exist within an intranet. That is why the parts of the intranet that extend out to the customer shake up this model.

Randy: So Patricia, where do you see the future taking intranets?

Patty: The most obvious future is right in front of us. It is the ability to do consultative selling. You can profile the customer from the interactions with the intranet. You can provide entry into your intranet to allow the customer access to information. Once the customer knows who you are, and how you do business, you can offer consultations that help the user see how your products, goods, and services fit into their business.

This kind of activity on the external Internet is exactly what will happen on the internal intranet as well. Your internal clients will know each other, what kind of information you wanted last time, and will be able to provide you with information you may be needing in the future.

Randy: You don't think people mind your collecting so much data on them?

Patty: Collecting demographic information has always been going on. The idea is to find a way in which the user won't mind your collecting it. For example, National Semiconductor has a parametric search engine for helping you search for chip designs to meet your needs. In your search streams, you pass specific information about your preferences back to National Semiconductor. You are almost unconscious of doing it, as you are satisfying your own needs during the search session. National Semiconductor simply maintains this trail of search terms. You get what you want; they get what they want.

Randy: In the last two years since the intranet first hit the trade press, the estimates for all sizes of companies moving their information needs onto the intranet have grown enormously. Many organizations clearly are dedicated to doing business over the internet, and now the intranet. Why do you think business people are getting it?

Patty: It's the global infrastructure that appeals to business. It's the possibility to do one-to-one marketing. Most importantly there is a lot of pressure in all walks of life to offer customized products. Using technology to deliver commodity products at a price point that produces incremental revenues will stay on everyone's mind for quite some time. It's a race between survival and profit.

Randy: What would be your investment advice then?

Patty: What you're going to see is a lot of web-enabled software applications that drive e-commerce. If the intranet is part of the process to develop impeccable, profitable business in a high speed, wireless, portable fashion for each consumer, then it will grow like a weed. If your intranet provides an environment of document management, business intelligence, and decision support groupware for both the employee and the customer, then, you'll be one of tomorrow's winners.

Randy: Thank you very much, Patty. This was a great cut on the intranet that most people aren't looking at. Very insightful. I look forward to your upcoming book *Customer.com*.

Patty: You're welcome.

Dr. Steve Telleen, Director, Strategy and Business Development, Intranet Partners

Steve Telleen, Ph.D., is director of Strategy and Business Development at Intranet Partners, a consulting firm that focuses on helping companies develop intranets and intranet strategies. At the time of this interview, Steve was responsible for developing the intranet at Amdahl, as it grew up from its humble cross-functional roots to the IntraNet solution that has transformed Amdahl.

Randy: Let me ask some basic questions. Why do you have a working intranet system in your organization?

Steve: We saw the potential this technology could make in our business processes, technically, but more importantly, organizationally. From an implementation perspective, I credit the successes we have had with the fact that we treated the implementation as an infrastructure development program rather than an application development project.

Randy: How is your infrastructure developed to support the intranet?

Steve: We focused on three major areas: management, technical, and content. We set out to create a decentralized control model so we could avoid traditional bottlenecks. The key to rolling out the decentralized model was the formation and training of the Web Council, which consisted of the publishers for each major line of business and functional area. We then encouraged the publishers to organize the editors and authors in their area. The publishers determined formal information their group would make available. Each group was free to define the specific editorial areas and authoring responsibilities for their own organization.

Randy: How do you manage content within your intranet?

Steve: In general we tried to develop a distributed, self-management model. We quickly discovered three distinct kinds of information being published on the infrastructure, each with its own management challenges:

1. Formal information, which is officially sanctioned and subject to review and approval cycles,

2. Project information, also departmental, which generally is related to the

operation of a specific area or development project,

3. Informal information, which belongs to specific individuals. Personal home pages are one example of this, but personal information often consists of white papers, individual presentation foils, notes, and so forth. Sort of the water-cooler information that gets passed around.

The formal information is managed just as it is on paper, with review cycles and approvals. The difference is the content generally is made available on the intranet, as project information, as it progresses through development and the reviews. The project information is managed by the project or department members responsible. Informal information is not managed.

However, as an intranet grows, it is a good idea to have icon markers on each page that identify the formal or official information so the viewer knows the status of the information being accessed. Icon markers are a good idea for identifying internal-only information too.

Randy: Do you have a central intranet web page in your organization?

S: Yes, we identified three separate high-level entry points into the intranet. The first we call the Enterprise Map. It is based on the organizational or accountability structure around the formal information. The majority of the map is a set of link pages, starting at the CEO level. The top page has links to the top-level map page for each of the lines of business and major functional areas. These map pages coincide with each publisher on the Web Council, and each is owned by one of those publishers.

The top-level publisher page in each organization has links to each of their editor's top-level map pages. The editors structure their pages to reflect the logical ordering of the content for the functions for which they have responsibility. This structure allows each area to organize and self-publish their information but provides a very low maintenance structure to all the formal information based on organizational responsibilities.

Since the upper map pages are simple links, when reorganizations occur, the map can be modified in a matter of minutes by the organizations affected.

The Enterprise Map can be a powerful tool that helps managers monitor the status, completeness, and quality of information that they make available to the enterprise or the world. However, we discovered that many users, who were not the audience for the map, found it to be very useful for informational browsing.

The second entry point we called the Yellow Pages. This is a functional view of the content and may contain informal pages as well as formal. Links in the Yellow Pages are generated at the author's request. The danger with allowing unmanaged pages into the directory, which the Yellow Pages does, is that it can become cluttered with abandoned pages and junk information.

To counter this we implemented a sunset policy for informal pages. After 60 days they are removed from the Yellow Pages unless a request is made to keep them. The processes for submitting link requests and monitoring and removing links can be automated with scripts.

The third entry point is the Index and Search Engine. Here publishing is done automatically by a discovery agent (a spider) and the user finds the information by submitting a search. This is an important tool, but policies and processes need to be put in place so authors can easily tag content they don't want the discovery agent to index.

Randy: I learned about your intranet methodology from your web pages. Can you briefly describe that methodology for us?

Steve: The methodology is based on four basic stages of development:

1. Executive awareness

2. Goals clarification

3. Implementation planning

4. Implementation support and guidance from experienced personnel.

The process is facilitated by providing web-ready policy and standards templates, role and organizational charter documentation, and processes for effective rollout.

The methodology is driven by business goals rather than technology and addresses what I call the five "Ss" of success: skills, structure, staffing, shared vision, and systems.

Randy: What do you see as the main difference between enterprise networking and intranets?

Steve: Enterprise networking is a technology-centric approach. An intranet allows that technology to be driven and managed by the business goals and the domain specialists. It became feasible with the advent of real vendor-independent standards for both communication and content. While the commercial vendors argued over enterprise networking standards, noncommercial users around the world developed standards that worked. We have seen the power of vendor-independent standards in the pace of development that has occurred over the past three years in both the commercial and the noncommercial arena.

Randy: What's the key to integrating enterprise networking and the intranet?

Steve: Build a business infrastructure that fully utilizes the enterprise network. The intranet standards and tools make this feasible. To be successful requires attention to the five "Ss" mentioned above. With an intranet, you have the potential to transfer the way the enterprise manages itself.

Randy: How'd the intranet get started at Amdahl?

Steve: In April of 1994 several of the technical developers in the open systems group obtained a beta version of Mosaic and began playing with it. About that time, the competitive analyst for open systems was looking for a better way to move information to the field salesforce. They hooked up and began a pilot to see if this technology might provide a solution. A lot of technical issues remained back then, beta Mosaic was not easy to install or configure, and it didn't have all the viewers integrated like today. There was also the issue of getting the information from our external suppliers into web format.

In the spring of 1994 my open systems strategic and market planning group began to look at what offerings might make sense for Amdahl based on this technology. At that time the media play was all on the Internet. Our view was that there were too many issues that needed to be solved, too much infrastructure that wasn't there yet, for the direct consumer Internet to be an immediate and sustained success.

However, we noted that most large enterprises had the same problems inside their firewalls that the Internet/Web was designed to solve on a global basis. The security issues were less profound, and the base infrastructures were already in place. So we focused on intraenterprise uses.

It also seemed obvious that the technology was not where the real challenge lay. The challenge was going to be how to manage the content and the effects on the organization.

In late July of 1994, we asked International Data Corporation (IDC) to run four focus groups, two on the east coast and two on the west coast, for us to look at potential customer reactions to the concept of employing web technology internally. In the group, we had started referring to the concept as an IntraNet, and as we were building the focus group scripts with IDC, one of the analysts asked if we had taken out a trademark on the term.

This prompted us to do a search, and the term was available; we were the first to use it. For a number of reasons, we did not register the term as a trademark, although we did use it widely with customers, editors, and analysts the last four months of 1994, starting with the 44 companies that participated in the focus groups.

In the fall of 1994 we also started to build our methodology for introducing an intranet into an enterprise. I wrote the first draft of a white paper on the subject in the fall, and a refined version went up on the Amdahl external Web in early 1995. It can still be found there, along with two subsequent papers.

In January of 1995 I approached the CIO at Amdahl and convinced her to sponsor an intranet rollout. We had been testing some of the ideas in my group and in the rest of the open systems organization, but this was the first test of our concepts on a large scale.

Randy: Just like that? You founded a methodology and then built your intranet?

Steve: Yes, the issue was not the technology. The basic technical infrastructure already existed in our enterprise network. Because the technology was so easy to use, almost anyone in the organization could set themselves up as a web server. They already were connected to an IP network, and the software was cheap or free. The real issue was how do you manage this information. And by manage, I mean manage the "life cycle" of the content, just like we do information on paper.

This was a fundamental paradigm shift for everyone, developers, publishers, authors, and users. We immediately saw that this technology enabled a self-service, pull model, rather than the classical push model. Developers needed to provide authors and publishers with tools that enabled them to do for themselves what developers used to do for them.

Authors and publishers needed to learn to publish without distributing. Users needed to learn to be responsible for determining their real information requirements, and accessing information themselves, rather than relying on others to push a river of information (much of little immediate use) across their desks every day. Of course the problem becomes, how do users find the information once they determine the need?

Randy: What did you do when you discovered information overload problems?

Steve: A pull model actually reduces information overload on the user's desk. And, the intranet makes accessing the information easy, once you know it exists. The problem is knowing what exists and whether it is quality information or not.

The solution here is in the concept of a broker. Brokers provide context for the mass of content out there. Brokers are focused on specific functions or audiences, and provide links and tools that help users efficiently find information in the context which the broker supports. We are familiar with brokers in many aspects of our everyday lives. For example, *TV Guide* is a broker for television shows.

What we did not want to do was fall back on models and technologies that forced or encouraged centralization and the potential for resource bottlenecks. Now many of us, myself included, spent much of our careers marketing the benefits of data sharing, and particularly database management systems.

However, shared database approaches are inherently centralized. The internet and web technologies are primarily message-based technologies. We wanted to see if we could develop models for solving the communication and coordination issues outside the shared-data model, using a messaging model.

Randy: How do you define a messaging model?

Steve: A messaging model is when you only send what is needed as a message, when it is needed, to the individuals who need it. Coordination and communication is more of a one-to-one activity. E-mail is a good metaphor for messaging, but the web technology uses the same standards and approaches.

One can look at a Web transaction as an e-mail request for specific information, and an e-mail reply. Each request can be to a different system. By contrast data in databases has to be managed either by a common system, or have highly structured interfaces engineered between systems. The difference really is that database approaches require a lot more coordination, engineering, and rigidity than messaging approaches.

Randy: Does the intranet compete with Lotus Notes?

Steve: Yes, it became apparent in our focus groups in August of 1994, that the intranet was going to go head to head with Lotus Notes. Notes is a good example of solving the same problem, primarily using a shared database approach as opposed to messaging. The underlying database sharing approach is why Notes had the "replication problem."

In August 1994, intranet technology did not have anywhere near enough functionality to compete with Notes, but it was apparent that the velocity of development was so fast that within a year, intranets would be able to hold their own in a direct confrontation. The rate at which intranet technology was developing versus Notes technology development was a very good example of the benefits of vendor-neutral standards over proprietary technology.

In April of 1995 the intranet appeared on the Notes radar screen, and by the fall of 1995 (one year after our focus groups) the intranet was considered by many to be the winner. Notes still has strengths in the workflow management arena, but I think this too may come under serious attack as many of the workflow requirements are recast in terms of messaging approaches.

In the long run the message-based technologies will not drive the data-based technologies to extinction. Instead, we will learn which functions and kinds of information are best supported with message-based approaches and which are best supported with data-based approaches. Already the two approaches are starting to work together allowing us to manage smaller databases and use intranet technologies to integrate the output in more flexible and manageable ways.

We can only gain the knowledge of how to architect these new solutions through experience, so expect a lot of noise as those people and companies with a vested interest in data-based approaches resist the attempts of those trying out the message-based approaches on previously sacred ground.

Randy: Okay, then, from experience talk about advantages of the intranet.

Steve: The first advantage is a very intuitive, single, user interface to the diversity of information and resources on the network. This ability to integrate asynchronously managed content is extremely powerful and flexible.

The second is the ability for anyone to publish and find information easily on the network. This breaks down the organizational barriers to communication, flattens the hierarchy, and eventually will make enterprises much more flexible.

The third is that it makes development faster, cheaper, and easier.

Fourth, and ultimately the most important, as managers in functional areas learn that they really are managing information, and then learn that by using the intranet they can quickly see the information for which they are responsible in contexts and combinations they never could before, we will see higher quality information, and eventually the knowledge will lead to more effective organizations. We are generating new knowledge about how information drives function, and how to manage knowledge creation processes more effectively.

Randy: Which tools do you believe are going to enable knowledge creation and knowledge management processes?

Steve: I favor tools that allow domain specialists to manage, manipulate, and publish their information themselves, without having to call in a technology specialist to do it for them. I also am a fanatic about tools supporting distributed decision making and management at all levels. This includes not forcing groups to all use the same brand of creation tools or management tools. Of course that means the vendors must adhere to the internet-standard outputs, or the output from the various groups won't be compatible.

The internet and web standards have taken us to this point. The object standards and technology are a natural fit to the intranet and will make diversity and distributed decision making even more powerful. Intranets appear to be the necessary infrastructure that finally makes object-based technologies compelling. And, the object-based technologies can provide us with valuable perspectives on how to manage distributed decision making in organizations. This is a very promising marriage.

Randy: What is going to make that marriage work?

Steve: Distributing decision making is the key issue. It is what an intranet enables, and it what it encourages. It takes conscious effort to stop distributed decision making and information management after an intranet infrastructure is in place. Therefore, when you start the implementation stage, you find yourself in a full-blown paradigm shift. When that happens, the entire corporation is affected. You find out that what you're doing is much larger than you expected.

Bottom Line: Putting together an intranet is really about how you make decisions in an organization and how you view control. Neither of these are trivial issues by any means.

Randy: There's a lot of resistance to distributing decision making. Talk about that resistance.

Steve: There are three reasons for resistance. Some managers don't understand the technology and don't know what to do with it, so they resist the unknown. The second form of resistance comes from those who have made legacy decisions, for example, a decision to take the whole company to Lotus Notes. They may or may not have implemented their decision, but they're worried about intranets affecting perception of their decision-making capabilities. The third group is made up of people who are control freaks. They don't like intranets because they fear losing their control. The big security risk arguments come from this group of resistors.

Randy: How do you explain to them the value of the intranet, then, in such a way as to break down the resistance?

Steve: It depends on the source of the resistance. For those who don't understand, you can try analogies, but the best way is to give them first-hand experience with a web browser and either a pilot or something that clicks on that light bulb in their consciousness. I find it interesting that for many people the light bulb goes on when they experience something totally unrelated to their primary work interests.

For one very accounting-oriented manager, it turned out to be the virtual frog dissection page where he suddenly saw the possibilities. Maybe that is because the defenses are down on non-work-related pages. The reality is, that some people are never going to have the conversion experience. This really is a paradigm shift that requires the "aha" experience.

Randy: How do you handle security over this communication structure?

Steve: Security is still a big concern for most managers and executives as they plan for an intranet. However, the security technology has come a long way in the last three years. We now are at a point where intranet security is probably better in many areas than it is for noncomputerized information and processes. The legitimate driver for security is risk, and risk, it turns out, is a very subjective phenomenon. The other driver is the attitude toward information and control.

The first question I ask in facilitating development of an intranet security policy is: As a company do you want to deny your employees access to all information unless an individual is specifically permitted, or do you want to allow your employees access to all information unless it is specifically denied? This tells you a lot about the attitude and culture of the enterprise. I can configure an intranet for those who want to make an exception for access rather than for restriction, but the benefits of an intranet are going to be greatly diminished.

Randy: How do you manage people playing on the intranet, and not getting work done?

Steve: When people first encounter the intranet, you have to expect them to play. Playing is how humans learn. It is through playing that they will encounter the "aha" that they need to use the technology effectively, and it is by playing that they will learn how to find things efficiently. Playing tends to drop off after the first six to eight weeks and they get back into their jobs, but now they've got an incredible communication tool to help them do their jobs better.

This isn't to say that there won't be any problems. Companies have trouble with some employees spending too much time on personal telephone calls, playing computer games, reading novels at work, or just socializing. These are management problems and should be dealt with by normal management processes.

Randy: Could you say that you're developing critical thinking skills in your employees?

Steve: Precisely. Kenneth Boulding, the Nobel Prize winning economist, made a comment in the 1960s about education models that seems very relevant today. Since ancient Greek times education has focused on learning all the facts about a subject. We became educated by memorizing everything to get the information in your head. But as the amount of information increased, we had to become increasingly specialized and narrow in our focus, until today many people are so focused they miss important integrating concepts and opportunities.

He suggested that education needed to make a radical shift away from the know-everything paradigm. Instead, education should focus on teaching students problem identification, solution strategy development, and information acquisition skills. The real value is in being able to identify and solve problems, and specific information is a tool that is accessed "just in time."

It seems that the intranet/internet culture that is emerging may both require and enable that approach. A friend of mine phrased this same phenomenon another way. He said, we used to learn to do, now we do to learn.

There is a great book to read on the relationship of information, biology, and economics, called *Bionomics*. It's by Michael Rothschild. It lays out a pretty interesting chart on how the evolution of information drives both biological and economic phenomena.

Randy: You must have a background in biology.

Steve: Sure do; my Ph.D. is in biology. I tell you though, it really helps hone your systems skills. Another good book that actually supports the connection between biology and business strategy is *The Death of Competition*, by James Moore. What's an intranet from the systems point of view? It's a complex of self regulating subsystems in a constant state of flux, operating on information in an environment that is always changing. As Moore says, managing these complex systems is more like gardening than engineering.

Randy: Yes, that's great. I quoted Moore a couple of times to describe these same phenomena. How do you think Netscape fits into all this? They are doing much more than just providing a browser.

Steve: Netscape is clearly moving into the server space, providing higher levels of functionality for large commercial enterprises. They also will continue to play in the lower-end space; they have to in order to protect their value-add space. In the browser space they also are moving toward incorporating operating systems on the client into the browser. Meanwhile, Microsoft is trying to incorporate browsers into operating systems. The users and enterprises will win as long as vendor-independent standards keep it so it doesn't matter whose browser you have, and diversity stays in the market.

Randy: Netscape, Sun, and Java are one side, Microsoft on the other. How do you see this playing out?

Steve: Java may or may not be the best tool for developing distributed object technology on the Web, but they certainly have gotten the mind share, and applications are starting to emerge. Microsoft is coming after them full steam with ActiveX, but as long as Microsoft technology only runs on Microsoft platforms, they are violating that principle of vendor-independent standards.

I guess we will see if the intranet has helped customers recognize the benefits they accrue from these standards. I'd never underestimate Bill Gates. He clearly has the market-leading share of all the base legacy technology on PCs. It's the old paradigm and he owns 70 percent of the marketplace. He recognizes that the new paradigm has shifted, and he's willing to play because he is selling lots of new stuff too.

I think he's playing multiple strategies right now, and his preferred strategy is to use this movement to grab a bigger share of the application market, and then use his near monopoly market share to migrate as many of the key pieces back into his proprietary control as soon as possible. The losers in this scenario are the application vendors whose space Microsoft invaded, and the users who lose the advantages of competition in a standards-based environment.

Randy: What is the future of intranets?

Steve: Intranets themselves are evolving a couple of directions. Internally they are becoming the standard computing infrastructure. As such, we will see less emphasis on basic intranets and the focus will move to higher-level applications and functions built on top of the intranets.

Also, intranets are opening up. Partners and distributors are being allowed access to parts of each other's intranets. Firewalls are becoming increasingly virtual as access is controlled through other means as well. Ultimately, intranets have the potential to drastically alter most aspects of our lives. If this really is the equivalent of the printing press, then look at what the printing press caused. The ability to reproduce nearly unlimited copies of the Bible in multiple languages removed the technology barrier that supported the power structure of the Catholic church and brought about a religious reformation.

The ease of publishing information in volumes spurred the education and literacy of the masses but also created problems with knowing what information was correct. The scientific method came into prominence to solve the information quality problem and led to the Scientific Revolution, which spawned the Industrial Revolution. The new egalitarian culture this flood of information stimulated brought about both a raft of cottage industries (garage operations) which led Adam Smith to theories of capitalism and the birth of modern democracy.

Intranet and web technology is opening the floodgates of information as never before. If the period after the printing press is any indication, we have an exciting, turbulent future to look forward to.

Summary of Key Points

This chapter included interviews with the technology CIOs, Webmasters, and other visionaries.

- CIOs

    Bill Raduchel, CIO, Sun Microsystems

    Larry Geisel, CIO, Netscape Communications

John Connors, CIO, Microsoft

- WEBMASTERS

  Bill Prouty, Chief Webmaster, Sun Microsystems

  Ken Trant, SGI Webmaster

  Tim Horgan, WebMaster Magazine Webmaster, CIO Communications

- VISIONARIES

  Patricia Seybold

  Chris Locke

  Dr. Steve Telleen

CHAPTER 10

Top Ten Lists

These top ten lists are for fun, for relaxing, for a celebration for making it through this whole book. Congratulations. I'm sure the journey was invigorating.

At times you just want to see the key points as a list of ideas. It's a way of testing yourself, or exploring your own thoughts on these key issues. We came up with these items during the numerous interviews conducted to write this book, and by harvesting some of the great quotable quotes that leading developers, designers and executive managers shared with us. It is a representation of what we saw and heard repeatedly. Enjoy.

Ten Intranet Truths

1. An intranet is an art, not a science.
"It's how you express human thinking and feeling that makes the intranet a communication and collaborative treasure."

2. Design around your business goals, not the technology.
"For 2,000 years we've succeeded with business goals, leadership, vision, and then enabling technology."

3. The use of the intranet is what distinguishes it.
"Like knowledge, it's not what you learn or remember, it's how you use

knowledge for creative performance."

4.   Intranet development is organic.
"Humans are the center of the intranet. Human values, principles, laws must predominate."

5.   Once the consumer becomes an expert at a software interface, they won't change quickly.
"Certainly we welcome the open standards of the Internet. It's not a question of mindshare, it's a question of leveraging off existing knowledge."

6.   Developers who make their intranet products customizable will gain the competitive advantage.
"The customer (both internal and external) is at the very heart of the intranet. Provide for the customer. Create the market of one."

7.   A centralized administration, decentralized infrastructure intranet provides a single point of access to be leveraged by employees and customers.
"Make this your credo. Consider nothing else."

8.   You must get on the intranet and give back to the intranet to learn how to use it well and to become a part of it.
"Create your own site, maintain it and deal with all the issues of dead links, moved sites, limitations, and bandwidth consumption."

9.   Employees will take over the intranet.
"Give employees information, they'll excel, they'll create, they'll reign in chaos, then they'll create a paradigm shift."

10.   The network is the computer—the intranet is the network.
"Prepare yourself for the digital economy."

Top Ten Intranet Business Issues and Answers

1.   **What is the value to my business of creating an intranet?**
"Being able to communicate, collaborate and transact on-line with all the company data."

2.   **How much does an intranet cost?**
"You probably have most of the intranet installed already. The costs of startup are fairly low. Watch out for the hidden costs though, content maintenance, and technology maintenance."

3.   **How do I guide my employees toward using the intranet to enhance business productivity?**
"Give them the tools. Show them what it can do. And, leave them alone to create."

4.   **How does an intranet compare with traditional networking?**
"An intranet is the evolution of your networking environment. Adapt to the evolution to survive."

5.   **What is a Webmaster and what do they do?**
"An evangelist, a knowledge manager, a teacher."

6.   **Will an intranet parallel my paper system or replace it?**
"Most likely parallel, at first, then replace fairly rapidly."

7.   **How are my competitors using their intranets?**
"To compete against you. They are, in essence, building strong internal models to help them react more quickly to customer change than you do."

8.   **How do I organize information to improve ease of use?**
"Keep it very simple. Keep screen real estate down to about five to seven concepts per page. Provide search tools, and agent technology to allow profiling of users."

9.   **What about Lotus Notes and other groupware?**
"They will assimilate with the intranet, bringing their expertise in collaboration to the table."

10. **What training will be needed by users and administrators?**

"A short 4-hour session learning how to access corporate data, then another 4-hour session to learn how to publish pages. Then, rely on self-paced learning."

Top Ten Intranet Issues

1. Is the Intranet secure?
Yes: The security issues are overhyped.
No: Insiders can easily hack into your intranet.

2. Can I outsource?
Yes: Outsourcing speeds up intranet development.
No: You can't outsource content management.

3. Will I need more hardware?
Yes: Some intranet-ready hardware is more efficient.
No: Initially you don't.

4. Do I need more bandwidth?
Yes: Especially for video, audio, and increasing traffic.
No: The cool stuff on the Net won't become popular for about 5 years. You can wait.

5. Should I centralize the maintenance and decentralize the content?
Yes. You'll control the network and web servers effectively.
No: Chaos will reign at the lower levels.

6. Do I have to rely on consultants?
Yes: Consultants can help analyze processes and workflow, and set up intranet sites fairly quickly.
No: The internal staff must rely on their combined knowledge to grow the intranet site from the employee's point of view.

7. Can I easily integrate existing legacy data?
Yes: If you've got the right legacy system.
No: Legacy applications must support HTML. The standards (OBDC or JDBC) are not yet decided.

8. Do I need to reskill the staff?

Yes: Everyone will learn how to navigate in the hypertext environment of the intranet. Also, they'll need to know how to publish, edit, and update websites.

No: Existing applications that are commonly used can be seamlessly integrated with web front ends. Information technology groups may be the only ones who need to know much about intranet technology.

9. Is content management as big an issue as everyone is making it out to be?

Yes: Content management is the biggest hidden cost. It requires a lot of people to keep information fresh and updated.

No: If the content resides in the hands of the individual staff members, localized at the same level, and managed by gatekeepers (editors), the process is fairly straightforward.

10. Is it easy to convert my existing data for the intranet?

Yes: Much of the data doesn't need to be converted, as browsers are capable of reading many different data types. But there are tools for converting about anything to the intranet.

No: Spreadsheet data with complex macros, heavily formatted desktop publishing documents, and hyperlinking are areas of complexity.

Top Ten Things an Intranet Buys You

1. Elimination of your complex operating system with integration at the desktop.

2. Internet standards for creating a full body of network-centric applications.

3. Interoperability between platforms to expedite workflow.

4. Increase in enterprise functionality and reliability, enabling e-commerce.

5. Corporate culture of shared knowledge and collaborative workers, resulting in productivity improvements.

6.   Integrated applications, data, multimedia, and e-mail for information sharing.

7.   Integrated databases, datamarts, data warehouses, legacy systems for access to corporate data worldwide.

8.   Standard access interface regardless of source.

9.   Integrated, uniformly updated support at the server side.

10.   A 21st century investment, yielding phenomenal returns on investment.

Ten Steps to Creating a Security Policy

1.   Think of the intranet as a *tabula rasa*, an empty space. Then, determine how to add back levels of needed security.

2.   Decide who will make the network site security policy.

3.   Conform to existing policies, rules, regulations, and laws that the organization is subject to regarding security. Then think of the ease of moving information over an intranet.

4.   Define procedures to prevent and respond to security incidents.

5.   Address remote sites, local hosts, and user.

6.   Identify organizational assets, threats, exposure risks, and tools and technologies to meet the risks.

7.   Develop a usage policy.

8.   Institute an auditing procedure to review network and server usage on a timely basis.

9.   Plan a response to violation or breakdown.

10.   Communicate the policy to everyone and review on a regular basis.

Top Ten Design Issues

1.   Understand your target audience's needs.

2.   Provide content in multiple media formats.

3.   Be mindful of bandwidth.

4.   Only link to other relevant and reliable sources of information.

5.   Provide searchable archives.

6.   Use interactive multimedia where there is demand for it.

7.   Use consistent organization.

8.   Layer the information.

9.   Adopt familiar icons.

10.   Give clear indication of available choices and menu items.

11.   Provide overview maps.

12.   Provide clearly readable short text.

13.   Create a back-end database to hold your data.

14.   Supply a browser interface for the client to interact with the database.

15. Usability test, release on server.

Who ever said the original design held? So there were supposed to be ten, but there isn't; there's fifteen. Typical of design, isn't it?

Bottom Lines

This is a list of all the bottom lines in the book.

1. The most impressive contribution an intranet will make to your organization is its communication and collaboration benefits (page 12).

2. An intranet is a single point of contact for your organization's knowledge (page 18).

3. The extranet integrated with interenterprise intranets is the wave of the future (page 22).

4. Intranets are merely the tool for shaping your organization into a 21st century powerhouse (page 31).

5. What separates the Internet and intranets is their use, not their technology (page 32).

6. The Internet focuses people on how to make money, and how to get smarter (page 32).

7. Intranets focus on improving business processes and reducing development life cycles (page 33).

8. Centralize your architecture, decentralize your content (page 39).

9. There is no revolution going on here. There is only evolution (page 47).

10. Now you know what to plan for (page 48).

11. Until easy application programming evolves on the Web, network-centric applications will be slow in coming (page 62).

12. Once Executives see how to use the technology for their own improvement, understand a clear cost benefit, and see a direct impact on customer perception and loyalty, then your intranet is on the way (page 92).

13.   Information at your fingertips is powerful. Knowing how to get it is career enhancing (page 93).

14.   You cannot create web forms that perform heavy on-line transaction processing with CGI scripts (page 109).

15.   There is a dichotomy between the ODBC and JDBC, threatening open standards and database integration (page 109).

16.   Any system can be broken into if the break-in artist is determined (page 116).

17.   Ideally, the security policy should strike a balance between protection and productivity (page 123).

18.   Remember two things about designing for the 21st century: intranets are organic and intranets integrate the enterprise with the public (page 125).

19.   Plan your site, execute your plan, review your plan, then revise it. Then, do it all over again (page 128).

20.   Your databases will most likely be more and more integrated into your intranet, perhaps even replacing older, antiquated systems. Plan for this transition (page 138).

21.   Quickly put the control of the content into the hands of your employees (page 151).

22.   Self-directed teams architect web sites that position them in the big picture, rather than in the little picture (page 161).

23.   Collaboration, either in large packages or small intranet packages, buys you a lot (page 178).

24.   On the intranet the quality of information is known as truth. Are you ready to use it? (page 179)

25.   What does the intranet buy you? It buys you a place in the 21st century economy (page 193).

26.   Prices and services vary widely worldwide and change rapidly. Three different price quotes will serve you well (page 216).

27.   Allow the unpredictable and the unknown. Creation is occurring (page 234).

28.   Allow your intranet to grow in every conceivable direction. You can prune later (page 234).

29.   Find a way to talk to the customer directly to measure the

usefulness of the intranet (page 242).

30. The site, either intranet or Internet, reflects or defines your strategic thinking (page 257).

31. It takes a global community all contributing their best to build an intranet (page 274).

32. Provide standards and processes for publication, but generally speaking, remain ultimately flexible (page 280).

33. Aligning goals to human performance improvement may prove the intranet to be the champion computer science discovery of the 21st century (page 296).

34. Web metrics improve human performance on your intranet (page 297).

35. The method for accelerating the interaction between the user and the server is a technique called "cookies" (page 306).

36. Process improvement accelerates workflow (page 307).

37. When intranets measure organizational goals against actual performance, your intranet is worth its weight in gold (page 308).

38. The organization that can analyze its performance can develop interventions for improving them (page 312).

39. Key industry analysts focus on the test architecture, the test infrastructure, and the test resources for the customers (page 319).

40. Hardware, software, bandwidth, and state are your big costs (page 335).

41. Successful companies are clearly disciplined with effective management and well-thought out business processes (page 347).

42. The executive's bottom line—it's really easy to put your information out there, so do it now (page 358).

43. If you don't have a clear idea where you're headed and what the pieces are that will need to be filled in over time, you'll wander (page 363).

44. The old industrial-era mandate to "check your brain at the door" is utterly dysfunctional in an economy driven by knowledge and innovation (page 369).

45. If control is what you're really after, you might as well go back to mainframes (page 371).

46. Intranets could blow corporations out of their counterproductive stove pipes and get people charged up to bring new knowledge into the company (page 376).

47. Putting together an intranet is really about how you make decisions in an organization and how you view control. Neither of these are trivial issues by any means (page 391).

Index